T0394081

SACRED HERITAGE

In this volume, Roberta Gilchrist critically evaluates the concept of sacred heritage. Drawing on global perspectives from heritage studies, archaeology, museology, anthropology and architectural history, she examines the multiple values of medieval Christian heritage. Gilchrist investigates monastic archaeology through the lens of the material study of religion and reveals the sensory experience of religion through case studies including Glastonbury Abbey and Scottish monasticism. Her work offers new insights into medieval identity and regional distinctiveness, healing and magic, and memory practices in the sacred landscape. It also reflects on the significance of medieval sacred landscapes as contested heritage sites which hold diverse meanings to contemporary groups.

This title is also available as Open Access on Cambridge Core at doi.org/10.1017/9781108678087

ROBERTA GILCHRIST is Professor of Archaeology at the University of Reading. A pioneer of gender and life course studies in archaeology, she was elected Fellow of the British Academy in 2008, voted Current Archaeology's 'Archaeologist of the Year' in 2016, and became an Honorary Fellow of Jesus College, University of Cambridge in 2018. She is the author of several books, including *Medieval Life: Archaeology and the Life Course* and *Gender and Material Culture: The Archaeology of Religious Women.*

SACRED HERITAGE

MONASTIC ARCHAEOLOGY, IDENTITIES, BELIEFS

ROBERTA GILCHRIST
University of Reading

CAMBRIDGE
UNIVERSITY PRESS

University Printing House, Cambridge CB2 8BS, United Kingdom

One Liberty Plaza, 20th Floor, New York, NY 10006, USA

477 Williamstown Road, Port Melbourne, VIC 3207, Australia

314–321, 3rd Floor, Plot 3, Splendor Forum, Jasola District Centre, New Delhi – 110025, India

79 Anson Road, #06–04/06, Singapore 079906

Cambridge University Press is part of the University of Cambridge.

It furthers the University's mission by disseminating knowledge in the pursuit of education, learning, and research at the highest international levels of excellence.

www.cambridge.org
Information on this title: www.cambridge.org/9781108496544
DOI: 10.1017/9781108678087

When citing this work, please include a reference to the DOI 10.1017/9781108678087

First published 2020

A catalogue record for this publication is available from the British Library.

Library of Congress Cataloging-in-Publication Data
NAMES: Gilchrist, Roberta, author.
TITLE: Sacred heritage : monastic archaeology, identities, beliefs / Roberta Gilchrist.
DESCRIPTION: Cambridge ; New York, NY : Cambridge University Press, 2020. | Includes bibliographical references and index.
IDENTIFIERS: LCCN 2019038170 (print) | LCCN 2019038171 (ebook) | ISBN 9781108496544 (hardback) | ISBN 9781108733915 (paperback) | ISBN 9781108678087 (epub)
SUBJECTS: LCSH: Christian antiquities–Scotland. | Archaeology, Medieval–Scotland. | Monasticism and religious orders–History–Middle Ages, 600–1500. | Archaeology and religion–Case studies. | Sacred space–Conservation and restoration–Case studies. | Material culture–Religious aspects–Case studies.
CLASSIFICATION: LCC BR133.G72 S264 2020 (print) | LCC BR133.G72 (ebook) | DDC 274.1/03–dc23
LC record available at https://lccn.loc.gov/2019038170
LC ebook record available at https://lccn.loc.gov/2019038171

ISBN 978-1-108-49654-4 Hardback

For Lynn Meskell

CONTENTS

FIGURES

TABLES

PREFACE

The idea for this book began with the Rhind Lectures delivered in Edinburgh in May 2017. It brings together two aspects of my work that until now have remained entirely separate: medieval archaeology and heritage studies. My academic research has focused principally on medieval social archaeology, with particular emphasis on gender and belief. Throughout my academic career, I have also worked in heritage management as a consultant, a member of national heritage conservation committees, as a trustee to a major heritage site, and as the Archaeologist to Norwich Cathedral (1993–2005). But for decades my work in these two spheres was disconnected, reflecting the general lack of engagement between academic archaeology and heritage practice. The gap between the two fields seems particularly pronounced in relation to medieval archaeology, despite the rich legacy of medieval material culture, archaeological sites, monuments and historic buildings that attracts both academic study and public appreciation. There is very little critical literature connecting the practice of medieval archaeology with heritage studies, although there are noteworthy exceptions (e.g. Bruce and Creighton 2006; Emerick 2014; James et al. 2008). My interests in medieval archaeology and heritage were finally brought together through sustained engagement with Glastonbury Abbey, first through my academic research on the abbey's archaeology, and secondly through involvement in the site's conservation and public interpretation. Glastonbury is an object lesson in 'living heritage', a medieval sacred site that has been continuously reimagined since at least the seventh century, and which is today valued for different reasons by diverse contemporary audiences (see Chapters 5 and 6). It is often said that Glastonbury exudes an irresistible 'sense of place', a distinctive quality linked to the local landscape, legends and heritage. Its enduring appeal to spiritual seekers has certainly caused me to think differently about the relationship between sacred heritage and medieval archaeology.

The timely coincidence of two invitations prompted me to reflect more deeply on the connections between medieval archaeology and heritage. First, I was asked by the Society of Antiquaries of Scotland to give the Rhind Lectures in 2017. I was reflecting on how to structure a series of public lectures on the archaeology of medieval beliefs, when an invitation arrived to give a Stanford Distinguished Lecture in Heritage. Lynn Meskell invited me to frame my work on Glastonbury Abbey within the context of global heritage studies. In preparing for the Stanford lecture, I realised just how little had been written on sacred heritage internationally, and how great was the gulf separating the practice of medieval archaeology, heritage management and heritage theory. This seemed a suitable challenge for the Rhinds – comprising six lectures delivered over a single weekend – the archaeological equivalent of Wagner's Ring Cycle!

But an additional gauntlet was thrown down by the Society of Antiquaries of Scotland: 2017 had been announced as Scotland's Year of History, Heritage and Archaeology, and they asked if at least one of my Rhind Lectures could be devoted to the topic of medieval Scotland. I had not worked previously on medieval Scottish archaeology, but, as a Scottish Canadian, how could I possibly refuse?! Foregrounding Scottish evidence prompted me to reflect more closely on issues of national identity, both in the construction of archaeological knowledge today, and in the regional expression of material religion in the past. The medieval Scottish experience permeates much of this book, and is given centre stage especially in Chapters 2 and 4. It was perhaps inevitable that I would find my way to Scottish monasticism eventually, where I discovered that 'Gilchrists' feature prominently: they turn up in historical sources as monks, hermits and the founders of monasteries. But this is not a simple case of nominative determinism: *Gilla Crist* means servant of Christ and was a popular Gaelic personal name in the twelfth and thirteenth centuries (Hammond 2013: 33).

The aim of this book is to connect medieval archaeology and heritage by focusing on the material study of religion, in other words, how bodies and things engage to construct the *sensory experience* of religion (Meyer et al, 2010; Morgan 2010). In developing this framework, I hope to advance three parallel but distinct objectives: first, to contribute a critical overview of the field of sacred heritage; second, to develop a practice-based approach to monastic archaeology that emphasises agency and embodiment; and finally, to stimulate social research questions for the archaeological study of later medieval Scotland. I would like to thank the Society of Antiquaries of Scotland and the audience for the Rhind Lectures, including friends who provided support throughout (especially Sally Foster, Mark Hall, Nancy Edwards and Rosemary Cramp). I would also like to acknowledge the audience and organisers of the Stanford Distinguished Lecture in Heritage (Archaeology Center, Stanford University, May 2016) and the Sune Lindqvist Annual Lecture (University of Uppsala, September 2016), for their thought-provoking questions and comments on material that was subsequently developed for Chapters 1 and 6.

Numerous colleagues have been kind enough to comment on draft chapters as my ideas have developed: Karin Altenberg, Janet Bell, Karen Dempsey, Dee

Dyas, Stephen Driscoll, Sally Foster, Mark Hall, Mary Lewis and Carole Rawcliffe, as well as very incisive comments from anonymous reviewers for Cambridge University Press. Gemma Watson provided invaluable research assistance with data collection for the Chapters 2–4 and prepared the tables, as well as assembling the illustrations and dealing with copyright. Karin Altenberg shared recent experience at the Swedish Heritage Board, including translation of public policy documents. For help with compiling illustrations, I would particularly like to thank Derek Hall, Mark Hall, Mick Sharp, Avril Maddrell, John Crook, Geoff Corris, Graham Howard, Liz Gardner, Sarah Lambert-Gates, Stephen Driscoll, Glastonbury Abbey, the Swedish History Museum and the Centre for the Study of Christianity and Culture at the University of York. I am grateful to the University of Reading for generously funding a subvention to enable Open Access publication and to the School of Archaeology, Geography and Environmental Science for a subvention towards the cost of illustrations. Chapters 5 and 6 draw on collaborative research projects on Glastonbury Abbey, funded principally by the Arts and Humanities Research Council. I would like to thank Beatrice Rehl of Cambridge University Press for her interest in commissioning this publication.

Finally, it is a great pleasure to dedicate this book to the inspirational Lynn Meskell, in warm appreciation of twenty years of friendship, feminist solidarity and shopping.

Illustrations:

The print on demand book is in black and white. For colour illustrations, please see the OA publication. For additional images and digital reconstructions of Glastonbury Abbey, please see: www.glastonburyabbey.org.

Data access statement:

Data supporting the results reported in this publication are openly available from the University of Reading Research Data Archive at http://dx.doi.org/10.17864/1947.152

ONE

SACRED VALUES: MEDIEVAL ARCHAEOLOGY AND SPIRITUAL HERITAGE

INTRODUCTION: 'LIVING HERITAGE'

This book aims to engage medieval archaeology with two distinct fields: heritage studies and the material study of religion. The focus is on medieval Christian heritage, principally later medieval monasticism in Britain, while this introductory chapter frames medieval sacred heritage in a global context. It reflects on how we define sites of sacred heritage and the basis on which we value and interpret them. What is the contemporary *value* of medieval European sacred heritage in an ostensibly secular society? The archaeological study of medieval Christianity has remained largely outside social, political and heritage discourses. Religion is frequently perceived as something separate from everyday life in the Middle Ages, the exclusive preserve of the church. As a discipline, archaeologists have also failed to consider the significance of medieval sacred heritage to contemporary social issues such as identity, conflict, cultural diversity and professional ethics. Why have medieval archaeologists failed to reflect critically on the sacred? How can we connect medieval archaeology with the sacred, to make it potentially more sustainable as a discipline and more meaningful to a range of audiences?

The first and final chapters of this book place the archaeology of medieval religion within a critical framework of heritage analysis, examining how archaeological knowledge is constructed in relation to belief and reflecting on the contemporary value of sacred heritage. The central chapters explore medieval monastic archaeology through the lens of the material study of religion, focusing on 'what bodies and things do, on the practices that put them to work, on the epistemological and aesthetic paradigms that organise the bodily experience of things' (Meyer et al. 2010: 209). Archaeology can make a distinctive contribution to understanding the *embodied experience* of religion through the study of material culture, bodily techniques and the spaces of ritual performance (Mohan and Warnier 2017). A practice-based approach to medieval monastic archaeology enables innovative perspectives on identity and regional distinctiveness, technologies of healing and magic, and memory practices in the sacred landscape. This introductory chapter reflects on how archaeologists have engaged with the sacred and considers why and how sacred heritage matters.

I will begin by briefly exploring the term 'heritage', a label which has multiple meanings and connotations. Heritage refers in one sense to the fixed material legacy of the past; in this case, the archaeology, material culture and landscapes of medieval belief. It also represents the contemporary use of this material legacy for social, economic and political agendas, that is, the use of the past to shape the present and the future (Harvey 2008). Heritage theory has developed in a piecemeal fashion over the past thirty years: two dominant strands have emerged, with one branch contributing critical commentaries on *heritage as a cultural process*, and the other addressing more applied questions in *heritage management* (Waterton and Watson 2013). The field of critical heritage studies examines how heritage as a cultural process represents power relations through language and cultural discourse, often applying a semiotic approach (Smith 2006). More recently, heritage theorists have reasserted the role of material things and the importance of the body in constructing the social experience of heritage (Harrison 2012; Holtorf 2013a). A third and alternative approach has interrogated *heritage as a political process*, for example investigating multilateral heritage bureaucracies, the political relationships between heritage and conflict, and how the material remains of the past are mobilised to shape new versions of post-colonial and post-conflict histories (Meskell 2012, 2016).

Among heritage professionals, two diverging philosophies on *heritage management* have developed over recent decades, resulting in a conflict between approaches that emphasise *evidential* value on the one hand, versus *social* value on the other (Emerick 2014: 219). The more established tradition in Europe is that of cultural heritage management, in which decisions are guided by professional assessments of the 'importance' of a monument according to qualities such as historical or aesthetic value, authenticity or relevance to a national story (Emerick 2014: 1–5). This prevailing model has been termed 'the Authorized Heritage Discourse' (AHD): 'a professional discourse that privileges expert values and knowledge about the past and its material manifestations, and dominates and regulates professional heritage practices' (Smith

2006: 4). A contrasting approach emphasises the 'significance' of a place according to the different contemporary values attached to it, often privileging social values over established national or international criteria based on age, attribution or connoisseurship. The 'living heritage' approach explores heritage in relation to living people and how they interpret and engage emotionally with their material world (Clark 2010; Emerick 2014; Holtorf 2013b). This more inclusive perspective was pioneered in Australia, the United States and Africa, to acknowledge and explore conflicts of meaning around indigenous heritage. Its influence spread rapidly following the adoption of the Faro Convention by the Council of Europe in 2005 (Holtorf and Fairclough 2013). Living heritage emphasises an interactive, community-based approach to heritage management. It champions local significance and sustainability and represents heritage as something made in the present and renewable, rather than something finite and inherited (Emerick 2014: 7). An emphasis on the changing meaning of heritage can also be seen in the French/Quebecoise approach to heritage as 'patrimonialisation', the dynamic process by which material remains *become* heritage, and how successive generations reinvent or reappropriate heritage by discovering new values in changing social contexts (Berthold et al. 2009).

The living heritage perspective emphasises diversity and multi-vocality – the legitimacy of different living voices to participate in heritage debates (Hodder 2008) – but it has seldom addressed the *spiritual* value of heritage or the voices of faith groups in interpreting their own heritage. However, the living heritage approach has been incorporated in strategies for the conservation and management of sacred sites inscribed on the UNESCO World Heritage list, such as Meteora in Greece (Poulios 2014), the Temple of the Tooth in Sri Lanka (Wijesuriya 2000) and Angkor Wat in Cambodia (Baillie 2006). The spiritual value of heritage is central to understanding the concept of '*intangible heritage*', which encompasses the oral traditions, myths, performing arts, rituals, knowledge and skills that are transmitted between generations to provide communities with a sense of identity and continuity (Nara Document on Authenticity, ICOMOS 1994; UNESCO 2003). The recognition of intangible heritage developed from non-Western understandings of heritage but offers interpretative potential globally. It places greater emphasis on empathy, present beliefs and the importance of local voices and communities in making decisions about heritage (Jones 2010, 2017). In summary, there is an increasing tendency for heritage practices to focus on recognition of the *contemporary significance* of the past based on its *social value* to living communities. While this perspective has been adopted in global heritage studies, it has so far had little impact on the archaeological interpretation of medieval sites and material culture. Further, neither archaeologists nor heritage practitioners have given sufficient consideration to *spiritual value* in shaping contemporary understandings of medieval European heritage.

This book aims to revitalise the archaeological study of medieval sacred sites by exploring currents in heritage studies, museology and the material study of religion. Prevailing archaeological approaches continue to prioritise constructs of value that have been challenged by social (constructivist) approaches to heritage. By privileging certain narratives – such as authenticity, economic value and 'rational' behaviour – archaeologists have failed to take adequate account of *spiritual value* and its relevance to people both today and in the past. Archaeological interpretations of medieval religion can be enriched by engaging critically with supposedly 'irrational' concepts like folk belief, magic and spirit, to develop compelling accounts that acknowledge multi-vocality and the popular appeal of intangible heritage. At the same time, these alternative perspectives reveal innovative insights that have been neglected by previous archaeological scholarship on medieval beliefs, such as materiality, sensory embodiment, gender, healing, memory and folk ritual.

SECULAR TRADITIONS: WHY ARE ARCHAEOLOGISTS AFRAID OF THE SACRED?

My opening premise is that medieval archaeologists have not engaged sufficiently with the sacred, either the beliefs of medieval people or those of our audiences today. The intellectual tradition of archaeology privileges a humanist or secular position, even when we study the remains of religious buildings and landscapes. This is not merely a methodological approach but an implicit theoretical position. For example, the standard textbooks of church and monastic archaeology typically focus on technology and economy, emphasising engineering feats such as water management and milling (e.g. Bond 2004; Coppack 1990; Greene 1992; Götlind 1993; Scholkmann 2000). Buildings archaeologists have explored medieval churches principally in terms of their construction technology and chronological development (e.g. Rodwell 2005), in contrast with the more aesthetic approaches of architectural history, which often focus on religious and iconographic meanings. This secular approach to medieval archaeology informs the interpretation of monastic heritage sites and their understanding by the public – a tendency particularly prevalent in Britain. It has been suggested that this attitude may stem from the severe treatment of monasteries by the Protestant Reformation in the mid-sixteenth century. The Belgian architectural historian Thomas Coomans makes the following observation: 'Monasticism was so deeply eradicated in England that few people today understand the spiritual dimension of abbeys. This is quite a paradox when we realise that the archaeological approach to medieval abbeys and the knowledge of material culture in Britain is one of the most developed in Europe' (Coomans 2012: 227).

The first century of monastic archaeology (*c.*1870–1970) focused on recovering architectural plans and documenting the variations associated with monastic 'filiation' (i.e. the respective monastic orders). From the 1970s onwards, monastic archaeology in Britain shifted away from studying the ritual life of the church and cloister to focus on the productive and service areas of the inner and outer court (Gilchrist 2014). For example, Mick Aston situated his work on monastic landscapes as 'an attempt to show monasteries as economic institutions coping with the difficulties and opportunities presented by the landscapes in which they were built' (Aston 1993: 16). Underpinning these studies is the model of the rural monastery as a self-sufficient organism, in keeping with the ideals expressed in the Rule of St Benedict, written at Monte Cassino in Italy by Benedict of Nursia (*c.*480–543 CE). Medieval archaeology experienced a significant paradigm shift in which the discipline consciously moved away from the study of religious belief and ritual. It was influenced by methodological innovations, such as the development of environmental and landscape archaeology, and by new scientific currents advanced by processual archaeology.

Monastic archaeology has focused almost exclusively on the study of discrete monuments and their buildings and landscapes. Archaeological questions have been addressed at the scale of the institution with relatively little attention directed towards the individual experience of the sacred. There are of course exceptions to the rule, including a number of important studies on monastic space and embodiment (e.g. Bonde et al. 2009; Bruzelius 1992, 2014; Cassidy-Welch 2001; Gilchrist 1994; Gilchrist and Sloane 2005; Williams 2013), complementing a broader corpus of archaeological work on the meaning and use of medieval religious spaces (e.g. Giles 2000; Graves 2000; Ó Carragáin 2010; Roffey 2006). The study of monastic landscapes is beginning to see a shift away from studies based on single monuments toward broader studies of multi-period landscapes which highlight the complex interrelationships between religious and secular sites (e.g. Pestell 2004). The dominant archaeological emphasis on the technological and economic roles of the monastery is being challenged by novel approaches that address ritual continuities and discontinuities over the long term (e.g. Austin 2013; Everson and Stocker 2011).

The 'economic turn' in medieval archaeology in the 1970s was important in opening up a new intellectual space for a relatively young discipline that had struggled to demonstrate a research agenda independent from the discipline of medieval history (Gerrard 2003). The study of agricultural and industrial landscapes offered a distinctively *materialist* enquiry, revealing an aspect of medieval life that was not accessible through historical documents. It differed from art-historical approaches that focused on the aesthetic qualities of material culture and privileged values of connoisseurship. Instead, it resulted in a privileging of economic themes and the projection of secular values onto the study of medieval religious settlements and material culture. This approach is characteristic of the study of monastic and church archaeology in Britain and much of Western Europe, but it is not a global trait. For example, a strong focus on ritual has continued to dominate archaeological scholarship on Eastern Christianity and Buddhist monasticism (Finneran 2012: 253; Shaw 2013a: 84). However, it is noteworthy that recent work by Western scholars has begun to prioritise the economic and technological landscapes of Buddhist monasticism (Ray 2014a: xiii).

This tendency to frame religion in terms of economic power relations is part of a wider intellectual tradition in Western archaeology. Severin Fowles has argued that archaeological approaches to prehistoric religion are characterised by a secularist position, one which pervades both the European archaeological tradition and the American anthropological school (Fowles 2013; Meier and Tillessen 2014). The last twenty years have seen an explosion of archaeological interest in prehistoric religions, but much of this work has deconstructed the concept of the sacred as a meaningful category. Some prehistorians propose universal definitions of religion focusing on symbolism and belief in the supernatural (e.g. Malone et al. 2007: 2), while others reconceptualise religion as an aspect of everyday life, or a holistic worldview. They have been influenced by ritual theorists who stress that even quotidian aspects of life are 'ritualised', dissolving the boundary formerly perceived between the sacred and profane (Bell 1992). Many archaeologists argue that there was no understanding of religion as a separate sphere of life in past societies ranging from prehistoric Europe to medieval Islam and pre-Columbian Central America (e.g. Bradley 2005; Graham et al. 2013; Insoll 2004). Some completely reject the idea that people in the past were motivated by a concept of the numinous. Research on Stonehenge is a prime example: the current orthodoxy of interpretation is framed in terms of the veneration of ancestors, rather than a celebration of the gods. The argument is that henge monuments were constructed in wood for ceremonial use by the living community and in stone to commemorate the ancestral dead (Parker Pearson and Ramilisonina 1998).

There is also a strong tendency in archaeology to focus on *ritual practice* rather than holistic understandings of the sacred. For example, Åsa Berggren and Liv Nilsson Stutz argue for the development of a practice-based ritual theory that will better connect with archaeological sources of evidence. They call for an emphasis on 'the traces of what people in the past were *doing* rather than with what those actions "meant", or signified' (2010: 173; original italics). Archaeologists of the medieval period have frequently reflected on the importance of formal liturgy in the design and use of churches. But 'ritual' extends beyond the codified ceremonies of the church to encompass the material aspects of everyday life. Prehistorians are more comfortable in engaging with ritual as a distinct *material process*, often emphasising ceremonial events such as feasting and funerals (Swenson 2015). However, ritual is usually conceptualised by archaeologists within a Marxist framework, as a means of legitimating power relations and extending social control (Swenson 2015: 331; Fogelin 2007). There have been calls for cross-cultural studies of ritual as a materially marked process that is susceptible to archaeological analysis (Swenson 2015: 340). Rituals have multiple meanings and they are constantly in flux: through rituals, people are able to transform religious belief and bring about change (Bell 1997; Fogelin 2007). An approach based on *practice theory* has been advocated to emphasise the role of human agency in shaping ritual experience (rooted in the works of Pierre Bourdieu, e.g. 1977). For instance, spatial studies have explored how architectural layouts have promoted ritual experience that favoured either monastic/clerical *or* lay experience, in contexts ranging from early Buddhist monasteries in southern India to parish churches in medieval England (Fogelin 2003; Graves 2000).

Recent anthropological approaches to religion have emphasised the centrality of the body and its interaction with material culture to produce religious knowledge and experience (Mohan and Warnier 2017; Morgan 2010). The '*matière à penser*' approach to material culture reasserts the role of techniques of the body (after Mauss 2006 [1936]), and takes new inspiration from cognitive neuroscience (Gowlland 2011; Warnier 2013). It proposes that two different types of knowledge are active in constructing religious practice: verbalised knowledge, focusing on creeds and texts, and procedural knowledge, based on sensory experience and 'bodily techniques that may or may not be immediately identifiable as religious' (Mohan and Warnier 2017: 371). Procedural knowledge requires a period of learning and apprenticeship in order to draw effectively on the material world to produce a religious imaginary. Medieval monastic training can be understood in these terms, requiring a novitiate of one year, plus four years of further training before final vows, during which time procedural knowledge was acquired. This ranged from sign language used in the cloister during periods of silence, to complex forms of liturgy and meditation that drew upon material culture to stimulate memory (Carruthers 2000). The '*matière à penser*' school advocates a new focus on the interaction between the material and the sensory and how together they mediate power relations. The approach emphasises the embodied religious subject but continues to project a secular framework. It assumes that devotees are 'marched' or compelled to belief: sensory experience persuades a subject 'who is often unaware of the process and, hence, uncritical about it' (Mohan and Warnier 2017: 381).

How did archaeology as a discipline come to be dominated by secularist reasoning? A key turning point is said to be an essay by Christopher Hawkes published in 1954, in which he set out the famous 'ladder of inference'. His paper is often taken as a warning to archaeologists against straying into the sticky realm of ritual and belief, effectively excluding this area from the legitimate questions to be addressed by archaeology. In fact, Hawkes carefully distinguished between text-free and text-aided archaeology, suggesting that historical sources and folklore should be used when available to illuminate questions of belief (Evans 1998). Nevertheless, 'Hawkes's ladder' had a major influence on how processual archaeologists approached religion and ritual. For example, burials were studied as social or economic status markers rather than as ritual deposits (Nilsson Stutz 2016: 16). Marxist perspectives had an even more pervasive influence on archaeology, beginning with the works of Vere Gordon Childe and continuing through processual and post-processual perspectives (Fowles 2013: 28). Archaeologists tend to frame religion in Marxist terms, as superstructure and false ideology, structural mechanisms of social control that aim to maintain hegemonic power relations (Swenson 2015: 331).

I include myself in this stereotype: as an undergraduate, I was fascinated by Childe and chose the topic of Marxism for a special project in my final year. Subsequently, I embarked on a PhD on gender in medieval archaeology, which led (inadvertently) to a focus on nunneries (Gilchrist 1994). It was only half way through my study that I began to reflect more deeply on how spiritual beliefs shaped the embodied experience of medieval religious women. This insight did not come from archaeology, but from an encounter with a contemporary community of enclosed nuns. There are very few substantial architectural remains of medieval nunneries in Britain. I was therefore keen to visit the site of Burnham Abbey in Buckinghamshire, where some of the claustral buildings remain intact. The medieval monastic ruins were acquired by the Society of the Precious Blood in 1916 and an Anglican convent was established on the site. I wrote to one of the sisters, who, serendipitously, was studying archaeology through a correspondence course; she encouraged me to visit the convent under the terms of a religious retreat. From my secular, academic perspective, I chose to structure my retreat as 'ethnographic fieldwork'. As well as examining the medieval fabric, I observed religious services and interviewed the sisters about their perceptions of sacred space and their current use of the convent's medieval spaces (Gilchrist 1989). But our conversations grew more intense, with some of the sisters discussing their personal experiences of vocation and the sacred, and their feelings about living apart from the world outside the convent. This episode had a profound impact on my doctoral research, inspiring a focus on female agency and the embodied experience of religious women. Previously nuns were seen as passive objects of feudal relations, daughters without dowries who were conveniently parked in family convents. I was already critical of previous androcentric perspectives that robbed medieval women of social agency, but, well-schooled in Marxist archaeological theory, I had regarded medieval nuns as hapless victims of false consciousness.

The experience of speaking with contemporary nuns about their vocation made me sensitive to the ethics involved in studying religion in both living and past communities. The ethical relationship between archaeologists today and the past peoples whom they study has been raised by Sarah Tarlow and Geoffrey Scarre in relation to archaeological treatment of the dead. Scarre argues that archaeologists do not need to share the religious convictions of people in the past in order to recognise a moral duty of care towards the remains of the dead. Archaeological practice that disregards the values and dignity of people in the past impinges on their status as previously *living beings* (Scarre 2003). Tarlow contends that through archaeological scholarship we participate in animating past people as social beings; we extend their social existence and therefore have an ethical obligation to be responsible in how we represent their beliefs (Tarlow 2006). My contact with a living community of nuns instilled an enduring respect for the beliefs and conscious agency of others, and the genuine spiritual convictions by which they live their lives. It made me think carefully about how I represent the beliefs and experiences of religious women in the past. This early encounter has influenced my engagement with contemporary faith communities and it has shaped my research on the medieval past, particularly in relation to problematic categories of belief such as magic (Gilchrist 2008).

Archaeology's privileging of secular values is particularly evident when discussing magic and 'odd' or inexplicable archaeological deposits (discussed in Chapter 4). Things that cannot be explained in functionalist categories of subsistence or technology are labelled as 'ritual'. Archaeologists stigmatise ritual in the past by framing it as a fallacy, something considered as irrational (Fowles 2013: 9). A classic example is the treatment of 'structured deposition', or 'placed deposits', such as whole pots or animals buried in ditches and pits, or objects placed at critical points in settlements, such as at boundaries, entrances or the corners of houses (Garrow 2012). Such deposits are widely regarded by archaeologists as intentional acts that appear to defy any rational explanation. Joanna Brück critically assessed the assumptions underlying such interpretations, arguing that a series of binaries is projected: secular/profane; rational/irrational; Western/non-Western, and that these attitudes are rooted in the legitimising discourses of European colonialism (Brück 1999). She argues that we need to interpret structured deposition within a different framework of values: placed deposits were *rationally* conceived according to past worldviews, directed towards specific practical purposes such as agriculture and technology.

Structured deposition was long considered by archaeologists to be a pre-Christian rite, confined to prehistoric and Roman contexts. Thus, an additional binary opposition is projected onto placed deposits dating to the medieval period: Christian/pagan joins the list of secular/profane; rational/irrational; Western/non-Western. Here too, a colonial discourse can be detected in the assumption that the conversion to Christianity erased long-standing practices and worldviews (Petts 2011). It is only in the last decade that medieval archaeologists have identified 'odd', 'special' or 'placed' deposits in medieval contexts, with similarities in the types of objects and materials selected for use across Europe, extending from pagan to Christian eras (Gilchrist 2012; Hamerow 2006). In Scandinavia and the Baltic, deposition appears to have been a common element of ritual practice in the home and the church (Hukantaival 2013). In medieval Denmark, for example, odd deposits comprised animal parts, metal tools and utensils, pottery vessels, coins, personal items such as jewellery, prehistoric lithics and fossils (Falk 2008: 207–8). The prevalent attitude of medieval archaeologists towards such deposits reflects their privileging of secular and economic approaches and their narrow conceptualisation of Christian ritual.

An instructive case is that of coin deposits in Scandinavian churches, with over 65,000 coin finds discovered below wooden floors in 600 churches. An interdisciplinary project based at the University of Oslo is examining coin finds in the context of the relationship between the church and monetisation, focusing on the best recorded church excavations (Gullbekk et al. 2016). Both economic and ritual perspectives are considered, with coins regarded as 'devotional instruments' (Myrberg Burström 2018). But the question of whether these coins were *deliberately* deposited is contested. The latest research concludes that these are accidental losses, for example incorporated during processes of floor renewal, or representing overflow from offertory boxes (Gullbekk 2018). Once again, archaeologists project the secular/profane; rational/irrational framework when interpreting inexplicable deposits. And yet, we have ample evidence that the medieval worldview incorporated a rich plurality of ritual practice performed as magic. We have specific archaeological evidence for the ritual use of coins, for example placed with the medieval dead (Gilchrist 2008; Hall 2016a). The historian Richard Kieckhefer proposed that magic should be perceived as 'an alternative form of rationality' that was consistent with medieval views of the universe (Kieckhefer 1994), a definition surprisingly close to Brück's discussion of prehistoric placed deposits (Brück 1999).

Archaeologists often dismiss as superstition any ritual performed outside the orthodox practices of the medieval church. For example, the burial of a complete cat was discovered beneath the foundations of the medieval church of St Mark's, Lincoln. But archaeologists chose not to report this find when the site monograph was published in 1986, because it smacked of 'superstition' (O'Connor 2007: 8; Terry O'Connor pers. comm.). The term 'superstition' has always been used pejoratively; it derives from antiquity and means the worship of the true god by inappropriate and unacceptable means (Cameron 2010: 4). More recently, archaeologists have recognised animal deposits in medieval Christian contexts across Europe. In Italy, for example, a complete cow was found buried in the nave of the mid-fifteenth-century Chiesa della Purificazione at Caronno Pertusella (Lombardy). The cow was placed in a kneeling position, with a coin in its mouth. It was interpreted as a foundation sacrifice – 'a very pagan-looking' ritual, which was perceived by the excavators as problematic in a Christian context (Travaini 2015: 221). In the Basque Country (northern Iberian Peninsula), a local rite has been identified in medieval churches and public buildings: chickens were buried in upturned pots as foundation deposits dating to the twelfth or thirteenth centuries. Rather than assigning a 'pagan' interpretation to these placed deposits, the practice has been evaluated within the framework of 'folk religion', in which traditional rituals were reworked to sit alongside the official liturgy of medieval Christianity (Grau-Sologestoa 2018).

There has been little scholarly attention paid to the archaeology of later medieval magic, a documented aspect of medieval Christian belief (see Chapter 4). The archaeology of magic has the potential to reveal intimate rites that were never documented in clerical texts and to provide a 'deep time' perspective on medieval ritual practice (Gilchrist 2019). Until very recently, archaeologists have stubbornly resisted the idea that medieval Christians engaged in such practices, in contrast with the burgeoning enthusiasm for magic shown by medieval and modern historians (Hutton 2016: 2). There is growing historical interest in the rise of magical practices after the Reformation, for example the ritual concealment of objects in buildings, such as animals, clothing and shoes, a practice which is generally interpreted as protection against witchcraft. This field of study has long been pursued by individual researchers like Ralph Merrifield in his landmark book, *The Archaeology of Ritual and Magic* (Merrifield 1987). However, the topic has remained on the margins of historical scholarship until relatively recently (Hutton 2016; Manning 2014). Historians now actively discuss the overt 'spiritual', 'sacrificial' and 'apotropaic' purposes behind acts of concealment (Davies 2015: 383), in contrast with the secular framework that archaeologists project onto placed deposits.

The use of folklore has met similar resistance in archaeological circles, although there is growing interest in using folk belief to interpret ritual in post-medieval contexts (Houlbrook 2015; Gavin-Schwartz 2001). A critical approach needs to be taken to collections of historical archives and material culture, which have been shaped by the interests and assumptions of folklore collectors (Cheape 2009: 88; Davies 2015: 385). Many of these collectors promoted the view that pagan religions persisted into the modern period and were reflected in a common belief in supernatural entities such as elves, fairies and siths (Hutton 2014: 379–80; Miller 2004). Archaeologists are more interested in how ritual was integrated in everyday life, such as local understandings of the landscape and the ritual use of objects, for instance the use of old coins to protect against the evil eye and metal objects to guard against fairies and witches (Gavin-Schwartz 2001). We should be cautious in making assumptions about the long-term continuity of beliefs and in projecting evidence from post-medieval sources back into earlier periods. Taking these caveats into consideration, folklore represents a unique source of evidence for investigating social memory, with potential to enrich our interpretations of medieval beliefs. Archaeology's failure to engage with this material results from the discipline's secular, rationalist perspective, which generally dismisses magic and folk belief as irrational superstition.

SACRED HERITAGE: VALUE AND AUTHENTICITY

Questions of the sacred have also been broadly neglected by the field of heritage studies. There has been relatively little critical reflection on the definition of sacred sites, how perceptions of their materiality and character change over time, and how they are valued by different contemporary audiences. This neglect of sacred heritage contrasts with the growing literature in history, anthropology, museum studies, geography, art and architectural history, law and tourism studies (e.g. Hutton 2014; Meyer and de Witte 2013; Maddrell et al. 2015; Coomans et al. 2012; Coomans 2018; Tsivolas 2014; Dallen and Olsen 2006). Sacred heritage sites are accorded high value internationally, indicated by the proportion awarded emblematic status as UNESCO World Heritage sites, deemed to hold 'outstanding value to humanity'. Around 30 per cent of the 1,000 sites on the World Heritage list can be broadly classified as sacred sites and at least 10 per cent of World Heritage sites are Christian monuments (http://whc.unesco.org/en/list/).

Landscapes and monuments defined as sacred heritage are said to follow some common criteria cross-culturally (Brockman 1997; Shackley 2001). They typically fall within the following categories, although many sacred sites meet multiple criteria:

- Locations associated with events in the life of a deity, saint or prophet (e.g. the Church of the Nativity, Bethlehem; al-Aqsa Mosque, Jerusalem)
- Pilgrimage landscapes associated with healing (e.g. Kumono Kodo, Kii Mountains, Japan; Canterbury Cathedral, England)
- Locales associated with religious visions and miracles (e.g. the Sanctuary of Our Lady, Lourdes, France)
- Venues of special religious rituals (e.g. Angkor Wat, Cambodia)
- Tombs of saints, prophets or founders (e.g. Basilica of San Francesco, Assisi, Italy)
- Shrines associated with relics or icons (e.g. Lumbini, Nepal, birthplace and early shrine of the Buddha)
- Ancestral or mythical homes of the gods (e.g. Gamla Uppsala, Sweden, home of the Norse gods)

- Landscapes manifesting the mystical power of nature (e.g. Sedona, Arizona; Uluru, Australia)
- Places of remembrance that commemorate persecutions and genocides (e.g. Auschwitz, Poland)

The distinctive character of sacred heritage resides in the integration of the *tangible* with the *intangible*: sacred sites are physical manifestations of religious myths and mystical beliefs, providing a material place to reflect on the immaterial. The interaction of sacred heritage with *place* is crucial; for instance, medieval monasteries were often located at dramatic, elevated spots that brought the community closer to God, while at the same time providing isolation from the secular world (e.g. Mont-Saint-Michel, Normandy; Rock of Cashel, Ireland; Monte Cassino, Lazio) (Coomans 2018: 85–9). The concept of the sacred is acknowledged as being culturally specific; however, it is frequently argued that sacred places share a cross-cultural quality of being set apart, by virtue of their mystical association with the gods. Sacred heritage sites provide a material connection to the numinous, to mythical personae and supernatural realms. Sacred places denote *otherness* and are perceived as being separate from everyday life (Coomans et al. 2012; Shackley 2001).

How do certain places come to be regarded as sacred? The 'deep time' perspective offered by history and archaeology provides critical insight to the processes by which certain places become sacred and how this is conveyed symbolically. Archaeologists use the term 'deep time' to refer to a *longue durée* approach, the extended time scale of archaeological analyses; the term is also employed in a religious context to challenge creationist narratives of Christian history based on biblical time. In the Judaeo-Christian tradition, places are not inherently sacred; they are sanctified through formal rites of consecration and spatial rules that set them apart from other locales. The spiritual and physical delineation of sacred space in Christian Europe was usually limited to the curtilage of a church or shrine. This was based on Christian concepts of bounded, consecrated space that developed from the ninth to eleventh centuries CE (Rosenwein 1999). Monastic precincts acquired a kind of immunity which allowed them to have control over their own boundaries as well as regulating access to the sacred; a similar concept of immunity was granted to Buddhist monasteries of the subcontinent from the second or third centuries CE, as a means of constructing sacred space and defining boundaries of jurisdiction (Ray 2014a: xvi). Formal consecration ceremonies conveyed both religious and legal status to Christian churches and objects directly associated with the sacraments. This concern to protect consecrated objects continues today in Catholic Canon Law, ensuring that sacred objects cannot be made over to secular use: chalices are melted down rather than sold; books and vestments are burnt and their ashes buried in consecrated ground (Brooks 2012: 17).

In contrast, Native American and Australian Aboriginal concepts of the sacred encompass the *entirety* of the land, rather than being limited to particular objects, spaces or topographical features (Shackley 2001). 'Sacred natural sites' are areas of land or water that hold special spiritual significance to peoples and communities. They are natural features including mountains, forests, rivers, lakes, caves, islands and springs, which may be regarded as inherently sacred, or become sacred through association with religious histories and pilgrimage traditions (Verschuuren et al. 2010: 2). The Aboriginal perspective reminds us that the concept of sacred heritage is culturally specific and may extend beyond the monumental expression of religious sites or cult centres. For example, landscapes associated with *conflict and loss* may also be regarded as sacred heritage, particularly where they represent transformative episodes that shaped a nation's or a people's history. European examples include the Scottish battlefields of Bannockburn (1314) and Culloden (1745) (Banks and Pollard 2011), the Battle of Waterloo (Belgium, 1815) and the First World War battlefields of Flanders Fields and the Somme (Picardy), the last of which became strongly linked with Canadian identity (Gough 2007). The conceptual status of a landscape is transformed by the bloodshed and mass sacrifice associated with war, so that battlefields may take on the status of hallowed ground. Sites of so-called dark heritage, such as battlefields, slavery sites and concentration camps, provoke a pilgrimage response, compelling us to visit landscapes where blood was shed and injustice was perpetrated (Biran et al. 2011; Colls 2015). These landscapes of sacrifice represent notions of sacred space that resonate with both secular and religious values, evoking an emotional response that may be regarded as a spiritual experience (Walton 2015: 34).

Many sacred sites fulfil a *memorial* function: there is a close connection between the burial and commemoration of the dead and the definition of sacred space. The presence of the dead attaches a layer of sanctity to a landscape – even contemporary, secular cemeteries take on the status of sacred space, with the disturbance of human remains generally perceived as desecration, regardless of whether the site is consecrated (Kinder 2012: 196). The strength of this association is demonstrated by the fact that cemeteries and funerary monuments may become terrorist targets during religious conflicts; for example, both Islamic and Christian monuments were destroyed during Da'esh's occupation of northern Iraq (2013–17) (Smith et al. 2016). The use of religious places for burial invests a human, biographical element to sacred space, in which cemeteries and places of worship come to represent the collective symbol for successive generations of a social community (De Dijn 2012: 43). It is significant that places of worship continue to be chosen today as the locale for rites of passage such as weddings and funerals – even among non-believers – and they are selected as the most appropriate venue for memorial services in times of national disaster and collective outpourings of grief (Voyé

2012: 81). The connection of sacred space to human biography is particularly clear in relation to life course rituals and rites of passage, key episodes in establishing memory and personal identity. These examples clarify that sacred sites are not the exclusive preserve of the gods, nor are they strictly perceived as being *other* or separate from everyday life (Shackley 2001; Coomans et al. 2012). Instead, sacred sites represent the coming together of the human and the divine, the tangible and the intangible.

The label of sacred heritage has also been attached to monuments that embody *national memory* and collective identity. In Greece, for example, sites of classical antiquity are referred to as 'sacred heritage' in both popular discourse and academic archaeology. Yannis Hamilakis and Eleana Yalouri have argued that classical antiquities represent a kind of secular religion to the Greek nation, noting the strong connections between nationalism and religious institutions (a theme discussed in Chapter 6). Evidence from archaeology and folklore was sought to justify perceived continuities between classical sites and medieval churches of the Greek Orthodox tradition (Hamilakis and Yalouri 1999: 129). The process of constructing or creating a sense of continuity was famously coined 'the invention of tradition' by the historian Eric Hobsbawm (Hobsbawm 1983). The wide definition and application of the category 'sacred heritage' indicates that cross-cultural, essentialist typologies are not helpful in elucidating the meaning of sacred places. Understandings of sacred heritage are culturally contingent and constantly evolving, drawing on local perceptions of the spiritual *authenticity* of landscapes and material culture.

Authenticity is culturally constructed and has multiple meanings that will be explored in the final chapter. Heritage professionals have traditionally assessed authenticity on the basis of the quality of material evidence according to academic criteria (Emerick 2014). These *materialist* models of authenticity have been challenged by *constructivist* (living heritage) approaches which acknowledge that concepts of authenticity vary in relation to social and cultural contexts (Clark 2010; Jones 2010; Holtorf 2013a). The authenticity of archaeological sites is typically defined by values including 'real, true, original, innate, reliable and aura'; the elusive quality of aura is that which distinguishes an original from a copy or fake (Myrberg 2004: 153–4). Nanouschka Myrberg Burström suggests that to be valued as authentic, monuments must be presented as 'frozen in time', with accretions and complexity pared down to reveal their true core. But the Western concept of authenticity, with its emphasis on originality and pristine preservation, may be inappropriate for application to some religious heritage. Even the principle that sacred heritage should be preserved is culturally relative: the Buddhist emphasis on the idea of *impermanence* implies that decay and renewal is necessary for continuation of life (Karlström 2005). Cornelius Holtorf has drawn attention to the importance of *patina* in perceptions of authenticity – the individual emotional response to ruins and their perceptible quality of dilapidation, wear and tear. He argues that the 'age-value' of a heritage object is more important than its chronological age or the specific nature of its origins (Holtorf 2013a; after Riegl 1982 [1903]).

Religious concepts of authenticity invest the value of *sanctity* in material objects, acquired through formal consecration or transferred through close proximity to saints and deities. Religious understandings of authenticity must be taken into account when dealing with the curation of sacred heritage. For example, when a religious site is deconsecrated, does it retain a sense of 'residual sanctity'? As religious buildings fall out of use, is it possible to perpetuate their spiritual heritage in processes of adaptive reuse (Coomans 2018)? To what extent should we respect the past uses of religious sites and buildings, long after they have ceased to be used for worship (Bell 2012)? A crucial question is whether the compass of archaeological ethics should extend beyond respect for the remains of the dead (Scarre 2003), to include respect for the *spaces* of past religious practices. These concerns impact on the curation of monuments and material culture that are regarded as holy by contemporary communities. Questions arise particularly around the treatment and status of religious relics: for example, proposals to conserve the Turin Shroud have been resisted because intervention would alter the perceived sacred *aura* of the object (Brooks 2012: 22). For pilgrims of any religion, the authenticity of relics is critical: the medieval church authenticated body parts as relics through a formal ceremony called *inventio* (Geary 1986: 176). Relic collections were curated over many generations and their connection to particular saints was recorded on *authentica*, labels of identification, illustrated by the large collection of medieval relics at Turku Cathedral in Finland (Immonen and Taavitsainen 2014). Unusually, the Turku relics survived the Lutheran Reformation and were rediscovered in 1924. Their authenticity has been tested archaeologically, using AMS radiocarbon dating, DNA and isotopic analysis. Archaeological science has served as proof of historical authenticity for the Turku relics, which were periodically re-wrapped in new textiles and containers, and bundled with other bones. Most of the Turku relics date to the fourteenth century but some were considerably older. Relic collections are sacred 'assemblages' that were subject to material processes of repeated ritual curation over centuries.

Heritage approaches based on authenticity have a tendency to divorce monuments from their historical and human context, presenting them as sterile and abandoned, frozen in time (Myrberg 2004). These observations are pertinent to the ruined medieval abbeys of Britain, Scandinavia, the Netherlands and northern Germany, which were dissolved in the Protestant Reformations of the mid-sixteenth century. Monastic heritage sites are often presented as if they were fossilised in the landscape at the point of their dissolution five centuries ago. In Britain, this approach to monastic ruins developed in the early twentieth century, when concern over the care of ruined abbeys contributed to the impetus for ancient monuments legislation. A distinction emerged between monuments perceived as 'dead' versus those which were regarded as 'living'. While 'living' sites could be restored to use, 'dead' monuments were 'frozen' to serve as documents for public education (Emerick 2014: 42, 53). The preservation ethic of the twentieth century aimed to present the main period of a monument's use and to strip away extraneous evidence to reveal the monument as a 'document' that was believed to 'speak for itself' (Emerick 2014: 85). The outcome was the generic presentation of medieval abbeys to illustrate the national story of medieval religion, with local stories and idiosyncrasies erased by conservation interventions. Keith Emerick concludes that the national preservation ethic of 'dead' monuments created ruins as the 'stage set for a consensual, safe, elite and manufactured past which over time became the established ("authorized") way in which the past was presented, understood and constructed' (Emerick 2014: 223). In other words, the 'frozen abbey' is the 'Authorized Heritage Discourse' through which heritage professionals have represented the medieval monastic movement.

Living churches and cathedrals are also framed in terms of authenticity, represented as unproblematic survivals of a living religion. Accretions and complexity of development are masked by restorations that project a false sense of timelessness: such spaces appear to embody seamless *continuity* and the stability of rituals and beliefs (Trigg 2005). These narratives of continuity belie centuries of social and religious change, even violent conflict and ritual discontinuity. For example, during the English Civil War of the mid-seventeenth century, the Anglican Church was suppressed and many cathedrals were sieged and partially destroyed by Parliamentarians (Gilchrist 2005: 229–31). At Winchester Cathedral, the medieval stained glass windows were smashed by Parliamentary troops in 1642, and the shattered fragments were reinstated in a new west window shortly after the Restoration of the English monarchy in 1660 (Figures 1.1 and 1.2). During the French Revolution (1789), religious houses, cathedrals and parish churches were closed in France and

1.1 Winchester Cathedral nave, looking west. Reproduced by kind permission of John Crook

1.2 Winchester Cathedral west window, restored shortly after 1660. Reproduced by kind permission of John Crook

Belgium. From 1794, the new regime tried to impose a civic religion centred on the Cult of Reason, with many churches turned into 'temples of reason'. Churches were reconsecrated following the Concordate (1801–2) (Coomans 2012: 224). Episodes of conflict and change, such as the English Civil War and the French Revolution, are masked by conservation interventions and heritage narratives that promote the false notion of continuity.

An example that has attracted recent controversy is Córdoba Mezquita-Catedral, a complex sacred monument in Andalusia (Spain) that has become a contested heritage site (Monteiro 2011; Ruggles 2010). This vast edifice is a unique hybrid of Moorish and Christian medieval architecture that draws over 1.5 million visitors each year. The Moorish mosque was built from the late eighth to the late tenth century on the site of a Visigothic cathedral, incorporating hundreds of columns reused from Roman buildings. It was converted to Christian use in 1236 by the Catholic conqueror Ferdinand III, when it was left largely intact but re-dedicated to the Virgin Mary. In the sixteenth century, a cruciform church was built into the centre of the complex, the iconic Christian symbol implanted in order to colonise Islamic space. This Christian core is enveloped and dwarfed by the Moorish complex, which retains Muslim ritual features such as the mihrab (Figure 1.3). The current display and interpretation of the Mezquita represent its Christian history exclusively, drawing on archaeological evidence for an earlier Christian church on the site. Archaeological authenticity is used to legitimate the cathedral's continuity of Christian use. The interpretation provides no commentary on religious change, conflict or tolerance, despite the reputation of Islamic Spain as a multi-cultural society (Monteiro 2011: 318). In recent years, tensions have developed when Muslim visitors have attempted to pray, kneeling in front of the mihrab. In 2010, several were arrested and charged with 'crimes against religious sentiment'. The Catedral has issued statements explaining that a Catholic church must not be used for prayers by other religions (Monteiro 2011: 321).

1.3 Córdoba Mezquita-Catedral (Spain) and its mihrab. Photographs by Toni Castillo Quero and Ruggero Poggianella / Wikipedia / CC BY-SA 2.0 and CC BY-SA 2.0

Conflict over ritual access is a recurring theme at sacred heritage sites, alongside the tendency to present a single narrative of the dominant religion, even where the site is considered sacred to multiple denominations (see Chapter 6). Again, a 'deep time' perspective can be useful in elucidating conflicting conceptualisations of sacred space and how these have changed over time. This is particularly pertinent in cases where a sacred site has been appropriated by another religion, such as Hagia Sophia in Istanbul, the

1.4 Southern aerial view of the Temple Mount in Jerusalem. Photograph by Andrew Shiva / Wikipedia / CC BY-SA 4.0

patriarchal church of Constantinople, built by the Emperor Justinian (532–7 CE). Hagia Sophia was converted into the imperial mosque following the conquest of Istanbul by the Ottomans in 1453. It was turned into a museum in 1935, following the secularisation of Turkey. Despite its status for the past eighty years as a secular monument, Hagia Sophia continues to be venerated as a sacred place by both Muslims and Christians. In recent years, Muslims have staged prayer-protests calling for its return to a mosque and Orthodox Christians have tried to conduct holy services (Avdoulos 2015: 189).

Jerusalem is perhaps the most deeply contested of sacred places: Temple Mount, or Haram ash-Sharif in the Old City of Jerusalem, has long been considered sacred to Jews, Christians and Muslims (Grabar and Kedar 2010; Silberman 2001) (Figure 1.4). The extent to which competing religions were allowed access to the site changed over time and there was no consistency of practice within a single religion. The site is regarded as the location of the First Temple, believed to have been constructed by King Solomon 3,000 years ago, and representing Judaism's most holy space. There is archaeological evidence for the Second Temple on the site, which is associated with several episodes in the life of Christ and is therefore an important sacred space for Christians.

A Roman temple was built in the second century CE on the site of the destroyed (Second) Temple. Following the Muslim conquest of Jerusalem in the seventh century CE, it became the site of the al-Aqsa Mosque, the Dome of the Rock and the Dome of the Chain. The site is one of the holiest in Islam, regarded as the location of Muhammad's ascent to heaven. During the Islamic phase, Jews and Christians were allowed access for prayer, in contrast with prohibitions introduced by Christians following the First Crusade in 1099. During the eighty-eight years of Frankish rule, Islamic shrines were Christianised, with the al-Aqsa Mosque transformed into the Temple of Solomon, while a Christian heritage was invented for the Dome of the Rock, which became known as the Lord's Temple (Kedar 2014: 13). These sites were re-dedicated to Islam following Saladin's victory in 1187, but earlier building fabric was reused, including figural sculpture from Christian monuments (Kedar 2014: 16). For one brief decade in its history, a compromise was negotiated that allowed open access to this sacred space for all three religions. Jews and Christians were allowed access to the site from 1229–39, which remained in Muslim control, while the remainder of Jerusalem was under Frankish rule. From the 1240s up to the present day, it has remained a Muslim shrine. While its Christian significance has declined over time, it remains highly venerated by Jews as the site of the destroyed Temple. During the twentieth century its status as a contested site intensified, sometimes erupting in violence, and frequently involving conflicts that implicated archaeology (Silberman 2001; Singh 2016).

SPIRITUAL VALUES: THE 'RE-ENCHANTMENT' OF RELIGIOUS HERITAGE

The failure of the disciplines of archaeology and heritage studies to engage with the sacred may result from perceptions of *value*: what is the value of sacred heritage in an allegedly secular society like Britain? This question was recently put to me very plainly by a trustee of the UK's National Lottery Heritage Fund: 'We live in the most secularised society in the world. What is the rationale for funding a sacred heritage site?' At one level this is clearly true – the majority of people in Britain (53 per cent) state that they have no religious affiliation (British Social Attitudes Survey 2017), but many of these same people actively seek out spiritual experiences (Heelas et al. 2005). There are several issues to unpick here: is there an appetite today for sacred heritage, and if so, by whom, and for what reasons is it valued? What are the different types of value attached to sites and objects of sacred heritage?

Heritage professionals may live in a secular world, but many politicians and intellectuals are concerned about the broader processes of de-secularisation and re-enchantment by religion. Rather than living in a post-modern, secular world, we may instead be entering a post-secular, religious world (Asad 2003). These concerns arise directly from the increase of Christian fundamentalism in the United States and Islamic extremism in Europe (Fowles 2013: 3). At the same time, there has been a 'spiritual turn' in Western societies, a shift away from organised religion towards an emphasis on the personal experience of spirit, mind and body and their connectedness (Heelas et al. 2005). 'Re-enchantment' is the term used to signal this new openness to areas previously regarded as irrational and non-scientific, such as New Age religion and individual spiritual experience. It counters the view proposed by Max Weber that modernity is characterised by the progressive 'disenchantment of the world' (Landy and Saler 2009). Examples of re-enchantment on the level of individual experience include the rise of 'transcendent tourism' and the resurgence of interest in Christian pilgrimage in Western Europe (Dyas 2004). Cathedrals have experienced a sharp increase in visitors over the past decade, with one quarter of England's population visiting a cathedral each year (Spiritual Capital 2012). Ethnographic study confirms that many of those visiting English cathedrals come to pray, but the majority seek out cathedrals to enjoy art and architecture and to experience an emotional connection with the past. Secular visitors to cathedrals engage in spiritual practices, such as lighting candles in thanks or memory of loved ones, and appreciating choral evensong in an inspirational space. The boundary between secular tourism and religious pilgrimage is fluid – cathedrals are places for personal, spiritual reflection that is not necessarily linked to institutional religion (Bowman and Coleman 2017).

What accounts for the contemporary appeal and significance of the religious past? Neil MacGregor argues that it defines who we are now, regardless of whether we align personally with institutional religion, and that it occupies the political centre stage as the focus of identity and global conflicts (MacGregor 2018). Spirituality is literally the new 'spirit of the age' (zeitgeist), at least among the prosperous sectors of the population that engage in cultural tourism. This is demonstrated by the marked increase in visits to religious buildings, the frequency in staging of temporary exhibitions focusing on the sacred, and even the foundation of new museums entirely dedicated to religious life in the past (Badone 2015; Brooks 2012, Buggeln 2012; Shackley 2002). At the time of writing, the British Museum in London and the Ashmolean in Oxford recently staged exhibitions on world religions and the Metropolitan Museum of Art in New York hosted an exhibition exploring the links between Catholic material culture and couture design. A new Museum of the Bible opened in Washington, DC in late 2017 and an outpost for this museum is in the planning at the redundant parish church of St Mary Le Strand in Westminster, London. An ambitious new project is also in development at Auckland Castle (Northumberland): the Faith Museum will be a permanent gallery dedicated to exploring the impact that faith of all denominations has had on the history and lives of people in the British Isles from prehistory to the present day. The project has received £10 million funding from the National Lottery Heritage Fund and additional funds from private individuals and charitable trusts. In Toronto, the inspirational Aga Khan Museum opened in 2014, combining a new Ismaili religious centre with a museum dedicated to the art of Islam. The aim is to achieve better understanding of Islamic history and culture and to promote research, artistic performance and discussion around diversity (Aga Khan Museum Guide 2014: 7).

The Aga Khan Museum is unusual in its integral physical connection with a living faith centre. Museums typically present religious artefacts removed from their social and spatial context of worship. Curators are careful to avoid presenting objects in a way that might encourage ritual behaviour in museum spaces (Buggeln 2012); for example, curators at the Victoria and Albert Museum in London were wary about setting up an altar space in the Medieval and Renaissance Galleries that opened in 2009 (Brooks 2012: 19). An exhibition that attracted a great deal of religious attention was itself subject to ethnographic study – the British Museum's 'Treasures of Heaven: Saints, Relics and Devotion in Medieval Europe', 2011 (Bagnoli et al. 2011). The Treasures exhibition was the UK's largest display of relics since the Reformation and it attracted high numbers of Catholic and Eastern Orthodox visitors. Some came specifically for the religious experience of venerating the relics, because they could get closer to the objects in the museum setting than in the concealed spaces that they usually occupy in churches (Berns 2016). Many kissed the glass cases or created contact-relics to take away, by pressing objects against the glass cases that contained the relics, a practice also seen at the Martyr's Museum in Tehran (Gruber 2012). Such intensity of public religiosity is rare in Britain and prompted extensive media comment (Brooks 2012: 19).

Why do people visit sacred heritage sites and how do they experience them? Some of the most popular tourist attractions in Europe are sites of medieval Christianity, such as the Cathedral of Notre Dame in Paris, which attracts nearly 14 million visitors per year, in comparison with 10 million visitors to Disneyland Paris (Stausberg 2011). Many visitors to sacred heritage sites seek a sense of the numinous or an appreciation of the 'spirit of place'; they quest for spiritual or imagined landscapes (Dallen and Olsen 2006). Recent reinterpretations of monastic heritage sites have begun to respond to this spiritual current: for example, English Heritage now presents Rievaulx Abbey (North Yorkshire) (Figure 1.5) as a place of spiritual nourishment and sanctity (Fergusson et al. 2016), while previously it was projected principally in terms of the economic success of the Cistercian order as sheep-farmers. Battle Abbey (Sussex) is represented as a monastery founded by William the Conqueror as an act of spiritual atonement following the Battle of Hastings in 1066 (Coad et al. 2017), and it has become a place of living commemoration for those lost

1.5 Aerial view of Rievaulx Abbey (North Yorkshire). Photograph by the author

in recent military conflicts (Michael Carter, pers. comm.). Public responses to Rievaulx Abbey comment on the value of medieval monastic sites as places for personal reflection: words such as 'evocative, serene, peaceful, magical, atmospheric, tranquil, awesome, mystical, breath-taking, solace, contemplation' stand out in Rievaulx's TripAdvisor reviews.

For many visitors to sacred heritage sites, personal experience is detached from any motive of denominational religion. People seek out holy places in their search for meaning and spiritual encounter, to give thanks and to remember loved ones, and to experience a sense of awe that takes them beyond their daily lives (Dyas 2017). For the secular-minded, the value of these sites may lie in the sense of *timelessness* and immortality that they convey: religious sites are 'anchors of collective memory' and a means for the non-religious to reconnect with the spiritual domain (Badone 2015; Voyé 2012). Visitors to living cathedrals, churches and monasteries experience a distinctive aesthetic of space; their access is controlled and they are asked to moderate behaviour and dress. Christian space is hierarchically ordered from east to west, with the most sacred (eastern) space of the high altar inaccessible to visitors. The scale and acoustics of cathedrals prompt a sense of awe, reverence and reflection. A sojourn in sacred space provides a reprieve from the chaos of the real world – this experience has been likened to Foucault's concept of 'heterotopia', a ritual space of 'otherness' that exists out of time (Foucault 1986; Shackley 2002).

This sense of 'timelessness' is palpable in Catholic and Orthodox monasteries that are still in use by contemporary monastic communities and open to visitors as heritage sites. Here, direct continuity can be observed in material spaces, artefacts, rituals and techniques of the body, such as monastic dress, fasting, celibacy and sexual segregation. This is exemplified by Mount Athos in Greece, a Byzantine monastery founded in 972 CE and thriving today as a theocratic monastic state of twenty Orthodox monasteries located on a peninsula 56 km (35 miles) long (Andriotis 2011). Strictly controlled access is permitted to male pilgrims and a small number of male visitors; in a true mark of monastic authenticity, all women (and female domestic animals) are excluded from the monastic peninsula. Konstantinos Andriotis argues that visitors to sacred heritage sites seek a specific type of authenticity: 'realness' at Mount Athos is confirmed by seeing living monks, observing their daily life, religious rituals and material spaces. Like other commentators on sacred heritage, he emphasises the importance of timelessness: 'visitors have a chance to step back in time and enter into an existential experience of unmeasured and uncontrolled time' (Andriotis 2011: 1622).

What is the value of sacred heritage to contemporary nations and communities? When the Cathedral of Notre Dame in Paris was ravaged by fire in April 2019, the value of financial pledges to rebuild was unprecedented, far exceeding donations to humanitarian crises. The speed and scale of the response reflects the cathedral's status as a national symbol, one which encapsulates national pride and identity, but also offers potential brand association to business donors. The 'value' of heritage is usually measured in terms of social, economic and political value, for example heritage may contribute to social and physical well-being, economic regeneration and conflict resolution (Holtorf 2013b: 17). Pilgrimage sites provide an instructive example: the revival of pilgrimage contributes to well-being, with contemporary pilgrims motivated by the physical challenge of the journey, therapeutic contact with nature and the promise of encountering the 'authentic past'. The physical experience of the pilgrimage journey is a significant part of the heritage value, exemplified by the arduous Camino to Santiago de Compostela (Spain), undertaken by 175,000 pilgrims each year. Local residents have benefited economically from the revival of pilgrimage and the Camino landscape has been restored and themed to complement the medieval pilgrimage narrative (Frey 1998; Maddrell et al. 2015: 10).

Sacred heritage is frequently invoked in nationalist narratives to contribute political value (see Chapter 6). For example, archaeological investigations of Buddhist sites in the nineteenth and twentieth centuries by colonial archaeologists provided powerful imagery for the independent state of India from 1947, such as the iconic Sarnath lion capital of Ashoka, adopted as a government insignia on stationery, passports and currency (Ray 2014b). Sacred heritage carries symbolic capital that can be put to good or ill effect; a negative consequence is the targeting of religious heritage in times of war or ideological conflict, for example the destruction by the Taliban in 2001 of the Bamiyan Buddhas in Afghanistan (dated to the late sixth century CE). There is a long tradition of targeting iconic sacred architecture as a strategy of war: for instance, both Islamic mosques and Catholic churches were destroyed systematically during the conflict in former Yugoslavia (1991–2001). Robert Bevan argues that the destruction of sacred heritage deliberately targets a nation's culture, together with its collective memory and identity, and that such acts should be viewed as being intrinsically linked to genocide (Bevan 2016). Sacred heritage is increasingly vulnerable to acts of terrorism which seek global impact by using social media to disseminate the destruction of cultural heritage that carries visual and symbolic capital (Smith et al. 2016).

However, sacred heritage can also contribute positive political value in post-conflict reparation and reconciliation, for example in Northern Ireland (Horning et al. 2015). Medieval Jewish heritage has served this purpose in Austria, a nation which has struggled to come to terms with its role in the Holocaust (Gruber 2002: 293–6). In 1995, the decision was taken to commission Austria's first Holocaust memorial, designed by the British sculptor Rachel Whiteread. The site chosen was the location of the medieval synagogue on Judenplatz, destroyed after a pogrom in 1420, when the Jews of Vienna were murdered, expelled or forcibly baptised. Research excavations revealed three phases of the synagogue as well as new information on standards of living in Vienna's Jewish ghetto. The archaeological evidence served as material witness for the earliest violent persecution of the Jewish community and provided a platform for Austrian reparation. The controversial monument was unveiled in 2000, a stark representation of lost lives as a library of sealed books in a 'nameless library'. More broadly, development of the archaeological study of medieval Judaism since the Second World War has contributed to a sense of identity and pride in the past for European Jews (Gruber 2002).

Despite the broad range of roles for sacred heritage discussed above, religious or spiritual value is rarely given explicit consideration in archaeological definitions of heritage value. However, it is central to the definition outlined by Siân Jones of the social value of heritage: 'including people's sense of identity, belonging and place, as well as forms of memory and *spiritual association*' (Jones 2017: 21; my italics). In evaluating the social value of heritage, Jones notes the importance of intangible heritage including spiritual associations, folklore, myth and family history in shaping how communities relate to specific places (Jones 2017; Jones and Leech 2015). The question of spiritual value has been addressed more explicitly in relation to built/architectural heritage, in response to the increasing number of places of worship that are falling out of religious use (e.g. the 1,600 Anglican churches in England that have been declared redundant). Thomas Coomans highlights the profound crisis facing contemporary Western monasticism as dozens of monasteries and convents close each year. He argues that intangible heritage adds heritage value and that the 'spirit of place' should be respected and protected in the adaptive reuse of former monastic architecture (Coomans 2018: 127, 154).

Lilian Voyé has considered the multiple values attached to religious buildings beyond their spiritual value to faith communities, noting a strong impetus to preserve religious heritage, even amongst non-believers. She explores the non-religious value of places of worship in terms of: aesthetic/artistic value; historical identity; collective memory; community identity; landmarks; and economic resources (Voyé 2012). Collective memory may focus on elements other than religion: for example, a study of the value of the Wearmouth and Jarrow monastic landscapes concluded that Bede's monastery was less significant to local identity than the nineteenth-century industrial heritage. Local memory and sense of place were more keenly attached to industrial landscapes that previously brought economic prosperity to the northeast region of England (Turner et al. 2013: 186).

Former Christian places of worship are being adapted for use by other faiths, such as a former Catholic church in Amsterdam, transformed into the Fatih Mosque (Beekers and Arab 2016). The changing landscape of urban religion offers an entry point to engage with contemporary social diversity through religious heritage – 'the tangible presence of religion and the co-existence of new and longstanding religious buildings, sites and artifacts in urban spaces' (Knott et al. 2016: 123). Historical perspectives take on increasing importance as contemporary religious spaces change use, responding to the current needs of migrant communities or networks of spiritual seekers. Rather than focus on the history of a particular site, new approaches to 'iconic religion' advocate study of the interactive nature of religious architecture and local communities – 'the ways in which places of worship are often interwoven with other religious and non-religious sites within a particular geographical space, both in the past and the present' (Beekers and Arab 2016: 141).

The resurgence of interest in pilgrimage amongst faith groups is clear evidence of the contemporary value of sacred heritage. There are strong traditions of pilgrimage at prominent sacred sites in Britain such as Lindisfarne (Northumberland), Iona (Scottish Inner Hebrides), Wearmouth and Jarrow (Tyne and Wear) and Glastonbury (Somerset), as part of a wider European movement of pilgrimage revival. New pilgrimage traditions are also actively being developed by faith communities as a means of revitalising local religion: for example on the Cowal peninsula in southern Argyll, a project focusing on 'faith tourism' incorporates medieval churches and carved stones (Márkus 2016). How do these local communities value and experience medieval sacred heritage? These questions have been addressed in Avril Maddrell's study of emerging pilgrimage practices on the Isle of Man (Maddrell 2015). She considers the annual pilgrimage which centres on the island's medieval keeills, tiny chapels that may have originated as proprietary (private) churches associated with each treen (land associated with a family group of small community). There are thirty-five keeills on Man and sixteen parish churches, many of which have place name elements connected with Celtic saints. However, they have little historical documentation to confirm their date or circumstances of foundation (Maddrell 2015: 137). 'Praying the Keeills' began in 2006 as an ecumenical movement, a means for individuals and communities of worship to connect through prayer walks focusing on medieval religious sites in the landscape. The participants are largely local, and while many are motivated by faith, others attend for the sense of fellowship, the physical experience of walking and interest in the island's heritage.

Maddrell concludes that the heritage of the keeills is treated as a 'spiritual resource' by the islanders. Heritage is central to the pilgrimage endeavour: local historians and Manx National Heritage curators provide public lectures to complement the prayer walks. Worship, walking and talking have 'reanimated' the keeills as sacred spaces and contributed to Manx national identity (Maddrell 2015: 135, 140). Archaeological authenticity is regarded as important because there is interest in the continuity of the keeills with earlier ritual practices (Maddrell 2015: 144). There is also a projection of the contemporary values of Celtic spirituality onto the past – the belief that the early Celtic church was closer to nature and less hierarchical and patriarchal than other church traditions (Maddrell 2015: 133; Power 2006). On the Isle of Man, local people have actively created a new purpose for medieval religious heritage that contributes spiritual value alongside well-being and cultural and economic value. Maddrell suggests that this kind of faith heritage is a good example of what has been termed 'heritage from below' (Robertson 2012), a local, grassroots movement which mobilises people and contributes to both the construction of identity and place-making.

PARTICIPATION AND PRACTICE: RE-ENGAGING MEDIEVAL ARCHAEOLOGY WITH THE SACRED

This chapter began by examining how the discipline of archaeology projects a secular framework of interpretation onto the archaeology of religion. I have reviewed cultural definitions of sacred heritage and the importance of the concepts of *authenticity*, *continuity* and *timelessness* in heritage narratives and visitor experience at medieval sacred sites. The value of sacred heritage in a secular society is often questioned, but there is ample evidence of increasing engagement with the spiritual through heritage, including growth in visitor numbers to religious sites and buildings, and increased participation in pilgrimage. The appetite for sacred heritage among cultural tourists is reflected in the growing number of exhibitions on aspects of religious life and in the founding of new museums dedicated to sacred heritage. Previous archaeological discussions of heritage value have tended to omit religious or spiritual value; however, this dimension is now gaining attention in definitions of value that place greater emphasis on intangible heritage. At the same time, we must acknowledge that there is no single perspective on spiritual heritage; the concepts of multi-vocality and contested heritage are crucial in evaluating spiritual values in relation to heritage. In concluding, I want to consider how we can apply the lessons of recent research in order to *re-engage* the practice of medieval archaeology with the sacred. There are two separate strands on which to reflect – how we engage more *actively* with living communities in adding value to sacred heritage; and how we engage more *meaningfully* with religious beliefs in our interpretations of medieval archaeology.

Classic definitions of sacred heritage emphasise the *otherness* of sacred sites: they are places associated with the gods and separate from everyday life (Shackley 2001). However, recent research on the *local value* of heritage demonstrates that religious sites and objects are fully integrated in contemporary life. Jones argues that the spiritual associations attached to a sense of place inform a community's collective identity and memory (Jones 2017). Maddrell's study of pilgrimage practice on the Isle of Man is a superb example of this process: the community has reanimated the heritage of the keeills to grow ecumenicalism, and at the same time, they have strengthened local and national identity in connection with medieval archaeology (Maddrell 2015). The Manx example helps us to tease out the values of sacred heritage: many people are drawn to the annual pilgrimage through a desire to share their faith, but secular participants seek companionship, local heritage and the sensory experience of walking the landscape. The 'spiritual' value of heritage is part of a more *holistic* experience and perception of religious sites and landscapes – one that is not exclusive to faith communities.

Religious heritage can evoke a 'spiritual' experience in secular individuals by prompting reflection on the numinous or on mortality and loss – for example, in the context of battlefields (discussed above). Another powerful example is the Lithuanian celebration of All Souls' Day (2 November): *Vėlinių Diena*, the season of spirit, is an annual pilgrimage to Lithuania's cemeteries to place flowers and light candles at the graves of the dead. Both secular and religious participants make the pilgrimage to remember loved ones, including Catholics, Orthodox and Protestant Christians, Jews, Muslims, followers of Baltic nature religions and Soviet-style atheists (Thorpe 2017). Secular engagement with sacred heritage may also bring a connection with nature, an appreciation of social memory, and the sense of well-being that comes from the 'timelessness' and 'stillness' that characterise medieval religious spaces. 'Spiritual' value is not incompatible with secular society or humanist values; it is closely bound up with *well-being and aesthetic value*, the sensory and visual qualities of heritage that are experienced on an individual basis.

Jones argues that the social value of heritage should be regarded as dynamic, a process of *valuing* heritage places rather than a fixed value category that can be defined and measured (Jones 2017; Jones and Leech 2015). Social value becomes an index of how local people engage with heritage, rather than the historical or material significance of a site or monument. Places of relatively minor historical value may accrue high social value; for example, when the tangible heritage of medieval carved stones and churches are animated in ecumenical pilgrimage practices (e.g. Maddrell 2015; Márkus 2016). To ascertain this value requires archaeologists to engage in participatory research, through ethnographic fieldwork, participant observation, focus groups, and drawing on oral history, historical and photographic archives (Jones 2017). Debates about authority and multi-vocality in geography, anthropology and archaeology are prompting a paradigm shift towards participatory methods that emphasise co-creation of knowledge and community engagement, as well as prioritising the ethical responsibilities of working with living communities (Meskell 2009). Participatory action research methodologies recognise that marginalised groups play an active role in the construction of identity and place (Kindon et al. 2007). These approaches resonate with the notion of 'heritage from below' – the use of heritage to mobilise and empower diverse groups that identify along axes of age, class, gender, ethnicity or faith (Robertson 2012).

Our interrogation of sacred heritage should also give critical consideration to its *political* use – to conflict and contestation. As Lynn Meskell reminds us, 'all heritage work essentially starts from the premise that the past is contested, conflictual and multiply constituted' (Meskell 2012: 1). A key characteristic of sacred places is that they are spaces of contestation, where legitimate ownership of sacred symbols is continually negotiated (Chidester and Linenthal 1995: 9–16). The archaeology of medieval churches and monasteries can appear deceptively *neutral*, *a-political* and *a-theoretical*. When archaeology is projected as heritage, however, it is never neutral, particularly where the subject matter is explicitly ideological. We recognise that prehistoric ritual sites like Stonehenge and Çatalhöyük are regarded as sacred sites by contemporary pagan and New Age communities, resulting in potential conflict with archaeologists and heritage managers (Bender 1998; Hodder 1998; Wallis and Blain 2003; White 2016).

Examples such as Córdoba's Mezquita and Istanbul's Hagia Sophia demonstrate that medieval sacred heritage can also be highly contested, revealing tensions and confrontations *between faiths* in the past and the present. These sites help us to better understand the deep histories of social diversity, to grasp 'that complex, messy cultural interactions are not new but have deep roots in European history' (Malik 2015). Sacred heritage is also used to legitimate contemporary authority *within faiths*, for instance along axes of gender. At the Greek Orthodox shrine of Tinos, church authorities cited historical precedents in their efforts to constrain female pilgrimage and to erase women's 'heightened emotionalism' from ritual spaces that they regard as public and male (Dubisch 1995: 219–23). Conflicts also arise *between dominant and alternative faiths*, as evidenced at Gamla Uppsala in Sweden, a site of national importance as the prime cult centre for both Old Norse religion and medieval Christianity. During the twentieth century, a grove of aspen trees became established near the medieval cathedral; in 2015, the Church of Sweden cut down the grove and destroyed the stumps, an act which was interpreted by some neo-pagans as an attempt to discourage their activities (John Ljungkvist, pers. comm.). Disagreements on strategies for heritage interpretation or conservation may result in conflicts *between heritage professionals and faith communities* (Jones 2010). For example, the reinstatement of the high altar at the ruined Cistercian abbey of Rievaulx took place in 2015, after a long campaign by senior Anglican leaders was successful in overcoming reservations held by English Heritage, the site's custodian.

My second question is how can we engage more meaningfully with the sacred in our interpretations of medieval archaeology? The connection is in the reflexive relationship between *archaeological knowledge and values* – how what we value informs what we seek to understand. I have argued that medieval archaeology follows the Western intellectual tradition in projecting a secular framework of values onto the study of religion (Fowles 2013), resulting in the prioritisation of 'rational' categories such as economy and technology over 'irrational' categories such as magic and folk belief. We have also seen that archaeological evidence is frequently used to underpin narratives of continuity and timelessness in relation to sacred space, with inadequate consideration given to *change, conflict and human agency* in shaping religious beliefs and practice. Some archaeologists have advocated an approach to the study of religion based on practice theory in order to emphasise agency and embodiment (e.g. Fogelin 2007; Petts 2011; Swenson 2015; Thomas et al. 2017). These approaches examine ritual as a *material process* and give priority to the active role of people in using sacred space and material culture, in contrast with secularist approaches that see religious participants as passive and controlled by elites.

The study of medieval pilgrimage is a pertinent example. Archaeological approaches have emphasised the economic dimensions of medieval pilgrimage, ranging from the production and sale of pilgrim souvenirs to the commercial and physical infrastructure developed at urban and rural shrines (e.g. Pestell 2005; Stopford 1994). In contrast, anthropological, historical and geographical perspectives on medieval pilgrimage emphasise embodiment and gendered experience (e.g. Bailey 2013; Bugslag 2016; Coleman and Eade 2004; Foley 2011). The historian James Bugslag has highlighted the intimate nature of the physical engagement between the medieval pilgrim and the shrine, which might involve kissing the tomb or relics; pilgrims thrusting their hands into foramina shrines to recover dust; ingesting blood, dust or water that was believed to have come into contact with the saint; bathing in water associated with the shrine; and sleeping at the saint's tomb in the hope of receiving religious visions. At Chartres, for example, pilgrims kept vigils in the cathedral, which was designed with a sloping floor and water system to sluice out the church each morning. Infirm pilgrims seeking a cure slept for nine nights in the cathedral crypt, which was staffed by female nurses in the fifteenth century (Bugslag 2016: 230, 233). Miracle stories at English shrines record men, women and children keeping nocturnal vigils in the churches at Reading Abbey and Beverley Minster, with women staying eight or nine nights at the shrines of Gilbert of Sempringham and St Frideswide of Oxford (Bailey 2013: 503). Pilgrims made offerings of candles and placed votives, often models of the afflicted body part for which they sought a cure. They also purchased cheap souvenirs or 'signs', which served as contact-relics to protect them on the homeward journey (see Chapter 4). Archaeologists have focused on these pilgrim signs as the most direct material evidence for medieval pilgrimage, recently extending this study to include practices of ritual deposition of pilgrimage souvenirs in the landscape (Anderson 2010; Spencer 1998). However, they have seldom considered the *embodied* experience of the pilgrimage journey or the ritual experience at the shrine (see Lash 2018 for an embodied perspective on early medieval Irish pilgrimage).

This is where archaeology might engage fruitfully with folklore, particularly in considering the rich evidence of folk belief in Scotland. Both archaeology and folklore reveal evidence for the persistence of material practices and embodied rites associated with pilgrimage, such as the construction of cairns and the placing of white pebbles. Cairns of pebbles on the beach at Columba's Bay on Iona were likely created by medieval pilgrims, a tradition that continues today; for example at Colmcille's Well, one of the three stations on the Glencolmcille pilgrimage, each pilgrim carries up three stones while saying prescribed prayers (Yeoman 1999: 77–9). Folklore sources suggest that these traditions continued into the eighteenth and nineteenth centuries as healing rituals associated with holy wells, where pilgrims gathered stones and placed them on cairns as part of the healing rite. These embodied practices appear to represent long-term continuities but they took on new meanings in a post-medieval context. Healing wells and pools, such as St Fillan's Well in the southeast Highlands (see Figure 5.3) and Loch Maree in the northwest, became associated with folk cures for insanity (Donoho 2014). At St Fillan's Well, the ritual involved circling the cairn three times and then placing an offering on the cairn, either a stone or a rag. The unfortunate sufferer was then bound and left overnight in the ruins of the chapel, with St Fillan's Bell placed on their head (Donoho 2014: 31). Emily Donoho argues that the religious aspect of the rite was lost as it became more medicalised in the eighteenth and nineteenth centuries, connected with the growing interest in cures for insanity that included cold water bathing and walking (Donoho 2014: 36).

On the Isle of Maree, pilgrims drank from the well and made offerings to an adjacent oak tree, or placed votives in chinks in the rock, such as coins, pins and buttons (Houlbrook 2015: 129). Rags and ribbons were tied to the tree in the eighteenth century, in the tradition of a clootie tree; in the nineteenth century it became more common to nail metal objects into the tree on Maree, including coins, buckles and nails (Figures 1.6 and 1.7). Ceri Houlbrook argues that this was part of a protective ritual, drawing on the Highland belief that metal repelled malevolent supernatural creatures such as fairies. The practice persists into the present day; however, the meaning of the ritual had changed by the late nineteenth century. The tree was originally central to healing rites involving the well and gradually became a wishing tree, a more secular ritual, but one still involving embodied practices of pilgrimage. In both these examples, folklore sources are used critically to assess the evolving meanings of rituals that appear superficially to represent long-term continuity, but in practice embody changing beliefs (Donoho 2014; Houlbrook 2015).

1.6 Coin tree on Isle Maree, Wester Ross (Northwest Highlands) in 2016 © Mick Sharp

1.7 Isle Maree, Wester Ross (Northwest Highlands) © Mick Sharp

1.8 The Witness Cairn at the Isle of Whithorn (Dumfries and Galloway) in 2007.
Reproduced by kind permission of Avril Maddrell

Contemporary pilgrims are drawn to the idea of *ritual continuity* at sites of medieval sacred heritage such as St Fillan's Well and Loch Maree. At the Isle of Whithorn, a new cairn was begun in 1997 as an ecumenical act to mark 1,600 years since St Ninian established the church in Scotland (Maddrell 2009). The cairn began as a local act of celebration, with school children placing stones that bore their names, later followed by pilgrims placing stones. It eventually grew to a substantial mound, with pilgrims of any faith – or no faith – placing a symbolic stone as an act of witness. Cairns are regarded by local people as an ancient communal rite, a means of marking a burial or a route through the landscape. Many of the stones placed at Whithorn's Witness Cairn are placed in memory of the recent dead, both human and animal companions (Figure 1.8). Placing a stone represents a personal, spiritual act, one that engages with the material practices and locales of medieval sacred heritage. Contemporary communities create their own value around medieval sacred heritage, which often involves 'the invention of tradition' (Hobsbawm 1983), and which engages both faith communities and secular pilgrims in creating a religious imaginary.

The themes introduced here are developed in the following chapters through more specific attention to medieval monastic archaeology and heritage. The geographical focus is British, drawing on comparative material from other regions of Europe. I have given particular priority to the archaeology of medieval Scotland, providing a case study through which to explore the regional character of monasticism (Chapters 2 and 4). Monasticism was a pan-European social movement driven to a large extent by powerful rulers and monastic orders. How did later medieval monasticism respond to *local* variations in belief, and to what extent did earlier, *indigenous* practices influence the local interpretation of monasticism? Chapter 2 begins by reflecting on the relationship between archaeological knowledge and values, particularly the role of Scottish national identity in shaping approaches to the study of medieval monasticism. The research agenda for monastic archaeology in Britain has given little consideration either to the Scottish experience of later medieval monasticism or to its distinctive material expression.

Chapters 3 and 4 pursue a 'practice-based' approach to monastic archaeology that emphasises agency and the active role of space, material culture and the body in medieval religious practice. Inspiration is taken from the emerging field of the material study of religion, which interrogates how bodies and things engage to construct the sensory experience of religion (Meyer et al. 2010; Morgan 2010). Archaeology provides insight to medieval religion as 'embodied, procedural knowledge embedded in the material world' (Mohan and Warnier 2017: 372), explored here through technologies that are characteristic of the monastic lifestyle. Geoff Egan compared the excavated assemblages of sixteen monastic sites in Britain and identified twenty-one categories of object that commonly occur (Egan 1997; Thomas et al. 1997: 107–11). The objects can be categorised in terms of *liturgical practice* (ornate metalwork), *personal devotion* (paternosters, papal bullae, burial goods, scourge), *music* (tuning pegs), *literacy* (styli, pencils, writing tablets, book mounts, parchment holders, spectacles, seal matrices), *hygiene* (taps and pipes), *privacy* (curtained beds evidenced by curtain rings), *textile-working* (spindle whorls, thimbles) and *trade* (jettons, weights, balances). None of these objects or technologies are exclusive to monastic sites; together, however, they represent a distinctive materiality of later medieval monasticism.

Monastic materiality is considered here in relation to ritual technologies of medieval medicine (Chapter 3), magic (Chapter 4) and memory (Chapter 5). While magic and medicine may appear to represent contradictory doctrines, both involved practices that aimed to protect, heal and transform the Christian body. The significance of magic and medicine to medieval monasteries is seldom explored in heritage interpretations of monastic sites, while academic approaches tend to study monasteries in isolation from hospitals and parish communities. These chapters challenge the traditional dichotomies of secular/religious and heterodox/orthodox, demonstrating the value of more holistic approaches to archaeological interpretations of medieval beliefs. They also detect regional differences in technologies of medicine and magic, reflecting local variations in monastic practice that may connect to earlier, indigenous beliefs. The incorporation and reworking of earlier indigenous beliefs is a theme that recurs throughout this book, revealing that later medieval monasteries drew actively upon their own concepts of sacred heritage.

Chapter 5 focuses on the monastic 'sense of place', how religious practices connected the body with material culture to create the sensory and emotional experience of sacred landscapes. A deep time perspective is taken to consider the monastic biography of place, evaluating the changing meanings of medieval sacred landscapes after the Reformation, and refuting the perception that medieval monasteries were 'frozen in time' (a theme discussed above). Particular attention is given to Glastonbury Abbey, an iconic monastic site that holds a unique place in English cultural identity. Glastonbury provides rich insights to the themes of place and memory and how sacred landscapes were actively *reimagined* by successive generations. Chapter 6 returns to the theme of sacred heritage, examining political and spiritual discourses and the role of archaeology in authenticating or challenging myths and narratives connected with medieval sacred sites. It draws together perspectives from heritage studies and medieval archaeology, to reflect on the changing meanings of authenticity and the value of archaeology in interpreting sacred heritage.

TWO

MONASTIC ARCHAEOLOGY AND NATIONAL IDENTITY: THE SCOTTISH MONASTIC EXPERIENCE

INTRODUCTION: REGIONAL RESEARCH TRADITIONS

This chapter considers archaeological approaches to the study of later medieval monasticism in Scotland, providing a case study through which to explore the regional character of monasticism and the factors that influence archaeological scholarship today. It reflects on how the construction of archaeological knowledge is shaped by national identity and the contemporary social value that we place on medieval heritage. Archaeology has played a salient role in the construction of national identities across Europe over the past 200 years, through the development of institutions such as museums, universities and national heritage agencies, and the selected versions of the past that they promote to the public (Díaz-Andreu and Champion 1996). National identity is understood here to refer to an individual's sense of belonging represented through collective culture, language, politics and heritage (both tangible and intangible), shared by a group of people regardless of whether the nation is formally constituted as a state (Greenfeld and Eastwood 2009). The archaeology of national identity often focuses on religious or sacred monuments and the perpetuation of 'Golden Age' narratives, periods celebrated for their artistic or technological achievements or military and political power (see Chapter 6). The primary function of nationalistic archaeology is to bolster the pride of peoples who feel deprived of political rights by more powerful nations (Trigger 1984: 360).

The chronological focus of this chapter is on the Scottish transition to reformed monasticism in the twelfth century, when Scotland embraced reformed orders of monks, canons and nuns, such as the Cistercians and Augustinians. The end of monasticism in Scotland is discussed as a case study in Chapter 5, examining the distinctive experience of Scottish religious houses following the Reformation Parliament in 1560. There was no formal dissolution of the monasteries in Scotland and these religious communities declined more gradually than in other Protestant regions of Europe. The reformed monastic orders of the twelfth century revived the communal model of Benedictine monasticism and placed greater emphasis on poverty and manual labour in monastic life. Medieval monasticism was a pan-European phenomenon characterised by powerful monastic orders and shared value systems. How did medieval monasticism respond to *local* variations in belief, and to what extent did earlier, *indigenous* practices influence the local interpretation of monasticism? This question has been considered by monastic scholars in examining the role of monasticism as a tool of conquest and colonisation, for example in the context of the Baltic crusades in Central Europe, the Reconquista in Spain and Portugal, and the Anglo-Norman colonisation of Ireland (e.g. Pluskowski 2017; Pluskowski et al. 2011; Lafaye 2018). Here, the aim is to place the Scottish monastic experience in comparative perspective, in order to identify what is distinctive and significant about monasticism in twelfth-century Scotland.

The archaeology of later medieval monasticism in Scotland remains a relatively under-developed field in comparison with many other regions of Europe. An archaeological research agenda is long overdue, but what factors have impeded its development? The subject has evolved in Scotland along a similar path to that travelled elsewhere in Europe: archaeological interest focused initially on the monastic core of the church and cloister, with more recent work expanding to include monastic landscapes, industry and buildings of the outer court (e.g. Hall 2006). The distribution of Scotland's monasteries was set out in the *Atlas of Scottish History* (McNeill and MacQueen 1996) and relevant archaeological information on individual sites can be found on Canmore, the database of Historic Environment Scotland. Excavations have taken place on numerous sites, although mostly on a small scale (ScARF 2012: 14), and important synthetic works on monastic archaeology and architecture were published over twenty years ago by Peter Yeoman (1995) and Richard Fawcett, respectively (1994a). Yet, despite significant investigations on individual sites and landscapes, monastic archaeology in Scotland lacks a critical framework of analysis to draw out its distinctive character. Nor has the study of religious institutions formed a major driver in shaping the archaeological research agenda for later medieval Scotland. Archaeological approaches to monasticism have remained principally descriptive and dominated by historical and architectural research questions. There has been relatively little interdisciplinary or theoretical engagement to address *social questions* about Scottish monasticism in the later Middle Ages or its wider *material character*.

In contrast, interdisciplinary studies have recently been undertaken on later medieval monasticism in Wales and Ireland. The 'Monastic Wales' and 'Monastic Ireland' projects feature web-based gazetteers that bring together historical and archaeological evidence for every monastic site and share them with a wide public audience. The 'Monastic Ireland' project contextualises monasticism at both the local and international level; for example, evaluating the extensive material remains of friaries in Ireland to consider how poverty was expressed through a distinctive mendicant materiality (Krasnodebska-D'Aughton and Lafaye 2018). The 'Monastic Wales' project aims to define Welsh monasticism in contrast to its English counterpart. The volume resulting from the project frames an important historical question which has immediate relevance to contemporary debates around Welsh national identity. It aims to explore the *significance* of monasteries in medieval Wales – how religious men and women shaped Welsh history and culture. Historical, archaeological and literary evidence is examined to begin to draw out the distinctive pattern of Welsh monasticism, and to make Welsh monasteries more 'visible', in terms of both scholarship and accessibility to a wider public (Burton and Stöber 2013a: xvii). There is currently no sister project in Scotland to those on the Welsh and Irish monasteries.

Regional research frameworks for monastic archaeology are rare internationally, although critical overviews have been undertaken for France (Bonde and Maines 1988, 2004) and Iceland (Kristjánsdóttir 2015a, 2015b, 2017; Monastic Iceland). In Italy, the archaeology of early medieval monasteries has been reviewed (Destefanis 2011), and the flagship project of San Vincenzo al Volturno (Hodges 1997) has opened up new comparative perspectives (Augenti 2016; De Rubeis and Marazzi 2008). Surveys of British monastic archaeology have tended to focus principally on England, with comparatively little coverage of Scotland and Wales (e.g. Bond 2004; Coppack 1990; Gilchrist and Mytum 1993; Greene 1992; Keevil et al. 2001). Regional overviews of monastic architecture are more numerous but generally prioritise particular orders, such as the Benedictines, the Cistercians and the friars (e.g. Bruzelius 2014; Carter 2015a, 2015b; Coomans 2001, 2004; Luxford 2005; Melville et al. 2015; Stalley 1987; Untermann 2001). The contemporary value and public visibility of monastic heritage has recently been addressed as part of European cultural patrimony (Coomans 2012; Coomans and Grootswagers 2016; Noppen et al. 2015), while historians have highlighted the role of monasteries as social and economic innovators in medieval Europe (Melville et al. 2014).

IN THE SHADOW OF THE 'GOLDEN AGE'

Why has the study of later medieval monasteries in Scotland failed to achieve a higher profile? Richard Fawcett argued that Scottish monasteries have been under-recognised due to the poor survival of architectural remains and because insufficient effort has been made to make information on them available. He also cited the historiographical tradition in Scotland: there was little interest in medieval architecture among Scottish antiquaries in the nineteenth century, in contrast with many other European traditions (Fawcett 1994a: 9). Chris Dalglish made a similar point to explain the late development of scholarship on Scotland's medieval countryside more generally: archaeological interest in Scottish prehistory emerged in the nineteenth century but there was comparatively little interest in understanding the medieval landscape (2012: 272). Scotland's medieval monasteries were also neglected by nineteenth-century, Presbyterian historians who were disinterested in Catholic heritage and viewed the reformed monasteries as morally corrupt, alien impositions. Their interest focused on the early medieval culdees, which were regarded as 'primitive and pure', and were considered to offer an historical precedent for Presbyterianism (Hammond 2006: 9). Scottish church studies were finally advanced in the 1950s by the Scottish Catholic Historical Association, with the development of the *Innes Review*. Scottish monastic history has been dominated until very recently by nationalist perspectives which focused on the medieval struggle for independence from England – for example, Arbroath Abbey (Angus) attracted historical interest as the setting for the Declaration of Arbroath (1320), and Melrose Abbey (Scottish Borders) (Figure 2.1) as the resting place for the heart of Robert the Bruce (d. 1329) (Jamroziak 2011: 35–7). The late Geoffrey Barrow (1924–2013) was influential in placing the history of the Scottish church and monasticism in a wider social framework, and recently historians including Emilia Jamroziak have situated Scottish monasticism in a comparative European context (Barrow 1973, 2004b; Jamroziak 2008, 2011, 2013).

Historiographical factors help to account for the late development of monastic studies in Scotland. But why does the subject continue to be neglected by archaeology? Why has medieval archaeology in Scotland failed to develop a critical framework for the analysis of later medieval monasteries? The crucial issue seems to be the role that Scottish national identity continues to play in selecting topics for archaeological study (Driscoll 2010). Later medieval monasteries have been neglected in Scottish archaeology because a lower *value* has been placed on them by heritage professionals, academic researchers and members of the public. 'Value' in this sense refers to the social significance placed on archaeological remains and their potential contributions to contemporary communities, culture, economy and political debates (e.g. Klamer 2014).

2.1 Melrose Abbey (Scottish Borders). Photograph by Michael Garlick / Wikipedia / CC BY-SA 4.0

The 'social value' of heritage relates more broadly to 'people's sense of identity, distinctiveness, belonging and place, as well as forms of memory and spiritual association' (Jones and Leech 2015). There is little doubt that Scotland's later medieval monasteries have been overshadowed by those of its 'Golden Age', the so-called Celtic monasteries of the sixth to ninth centuries.

Island communities such as Iona (Scottish Inner Hebrides), with its charismatic founder-saint Columba (*Colm Cille*), have captured the imaginations of historians, archaeologists and the wider public, including advocates of contemporary spirituality termed the 'new Celtic Twilight' (Power 2006). As Iain MacDonald commented: 'Scholarship has been traditionally weighted towards the early medieval period, where the search for the elusive "Celtic" brand of Christianity dwarfs anything published for the period after 1100' (2014: 17). Archaeological study of Scotland's early medieval monasteries is thriving, signalled by landmark publications on Portmahomack (Easter Ross), Inchmarnock (Argyl and Bute) and the Isle of May (Fife) (Carver 2016; Lowe 2008; James and Yeoman 2008). These excavations revealed early monastic centres that excelled in manuscript production, monastic teaching, healing and pilgrimage. Christian sculpture remains the key indicator for identifying the sites of early monasteries in Scotland (e.g. Foster and Cross 2005), in contrast with the shift to the patronage of buildings that characterises later medieval monasteries.

Scottish historiography bears close similarities with Ireland, where archaeological interests have focused predominantly on 'Ireland's Golden Age', *c.*500–900 CE. Early medieval monasteries have been valued as the apogee of native Irish culture, in contrast with later medieval monasteries that carry the negative overtones of Norman colonisation (O'Sullivan 1998). Throughout the twentieth century, archaeological scholarship on medieval Ireland was dominated by the 'Golden Age' narrative (O'Sullivan et al. 2014: 35). Even the most recent synthesis of archaeological excavations on medieval sites in Ireland covers the period up to *c.*1100 (O'Sullivan et al. 2014: 35), and there is no synthetic account for recent excavations on later medieval sites. The current 'Monastic Ireland' project, which focuses on the period 1100–1700 CE, therefore represents a major step-change in scholarship and may signal a corresponding shift in the social and cultural value that is placed on Ireland's later medieval monastic heritage (Krasnodebska-D'Aughton and Lafaye 2018). The focus on Scotland's 'Golden Age' is the legacy of a wider historical tradition that developed in the nineteenth century, beginning with the popularisation of Scottish history by Sir Walter Scott. The resulting narratives of medieval Scotland emphasise *ethnic differences* between Celtic and Anglo-Norman culture, a trope that was also explored by Welsh historians in the nineteenth century (Sims-Williams 1986). Matthew Hammond (2006) has examined the pervasive influence of this dualistic ethnic framework on the development and periodisation of Scottish history, which draws a sharp boundary at *c.*1100, separating Celtic Scotland of the eleventh century from Norman Scotland of the twelfth century. He argues that cultural and political projections of ethnic value that began in the nineteenth century continue to construct historical discourses around Scottish law, kingship, lordship and religion.

Within archaeology, the situation is exacerbated by the small number of later medievalists employed in Scotland. Later medieval archaeologists were appointed to posts in the Royal Commission on the Ancient and Historical Monuments of Scotland (RCAHMS) and the National Museum of Scotland, but they have been largely absent from university departments of archaeology. The higher value accorded to early medieval monasteries is reflected in the Scottish Archaeological Research Framework (ScARF 2012). This otherwise excellent document repeats the common tendency to under-value later medieval monasticism as a social and cultural phenomenon. Later medieval monasteries are omitted entirely from the chapter on 'mentalities' that addresses identity, ethnicity, gender and spirituality, although later medieval parish churches and pilgrimage are considered. Instead, later medieval monasteries are briefly cited for their potential to elucidate developments in agriculture and industry (ScARF 2012: 48, 55). ScARF identifies priorities for future research on religion exclusively in the early medieval period, including early medieval sculpture, early churches, early cemeteries and the relationship of protohistoric settlement to prehistoric ritual landscapes and practices. The period up to the later eighth century is described as 'the most inventive religious phase in Scotland', when 'belief was regional and creative' (ScARF 2012: 82). We can perhaps infer from its absence that archaeologists consider later medieval monasticism to be the inverse of the 'Golden Age', manifested by pan-European monastic orders such as the Cistercians, and lacking regional diversity, invention and creativity.

The research framework emphasises the importance of placing early medieval monasticism within a long-term perspective that connects it with prehistory, in the tradition of 'the long Iron Age' of Ireland and Scandinavia. This is informed by Martin Carver's compelling thesis that early medieval monastic practices in Scotland were influenced by prehistoric rites (2009). He notes precursors for early medieval monastic traits including the use of curvilinear enclosures, stone slab cist burials, stone markers and the curation of ancestral bones, which is continued in the Christian cult of relics. He concludes that early medieval people adopted archaic forms to reconcile changing beliefs and as a means of self-expression. Carver calls for early medieval monasticism to be placed within an interpretative framework that *looks back* at prehistory. In contrast, Stephen Driscoll argues for early medieval monasticism to be placed in a long-term perspective that *looks forward* towards the later Middle Ages and the modern, placing sites like early medieval Govan (Glasgow) in a framework of historical archaeology spanning 1,500 years, from the sixth to the twenty-first centuries (Driscoll 2010).

Driscoll contends that national identity has influenced the Scottish archaeological research agenda and in particular the drive to demonstrate *cultural distinctiveness* from England (Driscoll 2010: 443). The impact of national identity on the construction of archaeological knowledge helps to explain the low profile of Scotland's later medieval monasteries. They are accorded low cultural value because they do not figure in dominant discourses of Scottish heritage and national identity (Atkinson 1996). Reform monasticism of the later Middle Ages is often regarded as an English import – not an instrument of direct colonisation as it was in Wales and Ireland, but certainly not an expression of indigenous culture. The first step in developing a more critical framework for the study of medieval monasteries in Scotland is therefore to consider the construction of archaeological *value* in relation to national identity.

'VALUE' AND THE CONSTRUCTION OF ARCHAEOLOGICAL KNOWLEDGE ON MEDIEVAL MONASTERIES

How do later medieval monasteries look through the lens of archaeological 'value' that is projected in the Scottish Archaeological Research Framework?

2.2 The Great Drain at Paisley Abbey (Renfrewshire). © Crown Copyright: Historic Environment Scotland

To what extent are they 'inventive, regional and creative'? Later medieval monasteries are typically characterised as innovators in economy and technology (e.g. Aston 1993; Coppack 1990). In Scotland, later medieval monasteries introduced coal mining, intensified salt panning and operated granges dedicated to ironworking, lead, silver and gold mining (Hall 2006); they developed new approaches to sheep and cattle farming based on the monastic system of granges (Fawcett and Oram 2004). They stimulated local pottery production in the twelfth and thirteenth centuries in areas that were previously a-ceramic, as suggested by excavations at Tironensian Kelso (Scottish Borders) and Cistercian Dundrennan Abbey (Dumfries and Galloway) (Lowe 2005: 331; Ewart 2001: 39). And, of course, the often cited hallmark of monastic civilisation, they introduced high-quality plumbing and water management. This is vividly illustrated in Scotland by the superior engineering of the late fourteenth-century Great Drain of Paisley (Renfrewshire) (Figure 2.2), rediscovered in 1990 (Malden 2000), and the unique survival at Cistercian Glenluce (Dumfries and Galloway) of earthenware pipes, still in situ where joints and inspection chambers are exposed to view (Canmore ID 61214). However, the *cultural* contribution of Scotland's monasteries should not be overlooked, such as the essential role played by the friars in education and in the establishment of medieval universities at St Andrews, Aberdeen and Glasgow (Randla 1999: 249). There were great libraries at the cathedral of St Andrews (Fife) and the monasteries of Kinloss (Moray), Deer (Aberdeenshire), Scone (Perth and Kinross), Cambuskenneth (Stirling), Melrose, Dryburgh (Scottish Borders) and Culross (Fife), the last with a scriptorium which produced books sold for commercial profit (Curran 2015: 31). In the fourteenth century, campaigns of rebuilding at Melrose, St Andrews and Paisley stimulated a distinctive Scottish architectural style that blended influences from France and the Low Countries to produce architecture quite distinct from that of contemporary England (Fawcett 1994a: 76–81).

The following chapters will explore the inventive contribution made by Scottish monasteries to medieval technologies of healing and magic. There is one important contribution that I would like to stress here: reformed monasticism was truly transformational in providing new opportunities for *women* in Scotland to engage actively in monasticism. The florescence of Scotland's 'Celtic' monasteries seems to have been reserved principally, if not wholly, for men. In contrast with the early medieval monastic traditions documented for Ireland, England and Francia (Bitel 2013), there is little (documented) evidence for women's engagement with early monasticism in Scotland. The exception is the Northumbrian monastery at Coldingham (Scottish Borders), which followed the Anglian model of the double house: Bede records that it was in existence by the 660s presided over by Abbess Æbbe (Cowan and Easson 1976: 47; Bartlett 2003). Excavations have confirmed the presence of a ditched enclosure at Coldingham dating from the seventh century and the presence of Anglian sculpture strengthens the identification of Coldingham as Æbbe's monastery (Stronach 2005).

The monasticism of the reformed orders channelled the agency of medieval Scottish women as founders, patrons, nuns and hospital lay-sisters. The turning point both for women and monasticism was the involvement of Queen Margaret, second wife of King Mael Coluim (Malcolm) III and daughter of Edward the Atheling, who was son of the Anglo-Saxon king of Wessex, Edmund Ironside (Barrow 2004a). Margaret spent her early life in exile in Hungary before returning to England with her family, who fled to Scotland in 1066. She was married at Dunfermline (Fife) in *c.*1070 to Malcolm Canmore. She introduced reformed monasticism to Scotland, assisted by Archbishop Lanfranc of Canterbury, who sent three monks from Canterbury Christchurch (Kent) to establish a Benedictine cell at Dunfermline. The historian Geoffrey Barrow (1973: 196) argued that Margaret was the catalyst for the comprehensive transformation of Scotland under her sons and grandsons, in which monasticism was a key tool in nation-building, particularly under Alexander I (1107–24) and David I (1124–53). The so-called Canmore dynasty has been viewed as the breakpoint between Celtic and Norman Scotland and the stimulus for Scotland's process of Europeanisation (Hammond 2013: 2). Matthew Hammond (2006) has called for a critique of the Canmore concept and its impact on the periodisation of Scottish history. Nevertheless, the importance of Margaret as a religious innovator and role model for women remains convincing.

Margaret was buried in front of the high altar at Dunfermline, dying just three days after her husband was killed at Alnwick (Northumberland), in 1093. For at least one hundred years prior to her canonisation *c.*1250, she was venerated by the gentry as a blessed intercessor and holy queen (Hammond 2010). She is described as a servant of Christ and 'most pious mother', in Turgot's account of her life, written *c.*1100, suggesting that the cult of the Virgin Mary may have been influential in constructing popular devotion to Margaret. Based on her miracle stories, Robert Bartlett has described Margaret's cult as regional and with a strong masculine core (Bartlett 2003: xli).

2.3 Tomb effigy of Lady Dervorgilla at Sweetheart Abbey (Dumfries and Galloway). © Crown Copyright: Historic Environment Scotland

However, she was specifically called upon to assist women in pregnancy and childbirth: several Scottish queens gave birth at Dunfermline in order to wear the relic of Margaret's birthing 'sark' or chemise (Bartlett 2003: xxxix). Margaret's example was followed by Scottish women who established monasteries in pious acts of commemoration. Examples include Matilda d'Aubigny, who was co-founder of the Augustinian monastery of Inchaffray (Perth and Kinross) *c.*1200, together with her husband Gille Brigte, Earl of Strathearn, in memory of their son Gille Crist (Veitch 1999); Queen Ermengarde, wife of William the Lion, who established the small Cistercian abbey at Balmerino (Fife) *c.*1227 and was buried there (Hammond 2010: 74); and the romantic Lady Dervorgilla of Galloway, who founded Cistercian Sweetheart Abbey (Dumfries and Galloway) in 1273 in memory of her husband, John Balliol. The abbey was named in reference to his embalmed heart, which resided in an ivory casket bound with enamelled silver. Dervorgilla was buried with the casket in the sanctuary of the monastic church at Sweetheart Abbey and she is depicted on her effigy holding the heart (Richardson 2006: 20) (Figure 2.3).

Scotland's fifteen medieval nunneries were dismissed by twentieth-century historians as relatively poor and small (Cowan and Easson 1976: xii; Dilworth 1995). The emphasis on national politics in the historical study of Scottish monasticism (discussed above) has placed religious women at the margins of scholarship. Revisionist histories of medieval religious women have been written across Europe over the past forty years: the first historical study of Scottish nunneries was completed in 2005 by Kimm Curran (Curran 2005). Previous scholarly neglect of Scottish nunneries reveals a misunderstanding of the role and scale of institutions for medieval religious women, which were typically established to have a close relationship with the founding family rather than a national role (Gilchrist 1994). Prosopographical analysis confirms that Scottish nuns were recruited from the immediate locality of the nunnery, or were related either to the nuns or their tenants living on the monastic estate (Curran 2005: 148) (Figure 2.4). The Augustinian nunnery at Iona (Figure 2.5)

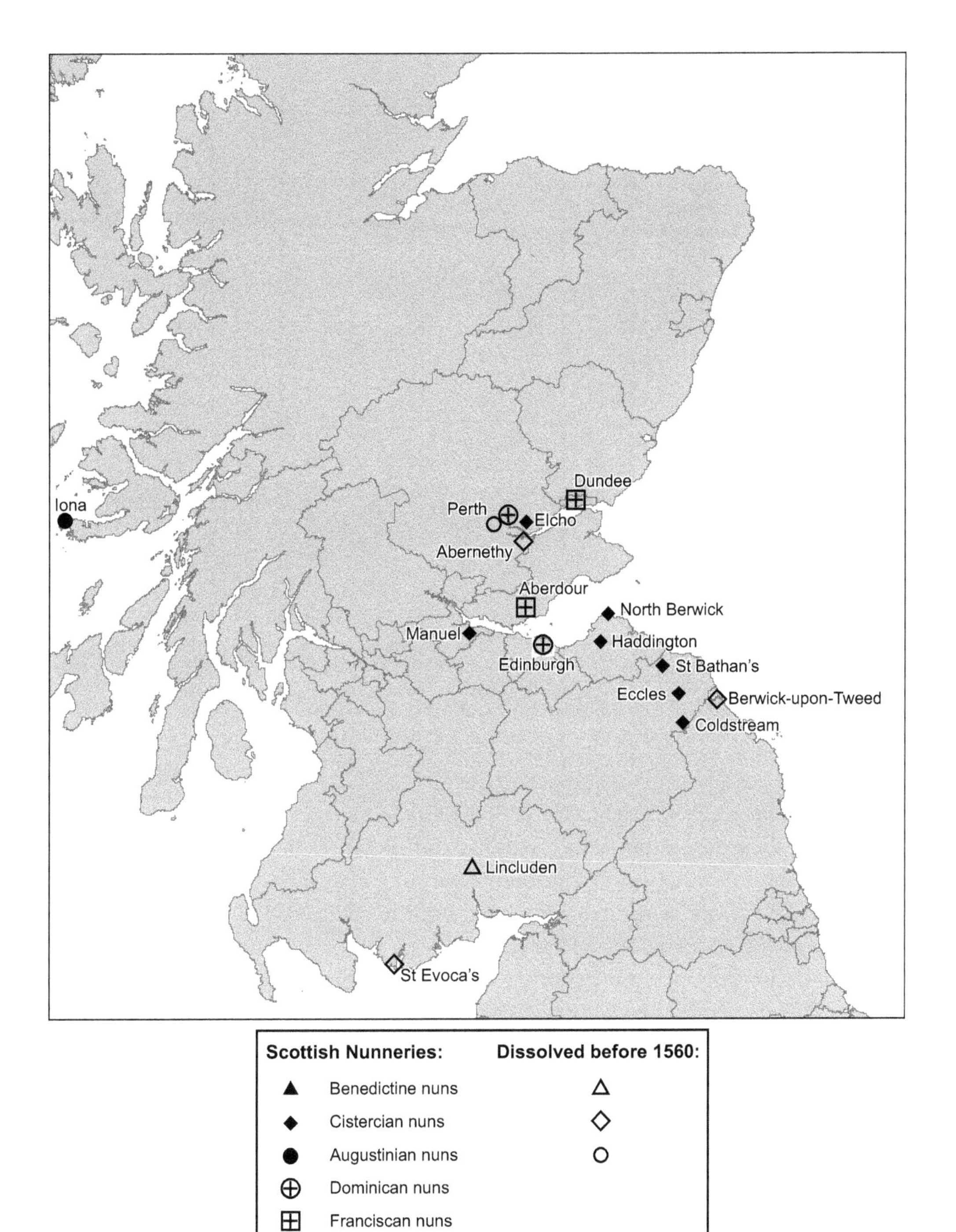

2.4 Map showing the location of medieval nunneries in Scotland (*c.* 1150–1560). After McNeill and MacQueen 1996 © Sarah Lambert-Gates

2.5 Iona Nunnery (Scottish Inner Hebrides). © Jean Williamson

was founded by Raghnall mac Somhairle in 1203, close to his foundation of the Benedictine monastery at Iona, and his sister, Bethóc, became the first prioress (Ritchie 1997). The well-preserved buildings of Iona compare favourably with surviving nunnery architecture in England, Ireland and Northern Europe, in terms of the quality and scale of architecture. Like their male counterparts, Scottish nunneries also promoted industry: the only example of a medieval tile kiln excavated in Scotland was in the grounds of the nunnery at North Berwick (East Lothian), which produced highly decorated floor tiles (ScARF 2012: 99; Hall and Bowler 1997).

The partially excavated site of the Cistercian nunnery of Elcho, outside Perth, is thought to have been founded in the thirteenth century by David Lindsay of Glenesk and his mother, Lady Marjory (Cowan and Easson 1976: 146). The site has yielded imported pottery comparable to that of the burgh of Perth and religious material culture including paternoster beads and window glass. There were three copper alloy book clasps, a mount possibly from a book cover, a nun's grave slab with inscription, and the base of a hanging bronze oil lamp (Reid and Lye 1988: 70) (Figure 2.6). This may appear on first glance to be a fragmentary assemblage, but it is actually a unique group of finds representing literacy from a British nunnery. Even thoroughly excavated

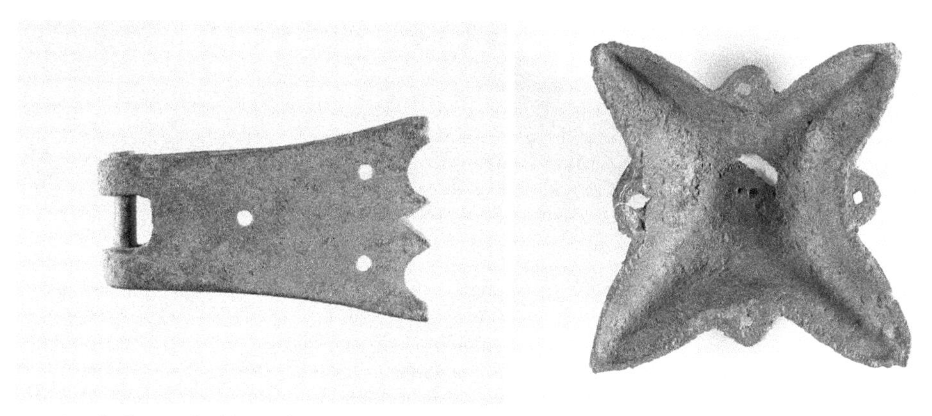

2.6 Book clasp and oil lamp from Elcho Nunnery (Perth and Kinross). Clasp: 30 × 22 × 4 mm; lamp: 201.5 × 54 × 20 mm. Images courtesy of Culture Perth & Kinross

English nunneries, such as St Mary Clerkenwell in London, have failed to produce material culture confirming literacy (Sloane 2012: 160). This contrasts with the rich assemblages of literary material culture that are typical of male religious houses, indicating that literacy was an important technology in shaping monastic experience (Egan 1997). The archaeological evidence for literacy at Elcho is a significant commentary on the spiritual life of Scotland's nunneries and the new opportunities that they provided for religious women. A number of books also survive from Scottish nunneries, including the Iona Psalter, the Sciennes Psalter, an English Bible from Elcho and a possible missal fragment from Lincluden (Dumfries and Galloway). The literacy of Scottish nuns may also have served a broader social purpose: Curran concludes that members of the laity were sent to the nunneries of Haddington (East Lothian), Elcho and Aberdour (Fife) to receive an education from the nuns (Curran 2015: 25).

MONASTICISM AND NATION-BUILDING

How did monastic foundations contribute to nation-building and to what extent was the Scottish experience distinctive? The Scottish Archaeological Research Framework identifies state formation as one of the key questions for future research in Scottish medieval archaeology: 'understanding why, where and how' Scotland emerged (ScARF 2012: i). Medieval monasteries were critical to Scottish nation-building in the twelfth and thirteenth centuries and their role in this process can be clarified in comparison with other regions of Britain and Europe. First, what did Scottish monasticism look like in the late eleventh century, on the eve of monastic reform? Monasteries of the 'Golden Age' had largely disappeared by the ninth century, such as Pictish Portmahomack, although communities of monks evidently survived. Sculpture dating to

2.7 Early monastic settlement at Sgòr nam Ban-Naomha ('Cliff of the Holy Women'), Canna (Scottish Inner Hebrides). © Royal Commission on the Ancient and Historical Monuments of Scotland

the tenth and eleventh centuries suggests the location of religious communities, for example an exceptional cross-slab at Dunkeld (Perth and Kinross) (Macquarrie 1992: 122). Turgot, the biographer of Margaret, described religious life in Scotland as 'very many men shut up in separate little cells in various places, who though they were living in the flesh practised denial of the flesh through extreme asceticism' (Barrow 1973: 190). His description may have been intended for political reasons to minimise the importance of monastic life before Margaret. Nonetheless, it places an important emphasis on the *eremitic* character of Celtic monasticism – a desert monasticism of the north Atlantic. In eleventh-century Scotland, eremitic monasticism was represented by both individual hermits and island communities of ascetic monks. It is likely that these communities continued to follow the Irish monastic lifestyle, living in individual cells such as those on Canna at Sgòr nam Ban-Naomha (Scottish Inner Hebrides), comprising the ruins of beehive cells in a stone enclosure (Dunbar and Fisher 1974) (Figure 2.7). Early churches have been excavated on the Isle of May and Iona (St Ronan's). Dating to the tenth century, these first stone structures were bonded in clay and built on a modest scale to accommodate small communities at worship (*c.* 3.5 m × 4 m internally) (Yeoman 2009).

There were communities of priests or *clerici* in eleventh-century Scotland who seem to have fulfilled some type of pastoral role and there were also

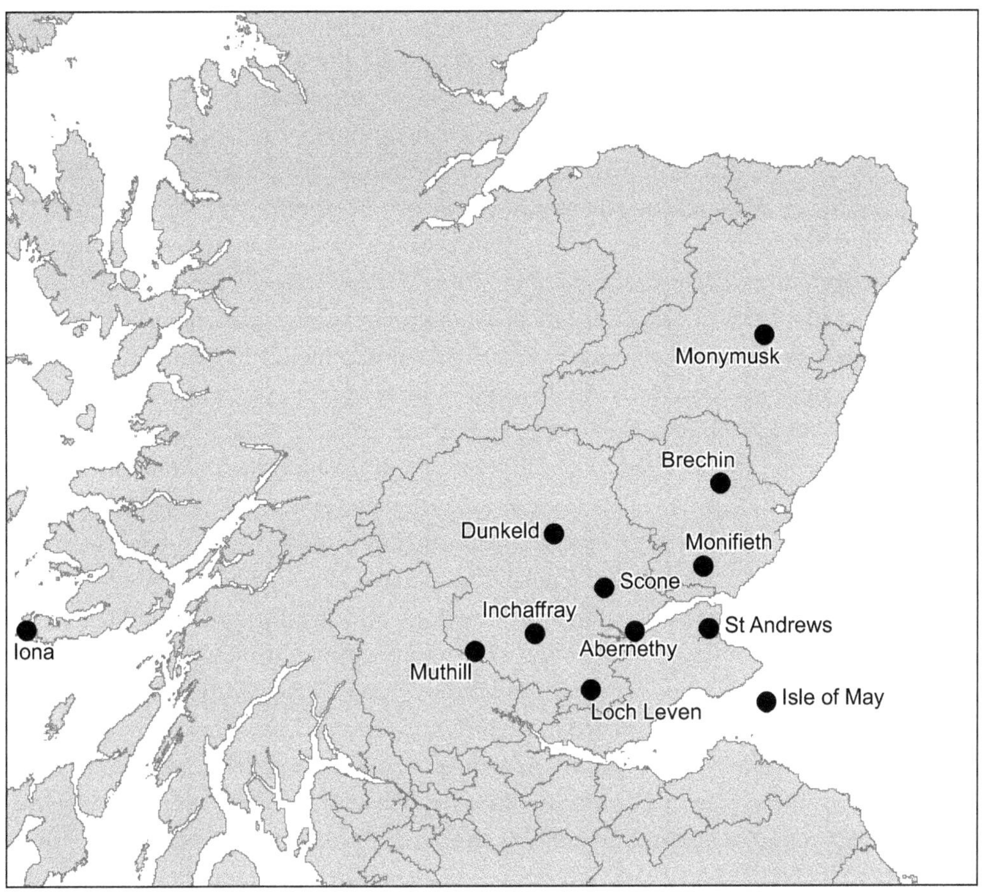

2.8 Map showing culdee and early monastic sites in Scotland (10th–11th centuries). After McNeill and MacQueen 1996 © Sarah Lambert-Gates

eremitic monks – the shadowy culdees, or *Céli Dé*. The term means companions or clients of God and was originally reserved for an elite class of eremitic monks and hermits. The reform movement of the *Céli Dé* originated in Ireland and was introduced to Scotland via Iona in the early ninth century (Clancy 1999). By the tenth or eleventh century, there were eremitic *Céli Dé* at remote sites such as Inchaffray and Loch Leven (Perth and Kinross), which Turgot records as receiving patronage from Margaret (Figure 2.8). However, the term *Céli Dé* was also applied to communities of priests, such as those serving the episcopal church at St Andrews, which appears to have comprised a group of married clergy based on hereditary succession (Macquarrie 1992). From the tenth to the thirteenth centuries, the term *Céli Dé* encompassed a wide diversity of monastic experience in Scotland (Clancy 1999). It seems that the spiritual needs of rural communities to the north of the Forth were served by the secular priests of monasteries that also incorporated *Céli Dé*, while the south followed the Northumbrian model of quasi-parochial minsters served by priests, such as Whithorn (Dumfries and Galloway) (Barrow 2004b: 592). There was nothing in Scotland that resembled the reformed, western monasticism of France and England; there was no regulation by bishops and very little contact with the papacy. The changes experienced by Scotland in the twelfth century were part of a wider pattern across Europe, in which local churches became more centrally controlled by Rome and local rulers used monasteries to consolidate their own power.

In Normandy, for example, the Norman dukes restored ancient monasteries that had been destroyed by their Viking grandfathers. Cassandra Potts argues that monasticism was central in forging Norman regional identity in the tenth and eleventh centuries. The dukes of Normandy appealed to local loyalties by rebuilding monastic heritage, reviving the cults of Merovingian saints and supporting the emergence of the reformed monastic orders. Monastic patronage was fundamental to transforming the perception of these rulers from Viking marauders into Norman princes (Potts 1997: 133–7). The Normans extended this strategy to England as part of the Conquest: William used Norman monasticism as an instrument of colonisation and consolidation in England, establishing new foundations and planting Norman monks in ancient monastic foundations such as Canterbury (Kent), Durham (County Durham) and Glastonbury (Somerset), in order to appropriate Anglo-Saxon sacred heritage. This process also involved major campaigns of rebuilding to establish the claustral plan at English monasteries. There is no archaeological evidence for a monastic cloister in England before the Norman Conquest – the commonly cited example of Glastonbury has recently been disproven by reanalysis of the archaeological archive (Gilchrist and Green 2015; see Chapter 6).

It is this Norman model of a Christian kingdom that was adopted by Scottish kings and Gaelic nobles in the twelfth and thirteenth centuries. Reformed monasticism was not imposed on Scotland; instead, the monastic cultural package was adopted as part of a proactive strategy of state-making that was intended to create a unified, European-style kingdom (Stringer 2000: 127). The establishment of a monastery conferred social status and prestige on the founder and identified them as a true Christian king or queen. For Kings Alexander I and David I, founding monasteries was a way of consolidating the kingdom of Scotland and bringing it into the mainstream of European culture (Jamroziak 2011: 47). Their foundations sustained close connections to the royal house by serving as royal mausolea, particularly Margaret's foundation of Benedictine Dunfermline (*c.*1070) and David's foundations of Cistercian Melrose (*c.*1136) and Augustinian Holyrood (Edinburgh; 1128). Royal palaces were also established at the monasteries of Dunfermline and Holyrood, which were foci for royal ceremony such as weddings and funerals (Ewart and Gallagher 2013). Burial practices reflect the close association of Melrose Abbey with royal and noble benefactors, in contravention of

Cistercian ordinances. Melrose permitted secular burial in the east end of the church in the twelfth and thirteenth centuries, in contrast with the strict observance of its mother house at Rievaulx (North Yorkshire), which did not permit lay burial until the mid-fourteenth century (Jamroziak 2011: 98–9). The burial of women was documented at Melrose in the thirteenth century and excavations in the chapter house uncovered a female interment in a sandstone coffin (Ewart et al. 2009: 269). In this respect, Scottish Cistercians were similar to those in Denmark, who welcomed the early burial of secular elites from the late twelfth century (McGuire 1982). The act of monastic foundation in Scotland was the exclusive preserve of the laity, in contrast with parts of Northern Europe and the Baltic, where bishops were often the key drivers of monasticism and the process of Europeanisation (Blomkvist 2004). Scandinavian kings and bishops established monasteries from the twelfth century in emulation of the 'Catholic core' of Europe (Nyberg 2000).

Monasticism in Scotland was rapidly transformed by the energy of the Canmore house, which spread its patronage widely (Figure 2.9). David I founded four Cistercian monasteries, three Augustinian, two Tironensian, two Benedictine and one Premonstratensian monastery; he established the first nunnery and introduced the Knights Templar and Knights Hospitaller to Scotland (Cowan and Easson 1976: 6). These monasteries had strong Anglo-Norman associations – they were often the daughter houses of English monasteries and staffed by English monks. They have therefore been regarded as a foreign (English) introduction, along with other aspects of feudalism established in twelfth-century Scotland such as burghs, sheriff courts and coinage. Recent historical research cautions against the simplistic binary framework of Gaelic = old *versus* Anglo-Norman = new, and the associated projections of cultural value that these ethnic oppositions promote (Hammond 2013). For instance, the Gaelic nobility founded monasteries and enrolled their sons and daughters as monks and nuns, while the local peasantry would have provided lay-brothers for Cistercian and Premonstratensian abbeys and lay-sisters for hospitals (Stringer 2000: 153).

Royal patronage was the catalyst for rapid growth in Scottish monasticism from 1100–65, followed by a period of fifty years of consolidation when new foundations were established by earls and magnates (Hammond 2010: 75). Gaelic nobles adopted the same cultural model of the Christian prince as monastic founder, perhaps in direct competition with the Canmores. Although Scotland in the twelfth century was united under a common monarch, it was still a highly fragmented nation (Broun 2007). In the west of Scotland, the Gaelic-Norse ruler, Fergus, Lord of Galloway, was associated with the foundation of two Cistercian, three Premonstratensian, one Augustinian and one Benedictine monasteries (Stringer 2000: 128). Gaelic nobles sponsored the conversion of *Céli Dé* into Augustinian communities, such as

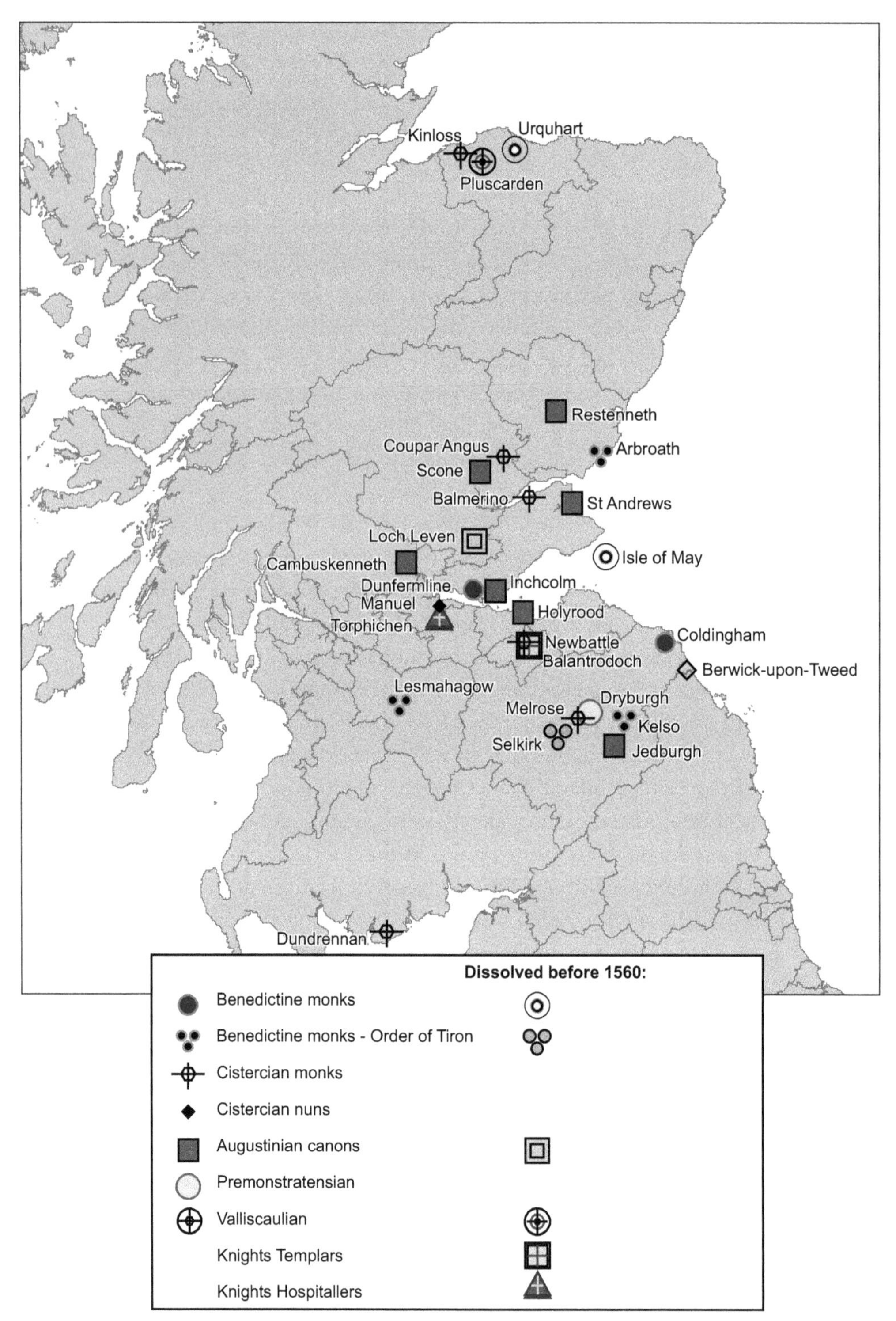

2.9 Map showing monasteries founded by the Canmore dynasty (1058–1286). After McNeill and MacQueen 1996 © Sarah Lambert-Gates

Earl Gille Brigte of Strathearn and Earl Gille Crist of Mar, respectively founders of Augustinian Inchaffray and Monymusk (Aberdeenshire), *c.*1200 (Veitch 1999: 21). A similar process was underway in Wales, where the sites of ancient Welsh *Céli Dé* were transformed into Augustinian monasteries by the royal house of Gwynedd, described by Karen Stöber and David Austin as a strategy 'to reform the practices of their cultural church and bring it more into line with European norms of monasticism' (Stöber and Austin 2013: 46). The Irish church became receptive to external influences from the mid-eleventh century and began the 'de-tribalisation of ancient monasteries', followed by the foundation of large numbers of new Cistercian and Augustinian monasteries in the twelfth century (Barrow 2004b: 602).

A defining characteristic of twelfth-century monastic foundations in Scotland was the *appropriation* of indigenous sacred heritage: reformed monasteries were created at ancient holy places and new foundations actively promoted Pictish and Celtic saints, alongside the new emphasis placed on Christ, the Holy Trinity and the Virgin Mary (Hammond 2010). Alexander I introduced the Augustinians to the ancient see of St Andrews and established the cathedral priory as Scotland's chief ecclesiastical centre. He also created an Augustinian priory at Scone (Perth and Kinross), a locale resonating with religious and political significance, as the ancient inauguration site of Scottish kings. Fergus of Galloway is credited with the transformation of Whithorn, the shrine of St Ninian's cult, into a cathedral priory staffed by the austere Premonstratensian order. David I gave the Celtic shrine on the Isle of May to the Benedictines of Reading Abbey, the foundation of his brother-in-law, the English King Henry I. David established new monasteries on or near the sites of Anglian minsters at Melrose and Jedburgh, respectively Cistercian and Augustinian foundations.

The reuse of ancient sites sometimes required adaptation and complex engineering to accommodate the claustral plan that was synonymous with reformed monasticism. For example at Jedburgh (Scottish Borders), excavations have shown that the choice to build on a steep river bank required the construction of terraces cut into the river bank to provide a level platform for the claustral complex. Siting of the cloister was clearly determined by the desire for visibility and dominance over the landscape. The cliff face was consolidated to protect the buildings close to the river and the Jed Water had to be diverted before the south range of the cloister could be built (Lewis and Ewart 1995). Why was it critical for monasteries of the reformed orders to be based around *cloisters*, even where sites were not well suited topographically? In functional terms, the cloister integrated four ranges of buildings and provided covered access between them. The cloister was also a powerful symbol of *coenobitic* monasticism and the Benedictine ethos of communal living. It represented a firm rejection of earlier forms of Celtic, eremitic monasticism, in which cells for solitary monks were arranged in concentric enclosures.

The cloister drew on Roman archetypes including courtyard houses and the galleried atria of basilican churches in Rome, and thus carried resonances of the Roman church. Its walks served as a performative space for processions, enhancing the monastic liturgy and integrating the church with the domestic buildings. It was connected to monastic ritual through observances carried out at the *lavatorium*, the washing place at the entrance to the refectory. It was the centre of daily life for the monks (or nuns) as well as a place of learning and contemplation, with carrels or benches provided for individual study (Gilchrist 1995: 66, 77–93). For example, the remains of seating can be detected in the cloisters at Inchcolm (Fife), Melrose and Iona (Curran 2015: 29). The cloister was at the same time a metaphorical space: the garden in the central space of the cloister garth represented the heavenly paradise that was the subject for monastic contemplation (Cassidy-Welch 2001: 48). The cloister served as a focus for monastic memory, with imagery selected to prompt monastic meditation and to evoke religious meaning (Carruthers 2000: 16). For example, the sequence and iconography of the historiated cloister bosses at Norwich Cathedral reinforced monastic concepts of time and communal history (Gilchrist 1995: 253–7). More than any other feature of monastic architecture, the cloister constructed embodied experience, bringing together material culture with monastic techniques of the body, including liturgical ritual, literacy and memory practices.

Even the oldest Celtic monastery in Scotland was subject to re-foundation at the close of the twelfth century: the sacred site of Iona, founded 563 CE, was the last to survive before its reform. As well as housing the shrine of St Columba, Iona was the burial place of Scottish kings until the late eleventh century, when it was eclipsed by Dunfermline. A Benedictine monastery was established at Iona *c.*1200 by Ranald (Rognvaldr), son of Somhairle, a Gaelic-Norse warlord who had seized control of the Kingdom of the Isles in the mid-twelfth century (Figure 2.10). The enclosure (vallum) of the early monastery at Iona is well-preserved and the remains show that Ranald was determined to stamp his new Benedictine cloister onto the centre of the ancient complex. The Irish *familia* of Columba are reported to have burnt down the new Benedictine monastery, while a contemporary poem laments the arrival of foreigners and records the cursing of the Somerled line (Hammond 2010: 83). However, Ranald's monastery evidently aimed to appropriate and promote the cult of Columba, rather than suppress it. The sanctity associated with St Columba and his grave-site was harnessed for the new Benedictine foundation by maintaining spatial *continuity of place* with its Celtic precursor.

Archaeological evidence suggests that the fabric of the existing shrine of St Columba was incorporated into the new Benedictine complex, tucked between the west end of the church and the west range of the cloister. This tiny chapel (4.3 m × 3.2 m) was rebuilt in the 1960s but the original walls

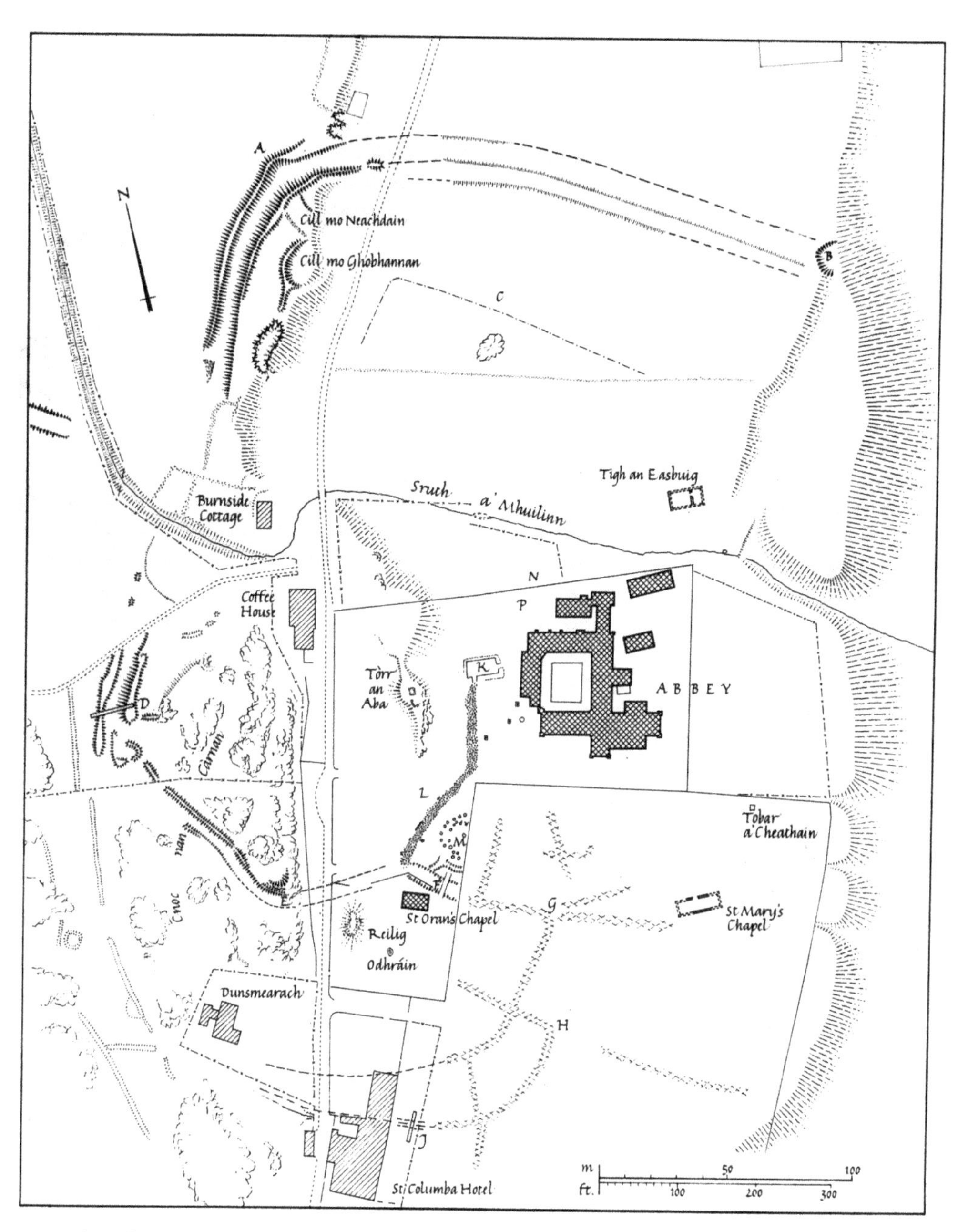

2.10 Plan of Iona Abbey (Scottish Inner Hebrides). © Royal Commission on the Ancient and Historical Monuments of Scotland

survived to 1 m in height in the nineteenth century (Ritchie 1997: 98). The antae of the shrine chapel survive at the northwest and southwest corners, a feature of early Irish churches in which the side walls project (RCAHMS 1982: 41–2). Columba's Shrine at Iona is the only extant example in Scotland of this characteristically Irish feature, which was also identified in excavations at

Chapel Finian (Dumfries and Galloway), which dates from the tenth or eleventh century (Radford 1951). Excavations at Iona have confirmed that the shrine pre-dates the Benedictine church. The shrine attracted other commemorative monuments, such as three high crosses and a stone-lined well (O'Sullivan 1999: 220). Excavations in the nave during the early twentieth century revealed traces of earlier structures associated with burials containing quartz pebbles (Yeoman 2009: 229). It is possible that the thirteenth-century crypt beneath the east end of the Benedictine church also incorporated earlier fabric. Reuse of parts of the existing church at Iona required compromises to be made in the Benedictine claustral plan: the cloister was placed to the north of the church, in contrast with the usual arrangement of a south cloister (Ritchie 1997: 105).

By 1200, the diverse forms of eremitic monasticism in Scotland had been replaced by liturgical uniformity and the Benedictine model of communal monasticism. The Church of Scotland was organised into dioceses led by a bishop and a direct connection had been established to the pope, with the Scottish church christened as the 'special daughter' of the Roman see (Barrow 2004b: 592). Scottish patronage had shaped a unique mix of monastic orders (Figures 2.11 and 2.12) showing a strong French influence: for example, the Tironensians favoured by David I were extremely rare outside France, and the obscure Valliscaulians were exclusive to France and Scotland. English monasticism was dominated by the Benedictines, while Scotland was principally Augustinian and Cistercian (Dilworth 1995). A new phase of religious reform around 1230 took place under Alexander II (1214–49), with the establishment of the friaries and the introduction of the austere Valliscaulian order at Pluscarden (Moray) (Hammond 2010: 75). The Scottish Wars of Independence resulted in the repeated devastation of monasteries in the fourteenth century, particularly in the Borders, but there was a resurgence of monastic foundations in the more prosperous period of the fifteenth and sixteenth centuries. A highly distinctive pattern of Scottish monasticism is the vibrancy of late mendicant foundations, with new friaries founded right into the sixteenth century (Randla 1999: 246), in contrast with the situation in England, Wales and Ireland (Figure 2.13).

SCOTTISH MONASTIC REFORM: THE CONVERSION OF THE *CÉLI DÉ*

State-building in medieval Europe was often supported by a process of monastic foundation that revived or appropriated the sites of ancient monasteries. What was the *material* manifestation of this cultural transformation and how did it impact on Scotland? Were the culdees (*Céli Dé*) and other early monasteries suppressed or absorbed? How did the appropriation of sacred heritage involve the preservation, destruction or modification of ancient sites? Considerable

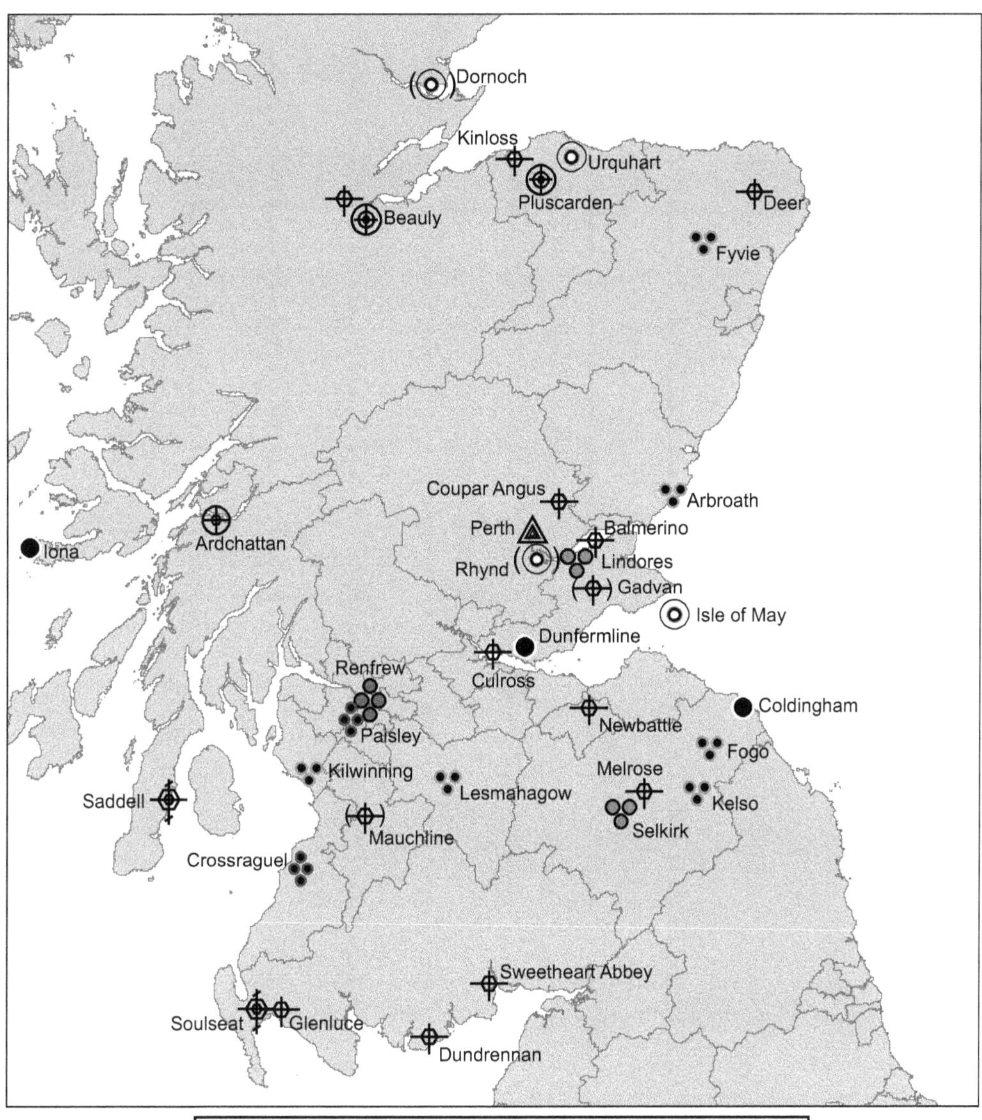

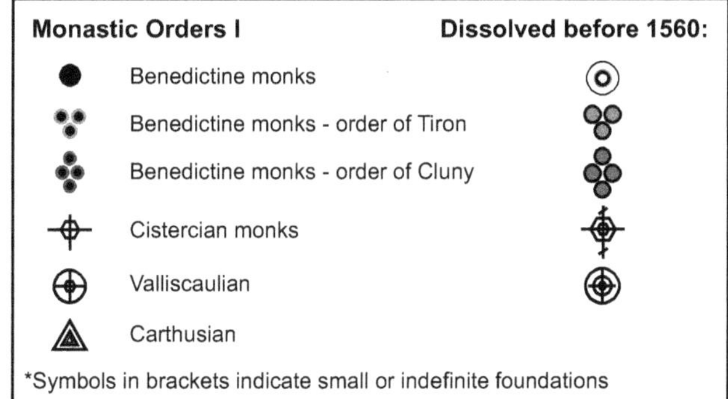

2.11 Map showing the location of later medieval monasteries in Scotland (1089–1560): Benedictine, Cistercian, Valliscaulian and Carthusian. After McNeill and MacQueen 1996 © Sarah Lambert-Gates

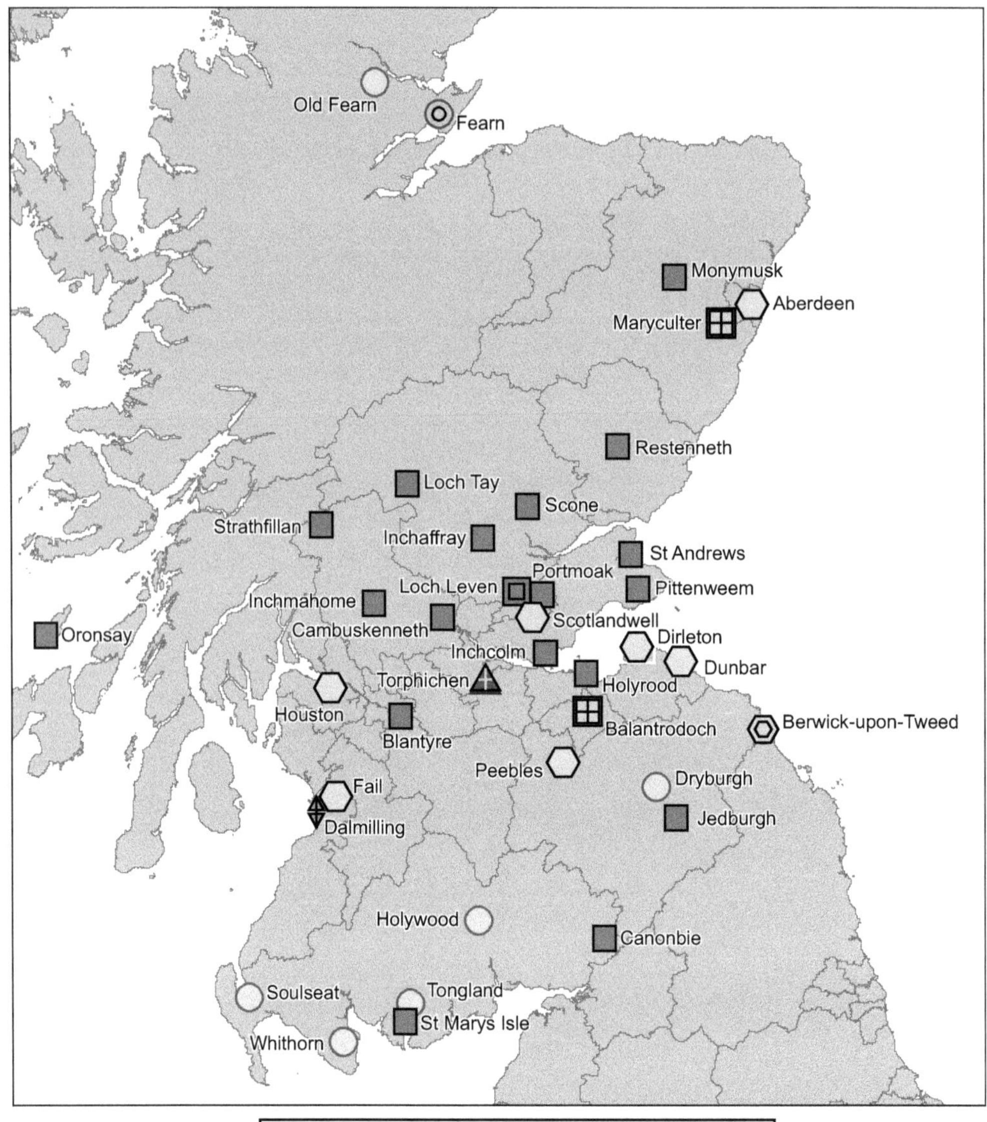

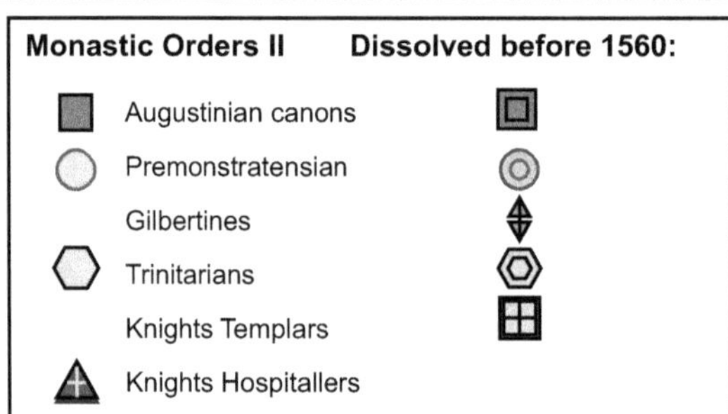

2.12 Map showing the location of later medieval monasteries in Scotland (1089–1560): Augustinian, Premonstratensian, Gilbertine, Trinitarian, Knights Templar and Hospitaller. After McNeill and MacQueen 1996 © Sarah Lambert-Gates

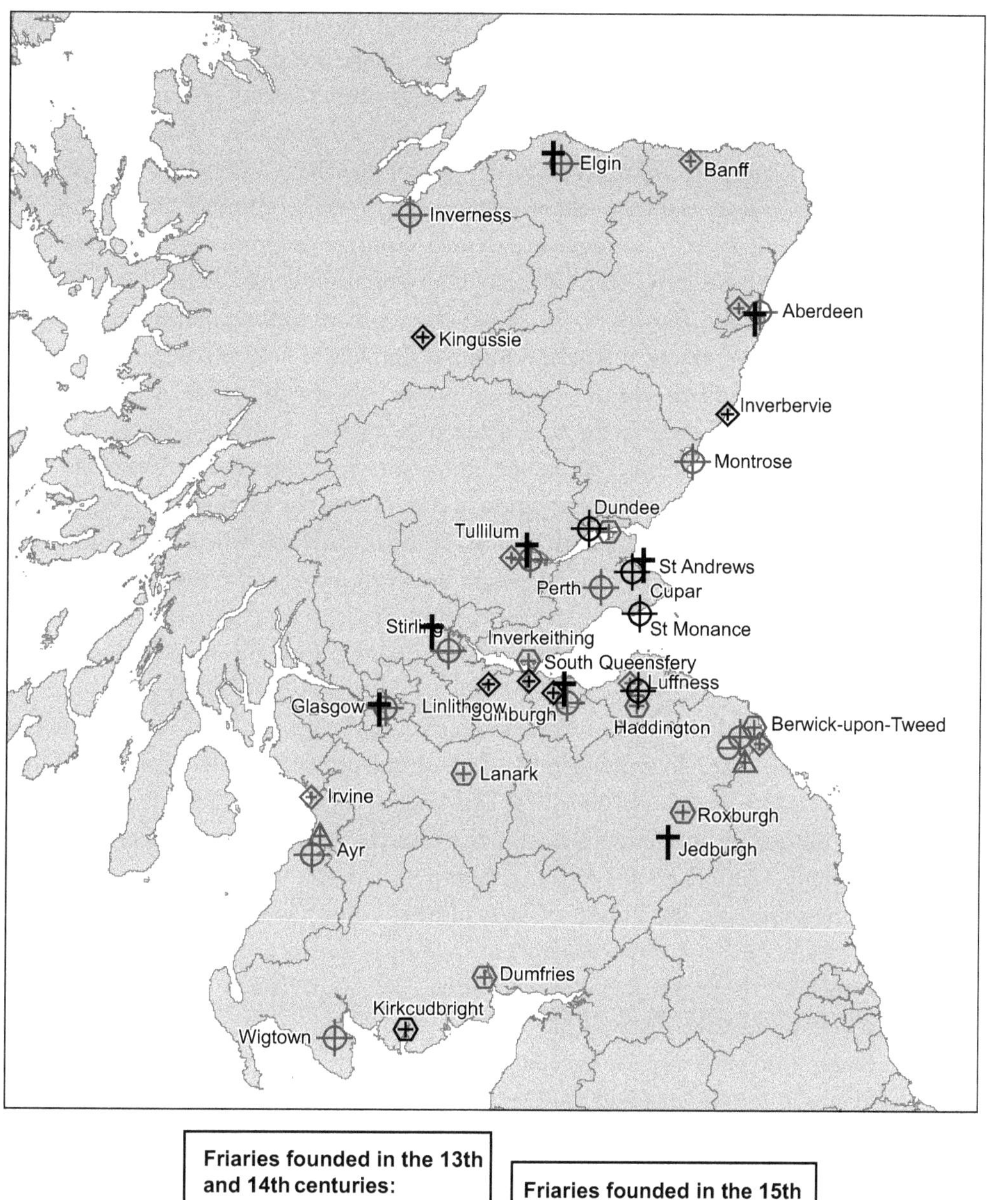

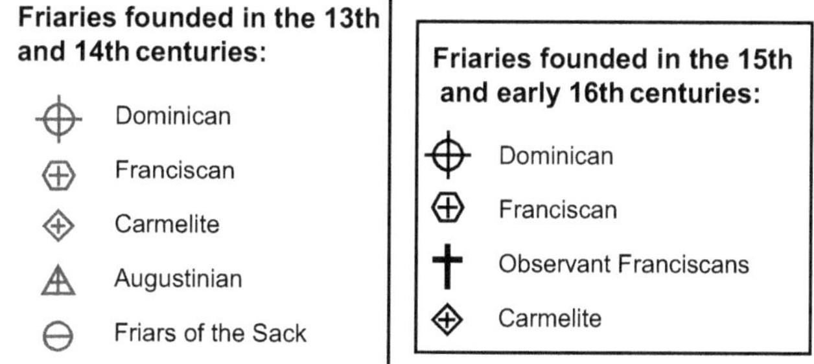

2.13 Map showing the location of medieval friaries in Scotland (*c* 1230–1560). After McNeill and MacQueen 1996 © Sarah Lambert-Gates

debate has focused on the question of the culdees and their possible continuity up to the end of the thirteenth century. They are key players in historical discourses that focus on the dualistic opposition between Celtic and Norman, stressing narratives of fierce Celtic resistance and pervasive Norman domination (Hammond 2006). Kenneth Veitch argued that continuity of settlement resulted in important aspects of religious and social continuity (Veitch 1999), while Geoffrey Barrow presented evidence for the institutional survival of the culdee at St Andrews for 200 years after the foundation of the Augustinian cathedral priory (Barrow 1973). What can we learn of the process of transition and the hybrid practices that developed at the sites of former culdees? A charter of David I confirms that the intention was to suppress the culdee at St Andrews and transfer its assets to the use of the new canons. Instead, it seems that the bishops converted the old culdee into a secular college of priests that was independent of the Augustinian priory and loyal to the bishop. For a time, two chapters existed at the cathedral of St Andrews, perhaps reflecting the internal political tensions that frequently arose between priors and bishops at cathedral priories. Barrow cites comparable situations at Canterbury and Dublin towards the end of the twelfth century and the beginning of the thirteenth century (Barrow 1973: 212–32).

Insight to the lifestyle of the converted culdees is provided by an episode documented at Monymusk in the early thirteenth century. The charter of the Augustinian priory established by Earl Gille Críst of Mar *c.*1200 confirms that the monastery was established 'in the church of St Mary in which *Céle Dé* formerly were' (Veitch 1999: 12). A dispute quickly arose between the culdee community and the bishop of St Andrews. Pope Innocent III authorised the abbots of Melrose and Dryburgh to investigate the situation and to broker an agreement between the warring parties. The outcome was that the bishop would protect the rights of the culdee if they followed certain stipulations. The community was not to exceed twelve brethren and a prior and they were expressly forbidden to adopt 'the life or order of monks and regular canons'. They 'should have only one refectory and one dormitory in common, and one oratory without cemetery, and that the bodies of the *Céle Dé* and of clerks and laymen who might die with them should receive the rights of sepulture at the parish church at Monymusk' (Veitch 1999: 14). This document confirms that the culdee at Monymusk was allowed to continue its independent existence at least for a generation, with continuity of personnel. It also records that the culdee had adopted a Marian dedication, in common with other communities such as Inchaffray, although it is not clear whether this allegiance was imposed or adopted, for either pious or political motives (Hammond 2010: 81). The Monymusk account reveals two further points that are important in understanding the transition to a community of reformed canons. The bishop insisted that the *Céle Dé* should live a *communal* lifestyle, following the model of coenobitic monasticism and sharing a single dormitory, refectory and oratory. He also withdrew the culdees' privilege to its own cemetery, a right that presumably would have been restored when the old community had faded away and conversion to the Augustinian priory was complete.

There is archaeological evidence relating to the transformation of some of the culdees; for example the round towers at Brechin (Angus) and Abernethy (Perth and Kinross) may belong to the period of their reform, rather than dating to earlier monastic occupation. Eric Fernie argued that they show the influence of Norman architectural style and date to *c.*1100 or later (Fernie 1986). They follow the Irish model of round towers that were current from the eighth to the twelfth century and may have been chosen to signal a nostalgic connection to the Celtic monastic tradition. However, archaeological analysis suggests that earlier fabric was incorporated in these structures and that their origins may be pre-Norman (Semple 2009). Excavations at Inchaffray provide insight to the colonisation of the former culdee by the Augustinian canons, *c.*1200, supported by the Earl and Countess of Strathearn. A major programme of landscaping was undertaken on the site of an existing church and community of brethren. Soon after 1200, the site was terraced to prepare for the construction of the new church and cloister. These were built over the remains of a 3 m wide earth bank, perhaps part of the enclosure of the earlier monastery. Temporary structures were identified in the southern part of the site: an early kitchen and oven were found beneath the later west range (Ewart 1996).

The process of colonisation is well-documented at Jedburgh, established jointly by David I and Bishop John of Glasgow. Excavations have shown that completion of the full monastic complex may have taken 120 years – four generations of the new community. It is possible that the Anglian minster remained in place while these works were underway, located to the north of the new monastic complex. The church of the Augustinian priory was constructed in stone, beginning in the customary manner at the eastern end. During building works, the canons were accommodated in a series of temporary timber structures located beneath the site of the west range of the cloister (Lewis and Ewart 1995: 3, 19–25). At both Inchaffray and Jedburgh, temporary monastic structures were located in the area that would become the west claustral range and which was typically the last monastic range to be constructed.

Excavations at the Isle of May have documented the process of converting the ancient Celtic shrine into a Benedictine cell of Reading Abbey from around 1145 (Figure 2.14). The monks colonised a site with a religious tradition stretching back at least 500 years, based around an existing stone church that was perhaps 150 years old. This church remained in use until a new one was built in the early thirteenth century. A cloister was constructed with

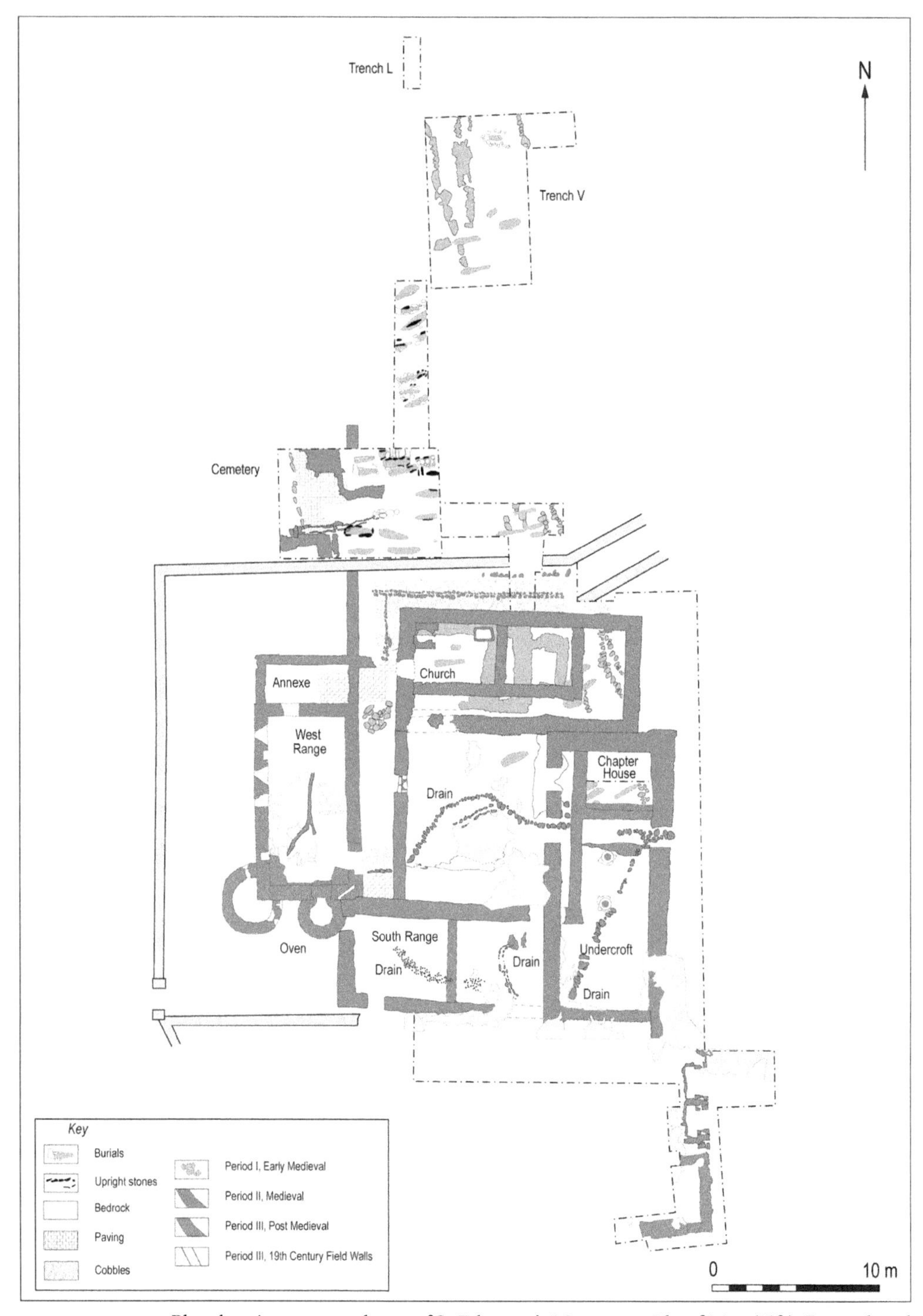

2.14 Plan showing excavated area of St Ethernan's Monastery, Isle of May (Fife). Reproduced by kind permission of Tayside and Fife Archaeological Committee

2.15 Excavation of burials within the cemetery platform at St Ethernan's Monastery, Isle of May (Fife). Photograph by Peter Yeoman © Fife Council Archaeology Service

the church as the north range; local dolerite stone was quarried for wall cores and dressed sandstone was brought from the mainland for the facings of windows and doors. Four different levels were engineered to create a cloister on this severely constricted site: the church, east range and cloister were on the lowest level; with a step up to the cloister walk and west range; another step up to the south range; and a fourth up to the latrine block (James and Yeoman 2008: 41). The effort required for construction at May demonstrates the importance of providing a formal cloister, even for a small cell of nine monks. The difficulty of living on the island may explain the early abandonment of the monastery in the thirteenth century, although it remained a popular place of pilgrimage for centuries.

The excavations at May also demonstrated continuity in the unusual burial practices of the island, which continued during and after monastic occupation. A burial ground to the north of the church contained layers of burials separated by beach stones in the manner of a cairn (Figure 2.15). This prompted one of the excavators, Peter Yeoman, to ask: 'why bury a Christian population under a burial cairn, a pagan form of burial, when there were other areas nearby where graves could be dug?' (Yeoman 1995: 27). At May, continuity with the early healing shrine was expressed by maintaining ancient burial traditions, despite their divergence from the orthodox mortuary traditions of reformed monasticism. At Iona, medieval burials were found crammed into the sandy rock crevices of the shoreline to the south of the abbey, some within roughly formed 'long cists'. The burials were principally of women and two radiocarbon dates suggest that the practice extended from the mid-first millennium up to at least the early second millennium CE (O'Sullivan 1999: 229). The control of burial rites and practices would have been an important factor in the religious transition of the twelfth century and is worthy of further study.

The extensive excavations at Whithorn provide insight to the conversion of the Northumbrian minster to a Premonstratensian cathedral priory from around 1177, associated with Fergus of Galloway (d. 1161). The archaeology of Whithorn has been characterised as 'urban' from an early date, with evidence of manufacturing, well-defined street systems, coinage and density of occupation (Hill 1997: 24–5). However, many of these traits can also be defined as characteristic of early monastic sites, such as the craft-working and manufacturing at Portmahomack and the system of streets and paths at Iona (Carver et al. 2016; Yeoman 1999: 82). The monastery at Whithorn, associated with the cult of St Ninian, became a Northumbrian minster in the eighth century and was destroyed by fire in the ninth century. Peter Hill's interpretation of the archaeological evidence emphasised shifts in the ethnic allegiances of Whithorn as the political and religious landscape changed over time, evolving from Irish to Hiberno-Norse, to Anglian, and demonstrating a 'Gaelic horizon' during the period of the monastic reform of the twelfth century (Hill 1997: 56). He used artefacts and building types as indicators of ethnicity; however, caution should be employed in using archaeology as a simple material correlate for ethnicity. It is likely that material culture was exchanged and adapted between social groups and that the religious and commercial communities at Whithorn were socially diverse throughout the ninth to thirteenth centuries.

Archaeological evidence suggests continuity of religious settlement at Whithorn during the largely undocumented period of the ninth to the early eleventh centuries, including the erection of a new timber church on a stone plinth. This provides an institutional context for the sculptured crosses of the Whithorn School. Some of the timber buildings of this phase incorporated hearths, pits and paving, and those in the northern sector produced finds including spindle whorls, ornaments and personal items (Hill 1997: 49). Medieval cultural imagery connected spinning with women and spindle whorls are one of the few artefacts that might be regarded as gender-specific at this date (Gilchrist 2012: 131, 146). However, spinning may not have been an *exclusively* feminine task: there is later medieval evidence for men spinning and spindle whorls are routinely excavated from later medieval monastic sites (Standley 2016: 289; Egan 1997). The spindle whorls from Whithorn may indicate that women resided at the minster in the tenth or eleventh century, consistent with the model of married clergy staffing the church. Archaeological evidence confirms major expansion at Whithorn in the eleventh to thirteenth centuries, when low-lying areas surrounding the minster were drained and new buildings were erected on reclaimed ground. Whithorn retained its curvilinear plan, with the early monastic precinct forming the central inner precinct and radial paths leading to an outer zone (Hill 1997: 55). Hill concludes that the most unexpected finding for this period is the lack of any clear evidence for the impact of the establishment of the reformed Premonstratensian cathedral priory, arguing that Whithorn remained ostensibly a commercial settlement (a 'monastic town'). However, some indications of significant change can be seen in association with the conversion of the minster to a reformed monastery.

A new church built in the mid-twelfth century seems to have been a simple cruciform with a short nave and long eastern arm. Ralegh Radford noted similarities between Whithorn's plan and the churches of converted culdees at St Andrews (St Mary of the Rock) and the Welsh site of Penmon (Anglesey) (Radford 1957: 184). The disproportionately long eastern arm was required for the stalls of the canons' choir. The location of the church at Whithorn is believed to coincide with the alleged site of St Ninian's tomb and perhaps replaced an earlier building (Hill 1997: 20, 56), much like the sequence at Iona. A further parallel between Whithorn and Iona is that both communities were provided with a cloister to the *north* of the church, an adaptation of the standard claustral plan perhaps necessitated by the reuse of the site of the earlier church. Whithorn's church was expanded considerably by the Premonstratensians after *c.*1200, with the nave and choir lengthened and crypts provided for veneration of the relics of St Ninian (Lowe 2009). Architectural fragments suggest that the church and cloister were complete by the mid-thirteenth century (Radford 1957: 186).

Artefacts from the inner precinct at Whithorn include writing implements (styli and parchment prickers) that may signal a new emphasis on literacy in the reformed community. Specialist workshops in the outer zone of the monastery were dedicated to comb production and smithing; these outer areas were depopulated by the end of the thirteenth century. This clearance may have been connected with the establishment of a more formal monastic precinct for the Premonstratensian cathedral priory, which is likely to have involved the large-scale relocation of people. Hill argued for social, economic and religious continuity between the minster and the reformed cathedral priory, proposing that the native clergy staffed the new cathedral priory (Hill 1997: 23–4, 56, 61). However, it is doubtful that the strict Premonstratensians would have tolerated married clergy or the presence of women in the monastic precinct. Some significant changes can be seen in the layout and zoning that reflect this transition but there was no wholesale redevelopment of the site. We know that the new Whithorn community remained ethnically diverse: in 1235, two generations after the Premonstratensian foundation, nearly half of the canons had Gaelic names, including the prior Duncan (Donnchad) (Stringer 2000: 153).

CONCLUSIONS: LATER MEDIEVAL MONASTICISM IN SCOTLAND – 'INVENTIVE, CREATIVE AND REGIONAL'

A critical, comparative framework of analysis assists in drawing out the distinctiveness of later medieval monasticism in Scotland, exploring how the model of reformed monasticism was 'Scotticised' in the twelfth century. The transition of the culdees seems to have been achieved gradually, involving flexibility and variation in local responses, to match the institutional diversity of early monasticism in Scotland. The archaeological evidence at Whithorn mirrors the historical evidence at St Andrews, indicating gradual change and assimilation rather than abrupt suppression. Excavations have shown that the conversion of Inchaffray, Jedburgh and May all involved rapid campaigns to construct cloisters, requiring terracing and engineering solutions to accommodate the claustral plan on challenging sites. The cloister was regarded as the *material cultural signature* of reformed monasticism, signalling Scotland's adoption of coenobitic monasticism on the Benedictine model and its rejection of eremitic monasticism rooted in Celtic sacred heritage. The early attention given to building formal cloisters reflects the financial investment that accompanied monastic foundation and perhaps confirms the impression of a peaceful transition to reformed monasticism in Scotland. It also demonstrates the importance of the cloister as an architectural space that structured the embodied experience of monasticism, together with the adoption of literacy as a monastic technology. For instance, the material culture of literacy is prominent in the thirteenth-century conversion of Whithorn and at the nunnery of Elcho. Archaeological evidence from Scottish nunneries confirms that claustral living and literacy were formative techniques of the female monastic body as well as the male. This contrasts with the female monastic experience in later medieval Ireland, where the masonry cloister was not considered to be an essential element of nunnery planning. Accommodation was sometimes provided in detached buildings or timber complexes, and where cloisters were provided, their irregular layout may suggest a more organic development (Collins 2018).

The model of coenobitic monasticism based around claustral living seems to have been fundamental to the conversion of the Scottish culdees. The cloister was also adopted in Ireland around the mid-twelfth century, replacing the concentric enclosures that had characterised Irish monasticism from the fifth century up to the reformed monasticism of the twelfth century (O'Keefe 2003: 104). The Welsh experience may have been different: in northwest Wales, eremitic sites were selected for the foundation of Augustinian priories in the thirteenth century at the sites of former Welsh culdees, such as Bardsey (Gwynedd), Beddgelert (Gwynedd), Penmon (Anglesey), Ynys Lannog (Puffin Island, Anglesey) and Ynys Tudwall (Gwynedd). Excavations at Tudwall revealed a cluster of simple buildings associated with a small church in a stone enclosure. Karen Stöber and David Austin argue that the first phase of Augustinian foundations at the Welsh culdees 'used the native motif of building clusters within enclosures' (Stöber and Austin 2013: 46). Traditional elements were also retained in the conversion of the Scottish culdees, for example the Irish-inspired round towers at Brechin and Abernethy, and the burial cairns at May. But the most significant indicator of continuity was the choice of location for the church: at traditional cult sites like Whithorn and Iona it was essential that the saint's grave and shrine were integrated within the rebuilding of the church, as it was at Irish monasteries such as Clonmacnoise (co Offaly) and Inishmurray (co Sligo). Direct *continuity of place* was also critical in establishing new monasteries at former minsters, such as Jedburgh, and culdees including Inchaffray and May.

The distinctiveness of Scottish monasticism can be found in the hybrid practices that connected reformed monasticism with Celtic sacred heritage. The time is ripe for archaeologists to critically reassess the significance of the perceived watershed of *c.*1100, just as historians are reflecting on the conventional framework of periodisation and its impact on historical scholarship (Hammond 2006; see Campbell 2013b for a material culture perspective). In 'understanding why, where and how' Scotland emerged (ScARF 2012: i), we must explore the longer transition of Scottish religious experience from the tenth to the thirteenth century. Documentation for religious communities in Scotland is exceedingly rare in the tenth and eleventh century (Hammond 2010: 62), increasing the value of an archaeological perspective. Recent excavations in Aberdeen suggest that monasteries were sometimes founded on early cemeteries that are undocumented: skeletons dating to the tenth or eleventh century have been excavated at the site of Aberdeen's Dominican Friary, founded 200 years later by Alexander II (*c.*1230–49) (Cameron 2016). To what extent did the new monasteries incorporate elements of Celtic monasticism that had borrowed from the prehistoric tradition? Carver (2009) suggested that the early Christian tradition in Scotland integrated prehistoric practices such as the use of curvilinear enclosures, stone slab cist burials, stone markers and the curation of ancestral bones. These elements continued in the reformed monasticism of the twelfth century, with the important exception of curvilinear enclosures, which were replaced emphatically by cloisters.

It is also imperative to develop more critical perspectives around *ethnicity* in twelfth-century Scotland: how were Gaelic, Scandinavian and Anglo-Norman traditions expressed and renegotiated through monastic material culture? Here, we could learn from medieval archaeologists who have explored diaspora identities such as the Hansa, the German merchants who settled in Baltic Europe, or the Normans in Anglo-Saxon England (e.g. Gaimster 2014; Naum 2015; Sykes 2005). These approaches have emphasised the potential of ceramic material culture and food remains in exploring cultural signatures connected with ethnic identity. A key source for exploring this theme in Scottish monastic archaeology is burial evidence (see Chapter 4). The Scottish case study demonstrates the value of comparative and critical assessments of regional monastic archaeology. By evaluating Scotland in the wider context of European monasticism, it also contributes to the development of an international research agenda for Scottish historical archaeology (Dalglish and Driscoll 2010: 314). A critical framework of archaeological analysis helps us to appreciate the value and significance of Scottish medieval monasticism – just like its Celtic precursor, later medieval monastic experience in Scotland was richly 'inventive, creative and regional'.

THREE

SPIRIT, MIND AND BODY: THE ARCHAEOLOGY OF MONASTIC HEALING

INTRODUCTION: THE MONASTIC HEALING REGIMEN

This chapter examines a specific aspect of the monastic lifestyle – how monastic identity and Christian ideas about the body influenced the prevention and treatment of illness. Spiritual and physical health were regarded by medieval people as indivisible: the very existence of disease was attributed to Original Sin and personal experience of illness was frequently understood as punishment for a bad life. Pain was believed to cleanse the soul of sin and to prepare the sinner for judgement after death (Rawcliffe 2002). To be truly healed required spiritual repentance: the medieval monastic regimen fully integrated treatment of the Christian body and soul, connecting the sensory and emotional with the material world. The prevailing view of medical historians is that treatment in the medieval infirmary was based primarily around spiritual succour and basic nursing care. What does archaeological evidence reveal about the nature of care in medieval monastic infirmaries and hospitals, and the differences between them? Can archaeology detect more active, *therapeutic technologies* in monastic healing? Can we discern regional or chronological patterns that may relate to earlier (indigenous) healing traditions and therapeutic landscapes?

The archaeology of monastic healing focuses on the full spectrum of healing technologies, from managing the body in order to prevent illness, through to the treatment of the sick and preparation of the corpse for burial. Monastic healing is examined here through a *practice-based* approach which emphasises agency and embodiment: archaeology and material culture are used to consider how monastic experience responded to illness, ageing and disability. This framework is influenced by the material study of religion, which interrogates how bodies and things engage to construct the sensory experience of religion (Meyer et al. 2010; Mohan and Warnier 2017; Morgan 2010), and by practice-based approaches in archaeology, which examine the active role of space and material culture in shaping religious agency and embodiment (Fogelin 2007; Petts 2011; Swenson 2015; Thomas et al. 2017).

Monasteries of the reformed orders lived communally, sharing daily liturgical routines in an enclosed space that was largely shut off from the world. The sixth-century Rule of St Benedict provided the blueprint for monastic identity and materiality: it disciplined the body through celibacy, fasting, and daily and seasonal routines for physical movement, prayer, work, study, talking, eating and sleeping. These 'disciplinary practices' (Asad 1987) or 'techniques of the body' (Mauss 2006 [1936]; Galliot 2015) constructed the monastic sense of self and created a programme for communal living. The monastic body was shaped by the interaction of bodily techniques and material culture, including monastic constructs of space, diet, health, hygiene and therapeutic treatments. A special place was reserved in each monastic community for the sick and elderly: 'before all things and above all things care must be taken of the sick, so that they may be served in the very deed as Christ Himself; for He said: "I was sick and ye visited me . . ."' (McCann 1952: 91). The strict monastic lifestyle was mediated by the need to care for the sick, with flexibility required especially around monastic rules that governed diet and communal eating and sleeping.

The Benedictine Rule emphasised the central role of hospitality and charity in monastic life, leading to the foundation of almonries located at the gates of monasteries. Independent hospitals were also established for the care of the poor and sick in medieval society, founded by prominent ecclesiastics, aristocrats, members of the royal family and, in the later Middle Ages, merchants, guilds and urban communities. These were not hospitals in the modern sense, providing medical intervention and emergency care – they provided 'warmth, rest, basic nursing care and nourishing food' (Rawcliffe 2011: 74). The larger and wealthier medieval hospitals were quasi-monastic institutions that followed the Augustinian Rule. They embodied Christian teachings on charity and offered welfare to the worthy and repentant poor. Care in the infirmary was based around the concept of the liturgy and a healing regime supported by the sacraments, holy relics, devotional imagery and sacred music. Both monastic and hospital infirmaries were provided with a chapel or high altar at which daily masses were performed; patient beds were placed so that they could witness the transubstantiation, the moment at which the Eucharistic wafer

3.1 A hospital ward in the Hotel Dieu, Paris, facsimile after a 16th-century original. Wellcome Collection, Public Domain

transformed miraculously into the body of Christ (Figure 3.1). This ritual was regarded as the most efficacious medicine for medieval Christians, impacting on all of the senses, like 'a powerful electric current coursing through the body' (Rawcliffe 2017: 78). Hospitals might be seen in one respect as a form of 'spiritual policing', reinforcing Christian compliance and enforcing a regimen of confession and prayer that promised health and salvation (Rawcliffe 1999: 7). However, these emotional and psychological elements are likely to have made a positive contribution to supporting therapeutic treatment (Horden 2007). Medieval monastic and hospital infirmaries demonstrate the integral relationship between ritual and healing technologies, and how Christian techniques of the body combined sensory, emotional and material experience to construct a religious imaginary.

Medieval monasteries had access to Ancient Greek medical texts, newly translated from the twelfth century onwards from Arabic, Greek and Hebrew into Latin. Pharmacological and surgical treatises from the Islamic world also figured prominently in their libraries. Monasteries built up impressive collections of medical treatises and herbals, guides to plants and their uses, which often included practical instructions for the preparation of therapeutic remedies (Green 2009). The instructions given in herbals relied on a strong element of tacit knowledge, indicating that substantial practical training underpinned the practice of herbal medicine (Van Arsdall 2014: 49). Medicine became more abstract and academic in the twelfth century, a more theoretical approach that broke with the earlier, empirical tradition (Rawcliffe 2011: 400). Influenced by the Greek physician Galen (*c.*129–200 CE), medieval medical theory was based on the four humours of the body interacting with the four 'natural' elements and the six 'non-naturals'. The human body was believed to be made up of four natural elements, which also made up the universe: fire, water, earth and air. Health and temperament were determined by the balance between the four humours, which corresponded with the bodily substances of phlegm, blood, yellow bile and black bile. Fire, which was hot and dry, produced yellow bile in the body, and led to a choleric complexion. Water, which was cold and wet, produced phlegm, and the phlegmatic complexion. Earth, thought of as cold and dry, was black bile in the body, and associated with the melancholic complexion. Air, regarded as hot and wet, made blood, and the sanguine complexion (Rawcliffe 1995). The 'non-naturals' were additional factors believed to influence health: ambient air, food and drink, exercise and rest, sleeping and waking, evacuation and repletion, and the emotions (referred to as the passions or 'accidents' of the soul) (Horden 2007: 134).

Monastic techniques of the body were an ideal fit with the medical concept of the *Regimen Sanitatis*, the proper management of the body to achieve an equilibrium through diet and moderation (Rawcliffe 2002: 58). This was based on the Greek model of the regimen of health, the idea that disease can be prevented through careful regulation of diet, hygiene and care for the body. The goal was to achieve harmony between body and soul through moderation of behaviour, with the regimen varied to suit individual 'complexions' that differed according to age, sex and the balance of the humours (Sotres 1998: 291–2). In practice, it involved eating a balanced diet, eliminating excess bodily fluids, living in a clean environment, taking regular exercise and rest, and avoiding stress (Bonfield 2017: 102). For medieval monastics, the regimen involved an emphasis on spiritual, mental and physical discipline, as well as attention to sanitation, fresh water, personal hygiene and the balancing of the humours through diet and phlebotomy (blood-letting). Exercise and recreation in green spaces were also considered to be important, for example walking in the monastic orchards, vineyards and gardens, where scented plants helped to rebalance the humours (Rawcliffe 2008). The Benedictine Rule encouraged gardens for contemplation and recreation, provided that they were enclosed and secluded (Skinner and Tyers 2018: 7). On average, each monk was bled every six to seven weeks, followed by three days' recuperation in the infirmary, where the rules governing diet and liturgical routines were relaxed. The division between academic and empirical approaches in medieval medicine was strengthened by the Fourth Lateran Council of 1215, which prohibited all clergy in higher orders from performing medical procedures involving bloodshed, in case they resulted in accidental murder or the pollution of the Eucharist when mass was celebrated. From this date onwards, monasteries employed laymen such as barber-surgeons to perform surgery and phlebotomy (Rawcliffe 2002: 46).

THERAPEUTIC LANDSCAPES

The medical historian Carole Rawcliffe has commented on the absence of documentary evidence for the foundation of specialist institutions for the care of the sick before the Norman Conquest. From 1070 to 1200, around 250 hospitals were founded in England (Rawcliffe 2011: 74). Of twenty hospitals known in Wales, only the site of Llawhaden (Pembrokeshire) has been excavated (Huggon 2018: 847). Derek Hall has found evidence for 178 hospitals in medieval Scotland, based on documents and place name evidence such as 'Spittal' and 'Maison Dieu' (Hall 2006: 44). The height of hospital foundation in Scotland appears to have been in the fifteenth century, in contrast with the twelfth-century boom in England. Some of these hospitals were specialist institutions for the care of 'lepers': skeletal evidence confirms isolated cases of leprosy in medieval Scotland, ranging geographically from Whithorn in the southwest to Orkney in the northeast. *Leprosaria* were founded in major burghs and in the countryside but there are no documented leper hospitals in the southwest, Highlands or Northern Isles (Oram 2011: 204–7). The relatively low level of institutional charity in Scotland before the fifteenth century may be explained partly by the Scottish social context. Clan chiefs were responsible for providing shelter for the needy and vulnerable and they sometimes maintained their own healers; parish clergy in the West Highlands were also expected to support the poor and to provide hospitality for travellers and pilgrims (Hamilton 1981: 35; MacDonald 2014: 21–2). It is also possible that Scottish hospitals recorded in the fifteenth century had been in existence for some time – the historical dates of hospital foundations are based on the earliest *surviving* documentary references. We know that the model of Christian charity was actively promoted in Scotland from around 1100: Turgot's life of Margaret presented the Scottish queen as an exemplar who served Christ by feeding the poor and supporting monastic communities (Hammond 2010: 68).

Historical models for the chronology of hospital foundation may be challenged by recent archaeological work at the sites of medieval hospitals in England. Excavations at three sites have identified specialist cemeteries *pre-dating* the Norman Conquest, suggesting that some medieval hospitals may have 'prehistories' as Anglo-Saxon healing centres. Excavations at the leper hospital of St Mary Magdalene, Winchester, have yielded structural evidence and radiocarbon dates confirming an early phase of cemetery and buildings at the site, prior to its formal foundation as a leper hospital in the mid-twelfth

3.2 Remains of the charnel chapel at St Mary Spital, London. © Museum of London Archaeology

century (Roffey 2012). Radiocarbon dating of two leprous skeletons from Winchester may place them before the Norman Conquest, disputing the conventional view that leprosy was not widespread before the twelfth century, and that the first leper hospital in England was Archbishop Lanfranc's foundation at Harbledown in Kent (*c.*1084). Radiocarbon dates from the hospital of St Mary Magdalene, Partney (Lincolnshire), suggest that some kind of charitable institution was in place before the medieval hospital was founded *c.*1115 on the site of a middle Saxon monastery (Atkins and Popescu 2010). Excavations at the site of St Mary Spital, London, also hint of earlier origins: the hospital was founded in 1197 on an existing cemetery that is undocumented historically and pre-dates the hospital foundation by approximately 100 years. Phasing is based on extensive radiocarbon dating and Bayesian statistical modelling. Before the documented foundation of the hospital, the site was used for mass burial in large pits, suggesting an emergency burial ground. An early fourteenth-century charnel chapel at St Mary Spital reused twelfth-century mouldings, perhaps indicating the symbolic incorporation of fabric to commemorate an earlier church on the site (Connell et al. 2012: 3–5) (Figure 3.2).

Taken together, these cases begin to question the traditional view that hospitals were a Norman revolution in health care. What types of charitable institution may have preceded the Norman hospital? What determined the selection of location for the foundation of medieval hospitals – could the choice have been influenced by earlier use of the locality? Medieval churches and monasteries often reused early medieval or Roman sites for symbolic reasons, even if there was no direct continuity of use (Morris 1989). Were medieval hospitals established at locales already esteemed as 'therapeutic landscapes', places with an enduring reputation for providing physical, spiritual and mental healing (Gesler 2003)? In Scotland, some hospitals may have been associated with earlier healing wells. For example, Trinity Hospital, Edinburgh, is believed to have been founded by King Malcolm IV (1153–65) at the site of a healing spring, and the *leprosarium* at Kingcase, St Ninian's Hospital near Prestwick (South Ayrshire), was said to have been founded by Robert the Bruce after he benefited from drinking the healing waters from the well (Walsham 2011: 51).

There were healing wells and springs located all over Scotland, as many as 600 in the later Middle Ages, and some of those in the Highlands remained associated with healing rites up to the modern period (MacKinlay 1893; Todd 2000: 140). St Fillan's Well (Stirling) in the southeast Highlands, and Loch Maree (Wester Ross) in the northwest, were both connected with folk cures for insanity, involving immersion and ritual practices (see Chapter 1; Figures 1.6 and 1.7). Both places are associated with Celtic saints and retain evidence for early medieval archaeology, suggesting a longstanding reputation as therapeutic landscapes. Near St Fillan's Well is the ruined church of St Fillan, and on Eilean Maree, the well is associated with a chapel and cemetery connected with St Maelrubha (Donoho 2014). Medieval wells may have developed on the sites of pre-Christian water cults: Adomnán's *Life of Columba*, written at the very end of the seventh century, describes how the saint converted wells that previously had been the focus of pagan worship. When visiting Pictland, Columba heard of a well that caused people to be struck down by leprosy or blindness after they came into contact with the water. He blessed the well in the name of Christ, before washing his hands and feet and then drinking water from the well. The *vita* records that 'after the saint had blessed it and washed in it, many ailments among the local people were cured by that well' (*Life of St Columba* Book II: 11; Sharpe 1995: 162–3).

The Isle of May (Fife) is a strong candidate for an early therapeutic landscape that continued in use over a thousand years. The Benedictine monastic cell at May represents a relatively short episode in the history of the island, founded in the twelfth century and abandoned in the thirteenth century. Skeletons excavated from the cemetery date from the fifth to the late sixteenth century, confirming that the island was a pilgrimage centre for a much longer period (see Figure 2.14). There is no firm historical evidence for a healing shrine at May but there is an early sixteenth-century record in the Aberdeen Breviary of a healing well, which drew female pilgrims to May who hoped to conceive a child (Willows 2015). Fifty-eight articulated skeletons were excavated at May, representing around 20 per cent of the total cemetery area. Over 80 per cent of these burials dated to the earlier phase of use, spanning the fifth to the mid-twelfth century, and pre-dating the foundation of the monastic cell. Analysis by Marlo Willows has shown that the skeletal population was striking in three respects: first, the skeletons were predominantly male (94 per cent of sexed burials); secondly, almost all of them showed at least one pathological lesion (97 per cent); and thirdly, there was a high proportion of young adults, aged under 25 years (22 per cent). The predominance of males suggests either a male religious community or that sexual segregation was observed in the location of burial. Only a fifth of the cemetery was excavated and it is possible that there was a designated area for female burial that was not located (James and Yeoman 2008: 16). The high incidence of disease among young adults may suggest something distinctive at May – perhaps a cult site that attracted infirm young men, both lay and religious male pilgrims in search of a cure (Willows 2015). We know that medieval cults sometimes appealed to particular social constituencies: for instance, the miracle stories of St Æbbe of Coldingham indicate that she attracted especially female, poor and younger pilgrims (Bartlett 2003: xxv).

THE ARCHAEOLOGY OF MEDIEVAL HEALING

Archaeology has enormous potential to contribute to the history of medicine but care is needed in how we define the framework for analysis. Archaeological insight to the more academic, theoretical constructs of medieval medicine is likely to be limited, but material sources provide new perspectives on the broader empirical tradition delivered by a diverse range of practitioners – physicians (often monks and priests), surgeons, bone-setters, apothecaries, herbalists, lay-sisters and midwives. As noted above, the archaeology of medieval healing focuses on the full spectrum of healing technologies, from managing the body in order to prevent illness, through to the treatment of the sick and the preparation of the corpse for burial. Monastic hospitals and infirmaries are the most direct form of archaeological evidence for medieval healing, providing the spatial context in which the sick were nursed. Material culture from these institutional contexts can sometimes be identified as having a specialist medical function. However, many objects such as knives and tweezers were multi-purpose and would not necessarily be considered to be medical objects if they were recovered from other spatial contexts. A small number of specialist therapeutic items have been excavated from graves in monastic and hospital cemeteries: the wider treatment of the corpse can also be seen in the context of the transformation of the Christian body in preparation for judgement and resurrection (see Chapter 4).

Skeletal evidence from excavated monastic and hospital cemeteries provides insight to disease, disability and care for the sick. My particular focus here is on possible evidence for *medical intervention* practised at medieval institutions, although this is difficult to discern. For example, at the Augustinian priory of St Mary Merton (Surrey), 13 per cent of the skeletal population of

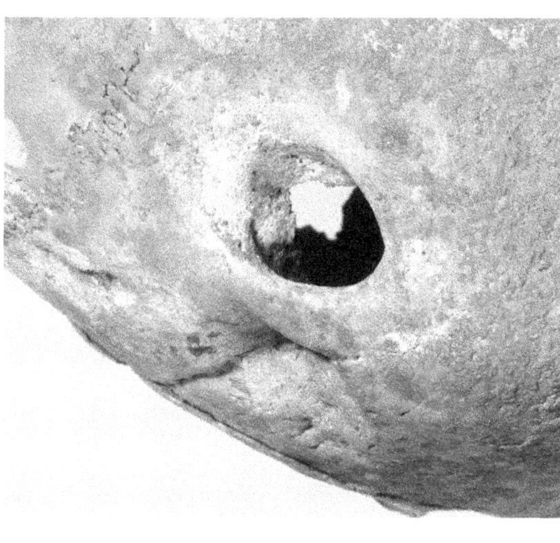

3.3 Skeletons from St Mary Spital, London, showing evidence for amputation and trephination. © Museum of London Archaeology

664 individuals showed evidence of healed fractures, most of which were well-aligned (Miller and Saxby 2007: 126). This suggests some degree of medical care, perhaps from bone-setters or barber-surgeons, and not necessarily by monastic infirmarers. In Scotland, well-healed fractures were recorded in skeletons excavated from the Carmelite friaries of Aberdeen, Perth and Linlithgow, and Cistercian Newbattle Abbey (Gooder et al. 2004; MacLennan 2001). Investigations at the Augustinian hospital priory of St Mary Spital in London represent the largest cemetery excavation undertaken in Europe, with 10,500 skeletons analysed (Connell et al. 2012; Harward et al. 2019; Thomas et al. 1997). There were 550 cases of fractured long bones, half of which showed some deformity in healing, and 8.5 per cent failed to heal. In rare cases, it is possible to detect the impact on the skeleton of other forms of therapeutic intervention: a high status, late medieval female from Ripon Minster (now Cathedral, North Yorkshire) showed abnormal changes to the bones of the thoracic cavity. The skeletal changes are interpreted as the result of compression bandaging to treat 'pigeon chest' (Groves et al. 2003).

There were five cases of surgical intervention at St Mary Spital: two amputations and three trephinations, in which a piece of the cranium is cut and removed (Connell et al. 2012: 202, 212) (Figure 3.3). It is likely in all of these cases that the surgery was intended to treat a head wound, for example to remove splinters of bone or release pressure following a head injury. Surgical intervention of this type was extremely rare, with only five certain cases of trephination and two of amputation recorded from other medieval sites in Britain, including hospitals in Chichester, Newark and Dublin (Roberts and Cox 2003: 251–2). The later medieval phase of Whithorn Cathedral Priory (Dumfries and Galloway) produced three further possible cases of trephination (Hill 1997: 529–30). Such operations were performed by surgeons who were members of the laity, rather than by monks or priests; both the surgeon and the patient received the sacrament of confession before the operation, revealing the overlap between religious and medical rituals (Rawcliffe 1999: 318). Further cases of amputation have been identified in skeletons excavated from *leprosaria*, indicating surgical intervention in advanced cases of leprosy. At St Mary Magdalen, Winchester (Roffey and Tucker 2012: 175), and St James and St Mary Magdalene, Chichester (Magilton et al. 2008: 258–9), there were single cases of lower leg amputations.

A small number of skeletons from monastic cemeteries indicate significant disability, suggesting that long-term care was provided for individuals with degenerative conditions. At Merton Priory this included cases of spina bifida occulta and conditions affecting the knee and foot that would have affected mobility (Miller and Saxby 2007: 276). At St Mary Spital there was significant evidence for impairments to major joints and long bones, including tuberculosis, as well as spinal anomalies. The majority of cases resulted from dislocations of the shoulder and hip. All age groups were affected, including children, and females were less likely to recover, perhaps suggesting that women received inferior care or were less able to take time out from daily work routines in order to heal (Connell et al. 2012: 190–2). At Newbattle Abbey (Midlothian), long-term care may have been required for an individual with an unreduced dislocated shoulder and another with a vertebral fracture that became infected (Gooder et al. 2004: 392). These cases confirm that individuals with impeded mobility were supported by their communities, but it is not clear whether they received *institutional care* or were instead nursed in the home environment. Because monasteries and hospitals accepted the wider lay population for burial in the cemetery, we do not know whether these individuals were cared for in the infirmary or in domestic contexts.

A systematic approach has been developed to consider individual cases of disability in detail: the 'bioarchaeology of care' is a framework for assessing the evidence and possible health-related care of individuals with pathologies that indicate long-term disease and disability (Tilley 2017). It advocates four stages: (1) diagnosing the pathology and its clinical implications; (2) assessing disability and its functional implications for everyday activities; (3) assessing the level of support and care required and the duration of care-giving; and (4) interpreting social context, identity and relationships, including the agency of both care-givers and recipients. Charlotte Roberts has applied the 'index of care' to an individual skeleton excavated from the leper hospital of St James and Mary Magdalene, Chichester (Roberts 2017). The male (aged 25–35) suffered from dental disease, respiratory disease, spinal degeneration and an infection, likely leprosy, which caused facial and postcranial bone changes consistent with lepromatous leprosy (Roberts 2017: 114). Roberts paints a vivid picture of the man's likely experience of disability; for example, dental disease would have made it painful for him to eat, while nasal congestion from leprosy would have resulted in loss of his sense of taste and smell, likely causing diminished appetite and weight loss. Nerve damage to his hands and feet would have made it difficult for him to walk and to complete basic tasks. The man would have needed shelter, sustenance and assistance with everyday tasks and mobility; his condition would have required constant encouragement to eat and drink, care for ulcers and skin lesions and protection to his hands and feet to guard against further damage. The 'index of care' model provides deeper insight to this man's *lived experience* of leprosy but the evidence does not allow his social context to be fully ascertained. As Roberts notes, we cannot assume that the man was a patient in the leper hospital – he may have been cared for elsewhere, before interment in the hospital cemetery. Social attitudes towards his disease, and his relationship to his care-givers, cannot be inferred directly from the archaeological context of his burial (Roberts 2017: 118). As further medieval case studies are documented using the index of care, it may be possible to make relative assessments of the care given to individuals with specific diseases in medieval hospitals, monasteries and domestic environments. However, it is not yet clear whether the framework will enable such comparative assessments or whether it is limited to more generic assessments of the lived experience of particular disabilities.

Diet was an important component of the monastic regimen, linked to both preventative medicine and therapeutic treatments: hot and cold humours were believed to be generated by the quality of food and drink (Bonfield 2017). In theory, the later medieval monastic diet was based around the staples of bread, cheese, vegetables, beans and cereals, with smaller quantities of eggs, fish and meat. The Rule of St Benedict forbade the consumption of the meat of quadrupeds, except by the infirm, but this was relaxed in all except the most austere monastic orders. Cereal carbohydrates were the mainstay, represented by bread and ale; the consumption of meat varied through the year, with more fish consumed on fast days and at Lent (Harvey 1993). The preservation of food remains at archaeological sites is represented principally by animal bones: the presence and varying proportions of different species has come to be recognised as a distinctive food signature of the respective medieval social orders. Monastic diets were usually devoid of large game, in contrast with evidence from castles, and fish remains are more abundant at monasteries than in towns and villages. Some monastic communities favoured beef and mutton over pork, according to a study of nine monastic sites in Belgium (Ervynck 1997).

The monastic infirmary was generally provided with its own kitchen and served an enriched meat diet in order to rebalance the humours after blood-letting. Waste disposal practices at monasteries were scrupulous by medieval standards and it is rarely possible to identify food remains deriving from specific areas. However, food waste was recovered from the infirmary kitchen excavated at the Augustinian priory of St Mary Merton, from floors and associated pits. Chicken bones were present in large quantities, alongside cattle, sheep and pig, with a few fragments of goose, duck and game birds. A very substantial and diverse assemblage of fish bones was recovered, with the major components including herring, cod and carp (Miller and Saxby 2007: 88). At Paisley Abbey (Renfrewshire), the rediscovery of the Great Drain yielded rare organic deposits dating to the fifteenth century (see Figure 2.2; Dickson 1996). Animal bone evidence confirmed a meat-rich diet of beef, pork and lamb, with remains of eel, cod and shellfish. Plant remains included leek, onion, brassica, wheat bran, apple, plum and walnut, all food stuffs found at other medieval sites in Scotland (Dickson and Dickson 2000: 196). There were also rare exotic imports: dried figs from the Mediterranean and nutmeg, likely from Indonesia.

Broad patterns in the consumption of food by different social groups can be refined to the level of individual life experience through isotope analyses of human skeletal tissue. Recent studies have confirmed the importance of marine protein to monastic communities in Britain (Müldner and Richards 2005, 2007). For example, two groups were studied from the Premonstratensian cathedral priory of Whithorn to reconstruct individual life histories and to compare diets and mobility (Müldner et al. 2009). A group of men buried in the presbytery, in close proximity to the likely location of the shrine of St Ninian, were identified as bishops or high-ranking clerics (see Chapter 4): they consumed significantly high levels of marine fish and had migrated to Whithorn from the east of Scotland. Lay-people buried at Whithorn consumed higher quantities of meat and their isotopic signatures showed a predominantly local upbringing.

Archaeobotanical evidence has potential for discerning herbal medical treatment in monasteries and hospitals but caution is needed in interpretation. Plant macrofossils may indicate evidence of food stuffs or seasonings, although the medieval culinary boundaries were blurred: foods such as garlic, onions, honey and almonds were considered to be medicinal. Plants generally perceived as ornamental may have been therapeutic, such as rose, violet and mint. Smells were regarded as material substances in vapour form; when inhaled, they were believed to act on the heart and brain, and could help to rebalance the humours (Rawcliffe 2002: 60). Plants and herbs were used in ointments, laxatives, purges and sedatives, with properties and traditional applications recorded in herbals. For example, the Herbal of Syon Abbey (*c.*1517) lists 700 herbal plants and provides a selection of 450 herbal remedies that make use of around 130 plants, together with animal parts, chemical and mineral materials. The author of the Syon Herbal, Thomas Betson, drew on the herbarium of John Bray and the Breviary of John Mirfield of St Bartholomew's Priory in London, both dating to the late fourteenth century, as well as Dawson's Leechbook, dating to the fifteenth century (Adams and Forbes 2015: 34). Eye complaints are the most common ailment addressed by the Syon remedies, followed by stomach problems, fever, dropsy, gout, toothache and loss of appetite. The symptoms of tuberculosis and cancer are also described, along with problems of conception and lactation, suggesting that the herbal was intended for use both within and beyond the celibate confines of the Bridgettine double monastery.

When extrapolating from archaeobotanical evidence, the argument for medical use is stronger where non-native plants are detected that are likely to have been introduced intentionally to monastic sites. In Norway and Iceland, recent studies have been undertaken of 'relict' plants on the sites of former medieval monasteries. Relict plants are regarded as medieval remnants that have survived at a specific locality since their medieval introduction (Åsen 2009). Historical, botanical and archaeobotanical evidence has been used to identify possible medicinal plants introduced to Iceland, such as madwort (*Asperugo procumbens*), garlic (*Allium oleraceum*), caraway (*Carum carvi*), yarrow (*Achillea millefolium*) and meadowsweet (*Filipendula ulmaria*). Archaeobotanical evidence from the excavated Augustinian hospital of Skriðuklaustur includes garlic, stinging nettle and brassicas, possible healing plants not native to Iceland. For example, wild cabbage (*Brassica oleracea*) was used to treat gout and rheumatism. Well-known medicinal plants from Southern Europe were also found at Skriðuklaustur, such as *Artemisia*, *Sanguisorba* and *Valeriana officinalis* (Kristjánsdóttir et al. 2014: 573).

The monastic regimen placed emphasis on the holistic prevention of illness through techniques of the body including the regulation of diet, physical activity and the practice of blood-letting (Horden 2007). Preventative measures also included care of the body through personal grooming and hygiene: the Syon Herbal provides a number of recipes for soap, both for washing the body and for general housekeeping (Adams and Forbes 2015: 51). Archaeological evidence for preventative hygiene includes tools such as ear-scoops and toothpicks. For example, excavations at Dunfermline Abbey (Fife) recovered a bone ear-scoop and an elaborate combination tool of tweezers and ear-scoop in copper alloy (Coleman 1996) (Figure 3.4). Tweezers were common tools for personal grooming but they could also be used for medical depilation or surgery (Bergqvist 2014). Examples have been recovered from Perth Carmelite Friary (Stones 1989), from the infirmary at Merton Priory (Miller and Saxby

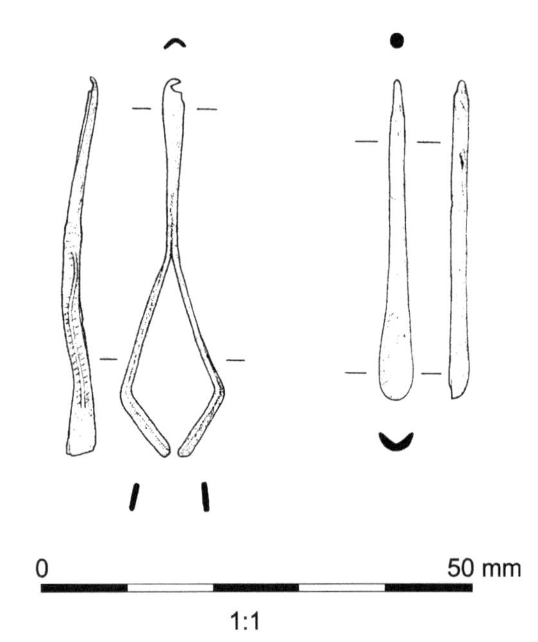

3.4 Illustration of bone ear-scoop and tweezers excavated from the area of Dunfermline Abbey (Fife). Reproduced by kind permission of Tayside and Fife Archaeological Committee

2007: 128) and from the hospital of St Mary Spital, where five sets of copper-alloy tweezers were found (Harward et al. 2019: 275). Small numbers of grooming tools are regularly recovered from monastic sites, for example two ear-scoops and a pair of tweezers from Kirkstall Abbey (West Yorkshire) (Moorhouse and Wrathmell 1987: 132–3), tweezers and two toothpicks from Battle Abbey (Sussex), one combined with an ear-scoop (Hare 1985: 154, 162), and an earpick and a fine pair of silver tweezers from the nunnery of St Mary Clerkenwell, London (Sloane 2012: 247).

THE MONASTIC INFIRMARY

The infirmary of a medieval monastery was generally reserved for the treatment of religious personnel who lived in the monastic precinct. Broader charity was dispensed at the almonry, a complex usually located at the main gates of the monastery, where food was distributed and hospitality and accommodation were provided for pilgrims (Gilchrist 2005: 182). The monastic infirmary housed elderly and infirm monks and those recuperating from illness, injury and the regular round of blood-letting. The well-documented case of Norwich Cathedral Priory reveals that 30 per cent of the monks would have passed through the infirmary in any single year (Rawcliffe 2002: 63). The Norwich infirmary was staffed by four to five attendants, including a keeper of the sick, a servant of those who had been bled, a laundress, a boy and a clerk of the chapel. Specialist members of the laity were retained to treat monastic personnel: a full-time phlebotomist was employed from the fourteenth century and local surgeons were occasionally bought in, together with physicians trained in the Galenic tradition (Rawcliffe 2002: 46–7).

The Bridgettine double house at Syon (Middlesex) was a community of nuns and canons, requiring two separate monastic infirmaries. The Syon Rule emphasises the importance of spiritual and physical care for the sick: the brothers' infirmarer should be 'strong and mighty to lift and move them ... often change ther bedding and other clothes, ley to her [their] plasteres, give hem ther medicyns mynster unto them mete and drynke, fyre water and other necessaryes nyght and day after the counsel of the physician'. He should 'exhorte and comforte them (the sick) to be confessyd and receive the sacraments of holy chirche'. The keeper of the sick should not be 'squames [squeamish] to handle hem and wash hem; not angry nor unpaciente, though one have the vomett, another the flyxe, another the frensy'. The Rule confirms that monastic observances were relaxed for the sick but discipline was renewed upon recovery from illness. A nun returning from a period in the infirmary was told to kneel before the abbess to seek penance, saying 'I have transgressed in meat, drink and many other ways, not keeping the regular times of eating, drinking and sleeping and the like, wherefore I do crave mercy and pardon' (Adams and Forbes 2015: 50–1).

The infirmary complex was usually sited to the east of the cloister for practical, medical and spiritual motives, while the precise location was determined primarily by the need for clean water (Bell 1998: 211–13). It was usual for the monastery's watercourse to pass first through the infirmary, in order to provide the purest water to this area. Water was connected with healing through the sacrament of baptism, bringing together the connotations of physical and spiritual cleansing, and recalling Christ's baptism by John the Baptist in the River Jordan (Mark 1:4–5). According to medieval notions of contagion, infections were transported by mists and noxious smells caused by stagnant water or sewage, and absorbed into the body through the pores. The siting of monastic infirmaries to the east of the cloister stems also from this understanding of contagion, following the Hippocratic notion that the healthiest location was in the east (Bell 1998: 220). The scale and complexity of the infirmary varied depending on the size and wealth of the monastic foundation. A larger abbey or cathedral priory was sometimes provided with a second cloister dedicated exclusively to the infirmary, around which were arranged the infirmary hall and chapel and specialist facilities. These might include a kitchen to prepare meat enriched diets, a dining room reserved for meat consumption, private chambers, a blood-letting room, a latrine block and possibly even a bath house, as at Ely and Canterbury Cathedral Priories. The monks of Norwich complained about the lack of tubs and other facilities for bathing and shaving but they benefited from a specialist pharmacy for the infirmarer to prepare medications from exotic ingredients listed in the account rolls. These ranged from the familiar to the exotic: ginger, cinnamon, peony, liquorice, fennel, rice, cloves, mace, cassia, aniseed, white turmeric, poppy seeds, prunes, nutmeg, frankincense and dragon's blood, referring to bright red resin from trees of the *Dracaena* species (Rawcliffe 2002: 60, 63).

Relatively few monastic infirmaries have been subject to significant archaeological excavation and the investigations that have taken place have focused on the main infirmary hall, rather than on ancillary buildings. We can also draw on architectural survivals such as the late thirteenth-century infirmary

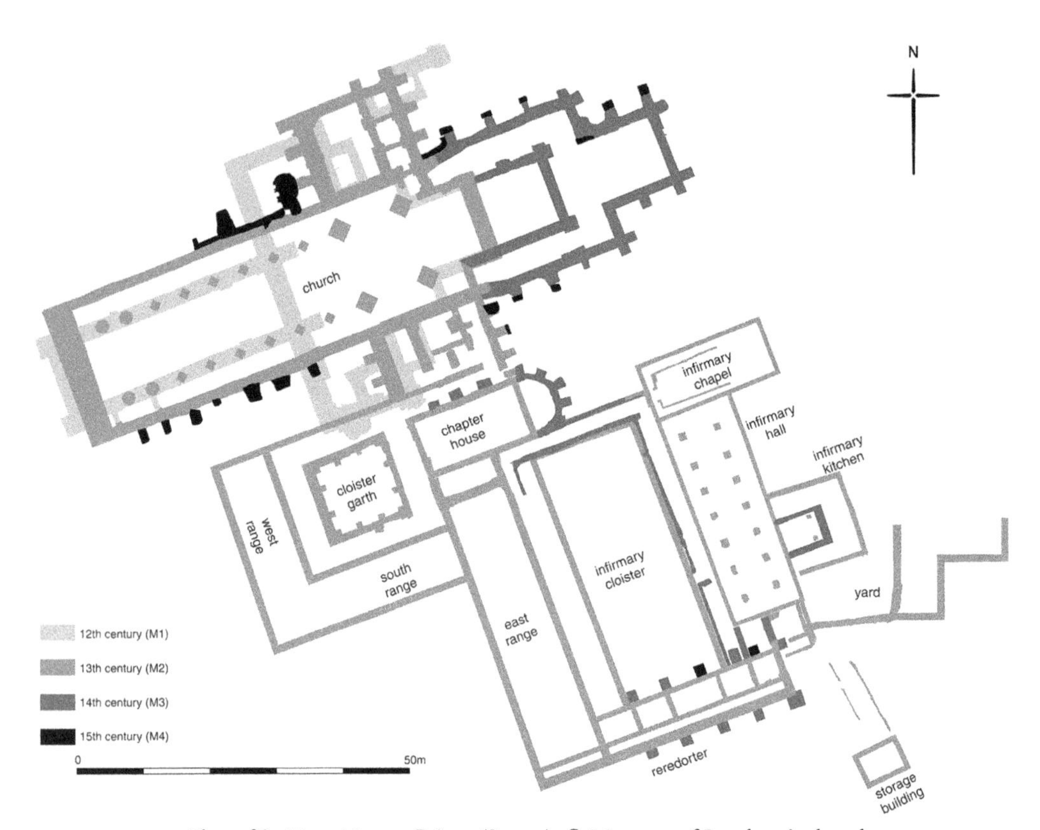

3.5 Plan of St Mary Merton Priory (Surrey). © Museum of London Archaeology

hall at St Mary's, Chichester, where the arrangement of the hall and chapel is much like the nave and chancel of a parish church (Gilchrist 1995). The infirmary complex at Merton Priory developed to the southeast of the main cloister, where an infirmary cloister was created between the monastic east range and the infirmary hall (Figure 3.5). A large latrine block was shared by the infirmary and the monks' dormitory and a chapel and kitchen abutted the infirmary hall. The typical arrangement for the infirmary hall was an aisled space opening into a chapel at the eastern end. The beds of the patients were located in the aisles, with the central space kept clear for the circulation of nursing staff. This arrangement is confirmed by archaeological evidence of wear patterns in the floors of infirmary halls: at St Mary Spital, the central area of the earth floor was eroded; at Merton, the floor tiles were more heavily worn in the centre of the hall (Miller and Saxby 2007: 125–6). The chapel may have been screened from the hall but direct visual access to the altar was important for the patients to benefit from the healing power of the Eucharist. Windows would have been glazed and fireplaces were sometimes provided, as at Merton, where there was also evidence for a cupboard in the western wall, perhaps a dispensary for medicines.

The infirmary hall at the Tironensian abbey of Kelso in the Scottish Borders was excavated to the southeast of the main cloister. The central space and eastern aisle were recorded, showing an arrangement of alternating circular and octagonal piers, closely comparable to the infirmary hall at Norwich Cathedral Priory. Kelso's infirmary was aligned north–south, rather than the more typical east–west, a pattern also seen at Waltham (Essex), Fountains and Rievaulx Abbeys (North Yorkshire). An impressive assemblage of cooking pots and jugs was recorded, confirmed by petrological analysis to have been made from local clays. The importance of lighting is illustrated by the find of a green-glazed cresset lamp, a form which is rare in Scotland (Tabraham 1984). In the later Middle Ages, monastic infirmary halls were often modified to create more private spaces for patients and special dining rooms were developed to accommodate the enriched meat diet. These private chambers were created by subdividing the aisles of the infirmary hall into separate compartments, as evidenced at Merton Priory, where single rooms were created in the aisles in the late fourteenth century (Miller and Saxby 2007: 126). Upper floors were sometimes inserted to provide additional spaces: at Norwich, a floor was inserted in the fourteenth century to provide a dining room on the ground floor and a private chamber above (Gilchrist 2005: 180). It was not uncommon for the comfortable spaces of the infirmary to be requisitioned by senior monastic officials, with private apartments developing at several Cistercian abbeys and cathedral priories (Gilchrist 2005: 181).

Arrangements in an Augustinian hospital priory are vividly illustrated by St Mary Spital in London, which shows both expansion over time and the accommodation of separate social groups within the community (Figure 3.6). Hospitals were commonly located on the edges of towns, near the walls and on main roads and bridges, in order to cater for travellers and pilgrims, and due to the greater availability of suburban land (Rawcliffe 2005). The priory of St Mary Spital was founded to care for pilgrims, sick poor, orphans and women in childbirth. The foundation of 1197 was for a small hospital of twelve to thirteen beds arranged in a simple rectangular hall. The re-foundation of the hospital in

3.6 Plan of St Mary Spital, London. © Museum of London Archaeology

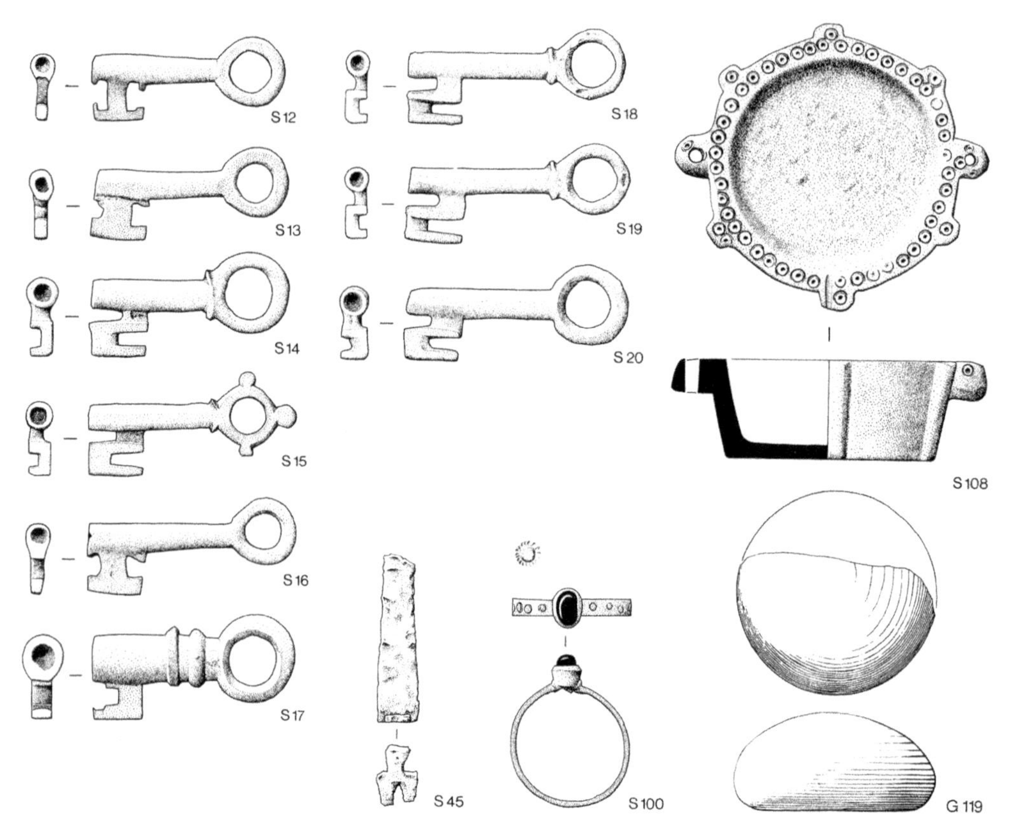

3.7 Small finds from the infirmary hall at St Mary Spital, London. © Museum of London Archaeology

1235 increased the number of beds to sixty. Both men and women were accepted by the hospital and they were segregated by splitting the infirmary into a T-shape, with the chapel in the centre and men and women housed in separate wards (Connell et al. 2012; Thomas et al. 1997). The T-shape was used for other mixed-sex hospitals such as St John the Baptist, Canterbury (Gilchrist 1995: 21). Large assemblages of keys were recovered from St Mary Spital (Figure 3.7) and also from the hospital of St Bartholomew, Bristol (Price with Ponsford 1998), perhaps indicating that lockers were provided to store patients' personal belongings. A new, two-storey infirmary was built at St Mary Spital *c.*1280, and the earlier hall was converted into a very large church. It is likely that men and women were segregated on different floors, as they were at SS John the Baptist and John the Evangelist, Sherborne (Dorset) (Gilchrist 1995: 21). A two-storey extension was added to St Mary Spital in the fourteenth century: at its height, the hospital catered for 180 beds (Thomas et al. 1997: 103–5).

The patients were cared for by a nursing staff of six to seven lay-sisters who were accommodated in a house next to the infirmary, built initially in timber and rebuilt in stone in the late fourteenth century. This housed the sisters' dormitory and refectory. These women nursed the sick and carried out daily chores: the main roles of hospital nurses were preparing meals for the sick, keeping the lamps lit in the infirmary, and changing and laundering the bed sheets (Rawcliffe 1998: 58). The sisters at St Mary Spital had their own private garden: finds from this area included thimbles and bone needles that the sisters would have used in mending, and personal dress accessories including buckles, a finger ring and possible headdress pins (Thomas et al. 1997: 109–10). Female artefacts found from other contexts in the hospital include three wire supports for headdresses (Harward et al. 2019: 274). Each lay-sister would have nursed up to thirty beds at St Mary Spital, with perhaps two to three patients in each one; a ratio of one nurse for up to sixty to seventy patients. Nursing sisters took the customary monastic vows of poverty, chastity and obedience, and were expected to dress in the most humble attire (Rawcliffe 1998: 48). Hospital ordinances frequently specified that virgins, chaste widows or women over the age of fifty should be selected for nursing sisters. They greeted and washed new patients when they arrived at the hospital, and in due course, washed and prepared the dead for burial in the hospital cemetery. Nursing was seen as an active spiritual vocation for women, but by the later Middle Ages, salaried nursing servants were beginning to replace nursing sisters (Rawcliffe 1998: 64).

The Augustinian canons of St Mary Spital were provided with a full monastic cloister to the north of the church, complete with dormitory, refectory, chapter house and their own private kitchen and infirmary. The canons' infirmary shows some signs of economy: it was a timber-framed building on stone foundations and it had no piped water supply (Harward et al. 2019: 154). However, the difference in status between the sisters and canons is all too evident in the accommodation and facilities provided for them. The higher quality of the canons' accommodation reflects medieval attitudes towards gender but also the greater value that was placed on the spiritual administrations of the canons, over the practical care for the body that was provided by the nursing sisters.

THERAPEUTIC CARE

Archaeology provides new evidence for the diagnosis and treatment of the sick in medieval monastic infirmaries and hospitals. The practice of more academic medicine is confirmed by the presence of fragments of urinals, or jordans, the common symbol of the medieval physician. Physicians used glass urinals to examine urine samples for consistency, colour, clarity and odour, which signified particular diseases or states of health. Uroscopy was the mainstay of the physician's diagnostic repertoire; the technique was closely associated with astrology, which influenced the diagnosis and the recommended cure

3.8 Ceramic urinal from Paisley Abbey's Great Drain (Renfrewshire). © Crown Copyright: Historic Environment Scotland

(Rawcliffe 2006). The extensive excavations at St Mary Spital located just two fragments of glass urinals dated to the fourteenth century (Thomas et al. 1997: 111). For comparison, two were recovered from the infirmary drain and latrine block at St Mary Merton (Miller and Saxby 2007: 128), five from the nunnery of St Mary Clerkenwell (Sloane 2012: 245) and twelve from the eastern range of Battle Abbey (Hare 1985: 141–2). The use of uroscopy in monastic contexts is also reflected in monastic book ownership and production; for example, the Syon Herbal has a full chapter in Latin on the use of urine for diagnosis, particularly in relation to women's health (Adams and Forbes 2015).

In Scotland, only ceramic urinals have been reported, including a complete example recovered from the Great Drain at Cistercian Paisley (Malden 2000: 175) (Figure 3.8), one from Benedictine Coldingham (Scottish Borders) (Laing 1971–2) and three from Cistercian Glenluce (Dumfries and Galloway) (Cruden 1950–1). Stephen Moorhouse suggested that ceramic urinals were not intended for medical purposes, but were instead used to separate liquid and solid human waste, with urine retained for industrial uses such as tanning. He noted the concentration of such vessels near latrine blocks at Melrose Abbey (Scottish Borders) and Kirkstall Abbey and explains them as accidental losses when emptying waste (Cruden 1952; Moorhouse 1993: 129). The absence of glass urinals in Scotland must have severely impeded the practice of uroscopy: a translucent vessel was required to see the colour of the urine and to observe sedimentation. Vessel glass is rarely recovered from Scottish medieval contexts although a few fragments have been reported from Perth Whitefriars (Derek Hall, pers. comm.). There is no evidence for the manufacture of glass in Scotland until the early seventeenth century, and imported glass wares are poorly preserved in Scotland's acidic soils.

Other specialist medical objects from monastic sites include spectacles, indicating the diagnosis and attempted correction of vision defects (Figure 3.9). An elaborate pair of bone spectacles was excavated from St Mary Merton, carved in the form of ecclesiastical tracery. Spectacles have also been recovered from Battle Abbey, the Dominican friary at Chester, Wells Cathedral, the

Bridgettine abbey at Syon and Alvastra in Sweden (Miller and Saxby 2007: 127). The importance of literacy in the monastic lifestyle would have resulted in a high value being placed on the correction of sight impairments. This is confirmed by the prominence of eye conditions in the Syon Herbal, representing the most frequently cited ailment in Syon's herbal recipes (Adams and Forbes 2015: 40). Medieval burials sometimes provide evidence of other types of therapeutic device. The great majority of Christian burials were simple interments of the naked corpse in its shroud, with no clothing or grave goods included. Very rarely, however, healing objects or prosthetics were left in place on the corpse after it had been washed and prepared for burial (see Chapter 4, for interpretation in relation to spiritual transformation of the body). For example, a bone paternoster bead was used as a tooth 'filling' in a medieval burial from Denmark (Møller-Christensen 1969). Three main types of therapeutic object have been identified in medieval burial contexts: copper-alloy plates used to protect and heal joint injuries or disease, other metal supports for limbs, and hernia trusses (Gilchrist and Sloane 2005: 103–4) (Figure 3.10).

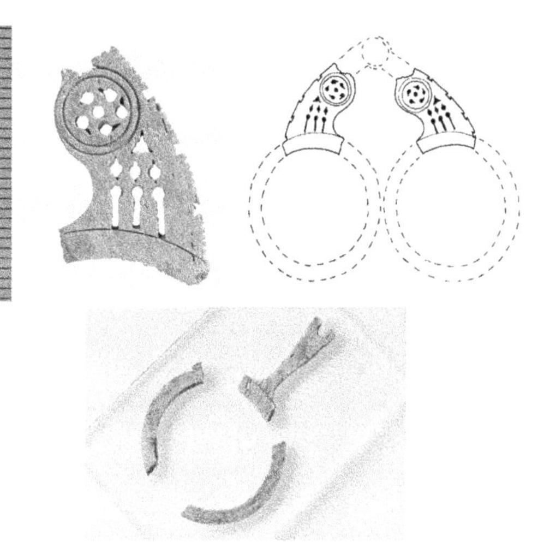

3.9 Bone spectacles from St Mary Merton (Surrey; © Museum of London Archaeology) and Alvastra monastery (The Swedish History Museum)

Pairs of support plates have been found with individuals from St Andrew's Gilbertine priory in York and from the *leprosarium* of St Mary Magdalene in Reading (Berkshire). The older male from York had a rotary fracture of the right knee: the plates were bound to the joint to provide support, fixed by stitched leather coverings (Knüsel et al. 1995). The female from Reading had a badly necrosed humerus; the plates contained dock leaves, perhaps applied as a poultice to the infection. Single plates have been found with burials at St Mary Stratford Langthorne (Essex), Pontefract Priory (West Yorkshire), St Mary Merton and St Mary Spital, where leaves were also found adhering to the plate. The dates of the burials range from the twelfth to the mid-fourteenth century. Contemporary sources confirm the medical use of herbal ligatures, for example cited in a healing miracle associated with St Æbbe (Bartlett 2003: xlviii). At Varnhem Abbey in Sweden, an almost pure copper plate was used to stabilise a possible sword or axe wound on a humerus (Hallbäck 1976–7: 80); similarly, a copper plate was found associated with the upper arm of a burial at the church of Vrasene, Belgium (Janssens 1987). A different type of support was present at St Mary Spital, where a plate of lead sheeting was wrapped

3.10 Therapeutic devices found in burials at medieval monastic sites: Hernia truss from St Mary Merton (Surrey; © Museum of London Archaeology), lead sheeting around right shin of female from St Mary Spital, London (© Museum of London Archaeology), bone with copper plate from Varnham monastery (photograph by Ola Myrin, The Swedish History Museum).

around the shin of a female who showed active periostitis of both legs. The lead sheet contained brown animal hair on its inner face, perhaps indicating a poultice, or alternatively, a charm of some kind (Connell et al. 2012: 208). Hernia trusses are known from early medieval graves in Britain and Europe (such as Llandough: Redknap 2005) but just one example has been identified from a later medieval monastic cemetery in Britain. An older male excavated from the north transept of the church at Merton Priory was found with a belt in situ, worn low on the pelvis, and interpreted as a support for a scrotal hernia. The Merton belt is made from iron and was bound to the body with woven textile and fixed with buckles (Miller and Saxby 2007: 101, 230). Both hands of the skeleton were clutching the strap, with some of the fingers laced over the belt and some behind it.

Burials sometimes contain evidence of certain materials believed to possess therapeutic or 'occult' properties (see Chapter 4). The materials of the copper plates from Varnhem and Vrasene and the lead sheet from St Mary Spital may have been selected for their therapeutic or humoral properties. Lead was also used in making amulets for healing or protective use (Gilchrist 2008: 125). Mercury, also known as quicksilver, was thought to have a cold, wet complexion; it was valued for its regenerative and purgative qualities and for its capacity to destroy infected flesh and remove unsightly blemishes (Rawcliffe 2006: 224). Mercury and cinnabar (mercury sulphur) were used to treat skin diseases such as scabies and skin lesions associated with leprosy and syphilis (Connell et al. 2012: 209). High levels of mercury have been found in the bones of skeletons excavated from Danish, German and Icelandic medieval cemeteries; analysis of associated soil samples indicates that the high mercury levels were not caused by post-mortem diagenesis (Rasmussen et al. 2013, 2015). At the Icelandic monastic hospital of Skriðuklaustur, eleven individuals exhibited elevated mercury concentrations and showed skeletal changes indicative of infection, including treponemal disease. Given the strong archaeological evidence for medical treatment at Skriðuklaustur (discussed below), it is likely that the raised mercury levels in these individuals resulted from medical therapies. However, exposure to mercury may also have resulted from use of cosmetics, ink or vermilion pigment, made scarlet red from ground mineral cinnabar. There were some individuals with raised mercury levels at Skriðuklaustur who showed no signs of pathological lesions, including a female buried in a prestigious location within the church. It has been suggested that she may have been a medical practitioner within the hospital, who would have been exposed to mercurial vapours while treating patients with mercury rubs (Walser et al. 2018). Mercury droplets have also been found on the skeleton of a young female buried in Exeter Cathedral Green in the late Middle Ages. Her skeleton reveals that she suffered from scoliosis and possibly miliary tuberculosis. The droplets were found on her right hip bone, causing blackening of the bone. It is possible that the droplets came from a medicinal vial hung from her waist that has since disintegrated (Kingdom, forthcoming).

Specialist surgical instruments (Figures 3.11 and 3.12) are remarkably rare finds in Britain, with no confirmed examples surviving from monastic sites, although two bronze objects from Glenluce Abbey are perhaps surgical hooks (Cruden 1950–1). General purpose objects such as scissors and knives may have been put to medical use: for instance, thirty-four knives and blade fragments were excavated from the hospital of St Giles by Brompton Bridge (North Yorkshire) (Cardwell 1995: 194–6). These could have been employed for medical purposes, such as phlebotomy, preparing medicinal ingredients and cutting up dressings; equally, they could have been used for domestic and craft-working activities. The paucity of specialist instruments from Britain can be contrasted with the recently excavated site of Skriðuklaustur, a remote Icelandic hospital and monastery following the Augustinian Rule. Medical

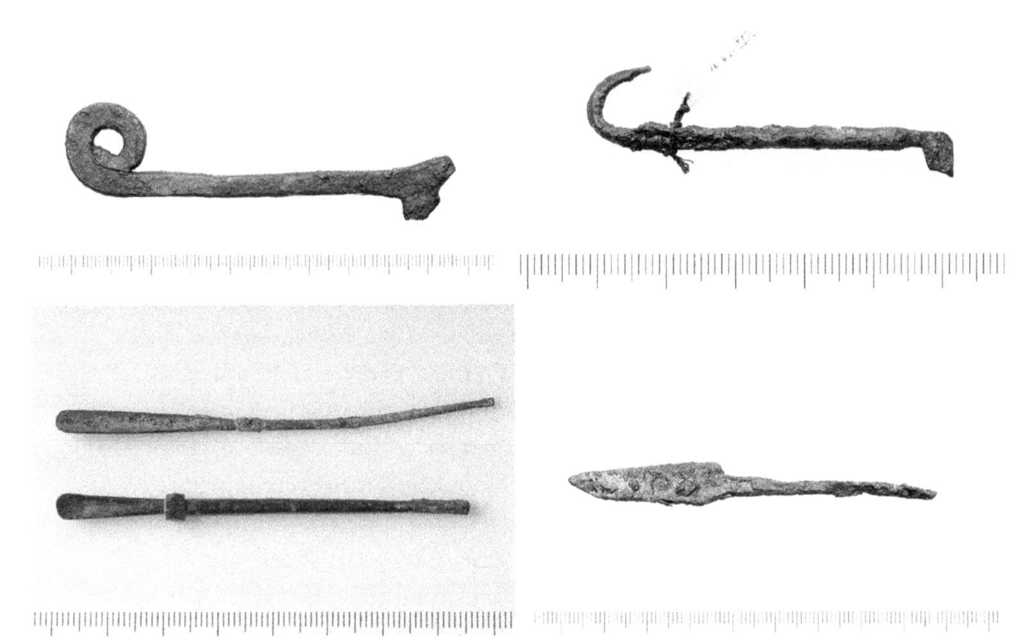

3.11 Surgical instruments excavated from Alvastra and Varnham monasteries: (clockwise) phlebotomy iron from Varnham, surgical hook, scalpel and probes from Alvastra. Photographs by Ola Myrin, The Swedish History Museum

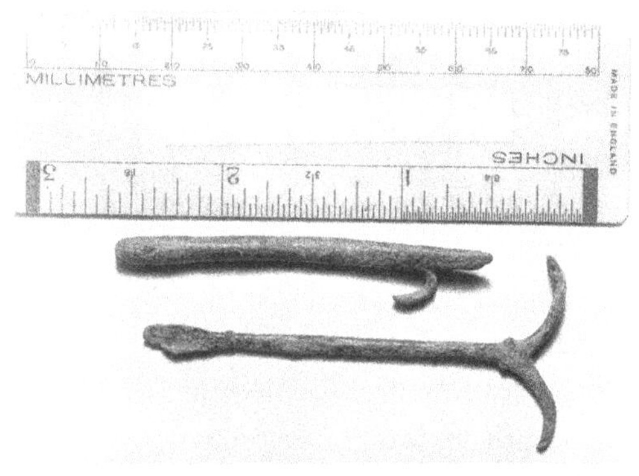

3.12 Possible surgical hooks from Glenluce Abbey (Dumfries and Galloway). © Crown Copyright: Historic Environment Scotland

care is indicated by the presence of implements for surgery or suturing, together with medical phials (Kristjánsdóttir 2010). The Cistercian monasteries of Alvastra and Varnhem in Sweden produced a range of medical objects including scalpels, phlebotomy knives, a cautery, a surgical hook, spatulas for applying medicament, probes and forceps for exploring wounds, and curettes for cleaning wounds (Bergqvist 2014: 91). The negative archaeological evidence for surgical instruments from Britain seems to confirm that surgery was not routinely practised in monastic infirmaries. Surgery was readily available to medieval religious, but it was either performed elsewhere, or visiting surgeons were scrupulous in their care and retention of instruments. Surgery would not have been performed in hospital wards which contained a chapel, due to the prohibition against shedding blood in a consecrated space. The archaeological evidence from Iceland and Sweden may indicate that the distinction between academic and empirical medicine was not as strictly drawn in Scandinavian culture, and that surgery was performed more routinely in monastic contexts.

The types of food vessels used in infirmaries may have been selected to help nursing staff in feeding the sick. The ceramic cooking pots and jugs recorded at both St Mary Spital and St Mary Merton were standard forms, with one possible exception. Both sites produced evidence of ladles in blue-grey ware that are rare in London. The ladles show external sooting, indicating that they were placed in direct contact with fire (Thomas et al. 1997: 59). It has been suggested that the ladles may have been used to reheat and serve individual portions of food for the patients. One of the ladles from Merton was subjected to subsurface residue analysis which indicated the presence of fats/oils and cereals (Miller and Saxby 2007: 128). Specialist vessels were also suggested at the leper hospital of St Nicholas in St Andrews (Fife), where an unusual form of flat-based open bowl was identified in the assemblage of Scottish East Coast Gritty Ware (Hall 1995: 60). The bowls were green-glazed internally and externally smoke-blackened – again, perhaps indicating the heating of individual portions by direct contact with the hearth.

A large assemblage of wooden bowls was found at St Mary Spital, some of which were shallow dishes that may have been used to feed the infirm (Thomas et al. 1997: 59–61) (Figure 3.13). One was an unusual double bowl that could be turned over and used again from the other side, perhaps for a second course. The wide rims would have helped to avoid spillage and may have been designed specifically for a second person to hold steady by the foot while an infirm patient was fed. Personal feeding bowls may have been common at medieval hospitals. During excavations at St Mary Magdalen, Winchester, fragments of two pottery vessels were found in the grave of an individual with leprosy who exhibited severe facial deformities. These have been interpreted as personal food bowls, perhaps indicating assisted feeding or the use of dedicated utensils (Roffey and Tucker 2012: 176).

3.13 Food vessels from St Mary Spital, London: wooden bowls and illustration of double bowl possibly used to feed the infirm, max. diam 170 mm. © Museum of London Archaeology

There is growing archaeological evidence for the use of herbal medicine in the treatment of the sick. Albarelli, or drug jars, have been identified at a number of monastic sites: these are specialist vessels imported from the Mediterranean containing exotic drugs for the dispensary. Possible examples have been reported from the Carmelite friary in Linlithgow (West Lothian)

3.14 Illustration of albarello excavated from St Mary Clerkenwell, London, height 164 mm (© Museum of London Archaeology), and a similar example in the Louvre Museum (photograph by Marie-Lan Nguyen / Wikipedia / Public Domain).

(Stones 1989), from Merton Priory (Miller and Saxby 2007: 128), and a near complete example from the nunnery of St Mary Clerkenwell (Figure 3.14), dated to the second quarter of the sixteenth century (Sloane 2012: 238). Chemical analysis of a jar fragment from Glastonbury Abbey (Somerset), dating to the early fifteenth century, has proven its origins in Tuscany (Blake 2015: 270). Two albarelli were excavated from the hospital of St Mary of Ospringe (Kent): one jar was Malaga Ware with a thin, tin glaze enamel with cobalt blue decoration, dating to the fourteenth century; the other had a deep yellow glaze and came from Dissolution levels (Smith 1989). There were no imported drug jars from the hospital of St Giles by Brompton Bridge but the ceramic assemblage was dominated by jars in domestic wares (37 per cent of the total pottery assemblage) (Cardwell 1995: 169–79).

Herbal plants were also grown in monastic gardens and collected from the local environment to be processed for medicinal use. Stone mortars from monastic sites were used for the preparation of foods and medicines, for instance three mortars in Purbeck marble were excavated from the nunnery of St Mary Clerkenwell (Sloane 2012: 245), and a very large assemblage of ten mortars from St Mary Spital in Purbeck-type marble and shelly limestone (Harward et al. 2019: 264–7). Monastic account rolls sometimes confirm the purchase of distilling equipment and it is often assumed that this equipment was used to transform herbs and flowers into perfumed oils, essences and waters. For example, the infirmarer at Norwich Cathedral Priory recorded the regular purchase of glass phials and distillation equipment in the fifteenth century, in addition to the purchase of a large alembic and the construction of a clay furnace to be fired by peat (Rawcliffe 2002: 61). Medical texts included recipes for distillation: notably, the early sixteenth-century Syon Herbal contained a complete chapter on herbal essences preserved in distilled alcohol, and the late fourteenth-century Breviary of John Mirfield of St Bartholomew's Priory, London, featured over fifty different distilled waters (Adams and Forbes 2015: 36). Aristocratic households also practised distilling, as evidenced in a late fifteenth-century manuscript associated with the Scropes of Bolton, the Berkeley Castle Muniments Select Book 89 (Voigts and Payne 2016). The first part of the manuscript comprises distillation recipes, while the second combines medical and culinary recipes, some of which required distillation. The recipes

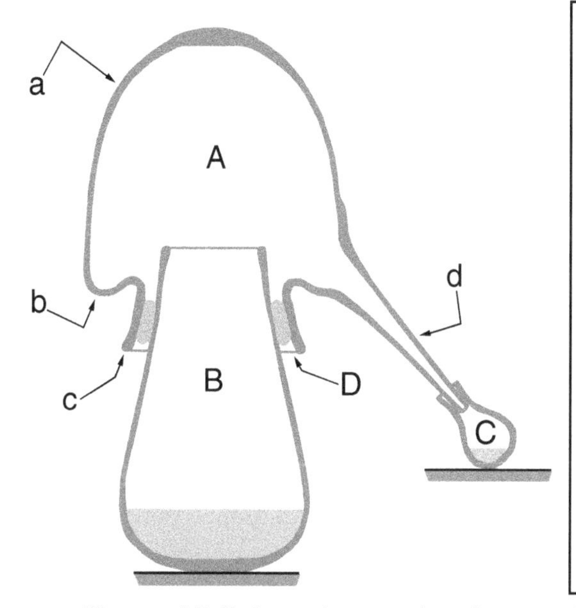

The complete apparatus is known as a still, alembic or limbeck, with variations in the spelling:

A Alembic: *alembic*, *stillhead*, *head* and *helm*

B Cucurbit: *cucurbit*, *body*, *matrass*, *flask* and *gourd*

C Receiver: *receptory*, *receiver* and *bolt-head*

D Lute: *lute*

Details of the alembic:

a Dome

b Collecting-channel

c Rim

d Spout: *pipe*

3.15 Diagram of distillation equipment and a 16th-century drawing showing similar equipment in use. After Moorhouse 1972© Sarah Lambert-Gates and Wellcome Collection, Public Domain

demanded exotic and costly ingredients, such as saffron, cinnamon, cloves, ginger, nutmeg, black pepper, caraway, cumin, camphor, musk and ambergris.

Distillation is a chemical process that harnesses the different boiling points of liquids in order to concentrate them for the production of fragranced oils and perfumes, strong alcohols and mineral acids (Booth 2016). Archaeological evidence for distillation in Britain dates from the thirteenth to fourteenth centuries onwards, comprising glass or ceramic alembics (stillheads), glass or ceramic cucurbits (distilling bases on which the alembic sat) and ceramic or glass flasks and phials that served as receivers for the distillate (Moorhouse 1972; Tyson 2000) (Figure 3.15). A liquid was boiled in the lower vessel, the cucurbit, and the vapour condensed in the domed head of the upper vessel, the alembic; the resulting liquid drained through a collecting channel into the receiver, termed the 'receptory' in vernacular documents. This technology remained unchanged until the development of metal stills in the seventeenth century (Booth 2016). Christopher Booth has surveyed the material culture evidence for the practice of chemistry published from twenty-three excavated monastic sites in Britain, distinguishing between the processes of distillation, cupellation and sublimation (Booth 2017). Distillation was used to produce alcohol and mineral acids; cupellation yielded silver from the melting of composite ores or man-made alloys; and the process of sublimation was used to transform a solid into a gas, for example mercury, sulphur or antimony, and is likely to indicate alchemical practice (Booth 2017: 197, 206).

The largest monastic assemblage of glass and associated ceramics for distilling came from Pontefract Priory, with significant concentrations recovered from Selborne Priory (Hampshire), Kirkstall Abbey and St Mary Spital. Some sites have yielded only ceramic evidence, such as the relatively poor Cistercian abbey at Hulton (Staffordshire) (Klemperer and Boothroyd 2004: 176) and wealthy Glastonbury Abbey, which has four possible cucurbits amongst its ceramic assemblage (Kent 2015). Many monastic excavations have produced one or more fragments of alembics or cucurbits, confirming that distilling was a widespread practice from the fourteenth century onwards (e.g. the hospital of St Mary Magdalene at Partney, Merton Priory, Battle Abbey, Hailes Abbey (Gloucestershire), Northampton Grey Friars and Leicester Austin Friary: Atkins and Popescu 2010; Moorhouse 1972, 1993; Hare 1985: 142; Oakley 1978; Woodland 1981). Excavations at Sandal Castle (West Yorkshire) produced a substantial assemblage of distillation equipment, the remains of a workshop dumped in the castle's barbican ditch (Moorhouse 1983). Sandal Castle and Pontefract Priory are located in close proximity and it is possible that knowledge was shared between monastic and secular households, resulting in regional clusters of distilling workshops. The scarcity of glass in medieval Scotland (discussed above) is likely to have inhibited the practice of medical distilling. To date, only three ceramic alembics have been evidenced from medieval Scotland, including a green-glazed example from Jedburgh Abbey (Scottish Borders) (Cruden 1955–6: 77; Moorhouse 1972), and one in Scottish redware excavated from the site of Aberdeen Franciscan Friary; ICP analysis confirmed that it was manufactured in the Perth area (Hall et al. in prep.). A basal fragment from the leper hospital of St Nicholas in St Andrews represents the first archaeological evidence of distillation at a *leprosarium* (Hall 1995).

What types of distillates were produced at medieval monasteries? Residue analysis on an alembic from demolition deposits in the infirmary drain at Merton Priory indicated the distillation of a fermented product (Miller and

Saxby 2007: 128). This could have been used for distilling wine into *aqua vitae*, which had a wide range of medicinal uses including relieving toothache, expelling poison and treating cancer (Moorhouse 1972, 1993). But not all distillation aimed to produce inert herbal liquors or perfumed oils: medical recipes and archaeological analysis of residues confirm that distillation was used in combination with the processing of chemicals and minerals. Excavations at St Mary Spital have produced evidence for three discrete areas of distillation (Figures 3.16 and 3.17), each of which employed heavy metals such as lead (Harward et al. 2019: 164–72). A cucurbit with a lead rich residue came from an early fourteenth-century deposit in the canons' infirmary at St Mary Spital. In the later fourteenth century, a possible pharmacy was built to the east of the canons' infirmary. This timber-framed building was identified as a distilling workshop on the basis of peat-burning hearths covering its floor; these are likely to be the remains of clay furnaces, a common industrial method employed by distillers and recorded in the infirmarers' accounts from Norwich Cathedral Priory (noted above). Residual evidence of arsenic, lead, copper and iron was detected in the building and a nearby pit yielded ceramic and glass distilling vessels. Tests on residues within the vessels revealed the presence of mercury, lead, iron, arsenic and copper; one deposit also contained calcium and phosphorus, possibly from a crushed bone. This building was used for specialist production up to the mid- or late fifteenth century. Another workshop using distillation was discovered in one of the tenements south of the cemetery at St Mary Spital, which contained a number of rooms with industrial hearths against the walls; a phial of mercury was found in the floor of a nearby structure. Six glass cucurbits were recorded from St Mary Spital, in addition to ceramic alembics, and bottles and kitchenware were reused for industrial or pharmaceutical processes. A silver litharge cake was also found in a building dating to the fifteenth century, which may have been used for medical or industrial applications (Harward et al. 2019: 178–9). Analysis of vessels from Pontefract and Selborne Priory also

3.16 Ceramic alembic from St Mary Spital, London, height 290 mm. © Museum of London Archaeology

3.17 Excavation of distillery at St Mary Spital, London: Canons' infirmary showing the distillery hearths (top left). © Museum of London Archaeology

confirmed the presence of numerous mineral elements including lead, copper, iron, silver and phosphorus, but no organic matter was detected (Moorhouse 1972: Table 1). At Battle Abbey, distillation vessels were founded in association with a small jar containing a mercury residue (Booth 2017: 207).

Were monastic chemists producing pharmaceuticals for human consumption? The process of distillation was employed for numerous purposes, including cosmetics that contained compounds of lead for whitening the skin (Adams and Forbes 2015: 38). The same equipment could also have been used to make nitric acid, used in metal refining to separate gold from silver, and for alchemical and metallurgical experiments (Martinón-Torres and Rehren 2005; Moran 2006). Lead and arsenic were used in medieval artists' pigments as well as in pharmaceuticals – and it can be difficult to distinguish between these two applications even where chemical analysis of residues has been carried out (Pérez-Arantegui et al. 2011). Metals and minerals were routinely combined with herbs in medical recipes: mercury was used in a large number of medicines, and lead carbonate was employed in the treatment of conjunctivitis (Connell et al. 2012: 210). Mineral materials such as arsenic, sulphur, gypsum, lead, mercury and iron were commonly used in the classical and medieval pharmacopeia for treating diseases of the skin, eyes and sexual organs (Lev 2002). For example, a recipe for distilled water in the Syon Herbal contained quicklime (calcium oxide) and ammonium chloride; this blue water was applied to the eyes to improve vision (Adams and Forbes 2015: 266). Another miracle water (*Aqua Mirabilis*) from the Syon Herbal was used to treat skin blemishes, leprosy and to preserve youth. The recipe explains that the ingredients should be mixed in a container of iron, steel, gold or silver, depending on the patient's wealth. It calls for scrapings of silver to be mixed with additional ingredients added on successive days: the urine of a boy on the first day; warm white wine on the second day; fennel juice on the third day; egg whites on the fourth day; breast milk on the fifth day; red wine on the sixth day; and egg whites again on the seventh day, distilling slowly, in combination with a prayer or charm (Adams and Forbes 2015: 267).

Further analysis of residues in distilling equipment is needed to improve our understanding of monastic chemistry. An additional route to identifying the medical ingestion of organic and inorganic materials is through trace residues contained in dental calculus (tartar or calcified dental plaque) (Warinner et al. 2015). Calculus is a complex bacterial deposit that adheres to the tooth enamel as plaque and mineralises quickly. Archaeologists have recently explored the potential for the study of calculus to reveal new evidence for prehistoric diet, but the micro-debris in dental calculus may also reveal plants and minerals that were ingested as medical preparations (Hardy et al. 2012). Very few studies have been published to date on dental calculus from medieval sites (e.g. Radini et al. 2016). However, promising results were obtained from the analysis of dental calculus from an adult male skeleton excavated from the medieval necropolis of Can Reiners (Balearic Islands, Spain) dated to the ninth or tenth century (Fiorin et al. 2018). The male was aged between 21 and 30 years at death and his skeleton showed no obvious signs of disease. Microscopic evidence was found for the sporangium annulus of a fern consistent with the species *Asplenium trichomanes* (maidenhair spleenwort). Historical sources confirm the widespread medical use of this species for treatment of the urinary tract (particularly kidney stones), conditions of the skin and as a decongestant. There are no published studies to date of dental calculus in individuals buried at medieval monastic and hospital cemeteries. However, an unpublished study of calculus from skeletons at the monastery of St Oswald's at Gloucester has provided preliminary evidence for raised mercury levels in three skeletons that showed pathological changes consistent with leprosy or syphilis (Flakney 2015).

Archaeobotanical evidence from monastic and hospital sites includes plants with specific therapeutic applications (Figure 3.18). At Merton Priory, exceptionally large quantities of black mustard (*Brassica nigra*) seeds were recovered from the infirmary area, recommended in Culpepper's Herbal for treatment of coughs, toothache or throat swellings (Miller and Saxby 2007: 128–9). The infirmary drain produced a large number of seeds of celandine (*Chelidonium majus*), suggested by Gerard's Herbal for treatment of warts and eye troubles (Miller and Saxby 2007: 128–9). Both Merton and St Mary Spital produced seeds of henbane (*Hyoscyamus niger*), a powerful sedative, but also a common local species that could have been intrusive in the assemblage. A number of plants present at St Mary Spital may have been grown specifically for medical use, including borage (*Borago officinalis*), catmint (*Nepeta cataria*), hyssop (*Hyssopus officinale*) and opium poppy (*Papaver somniferum*), which was typically prepared in a syrup administered for pain relief (Davis 2019). Henbane and celandine have also been found at the Isle of May and in the drain at Paisley Abbey (James and Yeoman 2008). Paisley Abbey yielded a variety of plants with possible medical uses, such as hemlock (*Conium maculatum*), which can be used as a strong sedative, and caper spurge (*Euphorbia lathyris*), found also at Reading Abbey, and well known as a purgative (Dickson and Dickson 2000: 198). Opium poppy was also present at Paisley and has been reported from Soutra (Scottish Borders) as an organic residue adhering to a jar (Moffat 1988–98, SHARP 3: figure 19).

Seeds of Valerian (*Valeriana officinalis*) and St John's Wort (*Hypericum perforatum*) have been reported from Soutra, an Augustinian hospital sited on the King's Highway between Edinburgh and London. In herbal medicine today, these plants are used for the treatment of mild depression, anxiety and sleeping disorders. In the Middle Ages, however, they seem to have been employed to promote healing in wounds and fractures (Moffat 2014). The Soutra project describes itself as 'archaeo-ethnopharmacological'; it considers archaeological evidence in tandem with historical sources, oral tradition and modern botany. The project has focused on the investigation of drains identified by geophysical survey in the 1980s, in search of medical waste such as human blood and exotic drug plants. Small-scale excavations focused on the cellar of an accommodation block, separated from the church by a major drain. The investigations have not been fully published but interim reports claimed pollen evidence for exotic spices such as cloves (Moffat 1988–98, SHARP 2: 32); while tests for haemoglobin confirmed the presence of vast quantities of human blood, supposedly contaminated with lead from the piped water supply (Yeoman 1995: 31–3). These results have not been replicated in tests undertaken at other hospital sites and the approach has not been taken up more widely. The identification of the presence of human blood at Soutra is of limited value, particularly in the absence of stratigraphic or dating evidence, as we know that phlebotomy was practised routinely at medieval infirmaries.

3.18 Pseudo-Apuleius, *Herbarius*; mid-13th-century herbal, folio illustrating Gladioli. Wellcome Collection, MS 573, f. 26v, Public Domain

Medieval healing also drew on magic and the use of amulets. The boundary between spiritual and magical practice was permeable even in monastic institutions, a theme that will be taken up in the next chapter. It is noteworthy that relatively few artefacts excavated from monasteries and hospitals can be identified as potential healing amulets, objects that were believed to possess special properties to protect or heal. Examples include objects made of occult materials such as jet or amber, or metal objects which carry sacred inscriptions. One candidate is a Roman intaglio recovered from the drain at Paisley Abbey (Malden 2000: 177). Antique cut gems were made into rings that were particularly favoured by medieval ecclesiastics and are sometimes found in the graves of bishops (Gilchrist 2008). The thirteenth-century *Book of Stones* by the Dominican Albertus Magnus described the special properties of images in stones, including antique cameos and intaglios, alongside agates and fossils. Albertus regarded the images or 'pictures' in cut gems as having been naturally created, with celestial powers channelled through astrological images (Wyckoff 1967: 127–35).

Amulets in more common use were found at St Mary Spital: a woman was buried in an ash-lined coffin with a silver ring dating to the fourteenth century. This has a two-line inscription around the outside of the ring, IASPAR MELCHIOR BALTACZAR IESUS NAZARENUS (Gilchrist and Sloane 2005: 99). This powerful charm combines the names of the three Magi, known for protection against epilepsy, with the formula Jesus Nazarenus, regarded as protection against sudden death (Gilchrist 2012: 163). Death without preparation was greatly feared by medieval people, since the last rites of confession, communion and the sacrament of extreme unction were required to send the soul on its journey. Seven gold 'angels' were also excavated from St Mary Spital, eight-shilling pieces which carry an image of the archangel St Michael defeating a devil or dragon; on the reverse is a ship with the mast depicted as the Rood. These coins were distributed ceremonially by the king to sufferers of the skin disease scrofula, known as 'the King's Evil'. The gold angels from St Mary Spital were found in a pit in a house within the hospital precinct (Harward et al. 2019: 279–80). 'Angels' were also used more widely to protect against illness and harm, as confirmed by their occurrence on the Tudor warship, the *Mary Rose*. Nineteen angels were recovered from the ship, seven of which were worn on mariners' bodies when the ship sank (Besly 2005).

CONCLUSIONS: MONASTIC HEALING TECHNOLOGIES

A practice-based approach to medieval healing reveals new insight to sensory experience in the medieval infirmary. In summary, the main classes of archaeological evidence for medieval healing are:

- preventative measures including diet, hygiene and care of the body;
- excavated infirmary complexes;

- potential medical objects from infirmary and cemetery contexts (including glass and ceramic vessels, medical tools, prosthetics and healing amulets);
- archaeobotanical evidence for herbal medicine;
- skeletal evidence for direct medical intervention such as bone-setting, amputation and trephination;
- skeletal evidence for disease and disability from which the extended social care of individuals can be inferred (Roberts 2017; Tilley 2017).

Each of these classes of evidence must be critically assessed according to their social and archaeological contexts. What do they tell us about differences in therapeutic treatment between hospitals, monastic infirmaries and (secular) domestic environments? Do they offer any commentary on the experience of patients, or who was responsible for treating them? Can we detect regional traditions or gendered differences in monastic healing technologies?

An interdisciplinary approach enables reconstruction of the sensory and material dimensions of the medieval infirmary. Attention to space confirms evidence for sexual segregation in hospital infirmaries and an increased emphasis on privacy in the later Middle Ages, including partitioned chambers and the possible provision of lockers to securely store personal belongings. Archaeology reveals patterns for the positioning of beds and the movement of nursing staff, engrained as wear patterns in floors at St Mary Merton and St Mary Spital, and highlights the importance of heating, lighting and sanitation in the infirmary (Miller and Saxby 2007; Harward et al. 2019; Thomas et al. 1997). At the hospital of St Mary Spital, the superior accommodation provided for the canons suggests that greater social value was placed on their spiritual ministry for the sick, above the practical vocation of the lay-sisters. Documentary evidence confirms that it was the sisters who performed the most basic care for the body: preparing meals for the sick, keeping the lamps lit, bathing patients and laundering bed sheets. Specialist vessels for feeding the infirm have been identified at the hospitals of St Mary Spital and St Nicholas in St Andrews, and ladles for heating individual portions were found at the monastic infirmary of Merton Priory. This suggests that individual meals were warmed and fed to patients as required, in contrast with the monastic model of communal dining at set times of the day.

As noted above, the prevailing view of medical historians is that medieval hospitals provided 'warmth, rest, basic nursing care and nourishing food' (Rawcliffe 2011: 74). Treatment within the monastic infirmary was more closely informed by academic medicine, revolving around a routine of uroscopy, astrology and blood-letting, to achieve a balance of humours in each individual monk or nun. Peregrine Horden stresses the emphasis placed on rhetoric in medieval medicine over practice or intervention; he suggests that prevention and 'talking cures' were valued over technological intervention, in contrast with the prevailing approaches of modern biomedicine (Horden 2007: 138–9). And yet, when the archaeological data are drawn together, there is considerable evidence for medieval healing, some of which was based around active intervention. Technologies of healing evidenced by archaeology include preventative care for the body, medical interventions such as surgery and bone-setting, the provision of prosthetics and specialist medicines (evidenced by archaeobotany and material culture), and extended social care for individuals with long-term disease and disability, evidenced by skeletons excavated from the cemeteries of hospitals and monasteries. The Syon Herbal gives insight to the range of expensive ingredients that enhanced sensory experience in therapeutic treatment, including richly fragranced exotics such as nutmeg, cinnamon, cloves and cumin (Adams and Forbes 2015: 40). It indicates that a strong emphasis was placed by monasteries on remedies to heal eye complaints, matched by archaeological evidence for spectacles found at Syon and elsewhere, reflecting the importance of sight in performing monastic liturgy and literacy.

A significant difference between hospitals and monastic infirmaries is that the latter were masculine environments, with care for the sick undertaken by the monk-infirmarer and male servants. The well-documented case of Norwich Cathedral Priory confirms that the only female servant was the laundress – she provided a supply of clean sheets but is unlikely to have interacted with monastic patients (Rawcliffe 2002). In contrast, nursing in hospital infirmaries was undertaken by lay-sisters who had taken monastic vows, gradually replaced in the later Middle Ages by female nursing servants (Rawcliffe 1998). Both environments produce significant archaeobotanical evidence for the use of herbal medicine in treating the sick. Rawcliffe suggests that medieval women were skilful herbalists and that the sisters' gardens at hospitals such as St Giles in Norwich were used to grow medicinal herbs (Rawcliffe 1998: 59). The cultivation and processing of herbs, in addition to the skilled preparation of herbal remedies, represent specialist technologies of healing. Nursing sisters drew on the empirical tradition of herbal medicine to treat hospital patients and they may also have been skilled bone-setters. Is it possible that the sisters' empirical knowledge included the distillation of herbal medicines? In the context of noble households in England and Germany, it has been argued that women were responsible for the distillation of medical recipes. This is based on women's ownership of recipe collections and distilling equipment (Rankin 2013) and the emphasis placed on women's health within manuscripts featuring recipes for medical distillation, such as the Berkeley Castle Manuscript and the Syon Herbal (Voigts and Payne 2016; Adams and Forbes 2015). Archaeological evidence suggests that medical distillation was carried out principally at monasteries for men; however, distilling equipment has been recorded at the Gilbertine double houses of Watton (East Yorkshire) and Haverholme

(Lincolnshire) (Moorhouse 1972: 113) and the Syon Herbal confirms the importance of pharmaceuticals to a Bridgettine double house. Excavated nunneries have also produced evidence for distillation, including a ceramic distilling base from Polsloe Priory, Exeter (Allan 1984: 67), a pottery receptory from Denny Abbey (Cambridgeshire) (Booth 2017: 202), and potential ceramic distillation vessels from a timber building at St Mary Clerkenwell (Sloane 2012: 45).

Urinals are commonly recovered from monastic sites, confirming the widespread importance of uroscopy in the monastic regimen, including nunneries such as St Mary Clerkenwell (Sloane 2012: 245). The rarity of vessel glass in Scotland must have limited the practice of both uroscopy and medical distilling. Only two fragments of glass urinal were recovered from the extensive excavations at the hospital of St Mary Spital, perhaps confirming that more academic approaches to medical diagnosis were employed only exceptionally in hospitals. Rare examples of therapeutic and prosthetic devices, ranging from spectacles to hernia trusses, seem to be more closely associated with monastic rather than hospital care. Healing plates were found associated with a burial at the *leprosarium* at Reading, but this hospital was located within the precinct of Reading Abbey. Clearly there was an overlap in nursing practice between the two types of institution, despite the gender difference in nursing personnel. However, monastic infirmaries seem to have been more likely to import exotic drugs for the dispensary, on the basis of drug jars identified from archaeological contexts to date, including an example from the nunnery of St Mary Clerkenwell.

The strongest indication of healing technology is in the likely production of pharmaceuticals, demonstrated by extensive evidence for glass and ceramic equipment for distillation. The practice was widespread at monasteries and has been detected at hospitals, with residue analysis at St Mary Spital confirming the use of heavy metals in distillations, including mercury, lead, iron, arsenic and copper. It is possible that distilling was carried out in connection with industrial processes such as assaying or in relation to alchemy, as the transmutation of metals was believed to hold the key to youth, health and eternal life (Principe 2013). Medieval monastic chemistry may not have clearly distinguished between practices aimed at pharmacy, alchemy and metallurgy (Booth 2017). However, the spatial and chronological contexts perhaps suggest a medical function: the large assemblages of distilling equipment recovered from Pontefract and Selborne Priories were concentrated near the monastic latrine blocks, in close proximity to the monks' dormitories (Moorhouse 1972: 90, 99). It is unlikely that metalworking processes would have been located so near the sacred space of the church and cloister, and in direct contact with the main water supply that was piped through the monastery. Monastic infirmaries were usually sited in precisely this area, to benefit from the purest water before it flushed the latrines of the dormitory and the drains of the kitchen. The medical application of these chemical compounds is confirmed by historical and skeletal evidence that metals such as mercury were used to treat leprosy and treponemal diseases such as syphilis (discussed above). Can we conclude that the hospital patients at St Mary Spital received chemotherapy, using chemical preparations produced at pharmacies within the precinct? The location of the distilling workshops is central to this question: two were adjacent to the canons' dormitory and infirmary, rather than sited with the infirmary of the sick poor. If these workshops were pharmaceutical, their spatial location suggests that the medicines may have been intended for treatment of the canons rather than the sick poor. The third distilling workshop at St Mary Spital was located in a more industrial area of the precinct and may have been operated by secular tenants; the association of a silver litharge cake suggests that this site is more likely to have been connected to assaying and metalworking.

To what extent were these medieval healing technologies exclusive to religious contexts? Herbals and medical manuscripts were also owned by aristocratic families and material culture confirms that uroscopy and distillation sometimes took place in castles and urban settlements, although they are found principally on monastic sites. Fragments of urinals have been excavated from London, Winchester, Southampton and Northampton, and at castles including Conisborough (South Yorkshire) (Thorn 1980). Herb gardens were also a prominent feature of castles and distilling equipment has been found in castle excavations, including an exceptional assemblage from Sandal (West Yorkshire) (Moorhouse 1983), and fragments from Bodiam (Sussex), Bramber (Sussex) (Moorhouse 1977), Wisbech (Cambridgeshire) and Weoley (Warwickshire) (Moorhouse 1972). The Weoley Castle evidence suggests the practice of chemical sublimation for alchemical purposes, comprising an aludel (the top vessel in sublimation apparatus) and a distilling base which retained a mercury residue. To date only one monastic site in Britain has produced an aludel, Byland Abbey (North Yorkshire), suggesting the practice of alchemy (Booth 2017: 204). Drug jars (albaralli) have also been recorded from castles, including Barnard Castle (co Durham) (Austin 2007: 407), while grooming tools are recovered from urban and castle excavations (Gilchrist 2012: 76–8). These technologies of the medieval body were not exclusive to monastic contexts, but in the medieval countryside, religious institutions were distinctive in their emphasis on clean water supply and scrupulous refuse disposal. In an urban context, English town corporations developed innovative public health strategies in the later Middle Ages, with an emphasis on water supply (Rawcliffe 2013). Both urban and rural monasteries engaged in a disciplined regimen of the body that included celibacy, hygiene, fasting and daily timetables that governed prayer, study, eating, talking and sleeping.

Finally, it is worth noting some possible regional and chronological traditions in monastic healing and technologies of the body. Preliminary observations suggest that the degree of medical intervention that took place in monastic and hospital infirmaries varied in different parts of Europe. Archaeological excavation of Icelandic and Swedish monasteries has yielded far more material culture for surgery and medical treatment (Bergqvist 2014; Kristjánsdóttir 2010). Johanna Bergqvist attributes the prevalence of these objects in Sweden to the wider 'medical culture' that existed in Scandinavian secular society, proposing that a strong vernacular tradition was already in place around the 'empirical art of healing' before the introduction of monasticism (Bergqvist 2013). What was the relationship of medieval monastic healing in Britain to earlier, indigenous traditions of care? Reformed monasticism introduced new ideas about care for the body and influenced the foundation of medieval hospitals dedicated to Christian charity. Recent archaeological investigations at the sites of English medieval hospitals have detected signs of earlier specialist cemeteries, dating to the late Saxon period. Archaeological evidence from Winchester, St Mary Spital and Partney suggests that we should be alert to the possibility that charitable institutions may have been in operation by the tenth or eleventh century, before Norman colonisation. We should also consider whether the locations of hospitals founded in the twelfth century or later may have been selected to harness the healing qualities of earlier therapeutic landscapes. In Scotland, the boom in hospital foundations appears to have been as late as the fifteenth century, on the basis of historical evidence. How many holy wells, shrines, hospitals and monasteries were re-founded at places renowned for an earlier healing tradition, such as the largely undocumented case of the Isle of May? A priority for future research is the investigation of regional differences in monastic healing and their relationship to earlier therapeutic landscapes.

FOUR

THE MATERIALITY OF MAGIC: THE RITUAL LIVES OF PEOPLE AND THINGS

INTRODUCTION: MAGIC AND RELIGION

This chapter explores the relationship between medieval magic and religion, with particular emphasis on the use of objects and material culture in rites of healing, protection and transformation. It extends the practice-based approach developed in the previous chapter (focusing on agency and embodiment) to consider ritual technologies and how they were made efficacious through the interplay of objects, materials, spaces and bodily techniques (Galliot 2015). The term technology is used here to refer to 'embodied, procedural knowledge embedded in the material world' (Mohan and Warnier 2017: 372) and applied for practical purposes in the healing and protection of the Christian body. Historical and archaeological scholarship generally separates monastic from lay experience and seldom considers shared beliefs and ritual practice. Archaeological evidence reveals that the ritual technologies of monasticism overlapped with those of the laity, particularly in relation to magic and burial. The dichotomy created between the study of 'institutional' (orthodox) and 'popular' (heterodox) religion has masked common beliefs and ritual technologies, as well as concealing important connections with earlier, indigenous traditions. Medieval archaeologists have begun to challenge this opposition by shifting their attention to the study of medieval 'folk', 'vernacular' or 'lived' religion, in a more holistic approach which considers the material practices of medieval people alongside the formal structures of Christian theology and liturgy (e.g.

Grau-Sologestoa 2018; Hukantaival 2013; Johanson and Jonuks 2015; Kapaló 2013).

How was belief in magic reconciled with the spiritual values of monastic life? The boundary between religion and magic can be elusive to twenty-first-century eyes, just as it was to medieval clerics, who debated the overlapping definitions of religion, science, magic and heresy (Rider 2012: 8). For example, charms recited over the sick made use of consecrated objects, together with herbs and animal parts, and in combination with religious language and ritual gestures, such as making the sign of the cross. If a cure was achieved, was it considered to have been brought about by miracle or magic? The key issue for theologians was in pinpointing the cause or agency of the marvel: was it effected by the intercession of saints, the occult power of nature or the intervention of demons? *Causation* was categorised by Thomas Aquinas in the thirteenth century as 'above nature', 'beyond nature' and 'against nature' (Bartlett 2008: 8). Any suspicion of demonic magic was prohibited by the church as illicit magic, while magic that drew upon the occult power of nature was accepted as licit and part of God's creation. The term 'occult' in the medieval context simply meant 'hidden from the eye', and carried no connotations of the supernatural or the paranormal, as it does today. Historians of magic identify the thirteenth century as a transitional point when the concept of 'natural magic' emerged, blending classical ideas regarding the virtues of natural substances such as stones, herbs and animals, with Christian ideas about the cosmos. Writing in the 1230s, the French theologian William of Auvergne saw natural magic as non-demonic, regarding it as an innocent consequence of the divine creation of the universe (Bartlett 2008: 21).

Medieval monks practised certain types of learned magic in which the potential for demonic agency was more problematic, such as divination, necromancy and image magic, rituals that were performed over an image to induce a spirit. The monastic fascination with magic increased in the twelfth and thirteenth centuries with the circulation of newly translated Greek, Arab and Hebrew texts. In monastic libraries, magic texts were grouped with astronomy, astrology, medicine and alchemy (Page 2013: 2, 5). Monasteries also collected herbal recipes (see Chapter 3), charms and lapidaries, books that explained the marvellous properties of stones. The ritual efficacy of charms relied on the power of substances, tools, sounds, smells and the procedural knowledge of the practitioner to transform their meaning. Charms consisted of powerful magic words or traditional Christian names, such as the three Magi – Caspar, Melchior and Balthasar – which were written on parchment or lead, on objects such as jewellery, spoons and bowls, or even on the body itself. Charms were used by medical and monastic practitioners but were most commonly associated with folk healers, often women (Olsan 2003). Their efficacy was achieved through the interplay of the body with material culture: the remedy was enacted by words ritually sung or chanted and often involving bodily gestures such as walking in a circle around an object. These rites were performed in domestic contexts, often by midwives and herbalists, but charms also played a part in mainstream medical and religious practice.

Magic and religion were brought together particularly around rites of healing, where ritual practice was intimately linked to the body, and in Christian life course rituals such as birth, marriage and death. This chapter considers the use of objects and material culture in ritual performances that may have been intended to heal, protect and transform the living and the dead. The geographical focus is on later medieval Scotland, to address one of the broader aims of this book to contribute to social approaches in the study of later medieval Scottish archaeology. It examines three specific ritual technologies: the use of amulets; the deliberate burial or deposition of objects in sacred space; and the placing of objects with the medieval dead. These practices raise a number of questions surrounding the use and meaning of objects, particularly around *agency* or *causation* (Gilchrist 2012: 216–18). The person–object boundary is often blurred in rites of magic: wonders are worked by relics that are both persons and things, while the agency of saints can be channelled through any material substance or object that came within close proximity to their remains, such as pilgrim badges, water, or even dust from the saint's tomb (Geary 1986).

Archaeologists studying prehistoric beliefs have challenged the pervasive dichotomy between 'sacred' and 'profane' that has characterised much archaeological thinking on ritual and religion (e.g. Bradley 2005; Brück 1999). Ritual is now regarded by archaeologists as an aspect of the *everyday*, imbuing all aspects of life (Insoll 2004: 159). Medieval archaeologists have begun to adopt this more holistic approach to the study of everyday belief in the medieval town and countryside (Gilchrist 2012). For example, Mark Hall has explored objects excavated from Perth High Street to show that everyday ritual practice in a Scottish burgh blended the cult of saints with traditional *apotropaic* rites, in other words, those intended to guard against harm or evil. Pilgrim souvenirs of Thomas Becket and St Andrew rubbed shoulders with occult materials such as jet, old coins, Roman glass and Bronze Age flints, some of which were deliberately deposited in a medieval hall (Hall 2011). With rare exceptions (e.g. Stocker and Everson 2003), this more integrated approach to everyday ritual has not been applied to medieval monastic contexts. Monastic ritual is generally equated with the formal liturgy of Christian worship, commemorative masses for the dead, and the monastic *horarium*, the daily timetable of religious services in the church. Archaeological evidence illuminates common technologies of magic and challenges the pervasive binary between monastic/institutional religion on the one hand, and popular/lay religion on the other.

STONES AND SACRED WORDS: THE OCCULT AND THE DIVINE

The intermingling of magic and religion in medieval Christianity may seem incongruous to us today; however, it was reconciled by the medieval framework of *natural magic*. Thomas of Chobham, a late twelfth-century English theologian, wrote 'natural philosophers say the power of nature is concentrated above all in three things: in words and herbs and in stones' (Rider 2012: 40). I would like to concentrate here on the power that medieval people attributed to stones and sacred words. Lapidaries – books of stones – were widely circulated from the eleventh century onwards. The most famous was Bishop Marbode of Renne's *De Lapidus*, a book of verse on the properties of sixty stones, dated *c.*1090 (Evans 1922: 33). Lapidaries were popular medical texts that explained the therapeutic applications of each stone, for example whether to wear it next to the skin or to consume it powdered in a drink. They describe the natural properties of gemstones, minerals such as sulphur and lignite, animal products and fossilized materials including coral, pearl, amber and toadstone, as well as mythical stones (Harris 2016: 185–7).

Belief in the power of stones drew on classical authors such as Pliny and Galen, who proposed that all materials of nature contained virtues that could be harnessed by those in possession of the correct knowledge (Kieckhefer 2000). Some of these properties were manifest and easily observed, while others were occult, with their qualities concealed or hidden from the eye. *Manifest* properties could be identified based on the doctrine of signatures, which proposed that nature marked objects with signs to indicate their use. For instance, red coral was the colour of blood and therefore believed to be an effective remedy to staunch wounds and bleeding. Examples of *occult* materials with hidden properties are magnetic minerals with a natural polarity that attracts iron; or jet and amber, fossilized organic materials that develop a static charge and emit a smell when rubbed. Medieval writers understood these natural materials as gifts from God, created for the benefit of humankind: to make use of stones was therefore a form of 'sacred healing', according to Marbode (Harris 2016: 195).

Medieval people believed in the efficacy of stones long before natural magic emerged as a conceptual framework in the thirteenth century. In Britain, the 'sacred healing' of stones pre-dated the circulation of medieval lapidaries based on classical knowledge. For example, Adomnán's *Life of Columba*, written at the very end of the seventh century, describes several miracles in which Columba made use of 'white stones'. These are indigenous quartz pebbles, rather than exotic gemstones such as rock crystal. Columba plucked a white pebble from a stream, saying 'Mark this white stone, through which the Lord will bring about the healing of many sick people among this heathen race'. He used the stone to bargain for the liberation of a female Irish slave held by the

Pictish king's wizard, Broichan, who was perilously ill. When asked to cure him, Columba replied:

> If Broichan will first promise to release the Irish girl, then and only then dip this stone in some water and let him drink it. He will be well again immediately. But if he is intransigent and refuses to release her, he will die on the spot.

According to the *vita*, the stone was kept in the king's treasury to cure sundry diseases among the people (*Life of St Columba* Book II: 33–4; Sharpe 1995: 181–2). In this example, the stone takes on curative properties by virtue of contact with the saint, in the manner of a contact-relic, and God is explicitly credited with causing the miracle.

There is strong archaeological evidence that in Britain white stones had long been regarded as having apotropaic or healing qualities. White, beach-rolled quartz pebbles were commonly placed with early medieval burials in Scotland, Ireland, Wales and the Isle of Man; for example, they are recorded in burials from Iona (Scottish Inner Hebrides) (O'Sullivan 1999), Llandough (Glamorganshire) (Holbrook and Thomas 2005), the Isle of May (Fife) (James and Yeoman 2008) and Whithorn (Dumfries and Galloway) (Hill 1997). Quartz is piezoelectric: when struck or rubbed together it will produce a faint glow (known as triboluminescence). Like jet and amber, quartz would have been regarded by medieval people as possessing occult properties. White stones evidently carried spiritual connotations associated with indigenous religious traditions, stretching back to the early medieval monasticism of Columba and much earlier, to prehistoric beliefs. For example, quartz pebbles are associated with Neolithic monuments in Scotland, such as Forteviot (Brophy and Noble in prep.), as well as in Ireland (Driscoll 2015) and the Isle of Man (Darvill 2002). It has been suggested that quartz carried the symbolic associations of the ocean and mountains. It may have been regarded as generative or transformative to prehistoric and medieval people, with its incorporation in mortuary and pilgrimage contexts conveying the symbolism of water and new beginnings (Fowler 2004: 116; Lash 2018). Quartz pebbles were occasionally placed with burials in Britain right into the later Middle Ages and beyond (Gilchrist 2008).

Jet was also regarded by medieval people as a powerful occult material. The deep black substance of jet is fossilized coniferous wood, easily carved into jewellery and objects such as gaming pieces (Hall 2016b). Jet occurs principally in two locations – near Whitby in North Yorkshire and in Galicia in northern Spain – and in both regions it was used to manufacture holy objects and pilgrim souvenirs. According to Marbode's lapidary, jet was efficacious if worn on the body, consumed as a powder, ingested through water in which the material had been steeped, or burnt to release beneficial fumes. The healing and anaesthetic properties of jet were recommended for easing conditions ranging from childbirth to toothache, and it was believed to possess powerful apotropaic value to protect from demons and malignant magic (Evans 1922). Jet crucifixes have been found in monastic burial contexts, for example from the priories of Gisborough, Old Malton and Pontefract in Yorkshire (Pierce 2013), St James's Priory, Bristol (Jackson 2006), and St John's Hospital, Cambridge (Cessford 2015). It has been suggested that jet objects were manufactured especially for monastic use: archaeological evidence confirms that small, jet crucifix pendants were produced in workshops at Whitby Abbey. A distinctive corpus of twenty-two crucifix pendants with ring and dot motif can be dated stylistically to the twelfth century (Pierce 2013). In Scotland, three jet pendants have been recovered as chance finds and declared as Treasure Trove, with examples spread geographically from the Borders to the Highlands (Canmore IDs 141341 (Dairsie Mains, Fife), 7952 (Hill of Shebster, Caithness), 5584 (Trabrown, Borders)). Jet was also commonly used for paternoster beads in England, but only a few examples have been found in Scotland: at Perth Carmelite Friary (Figure 4.1), Elcho Nunnery (Perth and Kinross) and at Linlithgow Carmelite Friary (West Lothian), although the latter may be a reused Bronze Age bead (Reid and Lye 1988: 78; Stones 1989: microfiche 12: E10). Jet was also worn by the laity and is found in domestic contexts: for example, a jet pendant and bead were recovered from High Street, Perth (Hall 2011).

4.1 Jet and glass beads found during excavations of Perth Carmelite Priory. Reproduced by kind permission of Derek Hall

Objects incorporating gemstones such as sapphires are occasionally found in Scotland and recorded as Treasure Trove. For example, a gold finger ring with a stirrup-shaped hoop with a sapphire cabochon, of twelfth- or thirteenth-century date, was found near Restenneth Priory (Angus: Canmore ID 89912), and another was found at Lamington (Lanarkshire: Canmore ID 339213). Sapphires were regarded as a cold stone to be used for the treatment of excessive bodily heat, ulcers and ailments. This perhaps explains the relatively common occurrence of sapphire rings in the graves of high-ranking ecclesiastics (Hinton 2005: 187), and it is likely that the Restenneth ring was associated with the priory. Objects incorporating blue glass have also been found, perhaps representing a proxy for sapphire, and used in combination with sacred names. A silver crucifix found at Loch Leven (Perth and Kinross) is a strong candidate for a monastic object (Figure 4.2): the front shows Christ on the cross and the reverse is decorated with a large cabochon blue glass gem and the remains of an inscription, which originally read 'IHESUS NAZRENUS

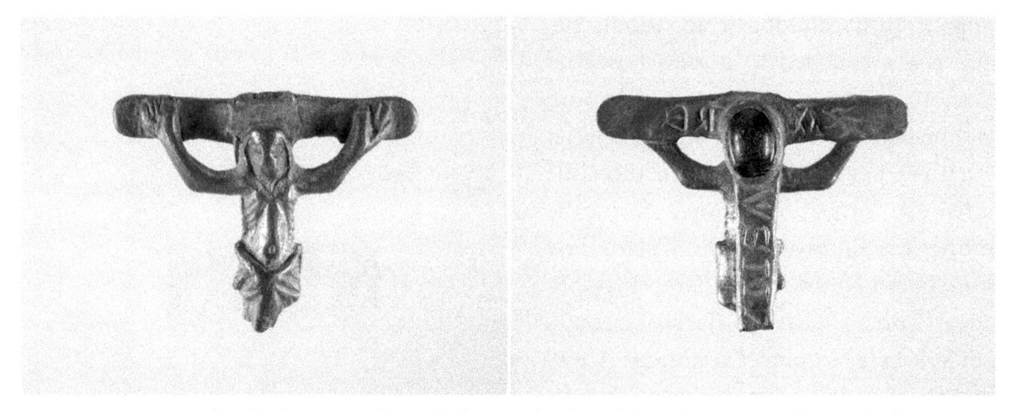

4.2 Medieval silver crucifix with large cabochon blue-glass gem and inscribed 'IHESUS NAZRENUS REX IOUDOREUM', found near Loch Leven (Perth and Kinross), 23 × 31 × 10 mm. Image courtesy of Culture Perth & Kinross

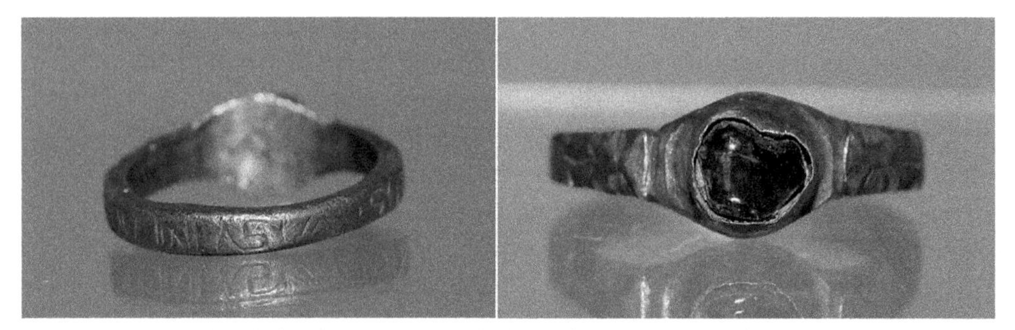

4.3 Medieval silver finger-ring set with a blue-glass stone and inscribed 'IESUS NAZA', found in Gullane (East Lothian). Reproduced with kind permission from East Lothian Council Museums Service

REX IOUDOREUM' or 'Jesus of Nazareth, King of the Jews' (*Treasure Trove in Scotland 2013/2014*: 10). The object may have been associated with St Serf's Priory or Scotlandwell Priory, which developed from a hospital and holy well into a Trinitarian priory in the thirteenth century. A silver fede ring from Gullane (East Lothian) (Figure 4.3) was set with a blue glass stone and engraved with the lettering 'IESUS NAZA', a contraction of Jesus Nazarenus (*Treasure Trove in Scotland 2015/2016*: 9). In both cases, two forms of magic were invoked for protection: the healing quality of sapphire (or proxy blue glass) and the holy name of Jesus.

The use of sacred names for healing and protection is part of the popular tradition of textual amulets and charms. Textual amulets were apotropaic formulae written on parchment or other materials (such as lead), while charms included brief inscriptions on a piece of jewellery or a household object. The inscription of holy words transformed these objects of material culture into charms, which were worn on the body and kept in the home to confer protection, good fortune and healing (Skemer 2006: 10). The name of Christ was used for general protection, including IHS and variations on Jesus, while the formula *Jesus Nazarenus Rex Judaeorum* was popularly believed to protect against sudden death, as documented in 'The Revelation of the Monk of Evesham', written in 1196 (Evans 1922: 128). The names of the Three Magi served as a verbal charm to protect against epilepsy, falling sickness, sudden death, and from all forms of sorcery and witchcraft (Hildburgh 1908: 85). Some medieval authors saw charms and sacred words as part of the conceptual framework of natural magic, including Thomas Chobham, quoted above. Most regarded charms as prayers – they were intended as religious invocations that were distinct from the natural world (Rider 2012: 42).

Fresh evidence for the medieval use of charms comes from the objects reported to the Portable Antiquities Scheme in England and Wales and the Treasure Trove system in Scotland. The examples from England are much more numerous, reflecting differences in both access to material culture by medieval people and the intensity of metal-detecting today (Table 4.1). Metal-detecting is a less popular pastime in Scotland but it is evident that fewer metal objects circulated in medieval Scotland (Campbell 2013a). At the time of writing, thirty-three medieval objects with sacred names have been reported through Scottish Treasure Trove, inscribed principally on rings (N=8) and brooches (N=8) and also on a range of objects including a sword pommel, a seal matrix, a pilgrim's badge and a crucifix (Table 4.2). The dedications are distinctive in the very strong representation of the names of Jesus, including IHS, IHC and Jesus Nazarenus inscriptions. Sacred inscriptions to Jesus account for nearly 80 per cent of examples in the Canmore database, nineteen of which are Jesus Nazarenus inscriptions (58 per cent). There is only one inscription to Ave Maria, one to the Magi, and one occurrence of the magic word AGLA (a Kabbalistic acronym for *Atah Gibor Le-olam Adonai*, meaning 'You, O Lord, are mighty forever'). This is significantly different from the amuletic objects in the English and Welsh Portable Antiquities Scheme, where IHS and IHC are much more frequently represented than Jesus Nazarenus, and inscriptions to the Virgin Mary are 5.5 times more common than Jesus Nazarenus (Gilchrist 2012: 274). The Treasure Trove objects have no archaeological context and little can be said of the circumstances or date of their loss or deposition. The majority are likely to have been possessions owned by the laity but objects with sacred inscriptions are also found at monastic sites. In addition to the Loch Leven crucifix already noted, a silver brooch with inscription is associated with Arbroath Abbey (Angus: Canmore ID 35645) and two silvered rings with inscriptions were found at Inchaffray Abbey (Perth and Kinross; *Treasure Trove in Scotland 2008/2009*: 16; Canmore IDs 339359 and 332582). An excavated example comes from the burial of an adolescent at the Carmelite friary at Perth, although the inscription was too worn to be legible (Stones 1989: 12).

TABLE 4.1 *Medieval objects with sacred inscriptions recorded in the Portable Antiquities Scheme (England and Wales) (as of 9 Jan. 2017)*

	Ave Maria	IHS	IHC	Nazarenus/INRI	Three Kings/Magi	AGLA
Seal matrix	48 (45 Cu A; 2 silver; 1 Lead alloy)	12 (11 Cu A, 1 lead)	47 (45 Cu A, 2 lead)	4 (4 Cu A)		
Purse	50 (50 Cu A)	18 (18 Cu A)	1 (1 Cu A)			1 (1 Cu A)
Pendant	2 (2 Cu A)	5 (2 lead, 1 Cu A, 1 lead alloy, 1 pewter)	3 (2 silver, 1 lead)	4 (3 silver, 1 Cu A)		17 (15 silver, 1 Cu A, 1 lead)
Badge	1 (1 silver)	4 (1 Cu A, 2 lead, 1 lead alloy)	2 (2 Cu A)	1 (1 Cu A)		
Ring	21 (17 silver, 4 gold)	21 (11 Cu A, 9 silver, 1 gold)	8 (5 silver, 2 gold, 1 Cu A)	6 (5 silver, 1 gold)	5 (4 silver, 1 gold)	3 (silver)
Buckle	13 (12 Cu A, 1 Silver)	12 (Cu A)	17 (Cu A)			
Brooch	23 (13 Cu A, 7 silver, 2 lead alloy, 1 gold)		1 (Cu A)	13 (8 Cu A, 5 silver)	2 (silver)	
Hooked tag		13 (Cu A)				
Strap-end	5 (Cu A)	29 (28 Cu A, 1 lead)	24 (Cu A)			
Mount	1 (Cu A)	12 (9 Cu A, 2 lead alloy, 1 silver)	6 (4 Cu A, 1 lead alloy, 1 silver)	1 (silver)		
Harness pendant	25 (Cu A)	0	0			
Harness mount	1 (Cu A)	1 (Cu A)	0	0		
Spur						
Vessel			1 (ceramic)			
Token	14 (12 Cu A, 1 lead, 1 lead alloy)	5 (3 lead, 2 lead alloy)	4 (3 lead alloy, 1 lead)			

Coin	0	29 (17 gold, 9 silver, 3 Cu A)	38 (35 gold, 2 silver, 1 lead alloy)	0		
Weight			1 (lead)			
Book fitting		5 (Cu A)	10 (9 Cu A, 1 silver)			
Plaque		2 (1 Cu A, 1 lead)				
Cross		1 (CuA)		7 (3 Cu A, 1 gold, 1lead, 1 lead alloy, 1 silver)		2 (silver)
Unidentified object	1 (silver)		1 (silver)	1 (Cu A)		1 (silver)
Total	205 (140 Cu A, 29 silver, 4 lead alloy, 1 lead, 1 gold, 59 unknown)	169 (113 Cu A, 7 lead, 4 lead alloy, 1 pewter, 19 silver, 18 gold, 5 unknown)	164 (104 Cu A, 5 lead, 12 silver, 37 gold, 5 lead alloy, 1 ceramic)	37 (18 Cu A, 15 silver, 2 gold, 1 lead, 1 lead alloy)	7 (6 silver, 1 gold)	24 (2 Cu A, 21 silver, 1 lead)

TABLE 4.2 *Medieval objects with sacred inscriptions recorded in Scottish Treasure Trove/Canmore (as of 25 Nov. 2016)*

	Ave Maria	IHS	IHC	Nazarenus/ INRI	Ihesus	Three Magi	AGLA
Ring		3 (2 gold, 1 Cu A)	1 (silver gilt)	9 (8 silver, 1 Cu A)	3 (1 silver, 2 Cu A)	1 (gold)	1 (silver)
Brooch	1 (Cu A)			8 (7 silver, 1 Cu A)	1 (silver)		
Seal matrix							
Sword pommel				1 (Cu A)			
Pilgrim badge				1 (lead)			
Total	1 (Cu A)	3 (2 gold, 1 Cu A)	1 (silver gilt)	19 (15 silver, 3 Cu A, 1 lead)	4 (2 silver, 2 Cu A)	1 (gold)	1 (silver)

TABLE 4.3 *Medieval objects with sacred inscriptions by material of composition (as of 9 Jan. 2017)*

	Copper alloy	Lead/Lead alloy	Silver	Gold	Other
PAS	379	29	102	59	2
Scottish TT/Canmore	7	1	19	3	

4.4 Silver heart-shaped brooch dating to *c.*1300, inscribed 'IHESUS NAZARENUS', found in Dalswinton (Dumfries and Galloway). Acc. No. DUMFM:2012.66 © Dumfries Museum

Also distinctive in Scotland is the high proportion of amuletic jewellery in precious metals such as silver or gold, in contrast with the more common base metal objects found in England (Table 4.3). Of the thirty metal objects with sacred inscriptions that have been reported as Treasure Trove, nineteen are silver, three are gold and eight are base metals. For example, two heart-shaped silver brooches (dated *c.*1300) from Kirkcaldy (Fife) and Dalswinton (Dumfries and Galloway) (Figure 4.4) have the inscription IHESUS NAZARENUS (*Treasure Trove in Scotland 2012/2013*: 8). The heart shape may denote a romantic gift but the form and material may also be apotropaic. Silver was

TABLE 4.4 *Fede rings with sacred inscriptions (as of 9 Jan. 2017)*

	Nazarenus/INRI	Iesus	Unknown	Total no of fede rings in database
PAS	2 (silver)	1 (silver)	5 (silver)	67 (61 silver, 4 Cu A, 1 gold, 1 lead alloy)
Scottish TT/ Canmore	7 (6 silver, 1 Cu A)	3 (1 silver, 2 Cu A)	3 (silver)	16 (12 Silver/silver gilt, 4 Cu A)

regarded in Scotland as powerful protection for newborns and heart-shaped pins were attached to children's clothing to guard against evil (Maxwell-Stuart 2001: 16; Miller 2004: 28). Sacred inscriptions occur on other types of silver jewellery with romantic connotations, such as fede rings, showing two clasped hands. A silver gilt example found within the scheduled area of Inchaffray Abbey has an inscription abbreviating Jesus Nazarenus (*Treasure Trove in Scotland 2002/2009*: 16). Fede rings with sacred inscriptions seem particularly well represented among the Scottish material, with nine in silver and three in copper alloy out of a total of sixteen recorded as Treasure Trove (75 per cent). Comparison with the English material emphasises the significance of this pattern (Table 4.4). Of sixty-seven medieval fede rings found in England and registered with the Portable Antiquities Scheme, only eight bear sacred inscriptions (all silver) (12 per cent). Fede rings (meaning faith) originated with the ancient Roman and Byzantine tradition for marriage rings that show a pair of clasped hands, perhaps referencing the Roman custom of concluding the marriage contract with a handshake (Hindman et al. 2007: 136).

'PLACED DEPOSITS': THE INCORPORATION OF OBJECTS

Prehistorians generally agree that people in the past deliberately 'deposited' objects in acts of ritual practice that were integrated with aspects of everyday life, such as the burial of selected materials at critical points in settlements, at boundaries, entrances or the corners of houses (Brück 1999; Garrow 2012; see Chapter 1). Medieval archaeologists are becoming increasingly alert to ritual deposits made in secular contexts – for example, the Bronze Age flints deposited in the medieval hall excavated at High Street, Perth (noted above; Hall 2011). But we have been slow to recognise deliberately 'placed' deposits made in medieval religious contexts, including parish and monastic churches.

An excellent example is the church at Barhobble, Mochrum (Dumfries and Galloway), where excavations uncovered a lost church built in the twelfth century on the site of an earlier church and cemetery, possibly monastic in origin (Cormack 1995) (Figure 4.5). The church went out of use after the

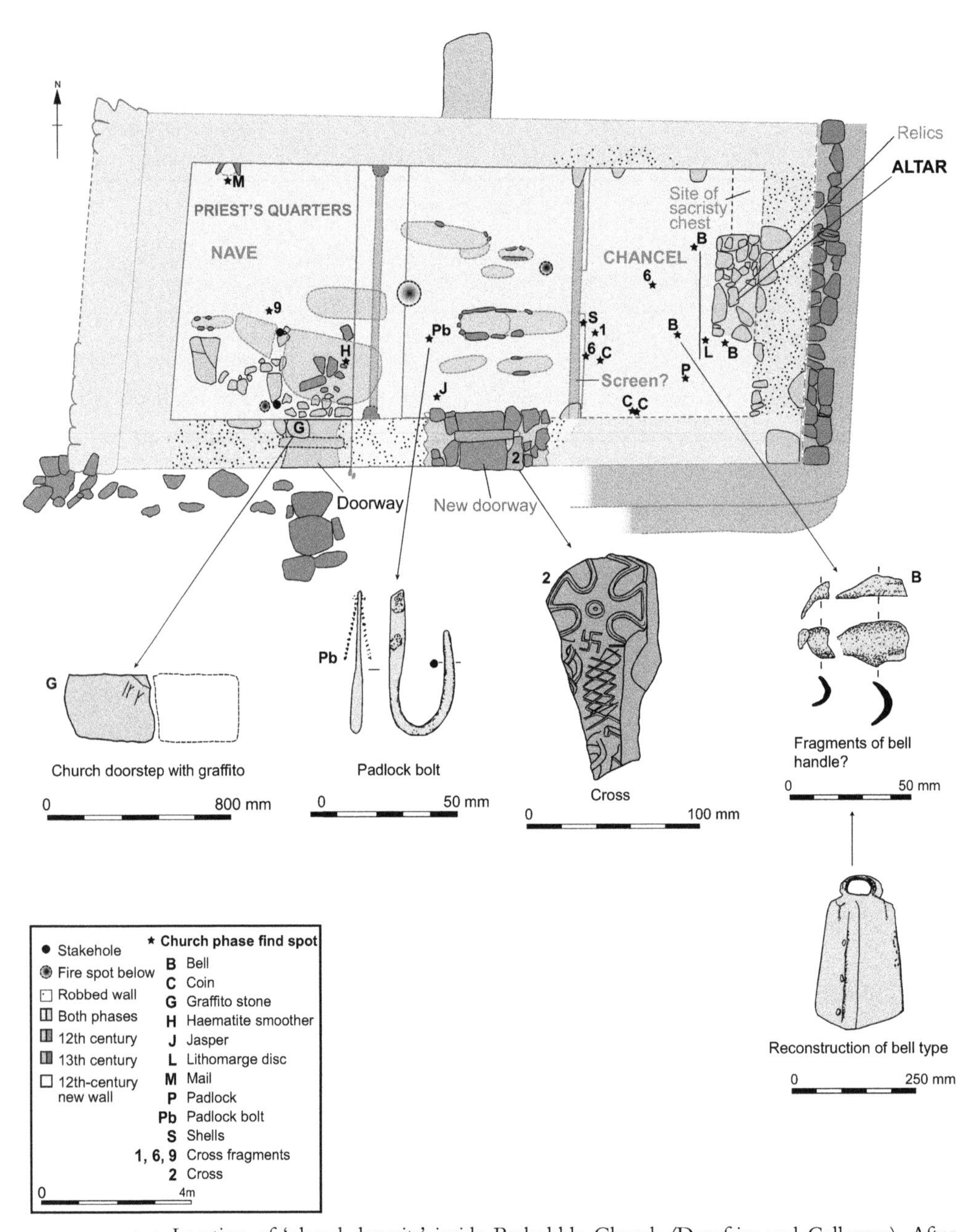

4.5 Location of 'placed deposits' inside Barhobble Church (Dumfries and Galloway). After Cormack 1995 © Sarah Lambert-Gates

thirteenth century; despite problems with dating, the placed deposits can be dated to the twelfth or thirteenth centuries. Several objects were recorded in association with the altar: an iron bell, a stone cross fragment, a kaolinite (lithomarge) disc and an iron padlock. Further objects were found in the area of the rood screen that separated the nave and chancel: a handful of sea shells, two further stone cross fragments and three coins. Two coins were also found

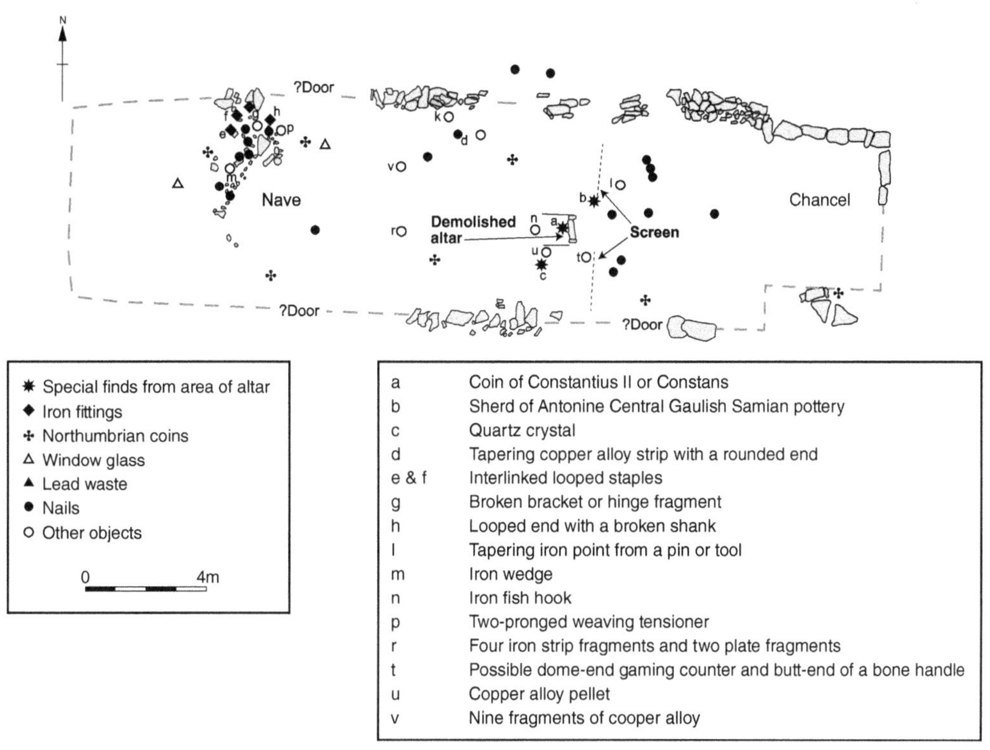

4.6 Location of 'placed deposits' inside the 9th-century church (*c*.835) at Whithorn (Dumfries and Galloway). After Hill 1997 © Sarah Lambert-Gates

together in a void against the south wall, and a lump of jasper and a copper alloy bolt for a padlock were found under the baked clay floor in the southwest corner. A western compartment, interpreted as possible priests' quarters, yielded further finds: a fragment of stone cross and a haematite burnisher. Of particular interest is a lump of decorated iron mail and mineralised textile, found deposited against the north wall of the structure near the northwest corner, within a V-shaped stone setting sunk into the clay floor. The textile was interpreted as a coif or headpiece with a linen cap, placed inside a grass bag.

The Barhobble deposits can be compared with those found in a number of early medieval churches where excavations have identified special objects associated with altars and screens. At Whithorn (Dumfries and Galloway), the church of the Northumbrian minster was 'deconsecrated' in the ninth century (*c*.835 CE). It was stripped of its ecclesiastical fittings and briefly used for secular purposes before it was destroyed by fire. A group of distinctive objects was found in association with the demolished altar at the eastern end of the chancel (Figure 4.6), including a sherd of Gaulish Samian pottery, a rock crystal and a Roman coin dating to the fourth century. Possible ecclesiastical artefacts were found at the eastern end of the nave, near the location of the chancel screen: a copper fragment with a cross motif and silver inlay and the possible handle of a spoon. Several flints were also recovered from the floor of the church (Hill 1997: 162–4). The Whithorn evidence may be compared to the Anglo-Saxon church at Raunds Furnells (Northamptonshire), where a Roman coin and prehistoric lithics were deposited in the chancel that was added to the church in the mid-tenth century (Boddington 1996).

At Glasgow Cathedral, two bronze mortars and an iron pestle were buried in the northwest corner of the Lady Chapel crypt, just east of the shrine of St Mungo, below the cathedral choir (Figures 4.7 and 4.8). The mortars were dated respectively to the late thirteenth/early fourteenth century and to the late fourteenth/early fifteenth century, while the pestle was later, dated to the sixteenth century (Driscoll 2002: 60). The mortars were placed on their sides in a pit, which appears to have been dug and filled in a single event, suggesting that it was dug specifically to contain the mortars. The mortars were well worn and several hundred years old when they were buried, explained by the excavator as a possible act of ritual concealment at the Reformation, located in the most sacred space of the cathedral (Driscoll 2002: 118). Similar cases have come to light at Cistercian abbeys in England, where the deliberate burial of religious sculptures has been interpreted as acts of concealment prior to the Dissolution (Carter 2015a).

In the nunnery church at Iona, a group of four silver spoons and a gold fillet from a headdress were found in 1923, wrapped in linen and placed beneath a stone at the base of the chancel arch (Curle 1924) (Figure 4.9). Stylistically the spoons are dated *c.*1150 and the hair-fillet is thirteenth-century (Zarnecki 1984: 280). The date of the deposit is unknown: the nunnery was founded in 1203, half a century after the spoons were made. A second deposit was buried in the chapel of St Ronan nearby, comprising a gold finger-ring and another gold fillet, with the fillet tightly folded up within the circumference of the ring and kept in position by a fragment of wire (Curle 1924) (Figure 4.9). When they were found, the examples from Iona were described as hoards, or perhaps as a thief's booty concealed for later retrieval. The Iona deposits can be compared with hoards from the site of St Blane's church on Bute (Argyll and Bute), found by workmen in 1863 (Figure 4.10). The deposit comprised two gold rings, three gold fillets and a small bar of silver, as well as twenty-seven coins associated with the Scottish kings David I and Malcolm IV, and the English kings Henry I and Stephen (Thompson 1956: 21). The date of deposit is unknown: the coin dates suggest some time after *c.*1150. The church of St Blane retains architectural evidence dating from the twelfth century onwards, but there are associated monastic remains possibly dating from the sixth or seventh centuries (Radford 1968). Part of the cemetery at St Blane's is known locally as having served as a women's burial ground (Canmore ID 40292), comparable to the nunnery at Iona. Although rings and fillets were found together at both sites, the Blane deposit is more obviously a hoard. It includes a

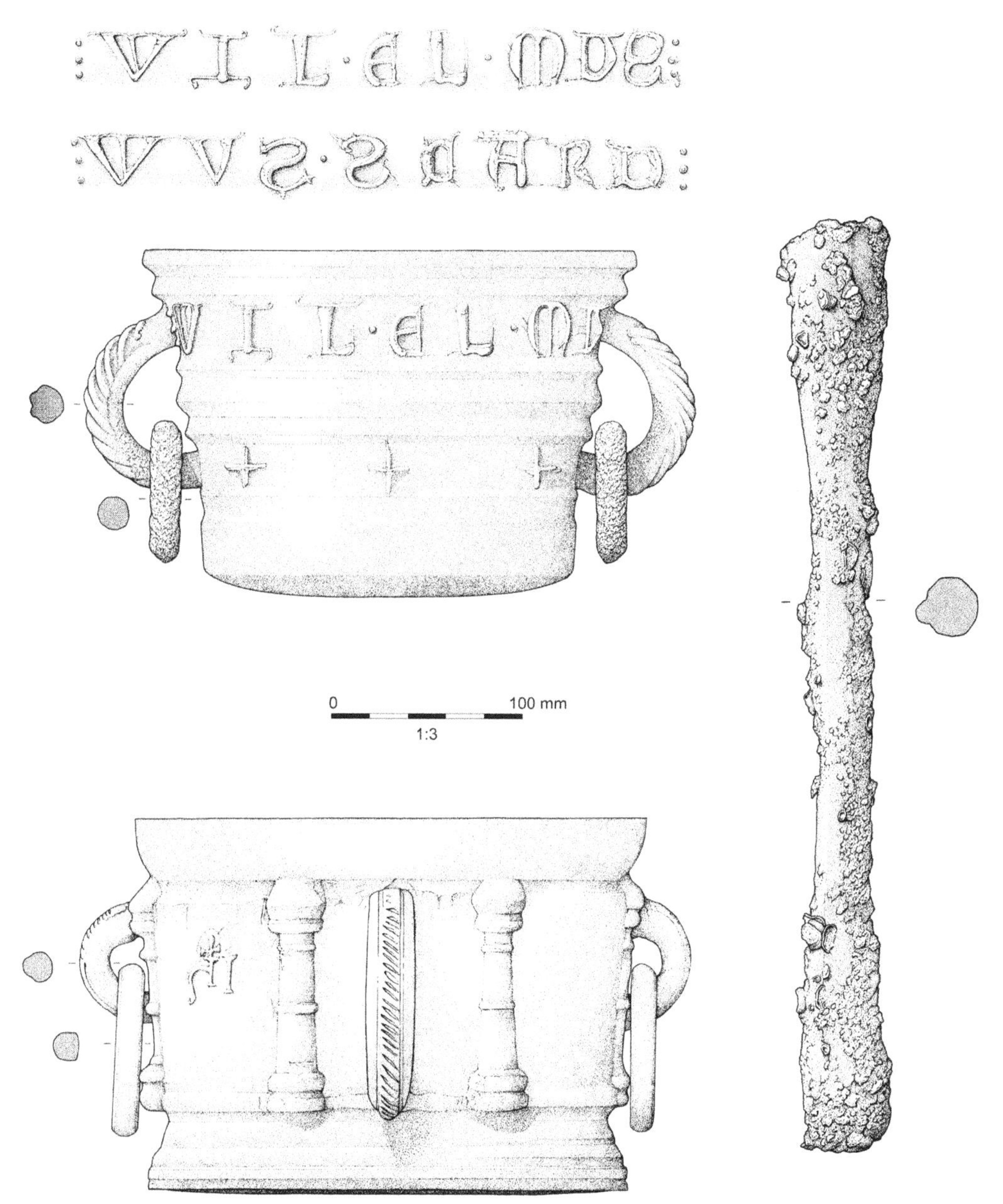

4.7 Medieval bronze mortars and iron pestle found buried in Glasgow Cathedral. Reproduced by kind permission of Stephen Driscoll

silver ingot and a large number of coins and it was buried extramurally, in contrast with the Iona deposits, which were deposited within the sacred space of consecrated buildings.

Objects deliberately buried in sacred contexts are often explained as hoards or precious artefacts concealed for protection at times of peril; such threats ranged from local military raids to the massive upheaval of the Reformation. At Glasgow and Iona, the objects deposited were of considerable *age* at the

4.8 Photographs showing the location of bronze mortars and iron pestle buried in Glasgow Cathedral. Reproduced by kind permission of Stephen Driscoll

time of burial, echoing the use of Roman and prehistoric artefacts in early medieval churches such as Whithorn and Raunds. These objects were placed at important liturgical points and they were items that possessed ritual associations. The bronze mortars from Glasgow are likely to have been liturgical objects, used for preparing incense burnt during the celebration of the Eucharist and other sacraments; mortars were also used for mixing medical or magical recipes and for alchemical experiments. The objects from Iona resonate with Christian life course rituals: the headdress fillets are the type worn by brides; spoons were given for marriage and baptism gifts; and the gold ring may be a wedding band (Gilchrist 2012: 94–5, 125–6). The Iona deposits may have been connected with individual life histories, perhaps even family heirlooms buried by a nun or widow entering the convent. The placed deposits at Barhobble combine liturgical objects such as the bell and stone crosses, with traditional amulets such as coins and seashells, while the chain mail coif may suggest the commemoration of a warrior. These examples confirm that special deposits were placed in Scottish churches dating from the ninth century right up to the Reformation.

Intentional deposits made in sacred contexts may be regarded as *ritual performances*: these material practices involved objects that held particular relevance to the collective life of the religious community, or perhaps to individual life histories. Some of the artefacts that were deliberately placed would have been highly revered *spiritual objects*. The spectacular Pictish shrine chest known as the St Andrews Sarcophagus is believed to have been deliberately buried to the southeast of St Andrews Cathedral (Fife), where its fragments were discovered in the nineteenth century (Figure 4.11). It has been suggested that its burial may have taken place prior to the twelfth century, perhaps when the eighth-century container was deemed redundant and the relics were transferred to a new receptacle (Foster 1998: 46). There are similarities with the recently discovered bas-relief panel of an angel in Lichfield Cathedral (Staffordshire). This is dated *c.*800 and interpreted as part of the shrine chest of St Chad, believed to have been broken and buried in or before the tenth century (Rodwell et al. 2008: 58–60). After prolonged physical contact with the relics of a saint, shrine chests would have been regarded as sacred objects, quasi-relics in their own right. There is some evidence that medieval monasteries may have extended this ritual treatment to sculptures that were particularly valued by the community. At the Benedictine Abbey of St Mary's, York, a set of life-size column-figures dating to the late twelfth century were discovered in 1829 in the nave of the former abbey church, carefully laid in a row with their faces down. The statues are likely to have come from a western portal of the Romanesque church and were carefully dismantled and interred during works to extend the Gothic church (Norton 1994: 275–8).

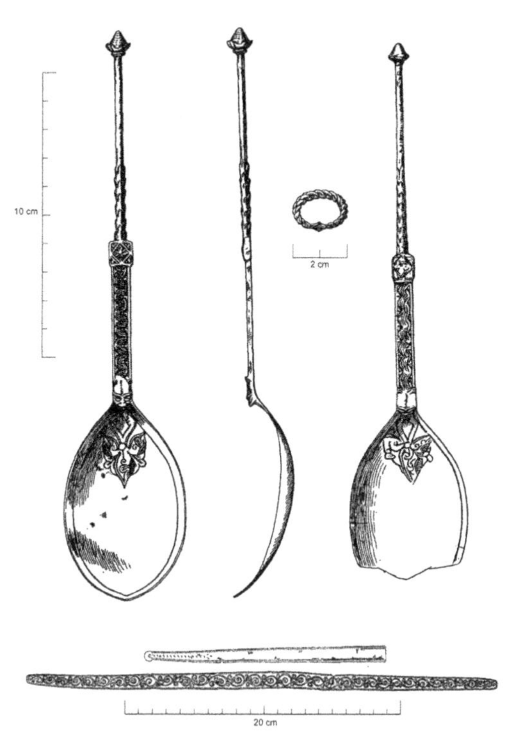

4.9 Objects buried in two separate deposits in the church and chapel of Iona Nunnery (Scottish Inner Hebrides), including silver spoons and two gold fillets. After Curle 1924, Proceedings of the Society of Antiquaries of Scotland 58

If a decision was made to replace a shrine or reliquary, care was needed in the disposal of the redundant object. A useful comparison can be made with disposal practices associated with materials that had become consecrated through their use in the sacraments. Strict rules governed the disposal of consecrated materials, ranging from the Eucharistic wafer and wine, to mass vessels and vestments, and the chrism cloth worn by baptised infants (Gilchrist 2012: 180–1). The careful disposal of disused medieval fonts illuminates this process, discussed by David Stocker (Stocker 1997). Fonts were not consecrated per se, but through prolonged physical contact with hallowed water, they acquired the status of sacred objects. It seems to have been common

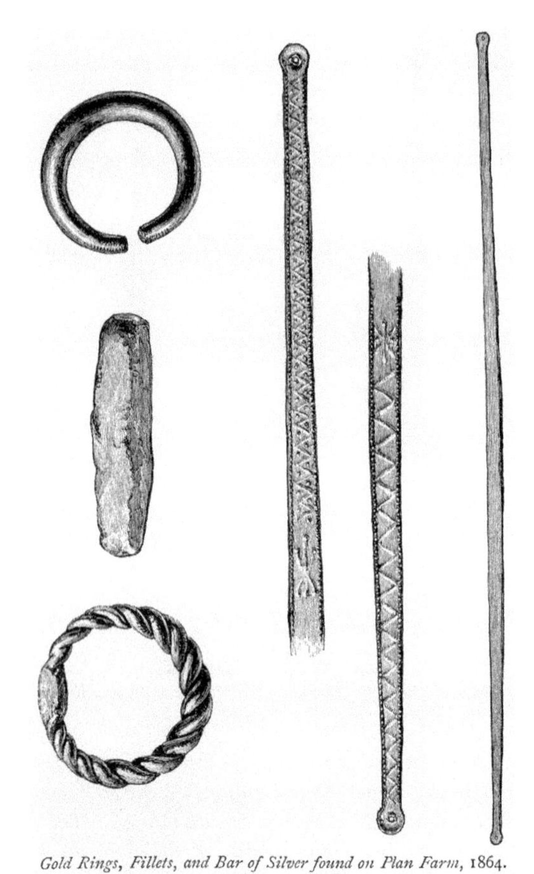

4.10 Objects from St Blane's Church, Isle of Bute (Argyll and Bute): gold rings, fillets and bar of silver. © Courtesy of Historic Environment Scotland

medieval practice to bury an old font beneath or near its successor in the nave of the church, with forty examples documented in England. Similar practices are observed in Scotland: nine examples of buried fonts include part of the rim of a decorated stone basin found under the ruins of the east end of the chapel at Loch Finlaggan (Islay – Argyll and Bute) in 1830 (Canmore ID 76281). Three disused fonts were deposited in watery locations (Canmore IDs 1765, 64298, 239026); four were reused in boundary walls (Canmore IDs 12254, 26165, 60040 and 97573); two were found in burial grounds (Camore IDs 4056 and 67206); and one was found deposited inside a cairn said to mark the site where St Kessog was martyred in Luss (Argyll and Bute, Canmore ID 42548). In common with vessels and textiles that had been used in the sacraments, it was essential to dispose of fonts in a way which prevented their reuse for profane purposes, for instance in illicit magic. The burial of shrine fragments at Lichfield and St Andrews may have been based on similar principles – the desire to remove sacred objects from circulation for safe-keeping, while at the same time reincorporating them within the religious community. This act can be likened to human rites of passage, classically framed by the anthropologist Arnold van Gennep as a three-fold process involving separation, transition and reincorporation (van Gennep 1960 [1909]). Seen in this context, the deliberate burial of objects in churches is consistent with Christian cosmology and ideas about sacred space, as well as the ritual treatment of both consecrated materials and the remains of the Christian dead.

Parallels can also be drawn between the burial of objects and people in sacred space and the incorporation of human remains within church fabric. For example, the church excavated at Barhobble had human bones incorporated into the altar built against the east wall, contained within the clay bonding of the structure of split stone slabs. The human remains comprised fifty fragments including the cranium, femur and tibia. It was originally proposed by the

4.11 St Andrews Sarcophagus, St Andrews Cathedral Museum (Fife). Reproduced by kind permission of Mark Hall

excavator that these were the relics of the sixth-century St Finian of Movilla (Cormack 1995: 15) but radiocarbon dating subsequently confirmed that the bones date to the mid-thirteenth century (Oram 2009). Incised stones were also incorporated in the fabric of the church at Barhobble: a small cross slab was built into the south doorway; a worn stone with possible graffito served as the doorstep. A paving slab incised with the gaming board for merrils was found in the balk between the two doorways and may have been built into the south wall. At Finlaggan on Islay, a bent coin of David II/Robert III was incorporated in the mortar of the southeast corner of the chapel (Hall 2016a: 149). Similar practices are seen in monastic contexts. At the nunnery of Elcho, one section of walling of the church reused a slab with cup and ring marks on its upper surface, likely dating to the Bronze Age; and human remains were deposited within a hollowed-out cavity in the wall (Reid and Lye 1988: 54–5). Insertion into church fabric was one method of reincorporating the bones of saints or earlier monastics within the community; this practice can be viewed as part of the cult of relics, and is also consistent with longstanding traditions of ritual deposition.

Fragments of disarticulated human bone were also buried in caskets and canisters, particularly where burials had been 'translated', in other words, moved from another site or deliberately disturbed and reinterred when churches were rebuilt (Gilchrist and Sloane 2005: 197–9). This practice is

4.12 Lead canisters excavated from the chapter house at Melrose Abbey (Scottish Borders). The Society of Antiquaries of Scotland – 0354: PSAS volume 139. p.272, Illus 13 Lead canister, grave 11 and p.273, illus 14 Heart canister

well-documented at Melrose Abbey (Scottish Borders), where three lead canisters containing body parts were recovered from the area of the east range (Ewart et al. 2009) (Figure 4.12). Two were excavated in the chapter house, which was the favoured place of burial for abbots (Gilchrist and Sloane 2005: 59). The Melrose chapter house also featured a pit near the abbot's seat, lined with a bed of charcoal; the pit was empty when excavated, but it has been suggested that it originally held translated human remains. These are likely to have been the bones of abbots buried in the chapter house and disturbed when it was extended in the thirteenth century. These mortuary practices belong to the mainstream repertoire of monastic death rituals and are also consistent with the tradition of placed deposits. Translated burials underwent an explicit sequence of separation, transition and reincorporation.

Coins were also employed as placed deposits in churches, either singly or in hoards, such as a deposit in the crossing of Glasgow Cathedral of fifty-eight half-crowns and sixty-two crowns (Hall 2012: 79). While coins are generally perceived as markers of financial transactions, they were also used for ritual purposes. Mark Hall has called for their study in terms of amuletic and 'prayerful' uses in spiritual transactions, while Lucia Travaini emphasises their significance for marking personal memory and recording chronology (Hall 2012, 2016a; Travaini 2015). Hall argues that coins were widely regarded as amulets connected to the cult of the Rood, based on the pervasive imagery of the cross or crucifix on the reverse of medieval coins. Throughout Europe, coin deposits occur in monastic churches, domestic and industrial buildings, and burials. The use of coins in foundation deposits in French and Italian churches (Travaini 2015: 218–20) can be compared with practices in Scotland. For example, a small vessel recovered from the foundations of the west front at Melrose Abbey contained a fifteenth-century denier of Charles VIII of France (14830–95) (Cruden 1952).

The incorporation of coins in building fabric is also common in Scotland. At Jedburgh Abbey (Scottish Borders), an Anglo-Saxon coin was found associated with a late medieval building (Lewis and Ewart 1995), and at the Carmelite friary at Perth, a mid-thirteenth-century coin of Henry III was associated with the foundation of a building dated to the thirteenth–fourteenth century

(Stones 1989). At Blackfriars in Perth, jetons and a coin were placed in the construction trench of a cellar and boundary ditch (Hall 2012). Two separate deposits were identified at Linlithgow Carmelite Friary: a groat of Robert II (1371–90) was found in the foundation trench of a building erected by 1430; and four coins were recovered from the chapter house (Stones 1989). At Whithorn, a group of four coins of Edward I was deposited in an oven in the southern section of the outer zone of the cathedral priory. The latest coin is the most worn, indicating that the deposit was made in the early to mid-fourteenth century (Hill 1997). Placed deposits in secular contexts have also been recorded in association with hearths and ovens, for example at High Street Perth, a Thomas Becket ampulla and scallop shell were associated with an oven (Hall 2011: 95).

One aspect in which monastic and lay practices seem to have differed is in the deliberate deposition of pilgrim badges and ampullae. These were usually cheap, mass-produced objects in lead or tin alloy, sold at saints' shrines. They are referred to in the archaeological literature as 'pilgrim souvenirs', perhaps conveying inappropriate parallels with modern tourism. The historian James Bugslag has recently suggested that they should instead be termed 'pilgrim blessings' (Bugslag 2016: 261). Badges and other small metal objects were blessed at the saint's shrine and acquired the status of quasi-relics or consecrated objects (Skemer 2006: 68). These objects were believed to trap the thaumaturgical (miraculous) power of the saint and their resting place, allowing the pilgrim to carry the healing essence of the saint away from the shrine. Ampullae were tiny containers that held water, oil or dust from shrines or holy wells, the most famous being ampullae from Canterbury associated with Thomas Becket, martyred in 1170. The monks of Canterbury Cathedral mixed Thomas's blood with water and it was widely believed that local water held the saint's healing power (Koopmans 2016). Ampullae from Canterbury were inscribed 'Thomas is the best doctor of the worthy sick' (Spencer 1998: 38).

Pilgrim badges were worn as amulets on the body and used in the home, fixed to doors and bedposts or fastened to textual amulets and books of hours. Archaeological evidence confirms that they were also employed in largely undocumented rites of deliberate deposition in the landscape. Pilgrim badges have been found in large quantities in rivers in England, France and the Netherlands, with particular concentrations recovered at the locations of bridges and river crossings (Spencer 1998). New evidence from the Portable Antiquities Scheme (PAS) provides evidence for badges from rural contexts, which serves to complement the urban evidence derived from archaeological excavations. Well over 300 examples are reported in the PAS, 250 of which can be attributed to particular saints or shrines. The geographical distribution of these badges indicates that the majority are found close to the shrine where they originated (Lewis 2016: 277). This pattern suggests that acts of deposition may have been an integral part of the pilgrimage rite itself, possibly completed on the pilgrim's return journey home. Some badges were purposefully destroyed and deposited in the landscape, perhaps as a thanks-offering to a saint for a cure or miracle, or as part of the performance of a charm.

In contrast, the distribution of ampullae recorded in the PAS suggests a very different pattern, based on over 600 recorded examples. It seems that these containers of holy water were sometimes taken home by the pilgrim and reserved for future ritual use. William Anderson has identified a pattern in which English ampullae dating to the fifteenth and sixteenth centuries were deliberately damaged before being discarded in cultivated fields (Anderson 2010). They were damaged by crimping or even biting, presumably to open the seal in order to pour the contents on the fields before discarding the vessel. Folded coins are also found especially in plough-soil, suggesting the possibility of a deliberate act of discard as an offering to protect or enhance the fertility of fields (Kelleher 2012). Ceremonies for blessing the fields are recorded in which parish priests sprinkled holy water and recited the biblical passage of Genesis 1:28: 'Then God blessed them, and God said to them, "Be fruitful and multiply; fill the earth and subdue it; have dominion over the fish of the sea, over the birds of the air, and over every living thing that moves on the earth"' (Kieckhefer 2000: 58).

The performance of magic frequently involved the modification or deliberate *mutilation* of objects, for example the bending of coins and pilgrim badges and the crimping of ampullae. This practice can be likened to the folding of charms written on parchment or lead: the act of folding increased the efficacy of the charm by preserving its secrecy and containing its magic (Olsan 2003: 62). The folding and discard of pilgrim souvenirs can also be compared with the deliberate destruction of magico-medical amulets, such as fever amulets thrown into the fire after the afflicted person had recovered (Skemer 2006: 188). The destruction of the amulet guaranteed that it was specific to the individual and could not be reused, while the act of folding or mutilation was also integral to the performance of magic. This premise is documented in relation to the practice of bending coins: miracles recorded at saints' shrines refer to the custom of bending the coin in the name of the saint invoked to heal the sick person (Finucane 1977: 44–6). In a study of folded coins from archaeological contexts, Richard Kelleher noted their occurrence in both religious and secular contexts, ranging from urban and rural settlements to castles and monasteries. However, folded coins occur most commonly at religious sites, including the chapel at Finlaggan, Glastonbury Tor (Somerset) and the monasteries of Jarrow (Tyne and Wear), Battle Abbey (Sussex), St James's Priory, Bristol, Whithorn and St Giles's Cathedral Edinburgh (Kelleher 2018: 73).

In contrast, the deliberate deposition of pilgrim badges and ampullae seems to be a ritual practice associated exclusively with the laity. Very few pilgrim signs are found in monastic contexts, with rare examples reported from burials in monastic and hospital cemeteries, for example at Cistercian Hulton Abbey (Staffordshire) and the hospital of St Giles by Brompton Bridge in Yorkshire (Klemperer and Boothroyd 2004: 133; Cardwell 1995; Gilchrist and Sloane 2005: 96–8). There are also significant regional differences, with very few pilgrim badges and ampullae reported in Scotland (Shiels and Campbell 2011: 84) or Wales (Locker and Lewis 2015: 60). Pilgrim souvenirs are completely undocumented for some major cult sites such as St Winefride of Holywell (Flintshire) and Glastonbury Abbey. It has been suggested that natural souvenirs may have been preferred over manufactured souvenirs at some cult centres, for example organic objects such as stones, shells and flowers (Locker and Lewis 2015: 59).

It is clear from archaeological evidence that pilgrim signs manufactured in metal were less common in Scotland. However, badges of St Andrew were made and circulated, confirmed by a stone mould for two St Andrew badges found in the churchyard of St Andrew's at North Berwick, on the pilgrim route to St Andrews (Hall 2007: 84–5). There are only eight examples of pilgrim signs reported as Treasure Trove on the Canmore database, in contrast with nearly 350 in the English PAS (Lewis 2016). This includes a rare example from Crail (Fife) of a lead pilgrim badge of St Andrew (*Treasure Trove in Scotland 2008/2009*: 15). Fewer than a dozen badges of this type are known, with the majority coming from the Thames foreshore in London. The evidence from Perth High Street demonstrates that pilgrim badges were used as placed deposits in secular contexts (Hall 2011). The assemblage includes a badge of St Andrew and two Becket ampullae, both of which had been crumpled, as well as scallop shells, a common pilgrim sign of St James of Santiago de Compostela.

Personal objects of jewellery inscribed with sacred names may also have been selected for deliberate deposition. Eleanor Standley has drawn attention to two possible cases from northern England. Two silver brooches were discovered near the foundations of a bridge at the Premonstratensian abbey of Alnwick (Northumberland), both with Jesus Nazarenus inscriptions. At the village of West Hartburn (co Durham), a silver brooch inscribed with a Jesus Nazarenus inscription was recovered near a circular hearth within a structure (Standley 2013: 82–3). This deposit combines several elements of meaningful ritual practice – deliberate burial, an amulet in precious metal with the Jesus Nazarenus inscription, and the selection of the hearth as a critical point for protection. The deliberate burial of amulets with sacred names raises the question of whether some of the apparently stray finds recorded by the Portable Antiquities Scheme and Scottish Treasure Trove may in fact be *ritual deposits* deliberately incorporated in the medieval landscape.

BURIAL: THE TRANSFORMATION OF THE DEAD

Medieval burials were sometimes accompanied by the same objects and materials that were used as amulets and placed as ritual deposits. Both monastic and lay funerary rituals employed objects associated with healing and protective magic; however, some significant differences are apparent between the two traditions. What was the purpose of magic for the dead: who placed these objects with the corpse and for what reasons? To understand the possible meanings behind these rites, we must appreciate the importance that medieval Christians placed on the *material continuity* of the body for its resurrection at Judgement Day. In 1215, the doctrine of literal resurrection was confirmed by the 4th Lateran Council: 'all rise again with their own individual bodies, that is, the bodies which they now wear' (Bynum 1991: 240). In confronting death, medieval people were highly anxious about the body and theologians debated the relationship between the corpse and the resurrected person. How was the soul in purgatory affected by the state of the corpse in the grave? Was individual identity retained, when dry bones had been reconstituted and resurrected as whole bodies at Judgement Day (Bynum 1991: 254)?

Monastic burial rites emphasised the religious identity of the deceased: clothing and grave goods were used to denote the consecrated status of their bodies and to distinguish them from those of the laity – in life, death and resurrection. Bishops, abbots and abbesses were buried with their croziers, the pastoral staves that were symbolic of their office. Priests were interred with signs of their clerical office: metal, ceramic or wax copies of the chalice and paten, the vessels used to celebrate the mass; while nuns went to the grave in their headdresses, signifying their role as brides of Christ (Gilchrist and Sloane 2005: 81–3, 160–5, 225). It was common to dress religious corpses in their monastic habits and possibly their robes of religious consecration: this clothing did not merely represent the status of the deceased, it was intended to *protect* the physical body of the corpse on its journey through purgatory (Gilchrist 2015).

A high proportion of the textiles and objects placed with the medieval dead have perished in the soil. Occasionally, however, ecclesiastical tombs illustrate the richness of medieval funerary rites. For example, excavations by Roy Ritchie at Whithorn in the 1950s and 1960s uncovered a group of ecclesiastical burials near the high altar of the cathedral priory (see Figures 6.1 and 6.2). Their re-examination and publication in 2009 included radiocarbon dating and scientific analysis of skeletons and artefacts (Lowe 2009). It was concluded that the burials dated principally to the thirteenth and fourteenth centuries and represented a group of three bishops, five to six priests and four to five lay benefactors, including two possible husband and wife pairs (Lowe 2009: 172). The grave goods from six burials contained textiles and ecclesiastical metalwork of outstanding importance, including the exceptional Whithorn Crozier, a copper-alloy, champlevé enamel crozier crafted in the second half of the twelfth century. The Whithorn grave goods included silver and silver-gilt sets of chalices and patens, as well as pewter examples, and gold and silver finger rings with gems of sapphire, amethyst, emerald and ruby, all highly valued for their occult properties. According to medieval lapidaries, the blue sapphire soothed fevers and pains; the purple amethyst supported wisdom and guarded against evil; the green emerald increased wealth; and the red ruby promoted health and protected against poisons (Evans 1922). Textile remains from Whithorn included gold braid, which was combined with spangles and glass beads in highly decorative liturgical vestments. Dress accessories included ring buckles, confirming that some burials were fully clothed. The clothed burials were interred in three stone cists, while the burials in wooden coffins had grave goods but no dress accessories, indicating their interment in shrouds (Lowe 2009: 105).

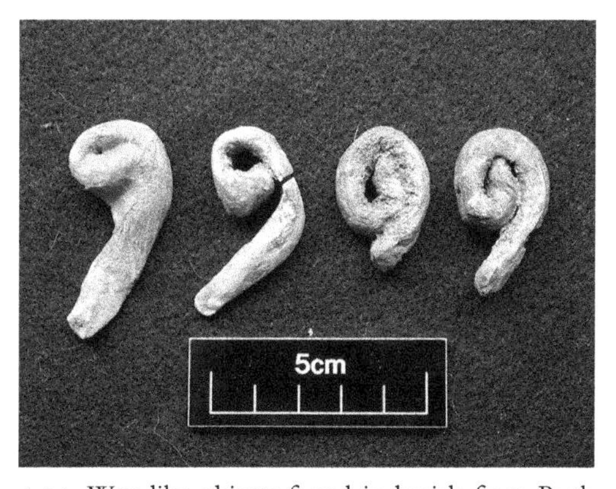

4.13 Wax-like objects found in burials from Perth Carmelite Priory. Reproduced by kind permission of Derek Hall

The majority of graves in medieval monastic and parish cemeteries would have been simple shroud burials, unaccompanied by objects. However, recent excavations have revealed new evidence for the use of clothing and grave goods in medieval Scottish burials (Figures 4.13 and 4.14). Many of these inclusions were organic and would typically fail to survive in the soil, while others may be overlooked by archaeologists as natural materials or residual objects in grave soils. Some of the most recently excavated sites have yet to be analysed fully, including nearly 500 medieval burials from the East Kirk of St Nicholas Aberdeen, dating from the eleventh to fifteenth centuries, and Perth Carmelite Friary, where excavations by Derek Hall recorded nearly 300 new burials, dating from the thirteenth century up to and beyond the Reformation (Cameron and Stones 2016; Derek Hall pers. comm.). Lay cemeteries excavated at Barhobble, The Hirsel (Coldstream) and Auldhame (East Lothian) provide

4.14 Lead-alloy cross suspended on a copper-alloy chain found around the neck of an individual buried in the East Kirk of St Nicholas, Aberdeen. Reproduced by kind permission of Alison Cameron

useful comparisons. The proprietary church at The Hirsel developed from around the tenth century, with the cemetery established from the twelfth century (Cramp 2014). Auldhame has been interpreted as a monastic settlement occupied from the seventh to ninth centuries, with the site later serving intermittently as a parish church and graveyard until at least the sixteenth century (Crone et al. 2016).

Lay burials at the East Kirk of St Nicholas Aberdeen included clothing or textiles associated with burials dating to the eleventh or twelfth century, including possible hair cloth, as well as grave goods such as coins and a lead alloy cross on a chain (Cameron and Stones 2016: 87) (Figure 4.14). At Auldhame, a grave contained a buckle with textile still adhering to it, suggesting that the corpse was interred fully clothed (Crone et al. 2016: 73). Clothed burials at the Carmelite friary at Perth were evidenced by the survival of leather shoes, while possible wax objects may represent skeumorphs of croziers or similar religious symbols (Figure 4.13). Graves excavated in the chapter house at Jedburgh Abbey confirm that a group of canons was given elaborate burial in the late fifteenth or early sixteenth century, including clothing represented by buckles and fragments of embroidered silk, as well as leather shoes (Lewis and Ewart 1995: 121, 124). St Nicholas Aberdeen and the Perth Carmelites also produced evidence for the placement of wooden staffs, rods or twigs next to the body, a funerary rite well known in England, Scandinavia, France and Germany.

4.15 Burial with wooden rod from Perth Carmelite Priory. Reproduced by kind permission of Derek Hall

More than twenty examples of wooden rods have been recorded at Carmelite Perth (Derek Hall, pers. comm.) (Figure 4.15). This rite was practised in Britain from the eleventh century up to the fourteenth and fifteenth centuries in both monastic and parish cemeteries; the largest comparable groups include eighteen staffs or rods from Glastonbury Abbey, twelve from Hull Augustinian Friary (East Yorkshire) and nine from Hulton Abbey (Gilchrist and Sloane 2005: 126, 171–4). The rods were usually made from coppiced hazel, ash or willow; the lack of wear and their insubstantial nature suggest that they were items made especially for burial. It has often been suggested that they represent a link with pilgrimage or journeying, or that the quick-growing coppices used for the poles symbolised the Resurrection and eternal life. Alternatively, they may have been objects used in Christian charms (Gilchrist 2008). In Scandinavia, the placement of burial rods in graves also develops from the eleventh century onwards and the rite has been interpreted as amuletic. Kristina Jonsson argues that the rods were used to measure corpses for magical purposes, perhaps connected with healing charms (Jonsson 2009: 115).

Coins were placed with the dead at both the East Kirk of St Nicholas Aberdeen and Perth Carmelite Friary. Coins are perhaps the most common amulet placed with the monastic dead in Scotland and numerous examples are also recorded from English monastic cemeteries (Gilchrist and Sloane 2005: 100). They were present in later medieval burials at Whithorn Cathedral Priory, St Giles's Cathedral Edinburgh, Jedburgh Abbey, Holyrood Abbey Edinburgh, Perth Dominican Friary, Perth Carmelite Friary and Elcho Nunnery (Lowe 2009; Collard et al. 2006; Lewis and Ewart 1995; Bain 1998; Hall 2012; Hall 2016a). There is also evidence for the use of occult materials as grave goods in Scottish monastic cemeteries: a female at Perth Carmelite Friary was buried with a necklace of jet and glass beads (Derek Hall, pers. comm.) (Figure 4.1) . The tradition of placing quartz pebbles in graves was maintained in some later medieval cemeteries in Scotland. At Inchmarnock (Argyll and Bute), ten graves with quartz pebbles were excavated, eight of which are considered to date after the twelfth century (Lowe 2008: 268). At Barhobble, graves dating to the eleventh and twelfth centuries contained quartz pebbles, with individual graves containing between one and twenty pebbles (Cormack 1995: 35). Quartz pebbles were observed in the majority of grave fills at Auldhame and a cist burial near the chapel contained quartz pebbles, shells and a possible gaming piece; the adult skeleton was radiocarbon dated to the eleventh or twelfth centuries (Crone et al. 2016: 21, 24, 91). Four graves at The Hirsel were associated with quartz pebbles: one located to the southwest of the church contained five quartz pebbles and a coin. This female burial had a folded coin placed in the mouth or near the chin: the coin was of William I (the Lion, 1165–1214) and stratigraphically the grave is consistent with a late twelfth- or early thirteenth-century date (Cramp 2014: 90). Another quartz pebble was found with a child's burial to the north of the church, which also contained an animal tooth, and was covered by large stones and an upright grave-marker (Cramp 2014: 93). Quartz pebbles placed in combination with a folded coin or animal tooth strongly suggest an apotropaic rite. Other types of pebble were also used as grave goods in nine cases at The Hirsel (Cramp 2014: 300), and at the Dominican Friary at Aberdeen, two older males were buried with large stones inserted in their mouths (Cameron 2016).

A number of graves from Barhobble included antique or exotic objects placed with the dead. For example, a child's grave had a piece of green porphyry placed at the head, a highly decorative, igneous rock that would have come from Greece. Another grave contained a fragment of Romano-British glass bangle (Cormack 1995: 36). Roman objects have been found in a number of later medieval graves in England, including a glass bangle from the parish church of Wharram Percy (North Yorkshire), a shale bracelet from St James's Priory, Bristol, and a copper-alloy bracelet from St Oswald's Priory, Gloucester (Gilchrist 2008; Heighway and Bryant 1999; Jackson 2006). The later medieval burial of a female at Perth Carmelite Friary contained a fragment of Samian pottery (Stones 1989) and Samian sherds were also deposited in medieval graves at Whithorn (Hill 1997: 296). The practice of placing 'old objects' in graves is part of an ancient tradition of using 'found objects' (*objets trouvés*) for healing and protection. Audrey Meaney first identified the magical use of Roman and prehistoric objects in Anglo-Saxon graves (Meaney 1981). This practice continued into the later medieval period, with Roman tiles, pottery, coins and bracelets occasionally buried with the medieval dead (Gilchrist 2008; Gilchrist and Sloane 2005).

Lay burials at Barhobble and The Hirsel also included iron objects in graves, a traditional rite which is not seen in later medieval monastic cemeteries in Scotland. At The Hirsel, an iron object was placed between the teeth of an individual buried to the north of the church (Cramp 2014: 103). At Barhobble, there were at least five examples of iron objects included with burials of children and adults. One of these was a knife, an object that was also associated with burials at Whithorn and Auldhame, noteworthy because knives and tools in general are rarely found as grave goods with medieval burials (Crone et al. 2016: 82). A remarkable case is an adult female in the nave of the church at Barhobble, located close to the entrance to the chancel, in a grave carefully constructed with side slabs and a cover stone. A pair of iron shears was placed over the woman's feet and she was surrounded by the graves of infants. The orientation of this group of burials is consistent with the twelfth-century phase of the church (Cormack 1995: 38). Scottish folklore suggests that iron objects were considered to provide protection from malevolent forces (Houlbrook 2015: 132), but these sources date considerably later than the funerary rites discussed here. Shears were the most common female symbol in the Middle Ages, believed to represent the woman's role as keeper of the house. They were used as a standard emblem to represent women on cross slab monuments dating from the twelfth century onwards (McClain 2010: 46). Domestic shears were used for textile working but could have many other uses, perhaps even medical applications. Midwives used knives, scissors or small shears to cut the umbilical cord and these tools were sometimes used in medieval art to symbolise the midwife (Greilsammer 1991: 290–1). The context of the grave at Barhobble may suggest the burial of a midwife or female healer, placed in a strategic position in the church, perhaps to provide protection to the infant graves with which it was associated.

Another gendered artefact was placed with a late medieval female buried in the cemetery at Coldingham (Scottish Borders) (Stronach 2005). This grave contained a lead spindle whorl decorated with a star motif. Spindle whorls were associated with textile working, which in rural, domestic contexts was a craft generally associated with women. Spindle whorls were occasionally placed in the graves of medieval men, women and children in England, Ireland and Scandinavia. Eleanor Standley argues that decorated lead spindle whorls such as the one from Coldingham were symbolic of the Virgin Mary and her association with spinning the thread of the life of Christ. In a burial context, the spindle whorl holds many potential symbolic meanings: a devotional object, a gendered artefact and a symbol of the thread of life being cut short (Standley 2016). A grave at Aberdeen contained an explicit Marian object: an elderly woman was buried in the fifteenth century with a badge depicting the Pietà, the Virgin Mary cradling the dead body of Christ (Figure 4.16).

4.16 Lead pilgrim badge decorated with an image of Our Lady of Pity found in the grave of a middle-aged woman buried in the East Kirk of St Nicholas, Aberdeen. Reproduced by kind permission of Alison Cameron

A number of medieval Scottish graves contained scallop shells, a popular organic pilgrim souvenir. The most dramatic is from the Isle of May: a young male in his 20s was buried near the high altar in the church, between the late thirteenth and mid-fifteenth century. Shortly after death, his mouth was wedged open with a sheep scapula and a scallop shell was placed in the palate (James and Yeoman 2008) (Figure 4.17). A perforated scallop shell was found near the head of a male burial at The Hirsel, aged 35–45 years old, and radiocarbon dated to cal AD 1260–1455 with peak in the fourteenth century (Cramp 2014: 106). Two burials from the East Kirk of St Nicholas Aberdeen included scallop shells: one had two scallop shells placed near the head; the other had a scallop shell placed on the thigh (Cameron and Stones 2016: 87) (Figure 4.18). The shells may have been pinned to a pilgrim's hat and pouch, which no longer survive. The scallop shell is a pilgrim sign symbolic of

4.17 Burial of young/middle-aged adult male from St Etheman's Monastery, Isle of May (Fife): his mouth is wedged open with a sheep tibia and a scallop shell has been placed in his mouth. Photograph by Peter Yeoman © Fife Council Archaeology Service

4.18 Skeleton buried with a scallop shell beside the left leg from East Kirk of St Nicholas, Aberdeen. Reproduced by kind permission of Alison Cameron

St James of Santiago de Compostela but is also found at early medieval Celtic shrine sites such as Illaunloughan Island (co Kerry) (White Marshall and Walsh 2005). Scallop shell badges may have been made in Scotland: an iron mould in the form of a scallop shell was found at Roseisle (Moray) and a scallop shell badge was found at Crail by metal-detectorists (Canmore IDs 33911, 215285). There was a strong later medieval connection between St James and the Scottish royal family: James was patron saint of five successive kings between 1394 and 1542 (Glenn 2003: 87). However, the scallop shell seems to have had more enduring significance as a pilgrim sign in Scotland: rather than expressing a specific connection to St James it may have carried resonances of earlier Celtic beliefs, comparable to quartz pebbles.

Many of these objects were placed in intimate contact with the corpse – on the body or even in the mouth. They must have been placed within the shroud when the body was washed and prepared before burial. In the case of a monastic burial, such preparations would have been completed by the monastic infirmarer; in a lay context, women of the family or perhaps a midwife would have carried them out, as depicted in contemporary Books of Hours (Gilchrist and Sloane 2005: 23). Why were certain individuals marked out for special rites at death? In some of the cases discussed here, palaeopathological evidence suggests that the individuals experienced impeded mobility. The woman buried with the Pietà badge at Aberdeen suffered from severe osteomalacia (adult rickets) (Cameron and Stones 2016), and the woman from Coldingham buried with a spindle whorl had bowed legs and signs of deterioration in her cervical vertebrae (Stronach 2005). The man buried with a scallop shell at The Hirsel had a bony tumour in his lower leg (osteochondroma of proximal tibio-fibular joint) (Cramp 2014).

Infants and children were also singled out for special treatment, both through the use of amulets and in the siting of graves. For example, at St Ninian's Isle (Shetland) in the tenth century, infants were buried in a series of stone compartments created by upright stones and then filled with stones and quartz pebbles. One of these infants was buried with a small water-worn, quartz beach pebble placed in its mouth (Barrowman 2011). At Auldhame, the burials of infants and neonates were clustered along the south walls of the building complex, with continuity demonstrated from the mid-seventh century up to the mid-twelfth century. Juveniles at Auldhame were buried at the western extreme of the site, with regularity in layout and orientation across 400 years (Crone et al. 2016: 31). At the East Kirk of St Nicholas Aberdeen, child burials were placed in a radiating arrangement around the exterior of the apse in the eleventh or twelfth century (Cameron and Stones 2016: 82). Children's burials had amulets placed with them at Barhobble and The Hirsel, including quartz pebbles, an animal tooth and a fragment of exotic porphyry. Children were also given special treatment in monastic cemeteries: at Linlithgow Carmelite Friary, only ten burials contained objects out of 207 excavated, and nine of these belonged to children or young adults. The objects included lace ends, wire twists, a copper-alloy ring and a strap end associated with a belt (Standley 2013: 105; Stones 1989). At St Giles's Cathedral, Edinburgh, a juvenile was buried in the fifteenth century with a folded coin and a pendant (Collard et al. 2006).

The placement of amulets with the dead may have been intended to guard or protect loved ones from the perils of purgatory, serving as the material equivalent of prayers and masses to protect their souls. It was noted in the previous chapter that therapeutic devices were occasionally placed in the grave, ranging from healing plates to support joint injuries, to hernia trusses (see Chapter 3; Gilchrist and Sloane 2005: 103–4). The presence of these therapeutic items in the grave strengthens the argument that the intention was to heal the corpse, just as the bodies of saints were known to heal in the tomb (Gilchrist 2008). Amulets were placed with men, women and children, a small number of whom showed skeletal evidence of impaired mobility. Is it possible that mourners placed healing and apotropaic objects with the dead to provide both *spiritual protection* and *physical assistance* during the arduous journey through purgatory?

SILENT WITNESSES: MAGIC, AGENCY AND THE LIFE COURSE

Both monastic and lay communities in medieval Scotland engaged in the ritual technologies explored in this chapter, confirming that some elements of 'folk religion' spanned the boundary that is often perceived between 'institutional' (orthodox) and 'popular' (heterodox) religion. All three rites involved deliberate acts of the body that followed established norms, ranging from the use of amulets, to the deliberate burial or deposition of objects in sacred space, and the placing of objects with the medieval dead. Their perceived efficacy relied on the interaction between objects, materials, spaces and bodily techniques. While monastic and lay communities drew upon a common repertoire of ritual acts, some significant differences can also be discerned, such as the greater range of objects placed with lay burials, the special treatment of children in lay cemeteries and the possible ritual deposition of pilgrim souvenirs by the laity.

Chronological patterns are also evident, with greater diversity in burial practices in the earlier part of the period discussed here, the eleventh to twelfth centuries. This coincides with a time of massive political and religious change in Scotland, including the introduction of reformed monasticism and the formalisation of local churches into parishes (see Chapter 2). During this period of major social change, hybrid practices flourished, with older traditions of folk religion reinterpreted and persisting alongside orthodox rites. Placed deposits are evident in monastic and parish churches in Scotland ranging chronologically from the ninth to the sixteenth centuries, including personal possessions and liturgical items, as well as continuing the indigenous tradition of depositing prehistoric lithics, Roman artefacts and quartz pebbles. A number of regional patterns are apparent in the use of amulets when comparison is made with England. For example, the association of sacred inscriptions with precious metals seems to be a distinctively Scottish regional pattern, together with the strong preference for Jesus Nazarenus inscriptions over dedications to the Virgin Mary. The frequency of the romantic fede symbol, in combination with Jesus Nazarenus inscriptions, may denote a Scottish betrothal or marriage custom, to protect the union by continually invoking the sacred name. Pilgrim signs are less common in Scotland, but badges of St Andrew were manufactured and scallop shells appear to have been widely adopted as a symbol of St James, or perhaps as an enduring symbol of Celtic pilgrimage traditions.

Comparison of three separate rites helps to draw out patterns and possible intended meanings behind the use of stones and sacred names, placed deposits and objects buried with the dead. An important distinction is that the use of stones and sacred inscriptions was well-documented by medieval writers; theologians rationalised these beliefs according to the cult of saints and the framework of natural magic that was formalised in the thirteenth century (Harris 2016; Kieckhefer 2000; Rider 2012). In contrast, medieval sources are completely silent when it comes to placed deposits and amulets buried with the dead. Even popular sources of natural magic, such as the lapidaries, make no mention of the use of materials such as jet or quartz in connection with the dead (Kornbluth 2016: 157). We have ample archaeological evidence that these rites were practised, but no documentary sources to confirm who was responsible for them, or what they were intended to achieve.

Does silence suggest that these were *illicit* magic practices that escaped the notice of the church? The contextual evidence explored here suggests that these were instead *licit* rites, magic easily reconciled with Christian beliefs. This is confirmed by the burial of ritual deposits at liturgically charged points in medieval churches, and by the inclusion of coins in even the most orthodox burials, such as an ecclesiastic buried in a stone cist at Whithorn Cathedral Priory (Lowe 2009: 112–13). Is it possible that these practices were so ancient, so deeply engrained, that there was no need to explain or justify them? Archaeological evidence confirms that these were *indigenous practices* with a long heritage stretching back to prehistory; in particular, the placement of quartz pebbles with the dead. However, continuity of practice does not necessarily indicate continuity of belief: these ancient rites were reinterpreted within a Christian worldview and would not have been perceived as pagan by medieval people. Medieval magic melded folk practices with classical medicine and Christian liturgies (Jolly 2002: 23). The archaeological evidence suggests that indigenous ritual practices were absorbed within the framework of natural magic, such as the placing of quartz pebbles and antique objects with the dead, and the burial of placed deposits in churches and domestic buildings. The spatial and social context of these rites suggests that they were licit magic – medieval people attributed their causation and perceived efficacy to agents of God's creation.

We may debate whether these rites should be termed 'magic' or whether they should be regarded instead as Christian 'pararituals', actions performed by the laity to complement the liturgy, such as processions on feast days and the adornment of religious images with clothing and jewellery (Duffy 1992: 20). I have considered them as magic 'technologies' because they required ritual knowledge, embodied practice and occult power to make them efficacious. Sacred names and occult objects such as stones were used in conjunction with the bodily performance of charms. Amulets and occult materials were placed intentionally as part of the ritual washing of the corpse that preceded a complex funeral liturgy (Gilchrist and Sloane 2005: 25–6). 'Placed deposits' in sacred space involved the act of burial and often the deliberate destruction of the object before its concealment. The breaking and mutilation was part of the ritual process to transform the object: the destruction of shrines at St Andrews and Lichfield before their burial can be compared with the crumpling of pilgrim badges before their discard, or the bending of coins before their deposition. The *age and biography* of the objects selected for ritual disposal are also significant and distinctive patterns can be observed that connect biographical artefacts ranging from metal objects to stone sculpture and human remains. Burial completed the ritual act and served two additional purposes: it removed the object from circulation and reincorporated it within the community (after Weiner 1992).

These ritual technologies also share close associations with life course rituals: stones and sacred names were used to protect births and marriages; pilgrim signs were deposited to support the well-being of individuals and the fertility of the fields. Amulets placed with the dead may have aimed to achieve the healing and transformation of the corpse, with particular focus on young and vulnerable members of the community. Human and object biographies are brought together in these rites, for example in the deliberate burial in sacred space of objects connected with rites of passage, including spoons, women's headdresses, and ecclesiastical vessels and vestments. Objects stood for the life histories of individuals, ranging from the chalice and paten of a priest to the iron shears of a woman valued by her community. The technologies of magic considered here were part of a common repertoire of belief and ritual practice that was shared by medieval monastic and lay communities, and which drew upon earlier, indigenous traditions. Archaeological evidence reveals the interleaving of magic and religion in all aspects of medieval life, illuminating beliefs that fell through the crevices of documented history.

FIVE

MONASTIC LEGACIES: MEMORY AND THE BIOGRAPHY OF PLACE

INTRODUCTION: LANDSCAPE AND MEMORY

Memory practices connected medieval sacred landscapes to embodied religious experience: monasteries were active in creating ritual landscapes as religious imaginaries, interweaving materiality, myth and hagiography. This chapter reviews recent approaches to the study of place and memory in the monastic landscape, before considering the biography of Glastonbury Abbey (Somerset) in detail. Physical space is transformed into social *place* through an 'organised world of meaning', combining topographical characteristics and physical features with the investment of social memory and individual experience (Tuan 2005: 179). A 'sense of place' develops through engagement with a landscape *over time*, connecting space with remembrance and emotional attachment to a specific locality (Feld and Basso 1996). Medieval monasteries were spiritual centres for 500 years or more – for nearly a millennium, in the case of early medieval foundations like Iona, Whithorn and Glastonbury. The Dissolution was not an abrupt end to these deeply-held beliefs, but rather a long process of renegotiating the meanings of medieval religious landscapes and their value to early modern communities. Monastic memory was reworked to serve post-Reformation narratives that operated at both local and national scales. Former monastic landscapes became *contested spaces*, with opposing creeds competing to control sacred heritage (Walsham 2011: 10). Social memory is based around collective ideas about the past: it is often used to legitimate authority and to reinforce the shared identity of communities. Ideological narratives around sacred heritage can also be used to emphasise differences between groups, serving as a tool of resistance or a weapon of conflict through the deliberate destruction of memory as an act of war or genocide (Bevan 2016).

Archaeological approaches to memory have focused principally on the 'uses of the past in the past', in other words, how ancient landscapes were invented, imagined and reimagined by successive generations (e.g. Borić 2010; Van Dyke and Alcock 2008). This approach is exemplified by Richard Bradley's study of the use of the past in prehistory (Bradley 2002) and Sarah Semple's examination of the Anglo-Saxon reuse of prehistoric ritual landscapes (Semple 2013). In contrast, historical (post-medieval) archaeologists have focused particularly on memory in relation to contested landscapes such as battlefields, and on broader landscapes of conflict and loss, such as those associated with the Highland Clearances (Horning et al. 2015; Jones 2012). There has been a strong emphasis in historical archaeology on the critical assessment and disruption of dominant narratives, to give voice to subaltern groups who were silenced by displacement, slavery and war (Orser 2010). These approaches highlight power relations and representation in memory practices but generally neglect the role of landscape and memory in negotiating changes in religious belief and attitudes towards the dead (Holtorf and Williams 2006). These questions are particularly relevant to medieval and post-medieval religious transitions, such as the impact of Norman colonisation on Anglo-Saxon monasticism and the shift from Celtic to reformed monasticism in twelfth-century Scotland (see Chapter 2). The Dissolution is especially significant in terms of memorial practices and the multiple meanings that were projected on the 'bare ruined quires' of former monasteries. Dissolution landscapes can also be perceived in terms of conflict and collective loss: monastic ruins held particular fascination for early antiquaries, perhaps because of their shared sense of the deep culture shock of the Dissolution (Aston 1973). Ruined monasteries served as mnemonic prompts but they also possessed active spiritual and political agency. Sacred heritage often serves an ideological purpose, stressing continuity or discontinuity, and harnessing material evidence to reinforce the authority of a particular version of the past (see Chapter 6).

MONASTIC 'BIOGRAPHIES'

Monastic landscape archaeology has been dominated by economic approaches, focusing on discrete elements of technology and land management such as fisheries, milling and grange farming (e.g. Bond 2004; Götlind 1993). However, recent work has examined two distinct aspects of place and memory in the monastic landscape. The first strand considers how medieval monastic communities actively shaped landscapes to forge *collective institutional memories*; the second addresses the *memorialisation and reuse* of monastic landscapes by post-Reformation communities. An excellent study of the monastic construction of memory is Paul Everson and David Stocker's analysis of the Premonstratensian landscape of Barlings in the Witham Valley of Lincolnshire (Everson and Stocker 2011). They reject the functionalist approaches that dominate monastic landscape archaeology, typically comprising the cataloguing of separate components of the estate identified by documentary sources. Instead, they integrate economic, symbolic and ritual perspectives on the landscape in order to explore the social construction of 'place' rather than 'space'. They consider how the Barlings monastic landscape related to the ritual landscapes that came before and after it. Their approach was prompted by the special character of the Witham Valley, which was the focus for the ritual deposition of weapons from the Bronze Age, right through monastic occupation, and up to the early modern period (Stocker and Everson 2003). Their theoretical framework is informed equally by post-processual approaches and Historic Landscape Characterisation (HLC), a methodology developed as a tool for the management and planning of the modern landscape. HLC evaluates landscape morphology and character by compiling evidence such as historic maps, aerial photography and satellite imagery. This essentially morphological approach can be used alongside a more nuanced process of interpretation to consider how landscapes are shaped by power, belief and identity (for debates on HLC see: Austin and Stamper 2006; Rippon 2013).

Studies of monastic landscapes have moved towards a 'biographical' approach to consider long-term developments following the Dissolution. For example, in their study of Cluniac Monk Bretton in South Yorkshire, Hugh Willmott and Alan Bryson frame the Dissolution as the starting point for the creation of new and evolving roles for former monastic landscapes. They are critical of previous approaches that emphasise the Dissolution as the final event in the lifecycle of a monastery, drawing a sharp division between religious and secular phases (Willmott and Bryson 2013). They focus on the micro-history of a single monastery which they describe as 'fairly unremarkable', reminding us that even minor monastic houses continued to reverberate on local landscape and memory. This point is demonstrated in David Austin's research on the Cistercian monastery of Strata Florida in Wales. Austin explores the significance of former monasteries in structuring local biographies of place and he also situates these local stories within a national perspective. He contrasts dominant national narratives of triumphal Protestantism with local themes and specific *biographies of place*. These local stories might include continuity in ritual practices, such as the use of holy wells and patterns of burial; local sentiments surrounding mortality and loss at the Dissolution; and political feelings associated with religious dissent (Austin 2013: 4). In Austin's study of Strata Florida, the writing of biography involves reconstructing the landscape from prehistory to the present day, to consider both the world that the monks inherited and the legacy that they left embedded in the landscape (Austin 2013: 11).

Monastic ruins continued to shape local and national stories into the modern period. In the first half of the nineteenth century they were integral to Romanticism, viewed by artists, writers and poets as a corrective to industrialisation and emblematic of the medieval 'Golden Age'. Some were used as symbols of national identity; for example, the Cistercian Abbey of Villers (Belgium) had been suppressed and sold by the French in 1796. From 1830, it became an important symbol of the independent nation state of Belgium; its controversial restoration in the late nineteenth and early twentieth centuries was highly politicised and connected with the promotion of Catholic identity (Coomans 2005). In Britain, abbeys were used to bolster local identity and civic pride in the face of growing urbanisation and industrialisation. For example, the well-preserved ruins of Kirkstall Abbey in Leeds were developed as an amenity space in the 1880s, attracting tourism and artistic responses in the form of painting and poetry (Dellheim 1982). The ruins of Reading Abbey (Berkshire) were incorporated into the Forbury Pleasure Gardens from 1856, connected by a tunnel to the garden, where some of the abbey's carved stones were reused in gothic follies. At the turn of the twentieth century, a Reading doctor and antiquary, Jamieson Boyd Hurry (1857–1930), encouraged civic pride by commissioning a series of ten oil paintings depicting Reading Abbey's most illustrious moments (Baxter 2016: 163). At the national level, concern for the conservation of medieval abbeys was key to the preservation ethic that fuelled the development of ancient monuments legislation in England (Emerick 2014: 42). The protection of England's medieval abbeys was regarded as an urgent priority in the first decades of the twentieth century: many monastic ruins were in danger of collapse, while others were at risk from wealthy American collectors who dismantled medieval buildings and shipped them to the United States as cultural booty (Emerick 2014: 72–5).

These biographical perspectives situate monastic archaeology within wider theoretical debates on landscape and memory, exploring themes of identity and cohesion, appropriation and legitimation, and contested and alternative readings of landscapes (e.g. Holtorf and Williams 2006). Historical studies of religious belief have also shifted towards long-term perspectives on landscape and memory. The contribution of Alexandra Walsham has been especially ground-breaking, tracing the broad canvass of changing perceptions of the landscape and the natural world at the Reformation and how relics of pre-Reformation belief structured new myths that transformed social memory (Walsham 2004, 2011, 2012).

MONASTIC MEMORY PRACTICES

How were material and embodied practices used to imprint monastic memory on the landscape? Monks were the memory specialists of the medieval world – they developed cognitive memory training, were ritual experts in commemorating the dead and designed architecture to monumentalise the Christian past. Monastic memory was 'locational', prompted by specific places and topographical markers, with architecture and landscape serving a cognitive purpose. Mary Carruthers has described monastic meditation as a form of 'craft knowledge', learned through imitation and practice, and prompted by constant recollection and memory (Carruthers 2000). It followed the Roman tradition of rhetoric and drew upon mental images such as architecture in order to stimulate memory (Carruthers 2000: 16). But monastic memory practices were not merely rhetorical, they were deeply material, performative and 'procedural' (Mohan and Warnier 2017). This point can be further elucidated with reference to Paul Connerton's classic study of memory and identity formation (Connerton 1989). Connerton was interested in how identity and memory were created through three types of bodily techniques or performance – calendrical, verbal and gestural. He proposed that the impact of these performances could be extended in time and space through memory practices that he distinguished as 'inscription' and 'incorporation' (Connerton 1989: 72–3). Practices of *inscription* include writing and other forms of recording which trap and hold ritual information. For example, inscription could include practices of naming, such as the dedication of monasteries to specific saints and the naming of places in the landscape. Naming is an active process in place-making: local stories are imprinted on physical terrain through names that fix collective memory in the landscape (Gardiner 2012). Practices of *incorporation* are more procedural and transient, and would include monastic liturgy and meditation, as well as ritual acts performed by the laity, such as grave-side rituals or pilgrimage to holy wells.

A key element of inscription was the writing of monastic chronicles and foundation narratives. It was not uncommon for these to be written over several generations: they represent a palimpsest of collective memory and often connected the identity of a monastic community to its founding saint and local topography. For example, the history of Selby Abbey in North Yorkshire, completed in 1174, claimed that its origins were divinely inspired by visions of St Germanus: the saint appeared to a monk in the French abbey of Auxerre and told him to travel to Selby to build an abbey in the saint's honour (Burton with Lockyer 2013). Selby's foundation legend claims that the monk Benedict left France to travel to Yorkshire in 1067, at the height of the uprising by the northern earls against William the Conqueror. He carried a relic of St Germain's finger in a golden box, a material vestige that connected Selby's origin story to the landscape of Auxerre. David Harvey describes monastic hagiography as 'profoundly geographical', a means of binding together real and imagined landscapes in order to create a sense of place and to shape collective memory (Harvey 2002). He argues that hagiography represents a selected version of monastic heritage that stressed continuity with a specific past; in other words, a carefully controlled and authoritative message of how a particular monastery or religious order wished its origins and allegiances to be perceived.

Dedications to saints represent a major source for investigating local memory, identity and patronage in the medieval landscape. Recent research has reassessed the religious landscape of medieval Scotland through dedications and place names. The evidence for Scottish saints' dedications has been critically assessed in a wider European context, demonstrating that devotion to insular saints such as Ninian, Kentigern and Columba was not incompatible with universal cults such as the Virgin Mary and English saints including Thomas Becket (Boardman and Williamson 2010). Place name evidence can be used to investigate how the cults of early medieval saints were perpetuated in the later Middle Ages. However, Thomas Clancy reminds us that place names are not 'fossil records of cult and church development'; instead, they are a vital source of evidence for the cult and 'afterlife' of a saint (Clancy 2010: 3). For example, he notes that most dedications to the fifth-century St Ninian actually post-date the twelfth century, coinciding with the period when Scottish clergy had increased access to Bede to inform their knowledge of Ninian's life (Clancy 2010: 8). Matthew Hammond has considered the dedications of Scottish monasteries in the twelfth and thirteenth centuries, which demonstrate a strong current of support for universal cults such the Virgin Mary and the Holy Trinity. He suggests that aristocratic foundations were more likely to favour insular saints while royal foundations supported universal saints. It has previously been argued that the popularity of insular Scottish saints in the later Middle Ages represents a 'nationalist' or anti-English sentiment (McRoberts 1968). David Ditchburn argues that their popularity is instead consistent with a wider trend common throughout Western Europe for devotion to local cults and their landscapes (Ditchburn 2010).

Choices in architectural form and style were also active in constructing social memory. The iconographical form of a building was used to signal sacred archetypes and religious allegiances. For example, the cylindrical piers in the nave at Dunfermline Abbey (Fife) have spiral and zigzag patterns that may have marked the location of the nave altar and possibly the original burial place of St Margaret (Figure 5.1). They are also part of a wider pattern in which spiral piers were used to highlight important locations at major churches in the late eleventh century, including Canterbury Cathedral crypt (begun 1096) and the nave altar at Durham Cathedral (begun 1093). Dunfermline was founded in 1070 by Queen Margaret to celebrate her marriage to Malcolm I. The abbey had close connections with both Canterbury and Durham: the first monks were sent to Dunfermline from Canterbury by Archbishop Lanfranc to establish the first Benedictine community in Scotland; Turgot (d. 1115), the prior of Durham, was Margaret's confessor and hagiographer, and was later appointed bishop of St Andrews (Bartlett 2003: xxix). Richard Fawcett dates the piers to after 1128 and suggests that the master mason may have come from Durham (Fawcett 2002: 165). In addition to signalling alliance to Benedictine Durham and Canterbury, the piers may have provided an iconographic reference to Old St Peter's in Rome. Eric Fernie has argued that spiral piers represented the ancient columns that marked the apse of the fourth-century basilica in Rome (Fernie 1980), a reference that would have emphasised the close link to the Roman church that Margaret and her sons promoted (see Chapter 2).

5.1 Cylindrical piers showing zigzag and spiral patterns at Dunfermline Abbey (Fife). Photograph by Mussklprozz / Wikipedia / CC BY-SA 3.0

In his study of English Benedictine architecture, Julian Luxford emphasised the importance that the Benedictines placed on demonstrating the ancient origins of individual monasteries. This included the deliberate retention of Saxon fabric in twelfth-century programmes of rebuilding at the West Country churches of Winchester, Malmesbury (Wiltshire), Tewkesbury (Gloucestershire) and Gloucester (Luxford 2005: 145–7). The practice continued into the later Middle Ages at Glastonbury Abbey, where twelfth-century fabric was re-incorporated in the choir extension dating to the mid-fourteenth century (Sampson 2015) and durable blue glass dating to the twelfth century was integrated in sixteenth-century glazing schemes (Graves 2015) (Figure 5.2). These incorporations may have been intended to reference the abbey's florescence under Abbot Henry of Blois, grandson of William I, nephew of Henry I and brother of King Stephen. Henry remodelled Glastonbury and commissioned sculpture that placed the abbey in the artistic context of European court culture. The Cistercians of northern England also used archaic style in architecture, manuscripts and

5.2 Durable blue glass from Glastonbury Abbey (Somerset) dated to the 12th century. Reproduced by kind permission of Cheryl Green

material culture to bolster Cistercian identity and privileges in the later Middle Ages (Carter 2015b). Archaic style was used more widely in ecclesiastical architecture to convey a sense of antiquity and to legitimate selected, authoritative messages of monastic heritage. For instance, the friars harnessed the ideological potential of architecture to signal their commitment to monastic reform and their return to the apostolic origins of monasticism. An example is Santa Maria in Aracoeli in Rome, where a late thirteenth-century nave was created with columns and round arches to mimic the appearance of an early Christian basilica (Bruzelius 2014: 189). The political use of archaic style can also be found in later medieval Scotland: Ian Campbell has suggested that Romanesque style was re-adopted in Scottish churches in the fifteenth century to evoke the 'Golden Age' of the Canmore dynasty (Campbell 1995). Round arches and cylindrical piers were incorporated in the rebuilding of Melrose Abbey (Scottish Borders), Dunkeld Cathedral (Perth and Kinross), St Machar's in Haddington (East Lothian) and the Church of the Holy Rood at Stirling.

MEMORY AND THE REFORMATION: REMEMBERING AND FORGETTING

Studies of the Reformation by historians including Andrew Spicer and Alexandra Walsham have highlighted complexities and contradictions in the treatment of sacred space and landscapes (Spicer 2005; Walsham 2011). These tensions are particularly evident in Scotland's 'long Reformation', which was an extended process that began twenty years after the final suppression of monastic houses in England, Wales and Ireland. The Scottish Reformation was launched in 1560 with 'rage and furie', when the preaching of John Knox inspired the lords of the Congregation and their followers to wreak havoc on monasteries and churches in the north and east of Scotland. It took just two days to gut the Carthusian, Dominican and Franciscan monasteries in Perth; and at St Andrews (Fife), the iconoclasts destroyed monastic gardens and orchards as well as religious buildings, statues and shrines (Walsham 2011: 100). The urban friaries were the main target for the reformers, with around half sacked and burnt (Randla 1999). However, the majority of Scottish monasteries were never formally suppressed. Although churches were cleansed of Catholic fittings, many monks and nuns were allowed to live out their lives peacefully in the monastic cloister for decades after the suppression (Fawcett 1994a: 120). Excavations at the sites of former monasteries such as Dundrennan (Dumfries and Galloway) confirm that limited occupation continued in the cloister up to *c.*1600 (Ewart 2001: 31).

In contrast, the typical treatment of English monasteries at the Dissolution involved the immediate demolition of the church, chapter house and cloister. This targeted the overtly sacred space of the church; the chapter house as the site of institutional memory; and the domestic space of the dormitory, to ensure that former monks and nuns could not re-occupy the ruins (Howard 2003). There were deliberate attempts to conceal religious artefacts in the grounds of monasteries, suggesting that monastic communities may have anticipated their eventual reinstatement: concealed sculptures have been recorded at Cistercian abbeys including Fountains, Byland (North Yorkshire) and Hailes (Gloucestershire) (Carter 2015a). The buildings most likely to be retained at the Dissolution were the gatehouse and the abbot's or prior's lodgings: these self-contained chambers suited conversion to new courtier houses and domestic uses (Phillpots 2003). The comparatively gentle treatment of many monastic sites in Scotland may suggest that by 1560 they were already regarded as having been secularised. At some Scottish monasteries, the monks were allowed to live in individual houses outside the monastic cloister. For example, the monks of Pittenweem (Fife) had small houses in the priory garden, and at Crossraguel (South Ayrshire) a series of small houses survives along the perimeter wall of the inner court to the south of the cloister, possibly private residences for monks (Fawcett 1994b: 109). The final phase of monastic Scotland saw the introduction of commendators, lay administrators appointed by the king, a system unknown in England but more common in Europe. These men built large mansions in monastic precincts, some of which were converted at the Reformation, such as the surviving example at Melrose, rebuilt at the end of the sixteenth century.

Paradoxically, the Scottish Dissolution combined localised, ruthless iconoclasm with a remarkably tolerant attitude towards the majority of former monasteries and their inhabitants. I would like to explore this contradiction through brief consideration of two specific material practices: the continued use of dissolved monastic sites for burial and the sustained use of holy wells for popular ritual use. There is archaeological evidence to confirm that monastic cemeteries in the west and north of Britain continued to be used for burial after the Dissolution. For example, excavations at Carmarthen Greyfriars revealed at least five graves to the north of the choir, cut through demolition deposits of the friary (James 1997: 191). Burial continued at the Carmelite Friaries of Aberdeen, Linlithgow and Perth well into the seventeenth century: at Linlithgow, there were six infant burials interred in the nave and chancel in the late sixteenth to seventeenth century (Stones 1989). At Inchmarnock (Argyll and Bute), the disused church continued as a burial ground in the sixteenth to seventeenth century, with the graves of perinatal infants dug into the ruined nave (Lowe 2008: 90–1). This pattern of reuse extended to disused parish churches and chapels. At Auldhame (East Lothian), an infant burial was inserted into the decayed west gable wall of the chapel, which had been abandoned around 1400 and left to tumble down and decay (Crone et al. 2016: 51). A similar case was recorded at the disused chapel on St Ninian's Isle (Shetland), where a neonate was interred close to the chancel wall (Barrowman 2011). The sites of former monasteries were sometimes used for the burial of Catholics (Walsham 2011: 181) but the archaeological evidence suggests a more select pattern of social use. At Aberdeen, Linlithgow, Perth and Inchmarnock, a high proportion of the post-Reformation burials are those of women and children (Stones 1989: 111, 42, 44, 114). Burial of children continued on the sites of some former Irish monasteries up to the nineteenth century (Hamlin and Brannon 2003), and on Iona (Scottish Inner Hebrides), women and children were interred at the site of the nunnery into the eighteenth century (O'Sullivan 1994). Post-medieval burials at Iona continued the traditional rite of placing quartz pebbles with the corpse (see Chapter 4). Similar practices took place at former parish churches: excavation at the burial aisle established in the sixteenth century at Auldhame suggests that the site was reserved for the burial of juveniles, and that the rite of placing quartz pebbles continued into the post-medieval period (Crone et al. 2016: 52). Continuity of burial within suppressed churches and monasteries is a clear expression of the sustained belief in the *sanctity* of a consecrated site, despite repeated attempts by the Kirk to outlaw the custom (Spicer 2000; 2005: 89).

Following the Reformation, people continued to visit sacred natural locations in the landscape such as springs, wells and trees. In Ireland, ruined monasteries remained significant places of pilgrimage, with some friaries in the west of Ireland continuing to operate well into the seventeenth century (Harbison 1991: 111–36; Moss 2008: 70). Pilgrims gathered at holy sites to perform the same embodied acts that they had rehearsed throughout the Middle Ages (Bugslag 2016), including circumambulation in the direction of the sun, sprinkling of water over infants and leaving offerings of scraps of cloth, pins and coins (Walsham 2012). Pilgrims also gathered stones and created cairns at Scottish sites including St Fillan's Well (Stirling) (Donoho 2014) (Figure 5.3), much as they had done at early medieval pilgrimage sites such as Iona and the Isle of May (Fife) (Yeoman 1999). The intensity of interest in these sites led to legislation by the Scottish Parliament in 1581, prohibiting pilgrimage to chapels and springs to perform illicit devotions. Heavy fines were imposed for the first offence and death for the second, although most found guilty of this offence were instead ordered to perform humiliating acts of public penance (Walsham 2011: 106). Legislation against such practices continued into the seventeenth century; nevertheless, rites of healing and pilgrimage continued at hundreds of sites throughout Scotland for centuries after the Reformation (Walsham 2011: 171; Donoho 2014). While some kirk sessions were determined to stamp out superstitious practices, many others were tolerant of pilgrimage to sacred sites in the landscape (Todd 2000). In Ireland, devotion at crosses and holy wells intensified in the seventeenth century, with the construction of new well-houses that incorporated Romanesque carvings taken from ruined churches and monasteries. These carvings may have been selected for their association with particular saints and sacred places, rather than for their style or antiquity (Moss 2008: 75).

Women and children seem to have been closely connected with rites at holy wells, mirroring the pattern noted above for the continued use of monastic cemeteries after the Reformation for the burial of women and children. This may signal some degree of continuity with earlier practice: the dedications of medieval holy wells are predominantly to the Virgin Mary and female saints including Bridget, perhaps indicating a female preference for devotion at holy

5.3 St Fillan's Holy Well (Stirling). © Mick Sharp

wells (Clancy 2013: 31). It is also striking that the objects left at holy wells and springs – such as coins, pins and headlaces (Walsham 2011: 107, 171, 457) – were similar to those placed with the medieval dead. Where pins and lace ends have been found in medieval graves, for example in association with children's graves at Linlithgow Carmelite Friary, they have been explained as shroud fixings (Standley 2013: 106). Pins continued to be used as offerings at wells throughout Britain into the nineteenth century, often bent before they were deposited, just as medieval pilgrims crumpled their badges before throwing them into rivers (Merrifield 1987: 112). The sustained use of such objects as offerings at holy wells suggests that even the most mundane objects found in medieval graves may have been placed with ritual intent.

This brief overview of two rites in the post-Reformation landscape questions two prevailing assumptions about early Protestantism: first, that it was intrinsically antagonistic to ritual and second, that it rejected the concept of sacred space. The idea that supernatural power was invested in sacred places remained an important element of popular Protestant religion (Walsham 2011; Spicer 2005), compelling burial at former monasteries and continued rites of pilgrimage in the landscape.

MYTH AND MEMORY: ARTHUR AND ARIMATHEA AT GLASTONBURY ABBEY

I will turn now to Glastonbury Abbey, an iconic landscape where myth has played a unique role in connecting the medieval monastery to broader discourses surrounding English cultural identity. In addition to its reputed association with King Arthur, the abbey cultivated an origin story to proclaim its historical and spiritual pre-eminence among English monasteries. The history, archaeology and ethnography of Glastonbury are complex and still evolving, particularly in relation to New Age re-imaginings of its past, a theme that will be picked up in the final chapter. The well-documented case of Glastonbury vividly demonstrates how material practices were employed by medieval monastic and later Protestant communities to fix religious memory in the landscape. I will focus here on two key narratives in the medieval abbey's biography: its *beginning* and *ending* and how these stories were re-imagined by subsequent generations. Detailed archaeological appraisal of Glastonbury Abbey can be consulted in a publication that reassesses thirty-six seasons of antiquarian excavations that were conducted at the site throughout the twentieth century (Gilchrist and Green 2015).

Memory practice documented at Glastonbury begins with the origin story that was recorded in the tenth century and further embellished from the twelfth century onwards. A series of accumulated tales linked Glastonbury Abbey to biblical and apocryphal characters and ultimately to the life of Christ. As was common elsewhere, Glastonbury's monastic heritage was projected through the medium of hagiography and the writing of chronicles. The abbey promoted its association with St Dunstan, abbot of Glastonbury 940–57 CE and later archbishop of Canterbury, who played a pivotal role in the reform of Benedictine monasticism in the tenth century (Brooks 1992).

The *Life of St Dunstan* was written *c.*995 CE by a monk known only as 'B', drawing on his earlier memories of the community from around the mid-tenth century. As well as recounting Dunstan's life, the *vita* places the abbey in its social and topographical context; it refers to the buildings constructed by Dunstan and presents Glastonbury in the tenth century as a place of great learning. It describes an ancient church, the *vetusta ecclesia*, and attributes its construction to divine agency: 'For it was in this island that, by God's guidance, the first novices of the catholic law discovered an ancient church, not built or dedicated to the memory of man' (Winterbottom and Lapidge 2012: 13).

This narrative was further developed two centuries later by the respected historian William of Malmesbury, a monk of St Albans Abbey, in his history of Glastonbury Abbey, dated 1129–30 and commissioned by Henry of Blois. The primary motivation was to prove the great antiquity and unbroken history of the monastery at Glastonbury. At the end of the eleventh century, Osbern of Canterbury had claimed that St Dunstan had been the *first* abbot of Glastonbury (Foot 1991: 163). The reputation of the monastery therefore depended on authenticating its early origin: William asserted that the monastery had been founded *before* the arrival of the Anglo-Saxons in Somerset and even hinted that Glastonbury originated in an apostolic foundation. He claimed that the ancient church had been built in the second century by missionaries sent by Pope Eleutherius in 166 CE. He cautiously noted a story that the church may have been founded even earlier, by the Disciples of Christ, and provided an eye-witness account of the ancient 'brushwood' church that they had allegedly constructed.

> The church at Glastonbury ... is the oldest of all those that I know of in England ... In it are preserved the bodily remains of many saints, and there is no part of the church that is without the ashes of the blessed. The stone-paved floor, the sides of the altar, the very altar itself, above and within, are filled with relics close-packed. Deservedly indeed is the repository of so many saints said to be a heavenly shrine on earth.
>
> (Scott 1981: 67)

The salient point in William's account is that a timber church of some antiquity existed on the site in the early twelfth century and that it was preserved as a relic of the early monastery and its founders.

Many Christians today believe that Glastonbury's Lady Chapel (consecrated 1186) was built on the site of this very early church, dating to the first or second century and founded by Joseph of Arimathea. Recent study of the archaeological archive has confirmed that there was indeed occupation on the site before the foundation of the Anglo-Saxon monastery. Fragments of late Roman amphorae imported from the eastern Mediterranean (LRA1) were

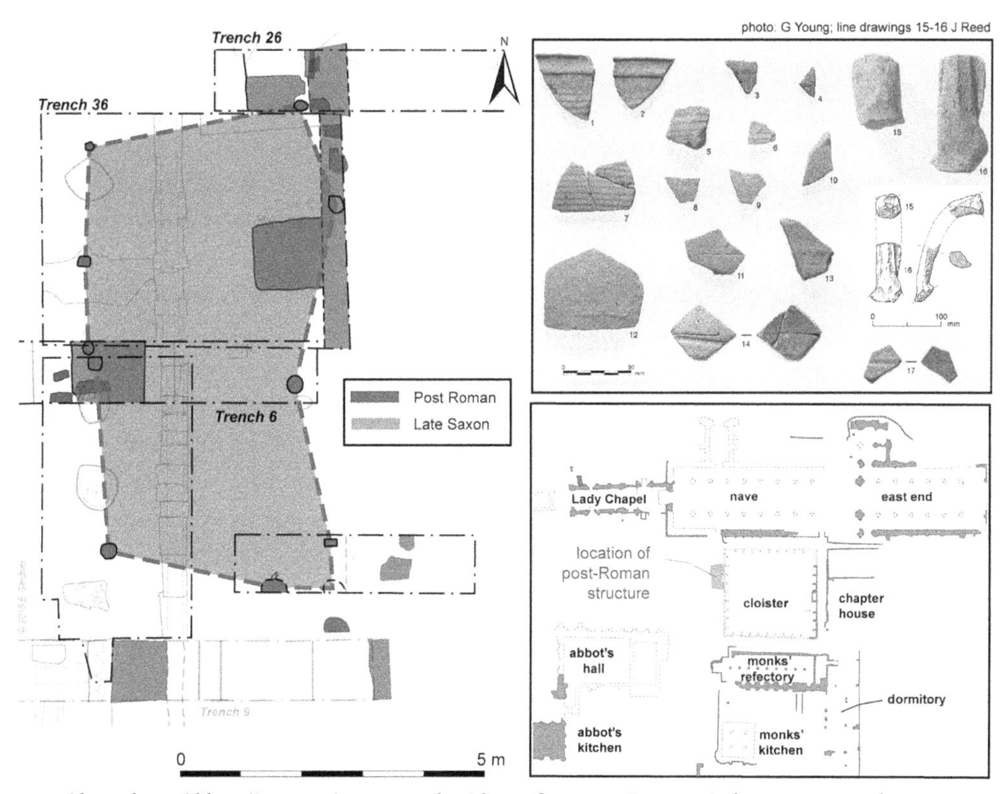

5.4 Glastonbury Abbey (Somerset): excavated evidence for a post-Roman timber structure and the location of LRA1 pottery, dated *c*.450–550 CE © Liz Gardner

associated with a roughly trodden floor and post-pits connected with one or more timber structures within the bounds of the early cemetery (Figure 5.4). In the southwest of Britain, this pottery occurs in contexts dating *c*.450–550 CE. A radiocarbon date from one of the post-pits dates the demolition of the timber building to the eighth or ninth century (Gilchrist and Green 2015: 131, 385, 416). It is possible that this structure was in use for a long period extending from the pre-Saxon occupation of the site *c* 500 CE, into the period of the Saxon monastery, for potentially up to 300 years. This would have required cyclical repair and renewal of the timber building once in each generation – the typical use-life of Anglo-Saxon earthfast structures is estimated to be around forty years (Hamerow 2012: 34–5). This new archaeological evidence does not prove the presence of an early church, but it does confirm that the Anglo-Saxon monastery was preceded by a high-status settlement dating to the fifth or sixth century. It may also suggest that the Saxon monastery 'curated' timber buildings that represented this antecedent community, just as the later medieval monks curated vestiges of their monastic heritage. Cycles of monument construction and reconstruction were employed by the Anglo-Saxons at secular elite complexes – such as Sutton Hoo (Suffolk) – to create social memory and forge connections to origin myths and genealogies (Williams 2006: 161).

Archaeological evidence for the earliest monastic occupation at Glastonbury comprises three phases of Anglo-Saxon stone churches, excavated 1926–9, when the entire width of the western area of the medieval nave was excavated. These were located to the east of the Lady Chapel and the presumed site of the old church. The churches can confidently be assigned a pre-Norman date on stratigraphic evidence: fragments of twelfth-century masonry sealed the Saxon remains. Three phases of church building were recognised on the basis of stratigraphic relationships and mortars characteristic to successive phases. The earliest phase can now be dated by radiocarbon dates associated with glass-working furnaces that provided glass for the windows of the first stone church. Bayesian analysis of the radiocarbon dates by Peter Marshall supports the proposal that the glass-making was a short-lived 'single-event', likely dating to the late seventh or early eighth century (Gilchrist and Green 2015: 131–46). This evidence complements recent historical analysis of the charter material by Susan Kelly which confirmed that the earliest charters from Glastonbury date to the final decades of the seventh century (Kelly 2012).

The old timber church described by William of Malmesbury was destroyed by fire in 1184 and the medieval Lady Chapel was rapidly erected on the same site. It was consecrated in 1186, just two years after the fire, and survives largely intact today (Figure 5.5). The Lady Chapel reflects the abbey's overall dedication to the Virgin and its strong promotion of her cult, which was strengthened

5.5 The Lady Chapel at Glastonbury Abbey (Somerset) consecrated 1186. © The Centre for the Study of Christianity & Culture, University of York

by the story of a miraculous statue of the Virgin and Christ Child which survived the burning of the old church. An interpolated passage in William of Malmesbury describes how the statue was damaged: 'Yet because of the fire heat blisters, like those on a living man, arose on its face and remained visible for a long time to all who looked, testifying to a divine miracle' (Hopkinson-Ball 2012: 15). The spiritual significance and location of the Lady Chapel resulted in an unusual arrangement of sacred space at Glastonbury. The focal point for pilgrimage was located at the *west* end of the abbey church in the Lady Chapel, the site of the former old timber church. Devotion to the Virgin was also reflected in material culture excavated in the twentieth century, including a copper-alloy plaque and a foil medallion, the latter possibly from Walsingham (Courtney et al. 2015: 294–5, Fig. 8.39: 7, Fig. 8.40: 9) (Figure 5.11).

The new Lady Chapel came to embody the collective memory and sacred heritage of the monastic community. It has been suggested that its form and decoration were deliberately archaic in order to recall Glastonbury's antiquity, perhaps modelled to resemble a contemporary reliquary, to contain and represent the saintly relics of Glastonbury's ancient past (Thurlby 1995). Despite its late twelfth-century date, the Lady Chapel is Romanesque in its proportions and exhibits distinctively archaic elements, including round-headed windows with chevron decoration and intersecting blind arcading of round-headed arches with chevrons (Sampson 2015) (Figure 5.6). Fragments of a sumptuous scheme of painted polychromy survive on the upper parts of the internal wall faces (Sampson 1995). The iconography of the door carvings represents the Life of the Virgin on the north side and an unfinished cycle of the Creation on the south side. The act of rebuilding a church is another form of monastic memory practice, particularly where fabric from the predecessor is incorporated in the new build. In writing about churches in early medieval Ireland, Tomas Ó Carragáin has described the act of rebuilding as the creation of an *associative relic* (Ó Carragáin 2010: 165). A useful comparison

5.6 Photograph of Glastonbury Abbey's Lady Chapel (Somerset) showing elements in the Romanesque style: round-headed windows with chevron decoration and intersecting blind arcading of round-headed arches with chevrons. Photograph by David Cousins © Glastonbury Abbey

with Glastonbury can be made with contemporary practice at Iona (see Figure 2.10), where fabric of the shrine of St Columba was incorporated into the new Benedictine complex, built *c.*1200 by Ranald Somhairle (Ritchie 1997: 98). At both Glastonbury and Iona, relics of the early monastic community were retained to the west of the rebuilt Benedictine churches and would have served as the main ritual foci for pilgrimage.

The fire that destroyed Glastonbury's old church in 1184 also set the scene for Glastonbury's role in the Arthurian myth. The monks claimed the discovery in 1191 of the shared grave of Arthur and Guinevere, famously recorded by Gerald of Wales in 1193, two years after the exhumation.

> Now the body of King Arthur ... was found in our own days at Glastonbury, deep down in the earth and encoffined in a hollow oak between two stone pyramids ... In the grave was a cross of lead, placed under a stone ... I have felt the letters engraved thereon ... They run as follows: "Here lies buried the renowned King Arthur, with Guinevere his second wife, in the isle of Avalon ...".
>
> (Rahtz and Watts 2003: 55)

Gerald went on to explain that King Henry II had informed the monks where to dig, having received the information himself from 'an ancient Welsh bard'. The historian Antonia Gransden argued that the monks staged a bogus exhumation in their desperate bid to attract funds to rebuild the abbey after the disastrous fire of 1184 (Gransden 2001). Indeed, there was reason to despair: Glastonbury had no major saint or cult of relics to attract pilgrims and they had recently lost their royal patron, Henry II, who died in 1189.

5.7 Lead cross, now lost, allegedly found in 'Arthur's grave' at Glastonbury Abbey (Somerset).

The account of Gerald of Wales described important *material* evidence which bolstered the monks' claims (Figures 5.7 and 5.8). The two 'pyramids' flanking the alleged grave were first described by William of Malmesbury in *c.*1130, who noted their great age and stated that they bore carved figures and names; these 'pyramids' were perhaps late Saxon cross shafts. The lead cross supposedly found in the grave is highly significant: it was probably a twelfth-century forgery of an earlier item, such as the mortuary crosses found in eleventh-century graves at St Augustine's, Canterbury (Gilchrist and Sloane 2005: 90). Gerald emphasises the

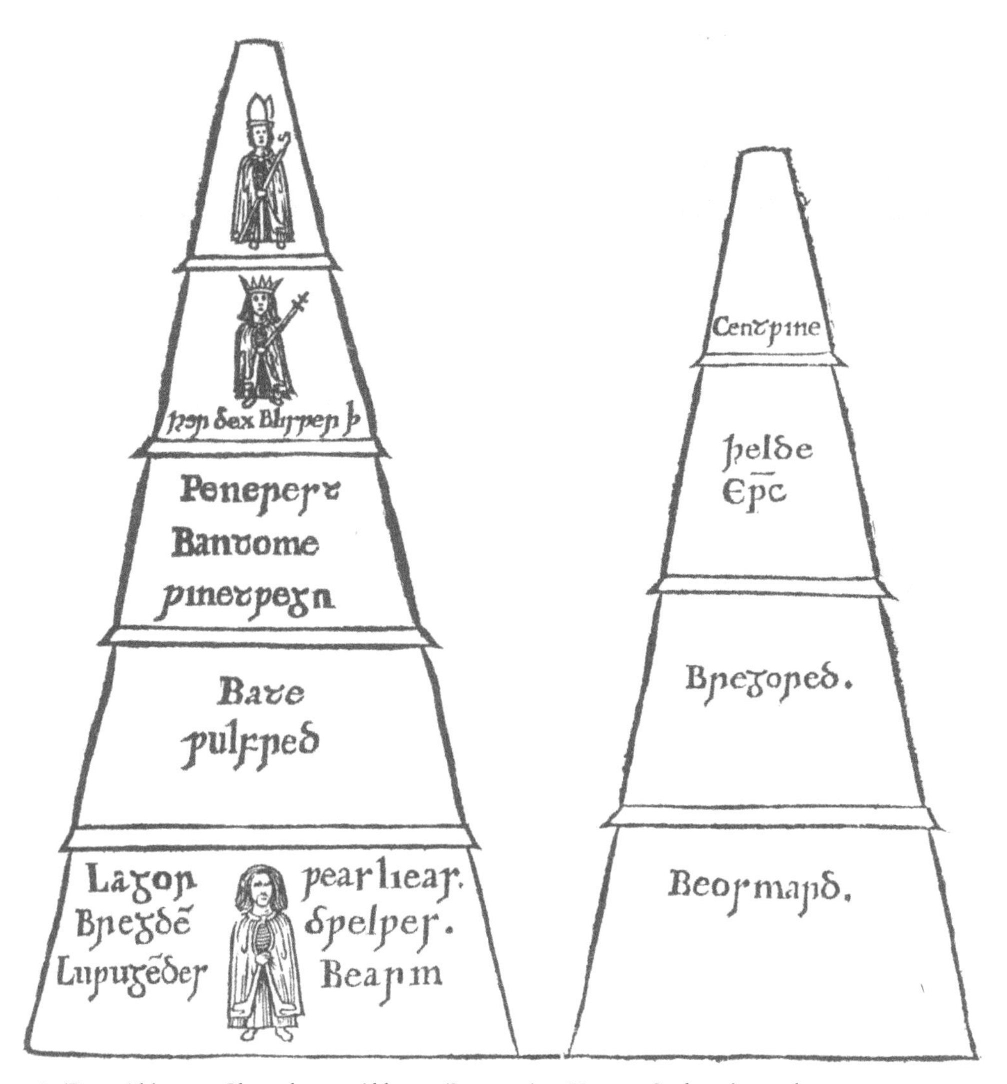

5.8 'Pyramids' at Glastonbury Abbey (Somerset). Henry Spelman's 17th-century reconstruction based on William of Malmesbury's description (*c.*1130).

materiality of the lead cross and the authenticity of its message: '*I have felt the letters engraved thereon*'. The Glastonbury lead cross survived up to the seventeenth century and was published in the 1607 edition of *Britannia*, by the antiquary William Camden. Arthur was known to have been taken to the Isle of Avalon after being mortally wounded, according to Geoffrey of Monmouth's *Historia Regum Britanniae* (*c.*1136). The lead cross associated with the exhumation of 1191 named Glastonbury as 'the isle of Avalon': this was the first explicit connection between Arthur's Avalon and the Glastonbury landscape.

Following the exhumation in 1191, the remains of Arthur and Guinevere were translated to a tomb in the abbey church. Contemporary chroniclers of the abbey, Adam of Damerham and John of Glastonbury, confirm that this was located 'in the choir, before the high altar'. The tomb of Arthur was placed in the most sacred space at the heart of the monastery, one reserved for burials of founders and patrons of the highest status. Julian Luxford has argued that Arthur was treated as the monastery's founder: a Saxon royal mausoleum was created in the choir, with Arthur's tomb flanked by those of Edmund the Elder to the north and Edmund Ironside to the south. In the later Middle Ages, Arthurian objects were displayed alongside saints' relics on a tomb to the north of the high altar (Luxford 2005: 170). The cult of Arthur brought international notoriety and royal patronage to Glastonbury Abbey, including royal visits to exhume and view Arthur's remains by Edward I in 1278 and Edward III in 1331.

Arthur's tomb was described by the antiquary John Leland in the 1530s, shortly before the Dissolution. Philip Lindley has suggested a possible reconstruction of the appearance of the tomb based on Leland's brief description, together with evidence in the Glastonbury chronicles and comparable examples of funerary monuments. The tomb was of black marble with four lions at its base (two at the head and two at the foot), a crucifix at the head (west) and an image of Arthur carved in relief at the foot (east). Lindley argues convincingly that the tomb described by Leland was the original monument constructed before 1200. Tomb-chests were unusual in England at the end of the twelfth century, making Arthur's tomb one of a small number of English monuments modelled on classical sarcophagi. The form and material were deliberately archaic, selected to place Arthur in a long line of ancient Saxon kings (Lindley 2007). An artist's drawing was recently commissioned to depict the choir of Glastonbury Abbey as it would have appeared in 1331 (Figure 5.9), for the visit of Edward III, based on archaeological evidence and ecclesiastical furnishings of contemporary date (see Chapter 6 for further discussion). The tomb reconstruction is inspired by Lindley's analysis and also draws on contemporary examples such as those in Córdoba Mezquita-Catedral (Andalusia, Spain).

The legend of the old church continued to evolve in the later Middle Ages: a revision of William of Malmesbury's history in 1247 attributed its foundation to Joseph of Arimathea (Carley 1996). According to the Gospels, Joseph was the man who donated his own tomb for the body of Christ following the crucifixion. The Glastonbury legend claimed that Joseph had been sent to Britain from Gaul by Christ's disciple, St Philip, together with twelve of his followers. A specific foundation date is stated for the old church as 63 CE and the dedication is noted as being in honour of the Virgin. However, the monks were not responsible for inventing the connection between Glastonbury and Arimathea. The link resulted indirectly from Glastonbury's Arthurian story and the emergence of Arimathea in the Grail legends of French romance. Around

5.9 Artist's reconstruction of the visit of Edward III to King Arthur's tomb at Glastonbury Abbey (Somerset) in December 1331. © Dominic Andrews www.archaeoart.co.uk

the year 1200, the author Robert de Boron brought together a trilogy of romances featuring Joseph of Arimathea, Merlin and Perceval. Joseph of Arimathea was used as the vehicle to explain how the Grail was brought to Britain, the vessel used to collect Christ's blood. He was cast as the guardian of the Grail and the father of English Christianity (Lyons 2014: 74–5).

By the mid-fourteenth century, the tradition had been established that Joseph came to Glastonbury and died there (Carley 1996). Arimathea and the Grail were fully incorporated in the Glastonbury story by *c.*1340, when John of Glastonbury wrote the abbey's chronicle. John quoted a pseudo seventh-century poem attributed to Melkin, claiming that Joseph is buried at Glastonbury and that in his sarcophagus are two cruets containing the blood and sweat of Jesus. Arimathea's place in Glastonbury's origin story was commemorated by an object known as the Magna Tabula, believed to date to the period of Abbot Chinnock (1382–1420). This still survives in the Bodleian Library: it is a hollow wooden box containing two hinged wooden leaves onto which parchment is pasted. It sets out the Glastonbury story from the foundation by Arimathea in 63 CE to the refurbishment of the abbey by Abbot Chinnock in 1382. Smoke stains indicate that it may have been displayed inside the church, perhaps attached to a pillar, and used to explain the sacred heritage of the site to pilgrims (Krochalis 1997).

The cult of Joseph of Arimathea was not fully developed at Glastonbury until the later Middle Ages, when the biblical association became more politically advantageous (Lagorio 2001). In the fifteenth century, representation at international Church councils was based on the antiquity and precedence of ecclesiastical foundations. The significance of an apostolic foundation was enormous and material evidence was sought to verify the connection to Joseph of Arimathea. In 1419, the monks were even planning to announce the discovery at Glastonbury of the graves of Joseph and his followers, but they later retracted their claim (Carley 2001b). The myth of Joseph of Arimathea was incorporated literally into the fabric of Glastonbury by Abbot Beere (1493–1524). He constructed a crypt chapel dedicated to Joseph beneath the east end of the Lady Chapel. The associated well of St Joseph was located to the south: the route for medieval pilgrims visiting the Chapel of St Joseph took them from the crypt to the well, via a stone passage. A brass plaque with early sixteenth-century lettering is likely to have been commissioned by Beere to explain its significance to pilgrims (Lindley 2007: 141; Goodall 1986).

DISSOLUTION STORIES: A MARTYRED LANDSCAPE

The events surrounding the suppression of the abbey in 1539 contributed a new narrative connected with sentiments of monastic loss and mortality. Glastonbury was one of the last monasteries to be dissolved: its enormous wealth proved irresistible to Henry VIII, valued in 1535 at £3301 17s 4d, second only to Westminster Abbey. The last abbot, Richard Whiting (1525–39), was arrested on a fabricated charge of treason in 1539 and found guilty of 'robbery' from his own church. He was hanged in front of the abbey gate and quartered on Glastonbury Tor, together with two of his monks, John Thorne, the treasurer, and Roger Wilfrid, one of the youngest monks. This level of violence was highly unusual: of approximately 220 Benedictine monasteries suppressed in England and Wales, only the abbots of Glastonbury, Reading and Colchester were executed. Their refusal to surrender their abbeys to the king was interpreted as a demonstration of loyalty to the Holy See of Rome.

Abbot Whiting's death produced a monastic martyr to the Dissolution, while the manner of his execution linked monastic memory to the broader landscape. Whiting was attached to a hurdle at the abbey gate and dragged through the town and up Glastonbury Tor. A remarkably similar ritual was played out at Reading, where Abbot Hugh Farringdon was dragged through the town and executed at the gallows with two of his monks (Baxter 2016: 134). Abbot Whiting's head was placed over the great gate of Glastonbury Abbey and the four quarters of his body were displayed at Wells, Ilchester, Bridgwater and near Bath (Carley 1996: 80–3). Among its multiple meanings, Glastonbury Tor became a mnemonic for the martyrdom of Whiting (see Figure 6.13). It has been suggested that Glastonbury's dissolution story also entered folklore through the nursery rhyme 'Little Jack Horner', a popular tale of opportunism. The earliest published version dates to 1735 (Opie and Opie 1997: 234–7):

> Now he sings of Jackey Horner
> Sitting in the Chimney-Corner
> Eating of a Christmas pye,
> Putting in his thumb, Oh fie!
> Putting in, Oh fie! his Thumb
> Pulling out, Oh strange! a Plum.

In the nineteenth century it was believed that this popular children's rhyme had its origins in the story of Thomas Horner, steward to Abbot Richard Whiting. Folk memory suggests that Whiting sent Horner to London with a great pie for Henry VIII, which had lucrative deeds baked inside as an incentive to persuade the king not to suppress the abbey. Instead, the rhyme insinuates that Horner kept the deeds for himself, including Mells Manor, thus sealing the fate of the doomed abbey (Roberts 2004: 3).

Archaeological evidence suggests that Henry VIII singled out the monastic precinct at Glastonbury for special treatment at the Dissolution. It was retained by Henry until his death in 1547 and there is evidence that the buildings of Glastonbury Abbey remained intact for a decade or more after its suppression. Reading Abbey was treated similarly in this respect, as well as in the execution of its abbot: Reading's cloister was not demolished until after Henry's death and the site was retained subsequently for royal use (Baxter 2016: 141). This was in sharp contrast with the frenzy of salvage and conversion that took place at the majority of former English monasteries. Historical sources confirm that the lead was removed from the roof of Glastonbury's chapter house in 1549 and the altars were removed from St Joseph's Chapel in 1550 (Stout 2012: 252). Study of the standing fabric and worked stone by Jerry Sampson has yielded evidence that the church may have been left standing and accessible after the departure of the monks. The rood beam was apparently removed from the eastern crossing piers and its sockets were repaired, implying that the work was done while the abbey church was still in use, or at least accessible to be visited (Sampson 2015).

The pattern of iconoclasm at Glastonbury may indicate that figurative sculpture was left in situ for a considerable time. The assemblage of sculpture from the abbey comprises detached heads or headless torsos, perhaps suggesting that systematic iconoclasm took place while the sculpture was still in situ. The nature of the damage is consistent with the wider pattern of iconoclasm that focused on the heads and hands of statues of the saints. Pam Graves has argued that the treatment of such images at the Reformation reveals that they were considered to have possessed conscious agency and that there was a desire to punish statues for their role in idolatry. The body parts selected for destruction – heads and hands – were the same as those targeted in cases of capital and corporal punishment. At the Reformation, these holy images were tried and held accountable for their false actions (Graves 2008). What is exceptional in relation to Glastonbury is the *chronological significance* of this particular type of iconoclasm. The nature of damage caused to monasteries at the Dissolution typically comprised demolition and the salvage of stone for reuse (Morris 2003). The ideological attack on images did not gain momentum until the late 1540s and 1550s (Aston 1988). The targeted attack on Glastonbury's saints may therefore suggest that the sculpture remained in situ in the church for a decade or more after its dissolution in 1539.

We may speculate whether the continued presence of the suppressed abbey was intended to be commemorative. The historian Margaret Aston highlighted the tendency for reformers to preserve evidence of broken images and ruined churches to serve as a visual reminder of the Protestant triumph over popery and superstition (Aston 2003). Did Glastonbury Abbey serve as a monument to the Dissolution – was Glastonbury intended as Henry's *memento mori* of the monasteries and the inevitable fate of their corruption?

POST-REFORMATION NARRATIVES: GLASTONBURY ABBEY AND PROTESTANT NATIONHOOD

Having set out the key stories of Glastonbury's birth and death, it remains to consider which of these narratives were remembered, forgotten or reworked in the years following the Reformation. Monastic ruins and landscapes were reshaped in the latter part of the sixteenth and seventeenth centuries as part of a national narrative proclaiming the triumph of Protestantism, the English state and the English economy (Austin 2013: 3). While memory of the Catholic monastery of Glastonbury may have been suppressed, its mythical founder-saint was harnessed in the creation of English nationhood.

Following Henry's death in 1547, the site and demesne were granted to Edward Seymour, Duke of Somerset. He chose the site of the former abbey for a Protestant social experiment, establishing a colony of 230 Walloon worsted weavers, French-speaking Protestant refugees from Flanders. The intention was that the Walloons would teach the craft of weaving to the local population, to create a centre of Protestant industry at Glastonbury. The weavers constructed houses within the precinct and their leader occupied the former abbot's lodging. In March 1552, the community comprised forty-four families and four widows; four houses were completely built and another twenty-two lacked only doors and windows (Cowell 1928). The historian Adam Stout has suggested that the Duke of Somerset chose Glastonbury to showcase the new Protestant religion, based on its mythical status as the 'cradle of English Christianity' (Stout 2014: 81). The Walloon community fled to Frankfurt following the accession of the Catholic Queen Mary in 1553. A number of small finds dating to the sixteenth century have their closest parallels in the Low Countries and could potentially be associated with the short-lived Walloon community (Courtney et al. 2015: 310). In 1556, four former monks of Glastonbury petitioned Queen Mary to restore the abbey and a legacy was made to support the work, suggesting that habitable buildings were still in place (Stout 2014: 79). Elsewhere, former monks and nuns were also hopeful that their monasteries would be restored: monks from Monk Bretton and nuns from Kirklees (West Yorkshire) continued to live communally in new secular surroundings, while the former abbeys of Roche (South Yorkshire) and Rufford (Nottinghamshire) anticipated full reinstatement under the Catholic queen (Carter 2015a).

Glastonbury's Arimathea legend was exploited by Archbishop Parker, John Foxe and Queen Elizabeth I to assert the independence of the English church from Rome. Elizabeth claimed Joseph of Arimathea as 'the first preacher of the word of God in our realm' (Stout 2012: 254). Joseph's foundation of Glastonbury's old church in 63 CE was cited as proof of the antiquity of the English church; it was argued that its distinct and reformed character had been established before 597 CE, when Augustine imposed the Roman church on Britain (Lindley 2007: 141; Cunningham 2009). A comparison can be made here with how the Presbyterian Church of Scotland claimed the early medieval culdees as its Protestant precursor. It was argued that the ancient and native church of Scotland did not have bishops and was therefore not truly Catholic (Hammond 2006: 26). The Anglican Church of Ireland used a similar argument in the nineteenth century, claiming that they were the true descendants of St Patrick, because Celtic Christianity had been corrupted by the Norman imposition of Roman Catholicism in the twelfth century (Hutchinson 2001: 513). In all three cases, medieval sacred heritage was pressed into service to provide spiritual authority for the Protestant church.

At Glastonbury, the material practices of dismantling the abbey ruins respected these political narratives. From his study of the standing remains of the church, Jerry Sampson has concluded that the process of destruction was controlled and systematic. The abbey buildings were used as a quarry for materials and there seems to have been a deliberate plan to create a symmetrical ruin of the church as the focal point of the site of the former abbey (Sampson 2015). The significant survival of paint fragments in the Lady Chapel suggests that it was roofed for an extended period following the Dissolution. From documentary sources, Stout has argued that the main demolition took place in the later sixteenth and early seventeenth century, when the precinct was owned by the Earls of Sussex (Stout 2014: 79). Further destruction took place throughout the seventeenth and eighteenth century, but a process of selective

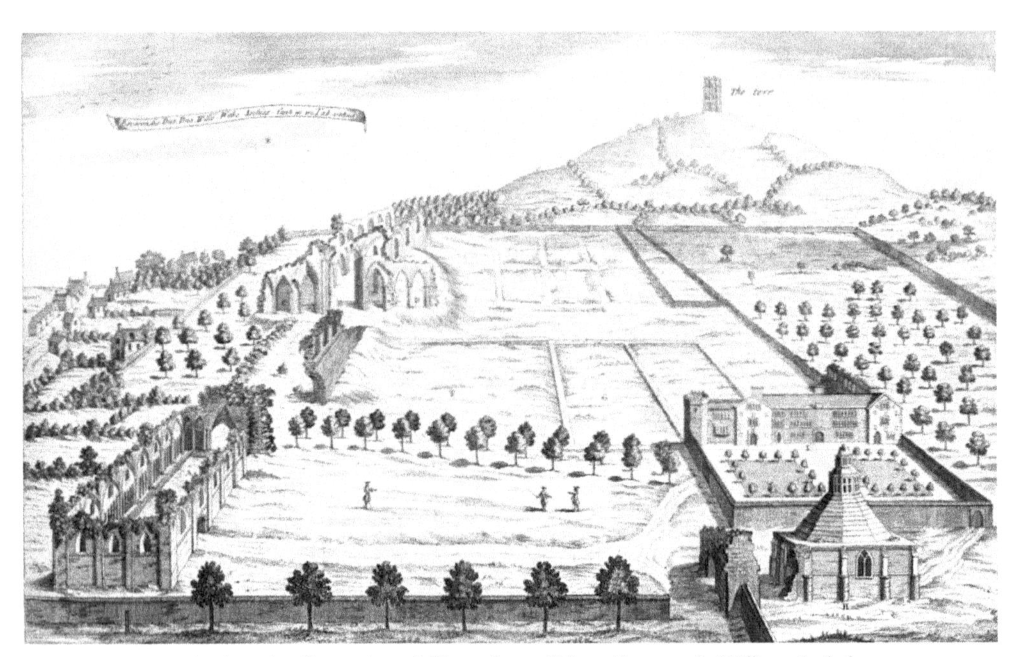

5.10 Antiquarian illustration of Glastonbury Abbey (Somerset): William Stukeley, 1724 eastern aspect. Reproduced by kind permission of Glastonbury Antiquarian Society

preservation was clearly adopted (Figure 5.10). The Lady Chapel was left largely intact and survives to the present day – the memorial to the old church and the antiquity of Glastonbury's foundation. By 1520, it was known as St Joseph's Chapel, and its special treatment is likely to have resulted from the importance placed on the Arimathea legend by the emerging Protestant nation. St Joseph's Chapel at Glastonbury was regarded as a Protestant shrine, for example, described in Camden's *Britannia* (1610: 226) as 'the beginning and fountain of all religion in England' (Stout 2012: 256). The abbey also continued to attract Catholic recusants well into the eighteenth century, some of whom created relics from the dense ivy thicket which had enveloped the chapel (Walsham 2011: 167).

In stark contrast, the importance of Glastonbury's Arthurian legend diminished after the Reformation. Arthur's tomb had been of singular importance to the monastery: when the antiquary John Leland visited in the 1530s, he accepted it as the *material proof* that verified the existence of King Arthur and his association with Glastonbury (Lindley 2007: 139). Leland was determined to prove the historical veracity of Arthur, which had recently been called into question by the Italian humanist Polydore Vergil, who had been commissioned by Henry VII to write a history of England (Higham 2002: 236). Leland used Glastonbury Abbey and the local landscape as material proof to authenticate the Arthurian connection. He recorded that Arthur had lived at Cadbury Castle and perpetuated the folklore belief that he remained asleep under the hill (Paphitis 2013: 3). The process of the Dissolution stimulated the development of antiquarian scholarship and the recording of medieval monuments, most notably by the seventeenth-century antiquary, William Dugdale (Dugdale 1817–30). And yet, Arthur's tomb disappeared from Glastonbury without trace: there is no surviving fragment and no clue to its fate. It must have been destroyed sometime after Henry's death in 1547, when demolition of the abbey began.

The 'pyramids' that marked Arthur's grave-site were treated similarly: the precise date of their removal is unrecorded but they had disappeared by the early eighteenth century (Stout 2014: 80). The lead cross that was allegedly found in the grave was held at the church of St John the Baptist, Glastonbury, for around 100 years after the Dissolution (Barber 2016). The forged artefact disappeared during the seventeenth century and was the subject of a modern hoax in 1981, when the British Museum was approached with an object supposedly found in the bottom of the lake at Forty Hall Park, Enfield, the site of a Tudor palace. The hoaxer was a skilled lead pattern maker capable of producing a copy. He served a prison sentence after refusing to produce the artefact for examination, which is believed to have been hidden or destroyed (Mawrey 2012). The failure to preserve Arthurian artefacts in the centuries immediately following the Dissolution suggests that the abbey's Arthurian legends were forgotten for a time. There was increasing scepticism about Arthur in the English court from the later sixteenth century and the English Arthurian cult declined significantly in the seventeenth century. In contrast, the Arthurian myth became more important in Scotland under James VI: Arthur was used to demonstrate Britishness and the political argument for political union under James I (Higham 2002: 238).

Meanwhile, the Arimathean legend continued to gather pace at Glastonbury during the seventeenth century, embodied by the Legend of the Holy Thorn. The story elaborates on Joseph's arrival at Glastonbury after his long journey from the Holy Land. It claims that Joseph paused on his way up Wearyall Hill and thrust his staff into the ground, whereupon the staff sprouted into a thorn tree. This motif of germination was shared with other British saints: for example, both Ninian and Etheldreda were associated with sprouting staffs that grew into trees (Walsham 2012: 35). Glastonbury Abbey also celebrated the cult of St Benignus, a follower of St Patrick who was associated with a sprouting staff. The staff of Benignus is perhaps represented by a tiny artefact from the excavations at the abbey: a gilt copper alloy rod with foliate decoration (Courtney et al. 2015: 294; Fig. 8.39: 4) (Figure 5.11). The Glastonbury Thorn and others grown from it was observed to blossom each year at Christmas. The thorn is a form of the Common Hawthorn, *Crataegus monogyna* 'Biflora', which flowers naturally twice a year, in winter and spring. In the local context of Glastonbury, the second flowering of the thorn was

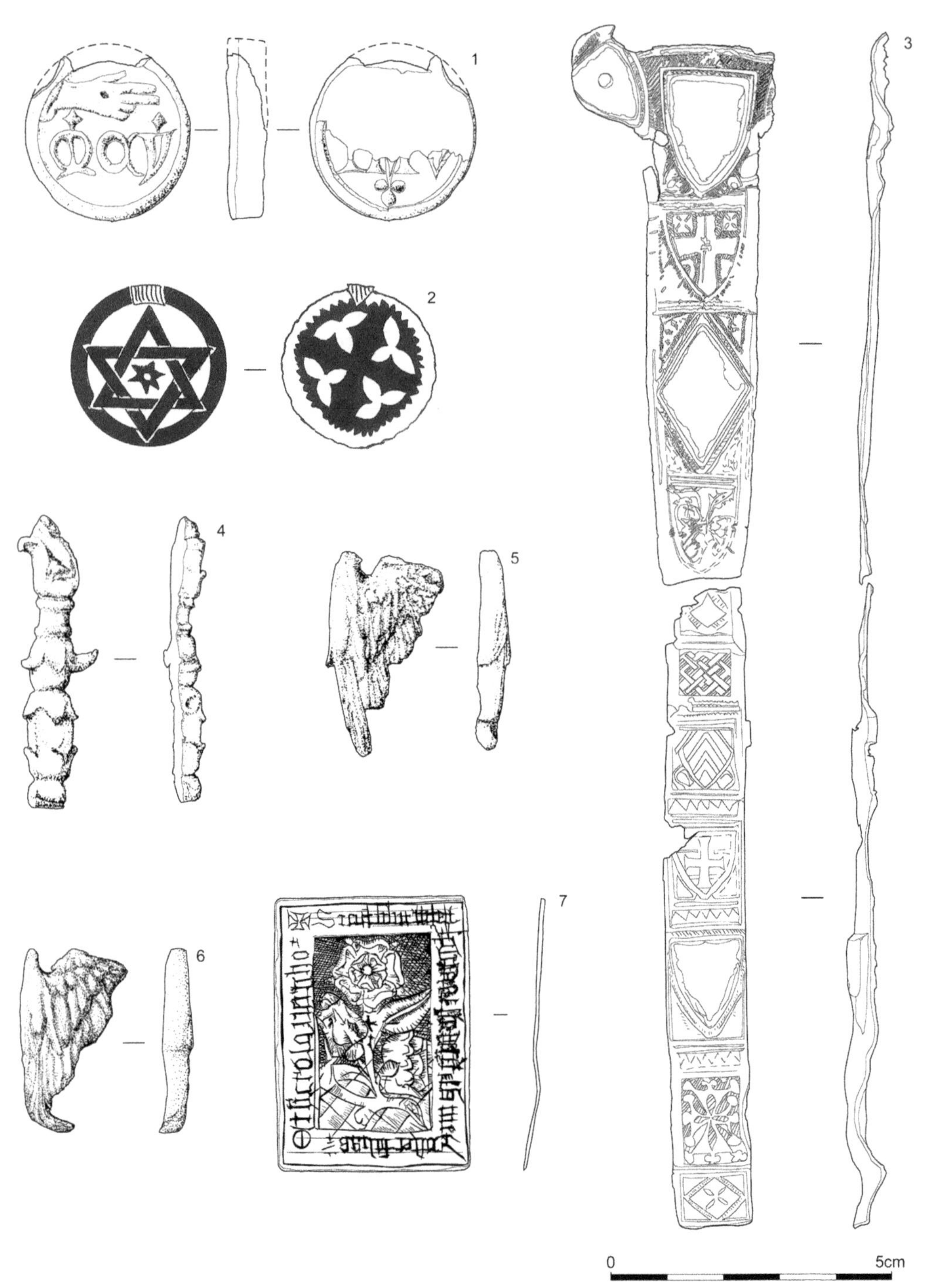

5.11 Devotional objects excavated from Glastonbury Abbey (Somerset): 1. Terracotta medallion; 2. Lead amulet; 3. Gilt copper-alloy decorative mounts, possibly from reliquary cross, box or book; 4. Gilt copper-alloy rod, possibly representing sprouting staff associated with St Benignus; 5&6. Gilded wings; 7. Copper-alloy plaque inscribed with Marian inscription SICUT LILIUM INTER SPINAS SIC AMICA MEA INTER FILIAS ET SIC ROSA I JERCHO ('As the lily among the thorns so is my love among the daughters and as a rose in Jericho') (Gilchrist and Green 2015: 294). © Liz Gardner interpreted as commemorating Christ's nativity. More widely, the Glastonbury Thorn is consistent with Protestant interest during the seventeenth century in the natural world and the miraculous properties of nature (Walsham 2012: 45).

Walsham has explored Glastonbury's Legend of the Holy Thorn and concluded that there is no evidence within medieval sources for the tradition (Walsham 2004). A flowering thorn is mentioned in the *Life of St Joseph of Arimathea*, 1520, but the specific link between the flowering thorn and the staff of Joseph did not emerge until the Jacobean period (Walsham 2011: 492–7). Popular interest in the Thorn coincided with the period when the destruction of the abbeys began to be regretted in some quarters. The Thorn was employed as a device in anti-puritan narratives: in 1653, Bishop Godfrey Goodman suggested that the tree may have begun flowering as a sign of God's anger against the 'Barbarous inhumanity' of the Henrician attack on the monasteries (Walsham 2011: 495). It became explicitly linked with the Royalist cause: the tradition began for the monarch to be presented with a sprig of the Glastonbury Thorn on Christmas morning, a tradition reinvented in the 1920s (Lyons 2014: 101). Glastonbury's Thorn was subject to iconoclasm by the Roundheads during the Civil War, prompted by both its Royalist associations and its connection with the celebration of Christmas, which was regarded as pagan by puritans (Walsham 2011: 134). This evocative symbol was vulnerable to both souvenir-hunters and iconoclasts, while it was venerated at the same time by both Protestants and Catholics. Stories circulated of misfortune that befell those who attacked it, transforming Glastonbury's Thorn into a Catholic symbol of resilience in the face of puritanism (Walsham 2011: 205).

The Holy Thorn also connected the Arimathea legend to the natural world and to the local landscape around Glastonbury Abbey. Nearby Chalice Well was drawn into the abbey's complex biography: this natural chalybeate spring was visited from Mesolithic times and became an important source of water supply to the medieval abbey. It was known in the Middle Ages simply as Chalkwell (Rahtz and Watts 2003), but its iron-rich water produced a red stain which became associated symbolically with the blood of Christ and the Grail legend. The medieval abbey funded the erection of a cover for the well, perhaps signalling the emergence of the cult (Walsham 2011: 56). It was popularly believed that Joseph of Arimathea had buried the sacred cruets near the spring and that the water had become tinged red by the healing blood of Christ (Mather 2009). In the mid-eighteenth century, Glastonbury was briefly celebrated as a healing spa focused on Chalice Well (Stout 2008). The Arimathea legend took on a new dimension in the nineteenth century, with the popular West Country story that Christ himself had come to England as a boy and had walked the Glastonbury landscape. The Bible gives no indication of where Jesus spent the majority of his life, from the age of twelve to thirty. This silence provided the opening for one of Glastonbury's most powerful stories:

the 'Holy Legend of Glastonbury' purported that Christ had been brought to Britain by his great uncle, Joseph of Arimathea, in pursuit of the tin trade (Smith 1989). This folktale became associated with William Blake's poem, '*And did those feet in ancient time*' (*c.*1808), which contrasted the heavenly Jerusalem that was created by Christ's visit to England with the 'dark Satanic mills' of the Industrial Revolution. The myth that Jesus visited Glastonbury remains significant for many English Christians today, immortalised in the country's unofficial anthem: Sir Hubert Parry's hymn, *Jerusalem* (1916).

MONASTIC AFTERLIVES: THE BIOGRAPHY OF PLACE

Glastonbury's stories demonstrate the highly stratified nature of monastic memory – how layers of meaning are added by successive generations to connect place with the past. The institutional identity of the abbey was commemorated both in hagiography and in the landscape – its birth and death were key themes in structuring the biography of place and fuelling later folklore, from the Holy Thorn to Little Jack Horner and the Holy Legend of Glastonbury. It is significant that the monks constructed legends of Arthur and Arimathea that included their interment at Glastonbury Abbey (Carley 2001b; Gransden 2001). It was not sufficient for the abbey merely to be associated with legendary figures; it needed to possess their mortal remains. The key memorial function of a monastery was as a *mortuary landscape*: the abbey fashioned itself as a mausoleum and reliquary for its legendary founders, while the presence of their graves strengthened the sacred heritage of place, bringing both spiritual cachet and economic potential for attracting pilgrims and patrons.

Narratives of closure and the finality of death helped to fix memory in the monastic landscape. Past and place were structured at Glastonbury through a range of material practices: the archaic styles of the Lady Chapel and Arthur's tomb, the use of ancient 'pyramids' to mark Arthur's grave, the forged 'antique' lead cross that identified Glastonbury as Avalon, the brass plaque and the Magna Tabula that conveyed to pilgrims the story of Joseph's foundation of the old church. Glastonbury's Dissolution story contributed darker elements to the biography: by the mid-seventeenth century, the abbey precinct was regarded as cursed and the area of the former church was believed to be haunted. The antiquary William Stukeley reported a local belief that those who quarried stone from the abbey ruins suffered ill fortune, while the economic decline of the town's market was blamed on the fact that the building in which it was held was constructed of abbey stone (Walsham 2011: 292). The monastery remained a key signifier of place, with these local tales resonating with monastic loss, betrayal and the 'bad death' of Abbot Whiting.

Post-Reformation narratives reworked the legend of Joseph of Arimathea, suppressing the Marian association of the Lady Chapel and its Catholic connotations. The Arthurian connection was eclipsed by the importance of Arimathea in providing spiritual authority for the Protestant nation. The monuments to Arthur, his tomb and grave-site, disappeared silently and without comment. In contrast, St Joseph's Chapel, Glastonbury's monument to the antiquity and purity of the English church, endured the ravages of the Dissolution and post-medieval speculators. The material practices of salvage and preservation were shaped both by national narratives and local sentiments. New connections were forged with the local landscape, grafting the biography of Glastonbury Abbey with elements of the natural world – the Tor, Chalice Well and the Holy Thorn (see Figure 6.14). These associations were consistent with wider Protestant practices in the seventeenth century, marking a return to the medieval view that certain places in the landscape possessed supernatural power (Walsham 2012: 35). Glastonbury's story is exceptional, but the abbey was not unique in extending its biography beyond the Reformation. The complex and celebrated case of Glastonbury Abbey demonstrates the enduring legacy of monasteries, their continuing power to inspire cultural imagination and to shape biographies of place. Glastonbury reveals the contested nature of place – why some memories are perpetuated while others are forgotten or erased – and how monastic afterlives continue to shape new versions of the medieval past.

SIX

SACRED MYTHS: ARCHAEOLOGY AND AUTHENTICITY

INTRODUCTION: SAINTS, SCHOLARS AND KINGS

This final chapter examines the role of archaeology in authenticating or challenging modern myths connected with medieval sacred sites. Sacred heritage sites are closely connected to nationalist narratives, both in the Middle Ages and today, for example through origin myths, the stories of saints and their martyrdom, military heroes and dynastic battles. Monasteries were centres of both religious and royal power, often serving as the burial place for saints and kings. It was common for medieval religious use to be just one phase of a longer-lived sacred landscape – certain places attracted a genuine continuity of ritual practice, while others were subject to the later 'invention' of sacred tradition, in order to legitimate a religious or political narrative (Shaw 2013b, after Hobsbawm 1983). My aim in this concluding chapter is threefold: first, to consider how medieval sacred heritage is used to construct myths connected with nationalist and religious identities; second, to review the role of archaeology in authenticating or challenging sacred myths; and third, to reflect on medieval sacred landscapes as *contested* heritage sites which hold multiple meanings to contemporary social groups. How have archaeologists contributed to the construction of myths at medieval sacred sites? In what ways have archaeology and material culture been used to authenticate religious narratives? What are the dominant and alternative myths that operate at sacred heritage sites, and what are the tensions between them? I will begin with some brief definitions of 'authenticity' and 'myth'.

Authenticity has been thoroughly explored in the heritage literature and remains a core principle for assigning heritage 'value'. Keith Emerick has commented that 'authenticity is an intellectual dead end' (Emerick 2014: 7); he argues that the 'sacred cows of conservation' – antiquity, fabric and authenticity – have outlived their usefulness and need to be rethought as we move towards more democratic heritage practices. He encourages heritage practitioners to focus instead on the relationship between people, story and place (Emerick 2014: 216). However, his critique is aimed at the traditional definition of authenticity as a construct of value defined by archaeological professionals, based on judgements of the quality of material evidence. It is now widely understood that authenticity is culturally constructed and varies between social groups and cultural contexts, following the wide definition of authenticity as set out in the Nara Document on Authenticity (ICOMOS 1994) as: 'that which embodies the cultural heritage values of the place'. Recognition of *intangible heritage* was an important factor in these debates: the oral traditions, myths, performing arts, rituals, knowledge and skills that are transmitted between generations to provide communities with a sense of identity and continuity (ICOMOS 1994; UNESCO 2003). Acknowledgement of intangible heritage has heightened awareness that concepts of authenticity are *culturally relative*; while European traditions of authenticity privilege fabric and antiquity, other traditions may emphasise people and spirit (Jones 2010).

European approaches to authenticity can be broadly divided into *materialist* and *constructivist* perspectives, the latter acknowledging that authenticity varies according to social and cultural contexts (Holtorf 2013a). Siân Jones has explored the constructivist concept of authenticity in relation to intangible heritage, which includes spiritual beliefs and related practices, artefacts and spaces. Jones focuses her discussion on the Hilton of Cadboll cross-slab, a Pictish sculpture dating to *c.*800 CE (Easter Ross, northeast Scotland) (Jones 2010). She reveals the strong local attachment to the object and the shared sentiment that it is a living thing – a member of the community – and integral to the local landscape and sense of place. Removal of the slab from its original setting created tensions between the local community and national heritage agencies, demonstrating how local voices may conflict with heritage managers and lead to the rejection of professional authority. Jones concludes that authenticity is not about the status of objects in themselves, but rather about the social relationships between people and things, 'a means for people to negotiate their own place' in a complex world (Jones 2010: 197). She emphasises the importance of the cultural biographies of objects – their life histories – in discussions of their authenticity. Cornelius Holtorf has responded to Jones by calling for constructivist approaches that reinstate the importance of *materiality* to authenticity, particularly how people respond perceptibly to the material qualities of objects in perceiving their 'pastness' (Holtorf 2013a). My aim in this chapter is to consider how authenticity is constructed in relation to *sacred* heritage: how do the *spiritual credentials* of a place relate to understandings of its materiality and historicity?

The term 'myth' is often used pejoratively, implying a false story or superstitious belief. Archaeologists in Britain have been wary of engaging with myth and folklore, even when investigating sites steeped in legend, such as the hillfort of Cadbury Castle (Somerset), popularly known as Camelot, the court of King Arthur. The site was investigated in the 1960s by the Camelot Research Committee, led by Leslie Alcock (Alcock 1972). The Arthur question dominated the project: Alcock rejected the site's folklore as romantic superstition, but he was firmly committed to the belief that he could tease out the historical 'facts' about Arthur as a genuine historical figure (Paphitis 2013: 15). More recently, the significance of myths to archaeological interpretation has been reasserted. In particular, archaeologists studying Celtic and Old Norse myths have emphasised the importance of reflecting critically on long-term continuities in belief. For example, Jim Mallory and John Waddell have explored the potential for using medieval Irish literature to discern elements of pre-Christian and Christian Celtic myth (Mallory 2016; Waddell 2014), while Anders Andrén and Lotte Hedeager have used Old Norse myths to explore beliefs prevalent in the Scandinavian Iron Age (Andrén 2014; Hedeager 2011).

The psychological basis of ancient myths has also been considered: Jordan B. Peterson examines myths from the perspective of neuropsychology, describing them as 'maps of meaning'. He argues that similar structures of storytelling have developed cross-culturally to explain human existence in terms of archetypes, enabling us to deal with the unknown and to defend our familiar territory from external threats (Peterson 1999). Religious scholars employ the term myth more neutrally, to describe a significant story, making no value judgements about its truth or veracity. Myths are seen as an ongoing narrative, the process of story-telling as a constantly evolving feature of religion (Bowman 2000: 85). Myths are integral to sacred narratives, representing our relationship with ancestors, the supernatural and the natural world. According to Roland Barthes, myth 'transforms history into nature' (Barthes 1994: 129), and for Jaan Puhvel, myth brings the sacred past to bear on the present and the future (Puhvel 1987: 2). I am particularly concerned here with 'origin' myths and how they relate to medieval sacred sites and the nationalist and religious narratives associated with them – what we might term 'Golden Age' stories.

THE 'GOLDEN AGE': AUTHENTICITY AND NATIONALIST NARRATIVES

The reciprocal relationship between archaeological practice and nation states was highlighted by Bruce Trigger over thirty years ago (Trigger 1984). He demonstrated that archaeology could serve alternative interpretations of the past, depending on whether the state concerned is nationalist, imperialist or colonialist in outlook. Subsequent work has emphasised the socio-political context of archaeology and how archaeological approaches and practices may lend themselves to nationalist arguments (Díaz-Andreu and Champion 1996; Habu, Fawcett and Matsunaga 2008). Nationalism seeks refuge in archaeology's emphasis on continuity and the rootedness of material traditions to particular places, territories and ethnic groups. Above all, archaeologists and nationalists share a 'profound concern with the authenticity of material culture' (Smith 2001: 441), resulting in archaeology's vulnerability to appropriation by right-wing groups who are drawn to 'Golden Age' narratives. Nationalist narratives look particularly to sacred sites to embody the 'Golden Age' when a nation was most heroic and authentically itself, before what may be perceived as later accretions caused by religious conversion, military conquest or mass migration (Smith 2001: 445). To give a contemporary example, far-right political parties in Scandinavia are promoting heritage in their attempts to combat the current forces of globalisation and non-Western immigration, with particular focus on Christian heritage (Niklasson and Hølleland 2018: 126). Recent shifts in global politics, in the UK including uncertainties around Brexit and Scottish independence, have once again highlighted the urgency of these questions for archaeologists. There is a renewed concern to understand the relationship between archaeology and nationalism and how this intersects with questions of identity, the study of migration and the practice and funding of archaeology (Brück and Nilsson Stutz 2016).

The most powerful evocations of nationhood bring together religious and secular power, for example landscapes of sacral kingship such as Tara, the traditional seat of the kings of Ireland, and Gamla Uppsala in Sweden, the burial place of kings and the cult centre of Old Norse religion (Bhreathnach 2005; Ljungkvist and Frölund 2015). Archaeologists were active in forging nationalist connections with monuments and landscapes in the eighteenth and nineteenth centuries, but nationalist myths have continued to interact with archaeological scholarship in the twentieth and twenty-first centuries. This process is particularly clear in the emergence of Irish archaeology around the Celtic 'Golden Age' narrative and its continued relevance in shaping research to the present day (O'Sullivan 1998). The central figure in this movement was George Petrie (1790–1866), the founder of scientific archaeology in Ireland but also a leading proponent of Celtic nationalism. His aim was to bring together Catholics and Protestants in a common love of their shared descent from the ancient Celts (Cooney 1996: 151–5; Hutchinson 2001: 506). Petrie collected objects for the Royal Irish Academy such as the Tara Brooch and the Armagh Chalice, both dated to the eighth century CE, and he worked with landscape artists to promote early medieval monastic landscapes such as Clonmacnoise (Offaly). His archaeological scholarship presented a new image of Celtic Ireland based on the Christian period of the eighth to eleventh century, before this (allegedly) utopian Celtic culture was shattered by Anglo-Norman invasion (Hutchinson 2001: 508). Christian artefacts were widely adopted as symbols of Celtic heritage in Irish architecture, arts and crafts and popular culture (Sheehy 1980). Far from uniting the sectarian divide, however, both Catholics and Protestants employed Early Christian archaeology to authenticate their own narratives. For Catholics, archaeology confirmed a vision of the sacred Celtic past, brutally undermined by the barbaric Normans; for Protestants, archaeology revealed the pristine Christianity of the Celts, before the corruption of Roman Catholicism in the twelfth century (Hutchinson 2001: 513). The 'Golden Age' narrative continued to impact on the development of medieval archaeology in Ireland throughout the twentieth century, by privileging the study of Irish ecclesiastical sites of the early medieval period over those of the later medieval period (O'Sullivan 1998; O'Sullivan et al. 2014).

Archaeologists in Britain were less overtly political in their use of medieval sacred sites and material culture, reflecting their cultural inheritance as the colonisers rather than the colonised. However, they were no less active in promoting 'Golden Age' narratives. For example, the renowned Egyptologist Margaret Murray drew on the evidence of sculptural carvings in medieval churches in Britain to argue that paganism had survived into the Middle Ages and subsisted harmoniously alongside Christianity (Hutton 2014: 347). She was the first to suggest that sheela-na-gigs, carved female figures exposing their genitalia, were icons of ancient fertility goddesses that continued to be worshipped by medieval people (Murray 1934). Around the same time, Julia (Lady) Raglan argued that the foliate carved heads common in medieval English churches were 'green men' and that they represented the persistent survival into the Middle Ages of a pagan fertility god (Raglan 1939). These interpretations were accepted for decades, before historians in the 1970s challenged the pagan reading of medieval church images and other sources of evidence. Despite scholarly critiques, these interpretations continue to inform modern Pagan Wicca beliefs, while sheela-na-gigs have been adopted as a feminist symbol and green men are a popular icon for the environmentalist movement (Hutton 2014: 347–51).

Following the Second World War, medieval archaeologists actively promoted British (Celtic) national heritage as distinct from Anglo-Saxon (Germanic) heritage. This is reflected in the popular search for Arthur, as demonstrated by the work of the Camelot Research Committee at Cadbury Castle (Alcock 1972; Paphitis 2013). Nationalist myths were connected to sacred sites such as Whithorn (Dumfries and Galloway) and Glastonbury (Somerset), where archaeological research agendas were shaped by Celtic

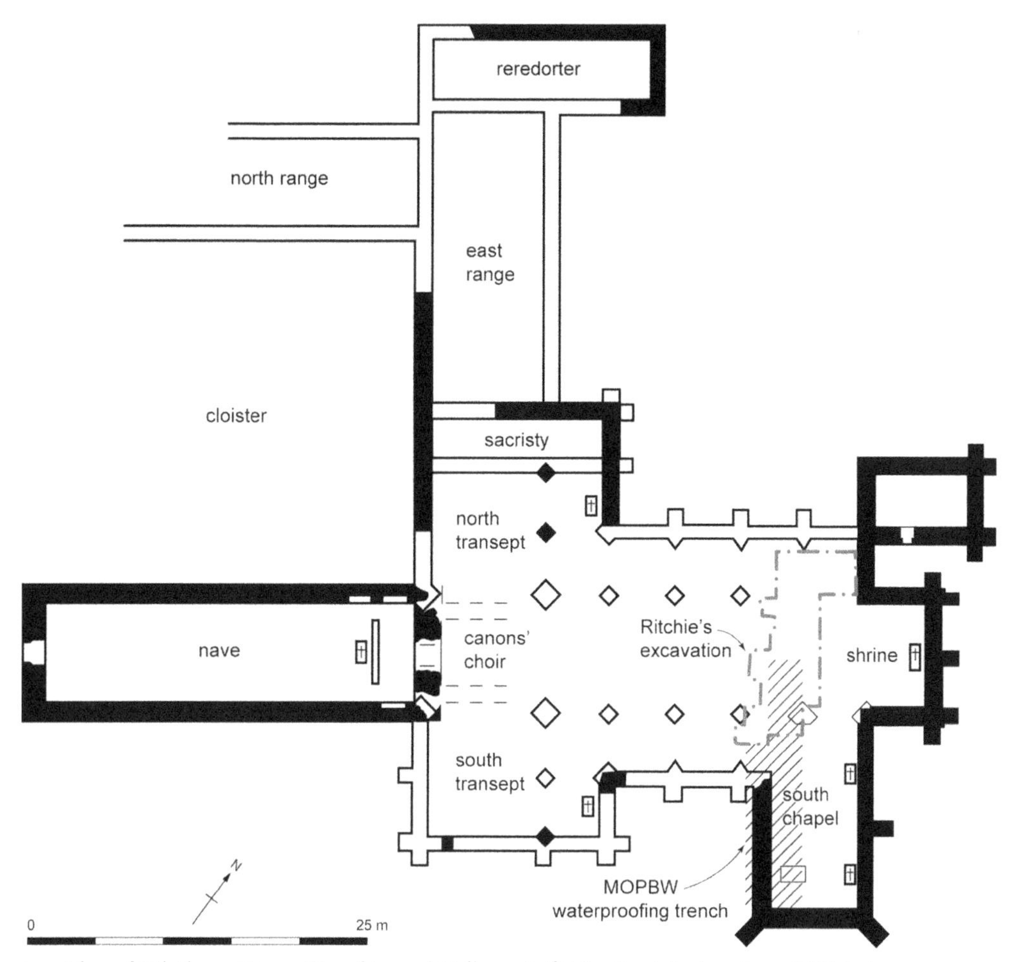

6.1 Plan of Whithorn Priory (Dumfries and Galloway). © Headland Archaeology (UK) Ltd

hagiography and narratives. Both sites are promoted as 'the cradle of Christianity', in Scotland and England respectively. St Ninian was first documented by Bede, *c.*731, and he is popularly regarded as having founded Whithorn (*Candida Casa*) in the early fifth century. Glastonbury's claim to religious primacy is based on the legend of the 'old church' (*vetusta ecclesia*) first recorded in the tenth century, and by the fourteenth century regarded as the earliest church in Britain, believed to have been founded by Joseph of Arimathea in the first century CE (see Chapter 5 for discussion). The sacred narratives attached to these sites have frequently clouded interpretations of the archaeological evidence.

From 1957–67, Roy Ritchie excavated a series of graves near the high altar of the cathedral church at Whithorn (discussed in Chapter 4) (Figures 6.1 and 6.2). The leading church archaeologists of the day assembled at Whithorn to pronounce their views on the sequence – Stewart Cruden, Ralegh Radford and Charles Thomas. They believed that the graves spanned a period of 1,000

6.2 Photograph of burials during excavation of Whithorn Priory (Dumfries and Galloway). © Crown Copyright: Historic Environment Scotland

years, connecting St Ninian's *Candida Casa* with the late medieval cathedral priory at Whithorn. They published interim statements claiming a late Roman cremation cemetery as well as Early Christian burials (Thomas 1971: 55). In his reassessment of Ritchie's excavations, Christopher Lowe describes their collective views as a 'suite of unsubstantiated claims relating to the origins of the site'. He suggests that Ritchie's failure to publish the excavations may have been caused by his inability to reconcile the archaeological evidence with the claims made by these very senior and influential figures (Lowe 2009: 177, 167). Fresh analysis and radiocarbon dating confirms that the Whithorn graves span a period of only 400 years, beginning in the twelfth century. They have no bearing on our understanding of Whithorn's origins, or the story of St Ninian's foundation. Lowe concludes that the complete absence of first millennium material from Ritchie's excavations demands reassessment of the presumed relationship of the medieval cathedral priory with the preceding Northumbrian ecclesiastical settlement (Lowe 2009: 178).

The figure most closely associated with excavations at Glastonbury Abbey is Courtenay Arthur Ralegh Radford, who excavated at the site from 1951–64 (Figure 6.3). As well as his involvement with Glastonbury and Whithorn, he excavated at numerous sites in southwest England, Scotland, Ireland and the Isle of Man. Radford was a committed Christian, describing himself as 'High Anglo-Catholic'. His personal beliefs were reflected in his scholarship: he

6.3 Courtenay Arthur Ralegh Radford (left) at Glastonbury Abbey (Somerset) in 1962. Reproduced by kind permission of Peter Poyntz Wright

advocated the study of the post-Roman period as 'Early Christian archaeology' and he pioneered the study of Celtic monasticism in western Britain (Gilchrist 2013). He was a strong proponent of Glastonbury's 'Golden Age', and presented the abbey's archaeology within a Celtic framework. He acknowledged that his excavations at the abbey had discovered virtually no evidence for a religious community earlier than the eighth century CE. This absence of evidence did not deter him: he described a Christian community at Glastonbury 'in Celtic times' and considered the abbey as one part of the 'holy city' of the Isle of Avalon (Radford 1981). He even ventured that Glastonbury was a pagan holy place of the ancient Celts, drawing on the tenuous evidence of early Irish saints mentioned in the abbey's later medieval chronicles (Radford 1968).

Radford interpreted the archaeological sequence at Glastonbury within a framework defined by Celtic hagiography and legend. His Christian beliefs also affected his field practice – for example, he was opposed to the disturbance of Christian skeletons, a rare ethical stance in the 1950s. After minimal recording, skeletons at Glastonbury were left in situ and covered over again with soil (Gilchrist and Green 2015: 425). Radford's site chronology was defined by historical references to individuals and events, in particular to St Dunstan (909–88 CE), the abbot who revived Glastonbury in the mid-tenth century and went on to reform English monasticism as archbishop of Canterbury. The twelfth-century historian William of Malmesbury recorded that St Dunstan had enclosed the cemetery and raised the ground level as part of his rebuilding of the abbey in the tenth century. Radford's excavations in the cemetery identified a layer of redeposited clay as the material that was laid down by Dunstan; he assigned a tenth-century date by virtue of the description in William of Malmesbury. Clay makeup layers in the cemetery were identified thereafter as a tenth-century horizon ('St Dunstan's clay'). Radford also interpreted structural remains through the prism of the tenth-century *Life of Dunstan* (dated *c.*955).

Glastonbury flourished under Dunstan, who substantially rebuilt and reformed the monastery. According to the *vita*, he 'first surrounded the cloisters on every side with solid monastery buildings' and enclosed the monks' cemetery with a stone wall (Winterbottom and Lapidge 2012: 50–1). Radford found structural evidence that could be dated to the late Saxon period – but his interpretation of the archaeology was shaped by his desire to locate Dunstan's cloister. He claimed to have found evidence for the earliest cloister in England, represented by narrow claustral ranges surrounding a courtyard measuring 55 m by 36 m (Figure 6.4). This evidence has been widely accepted and repeated as confirmation of the influence of Dunstan and the importance of Glastonbury in reforming the character of English monasticism in the tenth century (e.g. Fernie 1983: 85–6). Traces of the three claustral ranges were uncovered during separate excavation campaigns in the 1930s, the 1950s and the 1970s. Radford connected them on the basis of his personal memory of observed similarities in the masonry construction; there were no proven stratigraphic relationships and there is no evidence that they are all of the same date. When the excavated remains are mapped, it is clear that the eastern walls of the supposed eastern range are misaligned. There is no proof that the structures to the north and south of the refectory were connected or that the junction of two rooms to the south of the refectory represents the meeting of a south and east range. The archaeological evidence is insufficient to reconstruct a full cloister as envisaged by Radford (Gilchrist and Green 2015: 394–5).

Instead, it appears that several free-standing masonry structures were located across the area of the later west cloister, south of the refectory, and possibly below the later abbot's hall. The buildings in the area of the later west cloister and refectory are sealed by twelfth-century deposits and therefore may be late Saxon in date. However, the plan evidence based on recent study of the archaeological archive does not correspond with the cloister reconstructed by Radford. It is likely that his identification of a cloister relied heavily on the *Life*

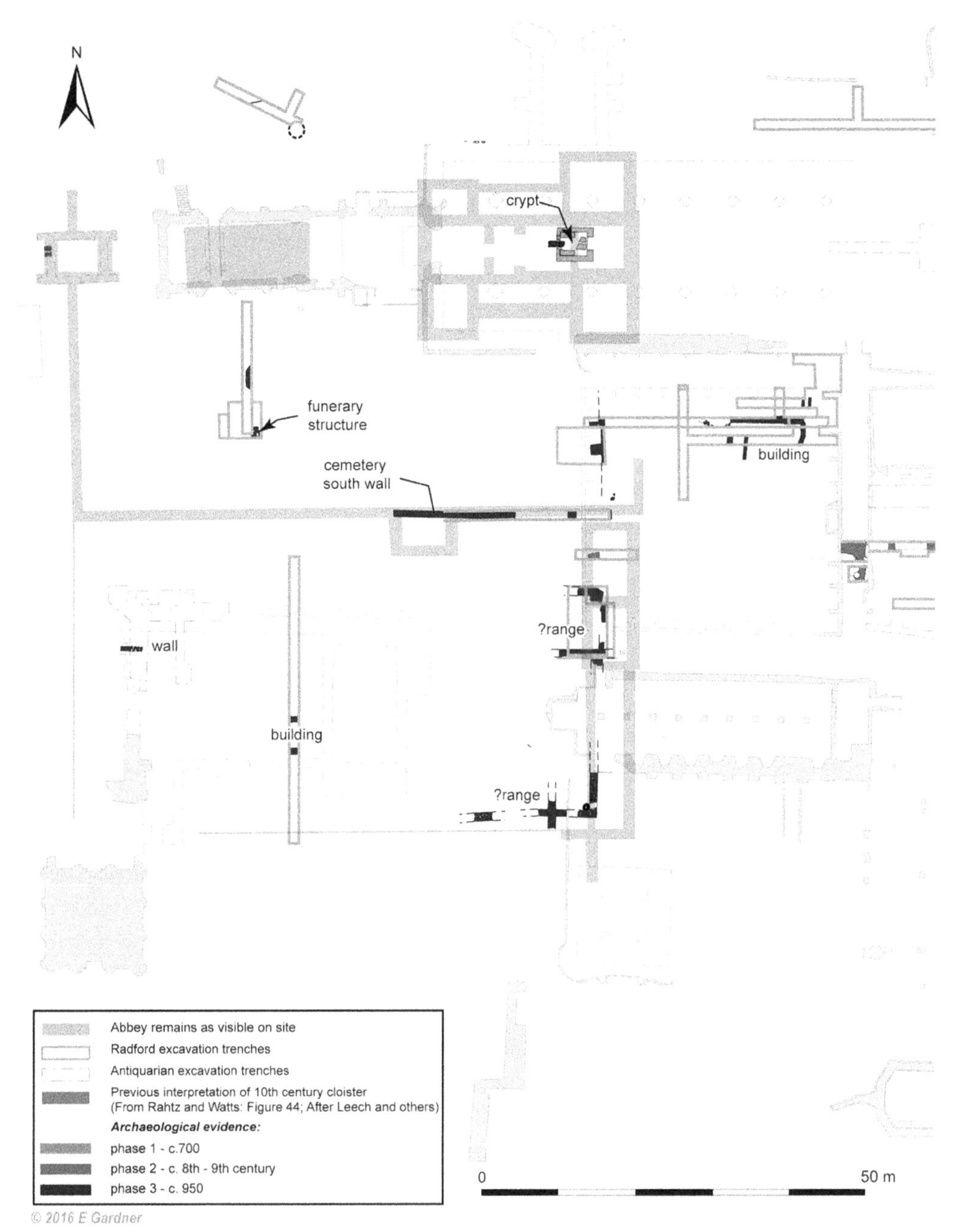

6.4 Plan showing archaeological evidence relating to Radford's Saxon 'cloister' at Glastonbury Abbey (Somerset) © Liz Gardner

of St Dunstan, which described Dunstan's devotion to the Rule of St Benedict and his building of a cloister. It is important to note that the Latin term *claustrum* can refer either to an enclosure or a formal cloister. On comparison with excavated monastic sites such as Jarrow (Cramp 2005), we know that free-standing stone ranges are more typical of accommodation at English monasteries right up to the late eleventh century. On the evidence available, it seems unlikely that Glastonbury possessed a formal cloister before the twelfth century (Gilchrist and Green 2015: 420). Dunstan's cloister is a Christian 'Golden Age' story, one perpetuated by Radford and repeated by subsequent archaeologists and architectural historians.

Radford also projected the Celtic 'Golden Age' narrative onto Glastonbury. He regarded the post-Roman period in the southwest of Britain as a heroic age linked to the figure of King Arthur; he investigated a series of sites with Arthurian connections, including Glastonbury, Tintagel, Castle Dore and Cadbury Castle (Radford and Swanton 1975). In 1962–3, he deliberately searched for Arthur's grave at Glastonbury Abbey, using medieval accounts to identify the approximate location in the cemetery. He located a large pit and reported to the press that this was the exhumation site of 1191, where the monks of Glastonbury claimed to have found the remains of Arthur and Guinevere (Gransden 2001; see Chapter 5). He argued that the pit had been dug out and then shortly afterward refilled in the 1190s. The evidence for his precise dating was based on the presence of chippings of Doulting stone, which Radford assumed was first used at Glastonbury in rebuilding the Lady Chapel shortly after the great fire of 1184. At the base of the pit were two cist graves that Radford believed to be sixth century in date. He claimed that the cist graves and the Doulting stone provided dating evidence for the supposed grave to be sixth century or later, and the exhumation event to be around 1190.

These dates matched the documented date of the alleged exhumation of Arthur by the monks in 1191, and the approximate date of the legendary king's death in the sixth century. In an interview with a local newspaper, Radford is quoted as saying 'I have always been one of the historians who believed Arthur to be an historical character and today I have added additional proof' (*The Western Morning News*, 15 August 1963). His findings were widely reported and accepted as conclusive evidence by the media, who in the 1960s displayed a touching confidence in the value of experts: 'to the untrained eye the discovery means nothing ... a patch of dark earth with a few stones protruding' (*Central Somerset Gazette*, 16 August 1963). Recent reassessment of Radford's archaeological archive has challenged his dating evidence and refuted the identification of Arthur's grave (Gilchrist and Green 2015: 394). The cist graves were cut into a layer of redeposited clay that was believed to be associated with levelling of the cemetery in the tenth century ('St Dunstan's clay'). In other words, the cist graves must be later than the clay, which is likely tenth century in date. Similar cists burials excavated at nearby Winchester Cathedral and Wells Cathedral have been dated to the later eleventh century (Rodwell 2001). Doulting stone is now recognised as the principal building material used in all phases of Glastonbury Abbey: Doulting has been identified among the

Anglo-Saxon carved stone from the abbey and was certainly used before the rebuilding of the Lady Chapel in the last decade of the twelfth century. Pottery associated with the pit dates from the twelfth to the fifteenth century. Fresh analysis of the archaeological archive therefore confirms that the feature Radford located in 1963 was merely a refuse pit and not a robbed early grave.

At Glastonbury and Whithorn in the mid-twentieth century, archaeologists were concerned first and foremost to authenticate origin myths, the stories that connected sacred sites to a 'Golden Age' of Celtic saints and heroic kings. Today, the pendulum has swung full circle, with archaeologists more likely to argue that early monasteries had their origins in secular, royal settlements (e.g. Thomas 2013). Excavations at Whithorn recovered a large quantity of imported, coloured glass from drinking vessels, perhaps more consistent with the consumption pattern of a secular site than a monastery (Forsyth and Maldonado 2013). Reassessment of the archive at Glastonbury Abbey revealed sherds of late Roman pottery (LRA1) confirming the presence of amphorae imported from the eastern Mediterranean carrying wine and oil, dated *c.*450–550 CE (Gilchrist and Green 2015: 416; see Chapter 5, Figure 5.4). The precise character of Glastonbury in the fifth or sixth century remains unclear, but it is possible that both Whithorn and Glastonbury originated as high status secular sites.

AUTHENTICATING SACRED SITES: PRESERVATION, REPLICATION AND THE PROOF OF ARCHAEOLOGY

In addition to feeding nationalist narratives, archaeological evidence has been harnessed by faith communities to authenticate the spiritual authority of sacred sites. Religious communities were reinstated on the sites of ruined abbeys throughout Europe in the nineteenth century, for example as part of the 'religious revival' in France and Belgium after the trauma and destruction of the French Revolution (Coomans 2012). Monasteries were also revived as an expression of regional identity; for instance, Landévennec Abbey was restored during the 1920s and 1930s by the Breton nationalist movement, as the symbol of historic Brittany (Tranvouez 2015). Three British case studies are considered here: Glastonbury, Walsingham and Iona were all reinstated as sacred sites in the twentieth century, with archaeology, preservation and replication playing different roles in each case.

The village of Walsingham in Norfolk is known as 'England's Nazareth' (Janes and Waller 2010). It was the site of a major medieval shrine to the Virgin Mary, second only to Canterbury as a destination for medieval pilgrimage in England (Marks 2004: 193–7). Souvenirs of Walsingham are amongst the most numerous examples of surviving medieval pilgrims' badges and ampullae, concentrated in East Anglia but distributed throughout Britain (Locker and Lewis 2015). The cult was sparked by a vision of the Virgin Mary, who appeared in 1061 to a wealthy Anglo-Saxon widow, Richelde de Faverches. The Virgin instructed Richelde to build a wooden replica of the House of the Annunciation, the site where Mary was visited by the Angel Gabriel, who brought news that she carried the Christ Child. The replica Holy House at Walsingham was believed to be modelled on the precise dimensions of the original in Nazareth, reproducing a biblical space in medieval Norfolk (Coleman 2004: 55). A statue of the Virgin was installed within it and an Augustinian priory was built on the site in 1153 (Knowles and Hadcock 1971). There was also a Franciscan friary and a wayside chapel for pilgrims, known as the Slipper Chapel, located 2.4 km (1.5 miles) from the village (Figure 6.5).

6.5 Slipper Chapel, Walsingham (Norfolk). Reproduced by kind permission of Graham Howard

Like Glastonbury, an example was made of Walsingham at the Dissolution, with eleven monks and choristers put to death following a rebellion in 1537. The priory and shrine were destroyed in the following year. In contrast with Glastonbury, however, the site and its legends lay dormant until the late nineteenth century, when interest was revived by the combined forces of Catholic emancipation, the Oxford Movement and the rise of antiquarianism. The Slipper Chapel was the first site in Walsingham to be restored as a focus for Catholic pilgrimage. It was purchased in 1896 by a wealthy local heiress, Charlotte Boyd (1837–1906), after she had visited Glastonbury Abbey and identified her life's work in the restoration of medieval monastic buildings (Coleman 2004: 55). She restored the chapel, and following her conversion to Catholicism, she placed it in the care of Downside Abbey (Somerset), the senior Benedictine monastery in England. Attempts were also made to purchase the site of the Augustinian priory at Walsingham but these were unsuccessful. The Slipper Chapel emerged as a major site of pilgrimage in 1934, when it was declared the Catholic National Shrine of Our Lady, in a national pilgrimage event attended by at least 10,000 people.

A rival Anglican shrine was established in 1931 by Walsingham's high Anglican priest, Alfred Hope Patten (1885–1958) (Yelton 2006). He secured land in the village and built his own replica of the Holy House, incorporating a statue of Our Lady of Walsingham (Figure 6.6). Patten's writings acknowledge the fierce competition between the Anglican and Catholic shrines throughout these years (Coleman 2004: 58). The Catholic shrine was located at the original Slipper Chapel, an authentic locale associated with the medieval cult of Walsingham. Patten's shrine had no direct spatial connection to the medieval site of the Holy House. Instead, he created a sense of authenticity through replication, using architectural reconstruction and incorporating medieval spolia. He collected 170 fragments of medieval carved stones from the sites of dissolved medieval monasteries and incorporated these within the walls of the new Holy House (Coleman 2004: 59). These stones were not from Walsingham but they were medieval and monastic, their materiality lending a borrowed sense

6.6 Anglican Shrine of Our Lady of Walsingham (Norfolk). Reproduced by kind permission of Graham Howard

6.7 Pilgrimage at Walsingham (Norfolk). Reproduced by kind permission of Graham Howard

of 'age-value' to the new shrine (Holtorf 2013a). In digging the foundations for his replica, Patten claimed that he had found archaeological evidence for a holy well associated with the medieval Holy House. He reconstructed the well next to the replica Holy House, implying that it occupied the original space of Richeldis's building. Patten even claimed to have experienced spiritual visions of medieval Augustinian canons, who materialised to confirm the accuracy of his reconstruction (Coleman 2004: 59). Today, religious competition at Walsingham is mediated by ecumenicalism and the concern with historical authenticity is less overt. The pilgrimage experience focuses instead on processions and movement through the landscape, including a barefoot pilgrimage of the 'holy mile' from the Slipper Chapel into Walsingham village (Figure 6.7).

Similar concerns with material authenticity can be seen at the sites of medieval monasteries that were reinstated as religious houses in the twentieth century. For example, the substantial ruins of the thirteenth-century nunnery at Burnham (Buckinghamshire) were acquired by the Society of the Precious Blood in 1916. An Anglican convent was established on the site and efforts were made to reuse the medieval spaces for their original religious purpose. The community adopted the Augustinian Rule that had been followed by the medieval nuns and they revived the most austere elements of medieval religious practice. For instance, they observe a daily watch before the Blessed Sacrament, lying prostrate before the altar, and at one time they supported an enclosed anchoress as part of the twentieth-century community (Gilchrist 1989). Comparisons can be made with the abbey of Pluscarden (Moray), originally founded in 1230 by Alexander II as a Valliscaulian priory (Fawcett 1994a: 70–2). The monastic ruins were extensive but poorly conserved when they were given in 1943 by Lord Colum Crichton-Stuart to the Catholic community of Prinknash Abbey (Gloucestershire). The site was re-established as an abbey in 1948 and continues to welcome visitors on religious retreat, many of whom engage in manual labour in keeping with the values of the medieval Valliscaulian order. At both Burnham and Pluscarden, authenticity is established through place, materiality and embodiment, nurturing a sense of continuity and personal identification with medieval religious experience. Continuity of place reinforces the sense of 'timelessness' that is a characteristic experience of sacred heritage sites (see Chapter 1), a ritual space of 'otherness' that exists outside of real time (Andriotis 2011; Shackley 2002).

6.8 George Fielden MacLeod (1895–1991). © The Scotsman Publications Ltd

Perhaps the most interesting case of medieval replication is that of Iona (Scottish Inner Hebrides), where the Iona Community was established in 1938 by George Fielden MacLeod (1895–1991) (Figure 6.8). MacLeod was Oxford educated and heir to a baronetcy, yet he was ordained as a Church of Scotland minister and developed a lifelong concern with social inequality, pacifism and ecumenicalism (Ferguson 2001). His ministry in Govan during the depression of the 1930s brought him into direct contact with the most austere poverty and social deprivation. His goal was to train ministers in a different way of thinking, to bring them together with working men in a common goal. His vision focused on rebuilding the monastic quarters of the medieval abbey of Iona, with the shared labour of reconstruction shaping a new religious movement. A contemporary observer recalls:

> George thought something new was needed – an experiment – and it came down to this: why not rebuild the ancient buildings on Iona where he'd often been on holiday? As Columba had experimented in Christian living and sharing, why not get a team and go there?
>
> (Uist Macdonald, quoted in Muir 2011: 15)

Iona had attracted artists, writers and antiquaries from the late eighteenth century onwards (Christian and Stiller 2000). The abbey church had been

6.9 Craftsmen at Iona Abbey reconstructing the refectory in 1939 (Scottish Inner Hebrides). © Newsquest (Herald & Times)

restored in the late nineteenth and early twentieth centuries: the choir, transepts and crossing from 1902–5 and the nave from 1908–10 (RCAHMS 1982: 55). This work pre-dated the Iona Community and was completed according to a different conservation ethic, with the work praised subsequently for its 'scholarly restraint' (RCAHMS 1982: 27). The monastic ruins were given by the Duke of Argyll into the care of the Iona Cathedral Trust on the condition that they were used for worship by all denominations (Power 2006: 38).

MacLeod persuaded the trustees to permit him to reconstruct the abbey buildings and he collected the funds and personnel to enable his vision (Muir 2011: 15). He recruited young ministers, while a master mason, Bill Amos, convinced skilled craftsmen to spend their summers in Iona working alongside them (Muir 2011: 19, 152) (Figure 6.9). The restoration was carried out to the design of architect Ian G. Lindsay (1906–66), and took place over summer months from 1938 to 1965 (RCAHMS 1982: 55). The abbey's medieval buildings were well-preserved; for example, parts of the east range and the refectory stood intact almost to the level of the wall-head (Figure 6.10). Only the west range was a completely modern addition (dated 1965) and did not reuse medieval footings. St Michael's Chapel, the infirmary (now museum) and the lavatory block were also reconstructed from medieval remains (Muir 2011: 125–37). The rebuilding copied medieval detail where possible; for

6.10 Iona Abbey (Scottish Inner Hebrides) before restoration (*c.*1874). © Royal Commission on the Ancient and Historical Monuments of Scotland

example, the cloister arcades built in 1959 were modelled on the early thirteenth-century cloister (Muir 2011: 123–4). Today, the church and monastic complex appear deceptively homogeneous, due to the consistent use of the same local building materials.

MacLeod's model for the lifestyle of the Iona Community was grounded in monasticism, as well as his own military training during the First World War. He forged a masculine community based on discipline, manual labour, daily worship and the communal life, which included sharing meals, labour and leisure (Muir 2011: 28). This fellowship was entirely male – married men had to leave their wives behind in Glasgow. The first woman was admitted to the Iona Community only thirty years later, in 1969, after MacLeod had stepped down (Power 2006: 39). MacLeod was influential in framing Iona as a 'thin place', a concept that has become central to the Celtic spiritual revival. This refers to the idea that in certain sacred places, the 'veil is thin' between this world and the next. He used this term repeatedly from the 1930s onwards, drawing on biblical references to the veil of the Temple (Hebrews 6:19; 2 Corinthians) to emphasise the thin separation of the material world from the spiritual realm (Power 2006: 45). In Celtic spirituality, 'thin places' are believed to allow spiritual seekers to hear and see God more clearly. It is a central concept in the development of Protestant pilgrimage practices in modern Britain, one which does not carry the Catholic overtones of medieval pilgrimage traditions. The concept of 'thin places' also resonates with the eremitic tradition of Celtic monasticism, with its close connection to nature and a sense of living on the edge of the world (Walton 2015: 34–5) (Figure 6.11).

MacLeod was interested in the spiritual authenticity of place and the physical act of reconstruction – but he was not troubled by specific details of archaeology. He manipulated historical and archaeological evidence to support his version of Iona's past, with apparently little challenge from the academic community (Power 2006: 48). A telling example is the reconstruction of St Columba's Shrine, completed in 1962 to the architectural design of Ian Lindsay. Archaeological evidence for a critical feature was omitted: the side walls originally extended to the west to form antae, or buttresses in the Irish tradition, that indicate a date of the ninth to tenth century (RCAHMS 1982: 42). This lack of attention to archaeological evidence is significant, given that the architect, Lindsay, was a close personal friend of J. S. Richardson, principal inspector of Ancient Monuments for Scotland. Richardson had intervened personally to ensure that Lindsay received the commission for the work at Iona (*Dictionary of Scottish Architects*).

Archaeological input came surprisingly late to Iona: limited recording took place in relation to clearance operations in the 1870s and architectural conservation in the 1940s (O'Sullivan 1999: 223; RCAHMS 1982: 137). Lindsay made some attempt to involve the architect and archaeologist Edwin William Lovegrove (1868–1956) in the work at Iona. However, this proposal was rejected by both the Iona Community and the Ancient Monuments inspectorate (Ian Fisher, pers. comm.). The first serious excavations did not take place until work for the Russell Trust, led by Charles Thomas from 1956–63 (RCAHMS 1982: 224; Campbell and Maldonado 2016). Rescue excavations in the 1960s responded to proposals for new buildings put forward by the Iona Community, with small-scale research excavations targeted on the claustral complex in the 1970s, after the architectural reconstruction was completed (Reece 1981).

The reinstatement of Glastonbury Abbey as a sacred site could not have been more different. Archaeology and preservation of fabric were central to the endeavour and efforts to reconstruct or replicate medieval fabric were limited. The site of Glastonbury Abbey was offered for sale in 1906, featuring the monastic ruins in the landscaped park of Abbey House, a gentleman's residence built in 1830. There was national interest and speculation that the ruins would be purchased either by the government for the nation or by the Catholic Church. The site was eventually purchased for the Church of England by the Diocese of Bath and Wells, for the sum of £30,000 (Gilchrist

6.11 Iona Abbey (Scottish Inner Hebrides). © Mick Sharp

and Green 2015: 9). This is a unique case of the Anglican Church actively acquiring a medieval monastic ruin, one perceived as a national shrine that they wished kept in Anglican control. A leading conservation architect, W. D. Caroe (1857–1938), was appointed by the abbey trustees and archaeological excavations were commissioned immediately to inform the site's conservation and interpretation. Frederick Bligh Bond (1864–1945), architect to the Diocese of Bath and Wells, was appointed as the first director of the archaeological programme, conducting excavations from 1908–21. The trustees intended the excavations to clear and consolidate the ruins and to trace the earliest Saxon and Norman churches (Gilchrist and Green 2015: 9–17).

However, the abbey's first archaeologist was driven by a personal research agenda linked to his own spiritual motives. Frederick Bligh Bond was intensely interested in the legendary history of Glastonbury and he is regarded as a pioneering figure of the New Age movement. His investigations integrated psychic experiments, dowsing and spiritualism, the belief that the spirits of the dead can communicate with the living. He developed his own interpretation of spiritualism, proposing that ancient memories from the unconscious could be channelled through the medium of automatic writing (Hopkinson-Ball 2007: 113). Automatic writing is an alleged ability to produce written words from a subconscious, spiritual or supernatural source. This psychic method gained currency in the late nineteenth and early twentieth centuries, with celebrated proponents including Sir Arthur Conan Doyle. Psychic methods also guided archaeological investigations at the Cistercian abbey of Villers (Belgium) in 1938, where the Jesuit Father Lepers used divination based on the alleged detection of emitted radiation (Coomans 2005: 54). At Glastonbury, Bond attempted to use archaeology both to verify Glastonbury's legendary history and to validate his methods of psychic research. He sought archaeological proof of the connection with Joseph of Arimathea and his foundation of a church at Glastonbury in 63 CE, after historians had begun to question the veracity of the documentary sources (Hopkinson-Ball 2007: 183). This approach can be compared with early biblical archaeology, and indeed one of Bond's patrons in this work was Sir Charles Marston, the wealthy chairman of Villiers Engineering, who was a great exponent of biblical archaeology.

Bond's second proof was more unorthodox: he used archaeological excavation as a method to prove the scientific value of automatic writing. This is best illustrated by the celebrated case of the Edgar Chapel, located at the eastern termination of the abbey church. Automatic writing suggested to Bond that the Edgar Chapel had an apsed termination, but this feature was not confirmed by his excavations. Despite the absence of archaeological evidence, Bond showed an apsed chapel on his published plans of the Edgar Chapel and reconstructed the apse on site in 1909, using large concrete blocks. In a book published in 1918, he revealed that his excavations at the abbey had been an extended experiment in psychical research: *The Gates of Remembrance: The Story of the Psychological Experiment which resulted in the Discovery of the Edgar Chapel at Glastonbury* (Bond 1918). Bond considered his psychical research to be entirely consistent with his commitment to Christianity; indeed, he argued that he was conducting 'sacred archaeology' at Glastonbury (Hopkinson-Ball 2008).

The Anglican trustees were surprisingly tolerant of these approaches. However, Bond was eventually dismissed in 1922, owing as much to controversy in his personal life and finances, as to irregularities in his archaeological field practice. Bond's reconstructed layout of the Edgar Chapel was quietly removed and the trustees appointed more traditional ecclesiologists to conduct excavations up to the outbreak of war in 1939, resuming in the 1950s and 1960s with the excavations led by Ralegh Radford (Gilchrist and Green 2015: 15). To the present day, Glastonbury Abbey has remained highly conservative in its site signage and presentation of the ruins to the public. There is no reconstruction of fabric and only minimal efforts have been made to show the layout of the church and cloister. The ruins are dominated by the Lady Chapel, also known as St Joseph's Chapel, which remains largely intact (see Figure 5.5). The chapel was built soon after the fire of 1184 destroyed the early church associated with the Arimathea legend (see Chapter 5). This hallowed structure represents the sacred heritage of Glastonbury Abbey and its claim to authenticity as the cradle of English Christianity. However, only those closely familiar with the Glastonbury legends would automatically connect the chapel with the Arimathea story. In their approaches to site presentation and conservation, the Glastonbury trustees have been starkly minimalist. The obvious question is this: why were the approaches of replication and reconstruction rejected at Glastonbury, when they were applied at Walsingham and Iona?

The answer lies in Glastonbury's engagement with emerging national policy on monument conservation and the impact of the Ancient Monuments Act 1913. The development of Glastonbury Abbey as a public monument took place at precisely the time when the English 'preservation ethic' was being established and when prominent medieval abbeys such as Rievaulx, Whitby and Fountains (North Yorkshire) were taken into 'guardianship' to preserve them for the nation (Emerick 2014). The key architect of this national plan was Sir Charles Peers (1868–1952), Chief Inspector of Ancient Monuments for the Ministry of Works. Peers promoted a distinctive approach to the preservation and display of ruins which aimed to preserve medieval authenticity – later fabric was stripped away to reveal the principal period of construction. Monuments were repaired or preserved 'as found', and set within simple, grassed lawns with minimal interpretation, projected as 'dead' monuments 'frozen' in time. Reconstruction was abhorrent to Peers and the emerging field of heritage professionals; replication was considered a threat to the integrity of medieval fabric (Emerick 2014: 83–98).

6.12 Glastonbury Abbey's Lady Chapel (Somerset) *c.*1900, before restoration. United States Library of Congress, Public Domain

The first phase of conservation work at Glastonbury disregarded the emerging philosophy on preservation. The conservation architect, Caroe, initiated major interventions to the Lady Chapel and the Galilee, reinstating a lost bay in the north wall, reconstructing the southwest corner turret and building a prominent new strainer arch to the east. Missing sections of wall-top were reinstated to their original height, possibly with the intention of re-roofing the Lady Chapel, a contentious proposal that was debated periodically by the trustees up to 1939. Caroe also undertook controversial works in the church which altered the profile of the ruin, rather than conserving it 'as found' (Figure 6.12). For example, he transformed the east wall of the crossing tower by facing the exposed core with ashlar in a series of curved corbels. The trustees' minutes indicate that they were not happy with the work and would have replaced it, had funds been available (Glastonbury Abbey Conservation Plan 2018).

Caroe's early work at Glastonbury (1908–13) was criticised locally and nationally. The Ancient Monuments Act 1913 provided the instrument for the state to intervene and Glastonbury Abbey was scheduled as a protected monument in 1915. Charles Peers reported his concerns about Glastonbury to the Ancient Monuments Board, describing Caroe's work as 'greatly in excess of anything needed for the preservation of ruins', and lamenting in private correspondence that Caroe's work to the Galilee was a 'beastly botch' (Glastonbury Abbey Conservation Plan 2018, citing PRO WORKS 14/691 071180/2 pt 1). Peers influenced work at Glastonbury from 1915 onwards, in his capacity as Chief Inspector of Ancient Monuments; he became more deeply involved as joint director of excavations at Glastonbury Abbey 1928–39, and subsequently as the abbey's conservation architect, following the death of Caroe in 1939. Under Peers's direction, the excavations at Glastonbury focused on the removal of building debris in order to consolidate the fabric, with very little disturbance to underlying deposits (Gilchrist and Green 2015: 12–15). Although Glastonbury Abbey is owned and managed by a private trust, it resembles an English Heritage guardianship site for all intents and purposes, even down to the Ministry of Works style signage that survives to the time of writing (2018). This reflects the personal involvement of Charles Peers and Glastonbury Abbey's close engagement with the national preservation ethic. The public presentation of Glastonbury Abbey projects a particular style of authenticity that emerged in the inter-war years, staging medieval monasteries as frozen in time and masking the substantial clearance and conservation works that were undertaken in the early twentieth century.

SPIRITUAL IDENTITIES: CONTESTED HERITAGE AND SACRED SITES

Multiple and competing religious narratives are frequently attached to sacred heritage sites: spiritual authority is contested and tensions emerge over access for the performance of religious rituals (see Chapter 1). These themes have been explored by archaeologists at World Heritage sites ranging from Stonehenge to Great Zimbabwe (Hodder 2008). At Stonehenge, pagan ritual engagement with the monument has come into conflict with the preservation ethic of heritage management. Votive offerings of candles and chalked symbols are regarded as a conservation threat to the stones and raucous celebrations are considered to compromise the quiet reverence deemed appropriate to a sacred site (Wallis and Blain 2003: 316). At Great Zimbabwe, interpretation and access are framed by the site's 'Authorized Heritage Discourse' (Smith 2006) as an early international trading site. There are also local understandings of the site among the Shona-speaking communities, including religious specialists (*masvikiro*) who claim to communicate with spirits who provide connections to ancestors (Fontein 2006). Joost Fontein's ethnographic study of Great Zimbabwe reveals that local religious understandings and sense of place have been silenced by dominant archaeological narratives. The local religious specialists believe that the ancestors have turned their backs on Zimbabwe due to desecration by archaeologists, including programmes of excavation, reconstruction and replication, and because traditional rituals are no longer permitted at the site. The ancestors used to whisper from the walls of Great Zimbabwe, but now they are silent.

Archaeologists have been alert to contemporary spiritual conflicts focusing on prehistoric sites, but they have not considered how these questions relate to sites of medieval Christianity. Medieval sacred sites in Britain are also subject to ongoing tensions over spiritual authority, ritual access and competing religious narratives. Early Christian sites such as Iona, Glastonbury and Lindisfarne remain highly significant to the Anglican and Catholic Churches, and they are also beacons for Celtic spirituality and neo-pagan beliefs. The 'new Celtic Twilight' movement emerged in the late twentieth century and in common with paganism, emphasises personal development and individual spiritual capabilities (Power 2006; Rountree 2006). Rosemary Power has set out the defining characteristics of Celtic Christianity. The movement emphasises: a focus on sense of place and interest in nature/environment; a connection with folk practices and the lives of early saints; belief that Celtic worship was spontaneous, incorporating dance, music and self-expression; belief in the equality of women in both the early Celtic church and today; a sense of liminality, being on the edge spiritually and organisationally; and distrust of ecclesiastical structures and rigid liturgy (Power 2006: 34). The Iona Community has found itself at the heart of this movement, although many of the values are completely opposed to George MacLeod's original vision, which was highly structured, institutional and male. The Community's commitment to ecumenicalism has enabled it to thrive and interact with late twentieth-century models of Celtic spirituality.

Glastonbury has attracted a diverse range of spiritual seekers for over a century. The abbey itself draws nearly 100,000 visitors each year, while the wider sacred landscape of Glastonbury entices many thousands more, followers of Christianity, Wicca and Druidry. The natural landscape is an important factor in Glastonbury's allure, combining with its religious ancestry to create a palpable sense of place. The abbey sits on a promontory above the surrounding marshlands; in the early Middle Ages, Glastonbury would have been a monastic island surrounded by water. A natural sandstone pinnacle towers over the abbey and town: Glastonbury Tor is visible for up to 25 miles (40 km) in all directions, crowned by the tower of the ruined medieval chapel of St Michael (Figure 6.13). In the early twentieth century, Glastonbury became the focal point for spiritual, creative and esoteric movements. A holy well located at the base of the Tor attracted a group of artists and spiritualists known as the Avalonians. The waters of Chalice Well contain iron oxides which leave a red deposit when dry – the red staining was explained through reference to the myth of Joseph of Arimathea (Mather 2009). It was claimed that when he arrived in Glastonbury, Joseph washed the Holy Grail in the spring, and

6.13 Glastonbury Tor (Somerset). © Mick Sharp

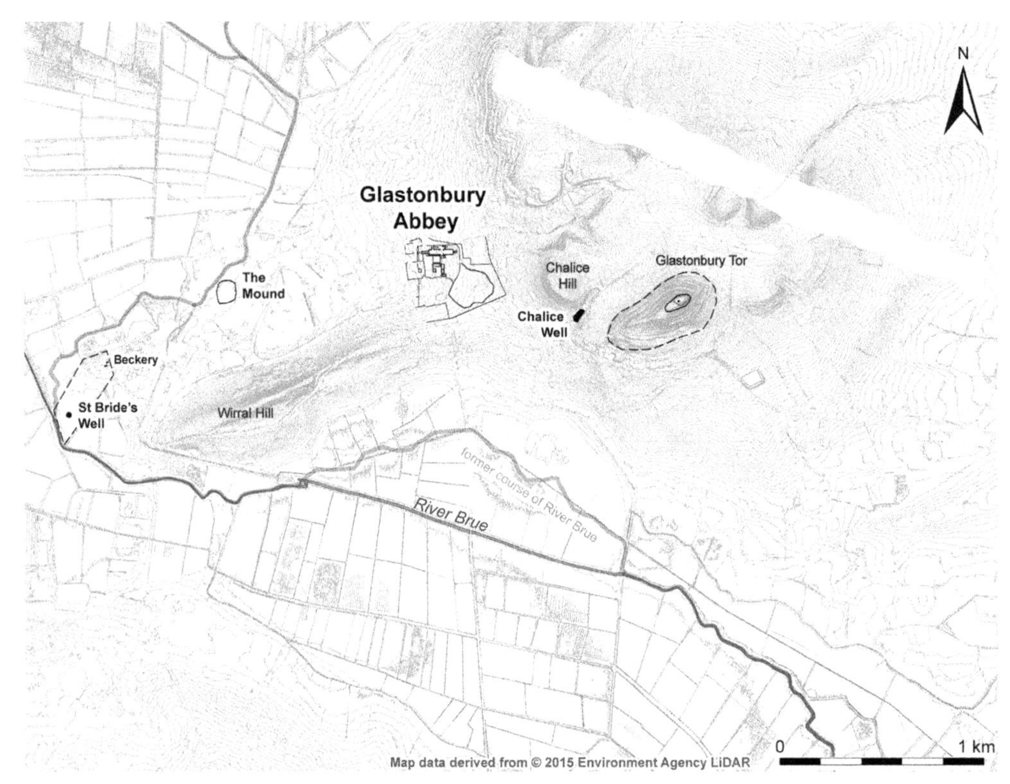

6.14 Sacred sites in Glastonbury (Somerset). © Liz Gardner

Christ's blood blessed the healing waters. The site was purchased by Alice Buckton in 1912, a Christian socialist, and she established a centre of traditional crafts at Chalice Well. Glastonbury became a place of pilgrimage for Christian mystics as well as a beacon for music and the performing arts (Hutton 2003: 63–4). Miss Buckton's Chalice Well School of Pageantry became the headquarters of the Glastonbury Crafts Guild and the Folk-Play and Festival Association. In 1914, the musical composer Rutland Boughton founded a community of musicians and artists at Glastonbury intended to rival London's musical establishment, and modelled on Wagner's Bayreuth. He established the first Glastonbury Festival, which survived until 1926, performing musical dramas based on Arthurian legends and taking inspiration from the abbey (Glastonbury Abbey Conservation Plan 2018). Glastonbury emerged as a magnet for the New Age from the 1970s, attracted by the modern Glastonbury Festival, which was established by Michael Eavis at nearby Pilton and has grown to be a leading international festival of performing arts.

Glastonbury is rare in the English religious tradition in representing a sacred landscape of multiple components, principally the abbey, the Tor and Chalice Well (Figure 6.14). It embodies the cult of 'topophilia', a term coined by W. H. Auden (1947) to describe how people experience a strong sense of place and how locations become integral to identity and belonging (Tuan 1990). Certain locations are believed to be inherently powerful and to have special qualities: the light, air, water and landscape of Glastonbury are believed to promote healing and creativity (Bowman 2000). Like Iona, Glastonbury is a 'thin place', where the boundary between the material and the spiritual is permeable. Many elements in the Glastonbury story appeal to currents in Celtic spirituality, such as identification with the landscape and a personal quest for enlightenment, embodied by the Grail legend. Alternative beliefs have developed surrounding the history of the landscape and they are stubbornly resistant to contradictory evidence from archaeologists. For example, it is widely accepted that ley lines were important in the laying out of the town, believed by some to be ancient or mystical alignments. The physical terrain itself is regarded as having been deliberately created for symbolic reasons: many believe that the landscape of Glastonbury Tor is shaped as a maze, zodiac or reclining goddess (Ashe 1979; Maltwood 1964). Since the 1960s, the terraces on the Tor have been popularly regarded as the remains of an ancient labyrinth, although archaeological survey has confirmed that the earthworks are medieval field systems likely dating to the thirteenth century (Hollinrake and Hollinrake 2003; Hutton 2014: 353–4). Glastonbury is heralded as both the site of an early Druidic university and a prehistoric centre of the goddess cult – these claims are promoted through web platforms and social media, without the need for supporting empirical evidence (Bowman 2009).

Glastonbury also appeals to the tendency in Celtic spirituality to celebrate a past 'Golden Age'. This manifests as a focus on the site's Celtic origins and the belief that Joseph of Arimathea founded a church of British Christianity, a purer form of native Christianity that pre-dated the Roman mission to England. Glastonbury's Arthur story also feeds the Celtic 'Golden Age' narrative: Arthur was a Celtic king who fought off Saxon invaders. Some still regard King Arthur as a messiah figure, who will rise again at Glastonbury to lead the New Age. Both Joseph and Arthur connect Glastonbury to an ancient, indigenous form of British religion, appealing to alternative spiritualities such as Druidry and Wicca, while alternative interpretations of the landscape have attracted feminist exponents of the goddess cult (Rountree 2006). There is also interest in the Celtic connections claimed by the medieval monks, in particular stories recorded by the abbey chroniclers that St Patrick and St Bridget visited the monastery in the fifth century. The medieval abbey claimed to have relics of St Bridget including a bag or wallet, a necklace, a small bell and some weaving implements (Carley 1996: 109). The legend of St Bridget is also associated with Bride's Mound, a small hill to the west of Wearyall Hill, in an area known as Beckery Island. Excavations at Beckery in the 1960s uncovered evidence for an early monastic site and cemetery of predominantly male burials, while the chronicle of Glastonbury Abbey records that an early nunnery had been located near Wearyall Hill (Rahtz and Watts 2003). Re-excavation of the site in 2016 was undertaken to obtain skeletons for scientific dating. Radiocarbon dates on seven skeletons revealed dates as early as the late fifth or early sixth century, continuing into the seventh to ninth centuries (Southwest Heritage Trust 2017).

The town of Glastonbury is a multivalent pilgrimage site that has generated a unique 'spiritual services industry', based on shops, galleries, spiritual therapies and psychic services (Bowman 2009). The religious scholar Marion Bowman describes it thus:

> Depending on whom you talk to, or what you read, Glastonbury is considered to be: the Isle of Avalon; the site of a great Druidic centre of learning; a significant prehistoric centre of Goddess worship; the 'cradle of English Christianity' visited by Joseph of Arimathea, and perhaps even Christ himself; the 'New Jerusalem'; a communication point for alien contact; the epicentre of the New Age in England; and the 'heart chakra' of planet earth.
>
> (Bowman 2000: 83)

6.15 Pilgrimage at Glastonbury Abbey (Somerset) in 2015. Reproduced by kind permission of Glastonbury Abbey

The historian Ronald Hutton sums up Glastonbury succinctly as 'the British capital of dreams'. Its two main streets are lined with shops purveying crystals, incense and New Age souvenirs, where 'characters from early Celtic literature rub shoulders with shamans, dowsers and The Goddess' (Hutton 2003: 59). Bowman argues that an 'alternative Christianity' has emerged at Glastonbury, with Anglican and Catholic practices influenced by 'vernacular' and 'integrative' (New Age) religions. The spirit of place is reflected in its continuing appeal to pilgrims of numerous faiths: the abbey attracts annual Anglican and Catholic pilgrimage processions (Figure 6.15); the

6.16 Goddess Festival at Glastonbury (Somerset) in 2015. Reproduced by kind permission of Geoff Corris

Tor is the focus of Beltane (May Day) celebrations; and the town hosts an annual, international Goddess Festival (founded 1996), in which goddesses process through the streets (Figure 6.16).

This magnet for spiritual energy has also attracted tensions between religious groups. A poignant example is the vandalism of the Holy Thorn on Wearyall Hill – the tree which is believed to have grown from the staff of Joseph of Arimathea. The legend of the Holy Thorn emerged in the seventeenth century and the tree was a symbol of conflict during the Civil War (Walsham 2004; see Chapter 5). An annual ceremony takes place in December each year, when sprigs are cut from the Holy Thorn at St John's parish church and are sent to the Queen (Bowman 2006). Bowman identifies the Holy Thorn as an essential element of Glastonbury's vernacular religion, which brings together diverse spiritual groups in the annual ceremony. The Holy Thorn on Wearyall Hill was vandalised in 2010 and attacked on numerous occasions until it was replaced with a grafted sapling in 2012, which was immediately snapped in half. The identities and motivations of the vandals have not been determined but both militant Christians and militant pagans have been blamed (BBC News, 4 April 2012). The attack on the symbol of Joseph of Arimathea brought the community together in shared grief and disbelief. However, it is important

6.17 Holy Thorns at Glastonbury (Somerset): Wearyall Hill and St John's Church (left). Reproduced by kind permission of Geoff Corris

to understand that there are five Holy Thorns in Glastonbury, all believed to be descendants from the original thorn, and periodically replaced with new grafted trees (Figure 6.17). For many in Glastonbury, authenticity is a relative concept; ancient symbols are valued but their historicity is not questioned too closely.

Bowman comments on how Glastonbury has become more ecumenical over the past twenty years. For example, she observes how the parish church of St John's previously put up railings to keep out the hippies – because it was believed that they posed a threat to the Holy Thorn located in St John's churchyard (Bowman 2006: 134). These barriers have now come down but access to sacred space in Glastonbury remains highly contested, particularly Chalice Well, the Tor and the abbey, with the abbey exerting strong control over what is permissible within its bounds (Bowman 2009: 167). In particular, non-Christian rituals are prohibited on abbey grounds, although illicit pagan offerings such as flowers and candles are frequently discovered, and abbey staff regularly intervene to stop pagan rituals from taking place in the grounds. Some local people complain that the abbey hides behind its medieval walls and that these should come down, to allow open ritual access and free entry to the sacred site of the abbey (Glastonbury Abbey Conservation Plan 2018).

The abbey trustees are also committed to increasing ecumenicalism but they are bound by the objects of the charity: to preserve the fabric and grounds; to educate the public in the abbey's historic and religious importance; and to 'use

Glastonbury Abbey to advance religion in accordance with the doctrines of the Church of England'. They have collaborated in research exploring multi-vocal perspectives on the abbey's archaeology (Smith 2013) and they have commissioned surveys to get a better sense of what motivates visitors to come to the abbey. All age groups are drawn by three themes especially – the abbey and its history, King Arthur and the spiritual connections of the abbey, notably the Arimathean legend (Gofton and McVerry 2014). A new interpretation strategy was developed in 2012 that stresses spirituality, both in the past and the present, together with the abbey's environmental resources (Bell and Smith 2012). This is a distinctive approach in comparison with other monastic heritage sites, which often focus on the economic aspects of medieval monasteries as the first global corporations (see Chapter 1). Glastonbury's interpretation strategy aims to develop compelling stories around the themes of spirit, space and society, including the abbey as a spiritual powerhouse and its place within the spiritual landscape; the changing use of space over time; and social themes of continuity, change and religious conflict. The emphasis on change, conflict and sacred space is unusual in the public interpretation of a monastic heritage site and reflects the abbey's close engagement with perspectives on monasticism informed by social archaeology (Gilchrist 2005).

For the first time, the abbey's spiritual value to other groups has been acknowledged in the interpretation strategy: 'spiritual stakeholders from different paths believe the abbey to be a sacred space and their beliefs should be respected' (Bell and Smith 2012). The trust asks visitors to respect that Glastonbury Abbey is a Christian site: non-Christian rituals are prohibited but all spiritual contemplation is encouraged. There is growing experimentation with multi-vocality through temporary art exhibits and projects involving local artists, such as a joy tree in the grounds. However, the interpretation of the site remains strongly rooted in the concept of *authenticity*, based on archaeological evidence verified by experts. In outlining their values as a charity, the trustees of Glastonbury Abbey give first priority to 'authenticity and sense of place', alongside sustainability, education and community (Glastonbury Abbey Conservation Plan 2018). Authenticity continues to hold particular value at Glastonbury Abbey, as a site that has been at the centre of competing religious narratives for centuries (see Chapter 5). Authenticity is viewed as a deliberate strategy for negotiating the grey areas between 'fact and belief' and maintaining a neutral middle ground between Christianity and alternative spiritualities (Bell and Smith 2012).

REPRESENTING LEGENDS: VISUAL RECONSTRUCTIONS AND AUTHENTICITY

Glastonbury Abbey's interpretation strategy acknowledges that new approaches are needed to present the complex history and myths accessibly and to explore the relationship between legends and archaeological evidence. The abbey collaborated with the Universities of Reading and York to create digital reconstructions that tell the story of Glastonbury through the lens of archaeology, improving visitors' understanding of the spaces of the site, their chronological development and how they relate to the site's myths (www.glastonburyabbeyarchaeology.org). The reconstructions focus on the Anglo-Saxon churches, the Lady Chapel, the cloister, the abbot's complex and Arthur's tomb. Stuart Jeffrey has commented on the general challenge of engaging audiences with digital reconstructions, which by definition lack a sense of materiality, time-depth and spatial context (Jeffrey 2015). He concludes that lack of authenticity is the central problem, which he defines in this context as a sense of aura, patina and proximity that is attached to material objects. The immaterial nature of digital reconstructions makes it difficult to feel a sense of ownership or connection with these images. They lack the tactile, material traces of 'age-value' that prompt emotional responses in the viewer (Holtorf 2013a). Jeffrey calls for a more democratic approach to heritage visualisation, involving co-creation with local communities and a stronger emphasis on 3D modelling and aesthetic values to increase the sense of visual authenticity.

The Glastonbury reconstructions involved co-creation with the abbey and were grounded in the aesthetics of medieval architecture. The abbey director stressed the importance of archaeological authenticity in developing the reconstructions: accurate, scaled models were generated from archaeological base recording; and lengthy discussions took place on every aspect of plan, form and materials. This level of archaeological detail added significant additional cost to the project, but the desire for *archaeological authenticity* overrode financial considerations. There are crucial aspects of Glastonbury's intangible heritage for which no archaeological evidence survives, notably the 'old church' associated with Joseph of Arimathea and King Arthur's tomb (see Chapter 5). These features are important in interpreting the site to the public and reconstructions were therefore requested by the abbey, to be based on descriptions in medieval documents. We took the decision to represent Arthur's tomb through the medium of a traditional artist's drawing (by Dominic Andrews), rather than a digital reconstruction. There is the risk of creating 'icons' when visualising intangible heritage and it is possible that digital reconstructions may be perceived as more objective than an artist's reconstruction. We used John Leland's description of the tomb from the 1530s (Lindley 2007), archaeological evidence for the appearance of the church and comparative evidence of surviving ecclesiastical fittings from contemporary churches. We chose to represent a particular event in 1331, when the relics of Arthur and Guinevere were visited by King Edward III and Queen Philippa. The representation of a specific moment in history may help to counter the timeless effect that is typical of visualisations (see Figure 5.9).

We also developed a digital reconstruction of the 'old church' associated with Joseph of Arimathea, based on the description by William of Malmesbury in 1130, before the old church was destroyed by fire in 1184 (see Chapter 5). There is a long tradition of visualisation associated with Joseph's church, beginning in 1639 with Henry Spelman's *Concilia*. Spelman reconstructed the building with wattle walls and reed thatch, and a later phase with upright wooden planks (Figure 6.19). His images conveyed an ideological purpose, emphasising the primitive simplicity of the structure, which served as a symbol of the early independence of the Anglican church, before the Roman mission to England (Stout 2012: 256). Spelman's approach was connected to a wider tendency in seventeenth-century, Protestant scholarship that sought to demonstrate the early origins of indigenous British religion. For example, antiquaries such as William Stukeley promoted monuments like Stonehenge and Avebury as evidence for a Druidic religion that was the true precursor to the British church (Haycock 2002). Spelman's images may have influenced later archaeological reconstructions, notably one by Judith Dobie for a publication by Philip Rahtz and Lorna Watts, first published in 1993 (Rahtz and Watts 2003: 95). Our reconstruction was influenced by archaeological knowledge of Anglo-Saxon domestic architecture and includes a nod to the features of early churches, such as double-splayed windows. The shape and ground-plan of the reconstruction are based on the surviving Lady Chapel, which was built on the site of the 'old church' in the 1190s. The only medieval depiction of the 'old church' is on a seal of Glastonbury Abbey dated 1171–8, showing the façade of a rectangular building with turrets similar to those of the later Lady Chapel (illustrated in Rahtz and Watts 2003: 96). We were conscious of the vernacular appearance of our reconstruction of Glastonbury's 'old church' but we were guided by medieval descriptions and influenced by earlier reconstructions (Figure 6.18).

Before launching the new reconstructions to the public in 2016, we trialled them at a workshop in Glastonbury involving representatives of diverse faith groups, including Anglican, Catholic, Quaker, Buddhist and New Age representatives. The reconstructions of the Anglo-Saxon churches, the medieval cloister, the Lady Chapel and the abbot's complex were all well received. Arthur's tomb prompted mixed responses, largely because people were surprised to see so much colour in the reconstruction, applied to both the fittings of the church and the tomb itself, which was described by Leland in the sixteenth century as 'black marble' (Lindley 2007: 150). However, responses to the reconstruction of the 'old church' surprised us: all participants at the workshop had expected to see a *round* church and they were shocked and disappointed by our reconstruction. We were initially perplexed by this response, but it soon became apparent that these faith groups were familiar with a different tradition of reconstruction of the 'old church'. Their

6.18 3D visualisation of the 'old church' at Glastonbury Abbey (Somerset). © The Centre for the Study of Christianity & Culture, University of York

expectations were shaped by a reconstruction by Frederick Bligh Bond, dated to 1939. Bond showed the 'old church' as a round structure at the centre of a palisaded compound, surrounded by twelve smaller round structures or cells (Figure 6.19).

Bond's image of Glastonbury in the first century CE was of an imagined early British monastery, following the form of an Iron Age village, and showing the apostolic number of twelve cells. He was clearly affected by the excavations at Glastonbury Lake Village, an Iron Age village constructed on a crannog in the Somerset Levels, 5 km northwest of Glastonbury. The Lake Village was excavated from 1892 to 1907 and Bond was closely familiar with the excavators and their findings (Bulleid et al. 1917). His reconstruction was evidently influenced by the paintings of the Glastonbury Lake Village by the artist Amédée Forestier, completed for the *Illustrated London News* (1911) (Figure 6.20). Bond depicted a round enclosure, consistent with both the Irish monastic tradition and with Forestier's representation of Glastonbury Lake Village. By representing Joseph's church at the centre of an Iron Age village, Bond emphasised the British origins of the early church at Glastonbury and its continuity with ancient traditions that pre-dated the Anglo-Saxon monastery. His image of the early church has been widely reproduced in New Age literature and has become the local symbol of the church reputedly founded by Joseph of Arimathea.

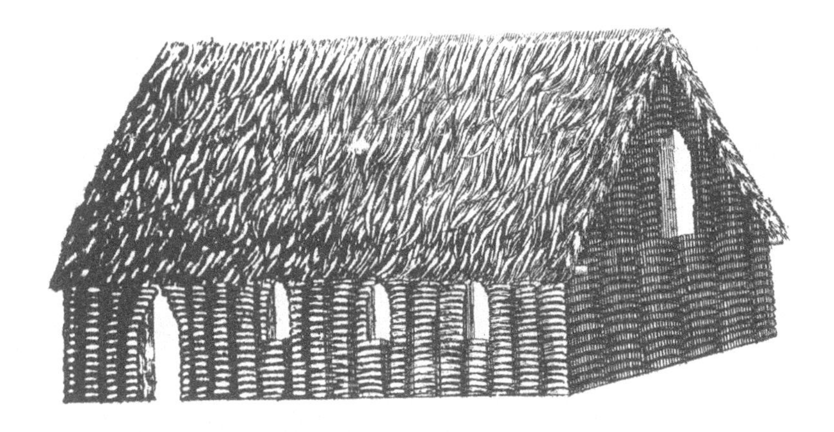

6.19 Reconstructions of Glastonbury's 'old church': by Spelman (1639) (above) and Bligh Bond (1939). Reproduced by kind permission of Glastonbury Abbey

The challenge of reconstructing Glastonbury's 'old church' highlights the complexity of authenticity, which can be informed by competing forms of knowledge and value, in this case archaeological scholarship versus local faith traditions of knowledge. It also illustrates the difficulties involved in democratising heritage visualisations when multiple communities and narratives are involved. Our reconstruction was based on co-creation, but with the abbey as the key stakeholder, an institution which places maximum value on archaeological authenticity. It was only through engagement with the wider

6.20 Artist reconstruction of Glastonbury Lake Village by Forestier (1911). Public Domain

community of spiritual groups that we became aware of the tensions and sensitivities around this reconstruction. Their response made it clear that the principle of multi-vocality (Hodder 2008) was essential in representing the 'old church' associated with Joseph of Arimathea. It also highlighted longstanding themes in the visual representation of Joseph's church and the spiritual significance of choosing to place it either within an Iron Age (Celtic) or an Anglo-Saxon building tradition. We concluded that no single image could convey the conflicting traditions of knowledge and representation that are associated with Glastonbury's 'old church'. We took the decision to reproduce Bond's image alongside our reconstruction: they are shown together in both the new printed guidebook of Glastonbury Abbey and digital resources on site, in an effort to convey the ambiguities and subjectivities involved in the research process that underpins visual reconstruction (Gilchrist et al. 2017: 29; www.glastonburyabbeyarchaeology.org).

CONCLUSIONS: 'DEEP TIME' AND 'THIN PLACES'

Archaeologists have long debated the role of material evidence in supporting nationalist narratives and they have appraised the meanings of authenticity in different social and cultural contexts. And yet, there has been virtually no critical reflection on how archaeology has been used to authenticate religious narratives at medieval sacred sites. This is in stark contrast with the extensive archaeological analysis of pagan engagement with prehistoric sacred sites such as Çatalhöyük (Hodder 1998). The archaeological study of medieval Christianity has remained largely outside social, political and heritage discourses (see Chapter 1). As recently as the 1950s and 1960s, archaeologists perpetuated myths at sacred sites to valorise 'Golden Age' stories, by seeking to demonstrate the saintly origins of sites such as Glastonbury and Whithorn. The archaeology was forced to fit a mythological framework, causing misrepresentation of evidence and leading to major delays in publication. These sites eventually reached publication decades after their excavation, achieved through scientific analysis and rejection of preconceived ideas about site origins (Gilchrist and Green 2015; Lowe 2009).

Heritage practice has recently shifted towards more democratic principles that challenge the pillars of academic archaeology: social value is increasingly regarded as more significant than the principles of antiquity, fabric and authenticity (Emerick 2014). However, these traditional designations remain important at sacred sites, where the authentication of early origins and the survival of original fabric are crucial in validating the unique sense of *place* and the *numinous*. Tangible and intangible heritage are brought together at sacred sites: authenticity represents a strategy for people to negotiate their own spiritual beliefs in relation to sacred landscapes, buildings, spaces and objects. The case studies discussed here illustrate how faith groups draw on archaeology selectively, both to authenticate their own versions of the past and to compete with alternative spiritual narratives. At Walsingham, for example, the Anglican Holy House built in the 1930s incorporated worked stone from medieval monastic sites, to rival the authentic medieval chapel that was the focus of the Catholic shrine (Coleman 2004). Replication was used at Walsingham and Iona in the twentieth century to reconstruct the authority of medievalism. The architectural reuse and replication of medieval fabric were strategies adopted to achieve 'age-value', a perceptible quality of 'pastness' that signals authenticity, regardless of age (Holtorf 2013a). In contrast, Glastonbury Abbey pared back interpretation of the ruins to minimal presentation based on professional judgements of archaeological authenticity. Through their involvement with the controversial figure of Frederick Bligh Bond, the trustees learned an early lesson in how archaeology can be appropriated to serve alternative narratives. The abbey's engagement with the heritage pioneer Charles Peers had a more lasting impact on the interpretation of the site: Glastonbury came to embody the national 'preservation ethic' that presented medieval abbeys as 'dead' monuments 'frozen' in time (Emerick 2014: 83).

Glastonbury Abbey demonstrates that a medieval monastic ruin can be a highly contested heritage site, with similar conflicts over access to sacred space and freedom to perform rituals that characterise UNESCO World Heritage Sites such as Great Zimbabwe and Stonehenge (Fontein 2006; Wallis and Blain

2003). Authenticity based on quality of evidence remains an important strategy for Glastonbury Abbey in mediating between 'fact and belief' (Bell and Smith 2012), a means of negotiating an interpretative position for an Anglican site immersed in legends and which serves as a beacon for New Age spirituality. As a heritage site, the abbey has been highly conservative in relation to its myths, wary of commemorating Arthur's tomb or the church of Joseph of Arimathea. This is now changing, with a more ecumenical approach that encourages spiritual reflection and creative engagement with the abbey's legends. Archaeological authenticity will remain a core value for the abbey – because an emphasis on scholarship and empirical evidence sets the abbey apart from alternative religious narratives at Glastonbury.

Marion Bowman argues that the Glastonbury landscape is the key spiritual focus for the Community of Avalon: New Age seekers are drawn to striking natural features such as the Tor with its contoured hill, the chalybeate spring of Chalice Well and the miraculous Holy Thorn that flowers twice a year (Bowman 2009). This strong attachment to landscape and the natural environment is more broadly characteristic of Celtic and pagan spirituality (Power 2006). However, I would argue that New Age interest in Glastonbury is equally concerned with 'Golden Age' stories that lend a sense of deep time, ranging from Arthur and Joseph of Arimathea, to the alleged Druidic university and prehistoric goddess cult. The Community of Avalon is not concerned with the archaeological authenticity of these stories, but they value the *antiquity* and *materiality* of Glastonbury, alongside its special qualities as a healing landscape and a 'thin place', where the physical and spiritual realms meet. Catholic pilgrimage to Glastonbury has also begun to focus on the abbey's long history as a Marian shrine and place of healing, in contrast with the twentieth-century Catholic veneration of Glastonbury as the site of Abbot Whiting's martyrdom at the Dissolution (Bowman 2009: 165).

I will conclude this discussion with a personal story about myth and authenticity. When the monograph reporting the new research on Glastonbury Abbey was published in late 2015 (Gilchrist and Green 2015), there was substantial national and international media interest. The tone of the coverage was largely set by the first article that appeared in *The Guardian* newspaper: an archaeological study 'has comprehensively demolished cherished myths about one of the most romantic religious sites in England' (Kennedy 2015). The article assumed that because I had challenged Radford's archaeological evidence for Arthur's grave (discussed above), my aim was to discredit the whole fabric of legends surrounding Glastonbury. Archaeology was characterised as 'myth-busting' science triumphing over outmoded religion. I was taken aback by this reaction, because I had under-estimated the cultural value that had been placed on Radford's evidential claims. In the early 1960s, a highly respected archaeologist announced that he had found material proof for the exhumation in 1191 of the legendary Arthur and Guinevere at Glastonbury. This news was heralded by the national press as 'one of the greatest archaeological finds of the century' with the story of Radford's quest described as 'almost as romantic as the very picture-book stories of Arthur himself' (*The Evening News*, 31 August, 1962). The discovery of the alleged exhumation site in 1963 drew crowds of tourists and boosted the local economy: visitors claimed that they had 'seen the grave of King Arthur in Avalon' (*The Times*, 18 August 1963). Radford's claim to have authenticated Arthur's grave had itself become part of Glastonbury's intangible heritage. My critical reading of his archaeological evidence was therefore perceived as undermining the authenticity of the whole Arthur story – a myth of nationhood that people *want* to believe.

I was concerned about how the Glastonbury community would respond to the media coverage and its representation of my research. The abbey was initially worried, given the high value that they place on authenticity based on professional judgement of archaeological evidence. However, they soon regarded the media storm as another compelling Glastonbury story – evidence of the enduring power of the myths of Arthur and Arimathea. The (New Age) Community of Avalon was interested to hear new archaeological findings but their personal beliefs about Glastonbury were not challenged. For them, there is no single truth about Glastonbury; its sacred quality lies in the personal, embodied experience of the place (Bowman 2000). For me, this was a lesson in the cultural relativism of authenticity even within a single locale, a small town of less than 10,000 people. Authenticity is a slippery concept in a place with five different Holy Thorn trees believed to descend from the staff of Joseph of Arimathea, and where archaeology has been actively used since the twelfth century to authenticate myths of the 'Golden Age' (see Chapter 5).

Glastonbury's contested heritage has shown me that authenticity is certainly not 'dead' (Emerick 2014: 7). Rather than pronounce its demise, we need to develop more fluid understandings of authenticity in relation to 'living heritage' (Holtorf 2013b; Jones 2010). For faith communities, principles of authenticity can serve as both 'neutral middle ground' and as confirmation of the *spiritual credentials* of a place, through nuanced understanding of its materiality and historicity. A deep time perspective demonstrates the layered and multivalent qualities of sacred heritage, changing meanings over time and between faith communities (see Chapter 1). The materiality of archaeology underpins these concepts of authenticity – the *enduring* quality of tangible heritage and its ability to connect the past with the present through entangled social relationships (Fowler and Harris 2015). In sacred landscapes such as Glastonbury, the material remains of the past enhance the effect of spiritual enchantment; authenticity becomes 'a way of expressing religious longing in a secularised world' (Fredengren 2016: 493). The living heritage approach has been criticised for its *presentist* framework, which prioritises the value of heritage as defined by contemporary communities and individuals. Critical appraisal of sacred heritage demonstrates that contemporary perceptions of value are also connected to the *materiality* of archaeology, its durability in connecting *present place* with the *deep past*.

We must also be more alert to the risks of *relativism* that come with the 'democratic turn' in heritage studies. Heritage can be appropriated to serve instrumentalist political agendas, in other words, using the past in attempts to solve contemporary social challenges (Swedish National Heritage Board 2016a). European heritage agencies have stepped up their attention to the relationship between contemporary social identity, social cohesion and national heritage. For example, Historic England has pledged 'to promote the past in a way that is inclusive to all and that celebrates the cultural diversity of England's heritage' (Historic England 2016: 8), while Historic Environment Scotland asserts the value of archaeology to 'help everyone celebrate the diversity of our heritage, regardless of their race, religion, gender or ability, and tell stories that reach beyond our borders, such as trade and migration' (Historic Environment Scotland 2016: 5). In Sweden, the Heritage Board has consciously stepped back from identity politics and has instead committed to more collaborative processes of *heritage management* through new models of participation and co-creation (Swedish Heritage Board 2016b). At the same time that heritage agencies are promoting social inclusion and collaboration, right-wing political parties aim to harness the power of heritage for exclusionary political agendas (Niklasson and Hølleland 2018: 139). The relativism of the living heritage approach provides no means of choosing between versions of the past and how they are used in the present.

Is it possible to achieve a balance between the democratisation of heritage and the interpretation of empirical archaeology, that is, social value on one hand (constructivist approaches), versus evidential value on the other (materialist approaches)? Critical reflection on different contemporary values and relative meanings of the past is one possible route of navigation through this complexity (Jones 2017; Jones and Leech 2015). An alternative is to consider the value of heritage sites in terms of their materiality, the power of archaeology to connect the present with the deep past and to provoke emotional and spiritual experiences (Fredengren 2016). Archaeology brings its own value to sacred heritage: the material study of religion is a distinctive contribution to understanding people's experience in the past – how bodies, things and spaces engaged to construct the sensory qualities of medieval religion. Focus on the material and sensory dimensions may help to make the past more accessible, opening up opportunities for people today to experience sacred sites and material culture and to draw their own meanings from them. This relational approach is relevant to both humanist and spiritual engagements with sacred sites, intersecting with social memory, an appreciation of landscapes, the aesthetics of architecture, personal well-being and individual reflections on the numinous, mortality and loss. The 'spiritual' value of heritage is part of a more holistic perception of religious sites and landscapes – one that is not exclusive to faith communities (see Chapter 1). We should be confident in crafting interpretations that are firmly rooted in archaeological evidence and also appeal to the strong contemporary desire to know more about spiritual beliefs in the past. This book began by commenting on the intellectual distance between heritage theory, heritage management and medieval archaeology. These separate fields can be drawn together in approaches that seek to be relevant and inclusive and at the same time are grounded in fresh interpretative perspectives on archaeological evidence. By reflecting more critically on spiritual beliefs in our interpretations, we may encourage deeper public engagement with sacred heritage and contribute greater sustainability to medieval archaeology.

BIBLIOGRAPHY

Abrams, L and Carley, J P eds (1991). *The Archaeology and History of Glastonbury Abbey: Essays in Honour of the Ninetieth Birthday of C. A. Ralegh Radford*, Boydell & Brewer.

Adams, J and Forbes, S eds (2015). *The Syon Abbey Herbal: The Last Monastic Herbal in England, c AD 1517 by Thomas Betson*, AMCD Publishers.

Aga Khan Museum Guide (2014). Aga Khan Museum.

Alcock, L (1972). *Was that Camelot? Excavations at Cadbury Castle 1966–70*, Thames and Hudson.

Allan, J P (1984). *Medieval and Post-Medieval Finds from Exeter, 1971–1980*, Exeter.

Anderson, W (2010) 'Blessing the fields? A study of late-medieval ampullae from England and Wales', *Medieval Archaeology*, 54, 182–203.

Andrén, A (2014). *Tracing Old Norse Cosmology*, Nordic Academic Press.

Andriotis, K (2011). 'Genres of heritage authenticity: denotations from a pilgrimage landscape', *Annals of Tourism Research*, 38(4), 1613–33.

Asad, T (1987). 'On ritual and discipline in medieval Christian monasticism', *Economy and Society*, 16(2), 159–203.

Asad, T (2003). *Formations of the Secular: Christianity, Islam, Modernity*, Stanford University Press.

Åsen, P A (2009). 'Plants of possible medical origin, growing in the past or present, at medieval monastery grounds in Norway', in J-P Morel and A-M Mercuri, eds, *Plants and Culture: Seeds of the Cultural Heritage of Europe*, Edipuglia, pp. 227–38.

Ashe, G (1979). *Glastonbury Tor Maze*, Gothic Image.

Aston, Margaret (1973). 'English ruins and English history: the Dissolution and the sense of the past', *Journal of the Warbourg and Courtauld Institutes*, 36, 231–55.

Aston, Margaret (1988). *England's Iconoclasts: Volume 1 – Laws Against Images*, Clarendon Press.

Aston, Margaret (2003). 'Public worship and iconoclasm', in D Gaimster and R Gilchrist, eds, *The Archaeology of Reformation, 1480–1580*, The Society for Post-Medieval Archaeology Monograph 1, Maney, pp. 9–28.

Aston, Mick (1993). *Monasteries*, Batsford.

Aston, Mick, Keevil, G and Hall, T eds (2001). *Monastic Archaeology: Papers on the Study of Medieval Monasteries*, Oxbow Books.

Atkins, R and Popescu, E (2010). 'Excavations at the Hospital of St Mary Magdalene Partney, Lincs, 2003', *Medieval Archaeology*, 54, 204–70.

Atkinson, J A (1996). 'Nationalism and material culture: decoding the Highland Myth', in J A Atkinson, I Banks and J O'Sullivan, eds, *Nationalism and Archaeology: Scottish Archaeological Forum*, Cruithne Press, pp. 59–66.

Auden, W H (1947). 'Introduction', in J Betjeman, ed, *Slick But Not Streamlined Poems and Short Pieces*, Doubleday, pp. 17–24.

Augenti, A (2016). *Archaeologia dell'Italia medievale*, Laterza.

Austin, D (2007). *Acts of Perception: A Study of Barnard Castle in Teesdale, Volume 2*, English Heritage and The Architectural and Archaeological Society of Durham and Northumberland Research Report 6.

Austin, D (2013). 'The archaeology of Wales and the Strata Florida Project', in J Burton and K Stöber, eds, *Monastic Wales: New Approaches*, University of Wales Press, pp. 3–20.

Austin, D and Stamper, P (2006). 'Editorial', *Landscapes*, 7(2), vii–viii.

Avdoulos, E (2015). 'Istanbul's Hagia Sophia: challenges of managing sacred places', in A Castillo Mena, ed, *Personas y Comunidades: Actas del II Congreso Internacional de Buenas Prácticas en Patrimonio Mundial*, Universidad Complutense de Madrid, pp. 180–203.

Badone, E (2015). 'Religious heritage and the re-enchantment of the world in Brittany', *Material Religion*, 11(1), 4–24.

Bagnoli, M, Holger, A, Klein, C, Mann, G and Robinson, J eds (2011). *Treasures of Heaven: Saints, Relics, and Devotion in Medieval Europe*, British Museum.

Bailey, A E (2013). 'Modern and medieval approaches to pilgrimage, gender and sacred space', *History and Anthropology*, 24(4), 493–52.

Baillie, B (2006). 'Conservation of the sacred at Angkor Wat: further reflections on living heritage', *Conservation and Management of Archaeological Sites*, 8(3), 123–31.

Bain, S (1998). 'Excavation of a medieval cemetery at Holyrood Abbey, Edinburgh', *Proceedings of the Society of Antiquaries of Scotland*, 128, 1047–77.

Banks, I and Pollard, T (2011). 'Protecting a bloodstained history: battlefield conservation in Scotland', *Journal of Conflict Archaeology*, 6 (2), 124–45.

Barber, C (2016). *King Arthur: The Mystery Unravelled*, Pen and Sword History.

Barrow, G W S (1973). *The Kingdom of the Scots: Government, Church and Society from the Eleventh to the Fourteenth Century*, Edward Arnold.

Barrow, G W S (2004a). 'Margaret [St Margaret] (*d* 1093)', *Oxford Dictionary of National Biography*, Oxford University Press [www.oxforddnb.com/view/article/18044, accessed 20 October 2016].

Barrow, G W S (2004b). 'Scotland, Wales and Ireland in the twelfth century', in D Luscombe and J Riley-Smith, eds, *The New Cambridge Medieval History, Volume 4: c.1024–c.1198*, Cambridge University Press, pp. 581–610.

Barrowman, R (2011). *The Chapel and Burial Ground on St Ninian's Isle, Shetland: Excavations Past and Present*, Society for Medieval Archaeology Monograph 32, The Society for Medieval Archaeology.

Barthes, R (1994). *Mythologies*, Grant and Cutler.

Bartlett, R (2003). *The Miracles of Saint Æbbe of Coldingham and Saint Margaret of Scotland*, Oxford University Press.

Bartlett, R (2008). *The Natural and the Supernatural in the Middle Ages*, Cambridge University Press.

Baxter, R (2016). *The Royal Abbey of Reading*, Boydell Press.

BBC News (4 April 2012). 'The mystery of who attacked the Holy Thorn Tree' [www.bbc.co.uk/news/magazine-17589575].

Beekers, D and Arab, P T (2016). 'Dreams of an iconic mosque: spatial and temporal entanglements of a converted church in Amsterdam', *Material Religion*, 12(2), 137–64.

Bell, C (1992). *Ritual Theory, Ritual Practice*, Oxford University Press.

Bell, C (1997). *Ritual Perspectives and Dimensions*, Oxford University Press.

Bell, D N (1998). 'The siting and size of Cistercian infirmaries in England and Wales', in M P Lillich, ed, *Studies in Cistercian Art and Architecture Volume 5*, Cistercian Studies 167, Cistercian Publications, pp. 211–37.

Bell, D N (2012). 'Spirituality and scholarship: sacred acts and sacred spaces', in T Coomans, H De Dijn, J De Maeyer, R Heynickx and V Verschaffel, eds, *Loci Sacri: Understanding Sacred Places*, Leuven University Press, pp. 13–28.

Bell, J and Smith, R (2012). 'Glastonbury Abbey: Interpretation Strategy', unpublished report for the Trustees of Glastonbury Abbey.

Bender, B (1998). *Stonehenge: Making Space*, Berg.

Berggren, Å and Nilsson Stutz, L (2010). 'From spectator to critic and participant', *Journal of Social Archaeology*, 10(2), 171–97.

Bergqvist, J (2013). *Leeches and Leechcraft: The Professionalization of the Art and Craft of Healing in Sweden During the Middle Ages and Renaissance*, Lund Studies in Historical Archaeology 16.

Bergqvist, J (2014). 'Gendered attitudes towards physical tending amongst the piously religious of late medieval Sweden', in E Gemi-Iordanou, S Gordon, R Matthew, E McInnes and R Pettitt, eds, *Medicine, Healing and Performance*, Oxbow Books, pp. 86–105.

Berns, S (2016). 'Considering the glass case: material encounters between museums, visitors and religious objects', *Journal of Material Culture*, 21(2), 153–68.

Berthold, É, Dormaels, M and Laplace, J (2009). *Patrimoine et Sacralisation*, Université du Québec à Montréal: Institut du patrimoine; Forum Canadien de recherche publique sur le patrimoine.

Besly, E (2005). 'Coins and jettons', in J Gardiner, ed, *Before the Mast: Life and Death Aboard the Mary Rose*, The Mary Rose Trust, pp. 250–7.

Bevan, R (2016). *The Destruction of Memory: Architecture at War*, Second Expanded Edition, Reaktion Books.

Bhreathnach, E (2005). *The Kingship and Landscape of Tara*, Four Courts Press.

Biran, A, Poria, Y and Oren, G (2011). 'Sought experiences at (dark) heritage sites', *Annals of Tourism Research*, 38(3), 820–41.

Bitel, L M (2013). 'Gender and the initial Christianization of Northern Europe (to 1000 CE)', in J M Bennett and R M Karras, eds, *Women and Gender in Medieval Europe*, Oxford University Press, pp. 415–31.

Blain, J and Wallis, R J (2015). 'Sacred sites, contested rites/rights: contemporary pagan engagements with the past', *Journal of Material Culture*, 9(3), 237–61.

Blake, H (2015). 'Italian wares', in R Gilchrist and C Green, *Glastonbury Abbey: Archaeological Investigations 1904–79*, Society of Antiquaries of London, pp. 270–2.

Blomkvist, N (2004). 'The medieval Catholic world-system and the making of Europe', in J Staecker, ed, *The European Frontier: Clashes and Compromises in the Middle Ages*, Almqvist & Wiksell, pp. 15–33.

Boardman, S and Williamson, E (2010). *The Cult of Saints and the Virgin Mary in Medieval Scotland*, Studies in Celtic History 28, Boydell & Brewer.

Boddington, A (1996). *Raunds Furnells: The Anglo-Saxon Church and Churchyard*, English Heritage.

Bond, C J (2004). *Monastic Landscapes*, Tempus.

Bond, F B (1918). *The Gates of Remembrance: The Story of the Psychological Experiment which resulted in the Discovery of the Edgar Chapel at Glastonbury*, Blackwell.

Bonde, S and Maines, C (1988). 'The archaeology of monasticism: a survey of recent work in France 1970–1987', *Speculum*, 63(4), 794–825.

Bonde, S and Maines, C (2004). 'The archaeology of monasticism in France: the state of the Question', in J Hamasse, ed, *Bilan et perspectives des études médiévales, Actes du Ile Congrès Européen d'Etudes médiévales*, Brepols, pp. 15–18.

Bonde, S, Maines, C, Mylonas, E and Flanders, J (2009). 'The virtual monastery: re-presenting time, human movement, and uncertainty at Saint-Jean-des-Vignes, Soissons', *Visual Resources*, 25(4), 363–77.

Bonfield, C (2017). 'The first instrument of medicine: diet and regimens of health in late medieval England', in L Clark and E Danbury, eds, *'A Very Parfit Praktisour': Essays Presented to Carole Rawcliffe*, Boydell Press, pp. 99–119.

Booth, C (2016). 'The stalled development of the still: material evidence for changes in distilling practice in Britain', *Post-Medieval Archaeology*, 50(2), 419–26.

Booth, C (2017). 'Holy alchemists, metallurgists, and pharmacists: the material evidence for British monastic chemistry', *The Journal of Medieval Monastic Studies*, 6, 195–215.

Borić, D ed (2010). *Archaeology and Memory*, Oxbow Books.

Bourdieu, P (1977). *Outline of a Theory of Practice*, Cambridge University Press.

Bowers, B and Keyser, L M eds (2016). *The Sacred and the Secular in Medieval Healing: Sites, Objects, and Texts*, Routledge.

Bowman, M (2000). 'More of the same? Christianity, vernacular religion and alternative spirituality in Glastonbury', in S Sutcliffe and M Bowman, eds, *Beyond New Age: Exploring Alternative Spirituality*, Edinburgh University Press, pp. 83–104.

Bowman, M (2006). 'The Holy Thorn Ceremony: revival, rivalry and civil religion in Glastonbury', *Folklore*, 117, 123–40.

Bowman, M (2009). 'Learning from experience: the value of analysing Avalon', *Religion*, 39(2), 161–8.

Bowman, M and Coleman, S (2017). 'Contemporary perspectives: understanding and supporting visitor engagement today', unpublished paper presented at *Cathedrals, Mission, and the Power of Place, Past, Present and Future*, Lambeth Palace.

Bradley, R (2002). *The Past in Prehistoric Societies*, Routledge.

Bradley, R (2005). *Ritual and Domestic Life in Prehistoric Europe*, Routledge.

British Social Attitudes Survey 2017 [www.natcen.ac.uk/news-media/press-releases/2017/september/british-social-attitudes-record-number-of-brits-with-no-religion/].

Brockman, N (1997). *Encyclopaedia of Sacred Places*, ABC-Clio.

Brooks, M M (2012). 'Seeing the sacred: conflicting priorities in defining, interpreting and conserving western sacred artifacts', *Material Religion*, 8(1), 10–28.

Brooks, N (1992). 'The career of St Dunstan', in N L Ramsay, M J Sparks and T W T Tatton Brown, eds, *St Dunstan: His Life, Times and Cult*, Boydell Press, pp. 1–23.

Brophy, K and Noble, K (in prep). *Death and Remembrance in the Valley: Excavations at a Prehistoric Monument Complex at Forteviot, Scotland 2007–2010*, GUARD.

Broun, D (2007). *Scottish Independence and the Idea of Britain: From the Picts to Alexander III*, Edinburgh University Press.

Bruce, D and Creighton, O (2006). 'Contested identities: the dissonant heritage of European town walls and walled towns', *International Journal of Heritage Studies*, 12(3), 234–54.

Brück, J (1999). 'Ritual and rationality: some problems of interpretation in European archaeology', *European Journal of Archaeology*, 2(3), 313–44.

Brück, J and Nilsson Stutz, L (2016). 'Is archaeology still the project of nation states?', *Archaeological Dialogues*, 23(1), 1–3.

Bruzelius, C A (1992). 'Hearing is believing: Clarissan architecture ca 1213–1340', *Gesta*, 31(2), 83–92.

Bruzelius, C (2014). *Preaching, Building and Burying: Friars in the Medieval City*, Yale University Press.

Buggeln, G T (2012). 'Museum space and the experience of the sacred', *Material Religion*, 8 (1), 30–50.

Bugslag, J (2016). 'Performative thaumaturgy: the state of research on curative and spiritual interaction at medieval pilgrimage shrines', in B Bowers and L M Keyser, eds, *The Sacred and the Secular in Medieval Healing: Sites, Objects and Texts*, Routledge, pp. 219–65.

Bulleid, A, Gray, H S G, Munro, R, Dawkins, W B, Jackson, J W, Andrews, C W and Reid, C (1917). *The Glastonbury Lake Village*, Glastonbury Antiquarian Society.

Burton, J with Lockyer, L (2013). *Historia Selebiensis Monasterii: The History of the Monastery of Selby*, Oxford University Press.

Burton, J and Stöber, K (2013a). 'Introduction', in J Burton and K Stöber, eds, *Monastic Wales: New Approaches*, University of Wales Press, pp. xvii–xix.

Burton, J and Stöber, K eds (2013b). *Monastic Wales: New Approaches*, University of Wales Press.

Bynum, C W (1991). 'Material continuity, personal survival and the resurrection of the body: a scholastic discussion in its medieval and modern contexts', in C W Bynum, ed, *Fragmentation and Redemption: Essays on Gender and the Human Body in Medieval Religion*, Zone Books, pp. 239–97.

Cameron, A (2016). 'Robert Gordon University and College, Schoolhill, Aberdeen AB10 1FT. Report on archaeological watching brief and excavation and data structure report', unpublished report, Aberdeenshire Council.

Cameron, A and Stones, J A (2016). 'Excavations within the East Kirk of St Nicholas, Aberdeen', in J. Geddes, ed, *Medieval Art, Architecture and Archaeology in the Dioceses of Aberdeen and Moray*, British Archaeological Association Conference Transactions for 2014, Routledge, pp. 82–98.

Cameron, E (2010). *Enchanted Europe: Superstition, Reason and Religion 1250–1750*, Oxford University Press.

Campbell, E and Maldonado, A (2016). 'Russell Trust Excavations on Iona led by A. Charles Thomas, 1956–63', unpublished Data Structure Report for Historic Environment Scotland.

Campbell, I (1995). 'A Romanesque revival and the Early Renaissance in Scotland, c. 1380–1513', *Journal of the Society of Architectural Historians*, 54, 302–25.

Campbell, S (2013a). 'Metal detecting, collecting and portable antiquities: Scottish and British perspectives', *Internet Archaeology*, 33 [http://intarch.ac.uk/journal/issue33/campbell_index.html].

Campbell, S (2013b). 'The language of objects: material culture in medieval Scotland', in M Hammond, ed, *New Perspectives on Medieval Scotland 1093–1286*, Boydell Press, pp. 183–201.

Canmore, database of Historic Environment Scotland [https://canmore.org.uk/].

Cardwell, P (1995). 'The hospital of St Giles by Brompton Bridge, North Yorkshire', *The Archaeological Journal*, 152, 109–245.

Carley, J P (1985). *The Chronicle of Glastonbury Abbey. An Edition, Translation and Study of John of Glastonbury's Cronica sive Antiquitates Glastoniensis Ecclesie*, Boydell Press.

Carley, J P (1996). *Glastonbury Abbey: The Holy House at the Head of the Moors Adventurous*, Gothic Image.

Carley, J P ed (2001a). *Glastonbury Abbey and the Arthurian Tradition*, D. S. Brewer.

Carley, J P (2001b). 'A grave event: Henry V, Glastonbury Abbey and Joseph of Arimathea's bones', in J P Carley, ed, *Glastonbury Abbey and the Arthurian Tradition*, D. S. Brewer, pp. 285–302.

Carruthers, M (2000). *The Craft of Thought: Meditation, Rhetoric and the Making of Images, 400–1200*, Cambridge University Press.

Carter, M (2015a). '"It would have pitied any heart to see": destruction and survival at Cistercian monasteries in northern England at the Dissolution', *Journal of the British Archaeological Association*, 168(1), 77–110.

Carter, M (2015b). '"So it was abowte iiiic yeres agoo": retrospection in the art and architecture of the Cistercians in northern England in the Late Middle Ages', *Journal of Medieval Monastic Studies*, 4, 107–32.

Carver, M (2009). 'Early Scottish monasteries and prehistory: a preliminary dialogue', *The Scottish Historical Review*, 88(2), 332–51.

Carver, M, Garner-Lahire, J and Spall, C (2016). *Portmahomack on Tarbat Ness: Changing Ideologies in North-East Scotland, Sixth to Sixteenth Century AD*, Society of Antiquaries of Scotland.

Cassidy-Welch, M (2001). *Monastic Spaces and their Meanings: Thirteenth-Century English Cistercian Monasteries*, Brepols.

Cessford, C (2015). 'The St John's hospital cemetery and environs, Cambridge: contextualizing the medieval urban dead', *Archaeological Journal*, 172(1), 52–120.

Cheape, H (2009). 'From natural to supernatural: the material culture of charms and amulets', in L Henderson, ed, *Fantastical Imaginations: The Supernatural in Scottish History and Culture*, Birlinn, pp. 70–91.

Chidester, D and Linenthal, E T eds (1995). *American Sacred Space*, Indiana University Press.

Christian, J and Stiller, C (2000). *Iona Portrayed: The Island Through Artists' Eyes, 1760–1960*, The New Iona Press.

Clancy, T O (1999). 'Reformers to conservatives: *Céli Dé* communities in the north east', in J Porter, ed, *After Columba – After Calvin: Community and Identity in the Religious Traditions of North East Scotland*, The Elphinstone Institute Occasional Publications 1, University of Aberdeen, pp. 19–29.

Clancy, T O (2010). 'The big man, the footsteps and the fissile saint: paradigms and problems in studies of insular saints' cults', in S Boardman and E Williamson, eds, *The Cult of Saints and the Virgin Mary in Medieval Scotland*, Boydell Press, pp. 1–20.

Clancy, T O (2013). 'Saints in the Scottish landscape', *Proceedings of the Harvard Celtic Colloquium*, 33, 1–34.

Clark, K (2010). 'Values in cultural resource management', in G S Smith, P M Messenger and H Soderland, eds, *Heritage Values in Contemporary Society*, Left Coast Press, pp. 89–99.

Coad, J, Carter, M and Porter, R (2017). *Battle Abbey and Battlefield*. English Heritage Guidebooks, English Heritage.

Coleman, R (1996). 'Excavations at the Abbot's House, Maygate, Dunfermline', *Tayside and Fife Archaeological Journal*, 2, 70–112.

Coleman, S (2004). 'Pilgrimage to "England's Nazareth": landscapes of myth and memory at Walsingham', in E Badone and S R Roseman, eds, *Intersecting Journeys: The Anthropology of Pilgrimage and Tourism*, University of Chicago Press, pp. 52–67.

Coleman, S and Eade, J eds (2004). *Reframing Pilgrimage: Cultures in Motion*, Routledge.

Collard, M, Lawson, J A and Holmes, N (2006). *Archaeological Excavations in St Giles' Cathedral Edinburgh, 1981–93*, Scottish Archaeological Internet Report 22, The Society of Antiquaries of Scotland, Historic Scotland and the Council for British Archaeology.

Collins, T E (2018). 'Archaeologies of female monasticism in Ireland: becoming and belonging *c*.1200–1600', in E Campbell, E FitzPatrick and A Horning, eds, *Becoming and Belonging in Ireland 1200–1600 AD: Essays in Identity and Cultural Practice*, Cork University Press, pp. 69–87.

Colls, CS (2015). *Holocaust Archaeologies: Approaches and Future Directions*, Springer.

Connell, B, Gray Jones, A, Redfern, R and Walker, D (2012). *A Bioarchaeological Study of Medieval Burials on the Site of St Mary Spital: Excavations at Spitalfield Market, London E1, 1991–2007*, Museum of London Archaeology.

Connerton, P (1989). *How Societies Remember*, Cambridge University Press.

Coomans, T (2001). 'L'architecture médiévale des ordres mendiants (Franciscains, Dominicains, Carmes et Augustins) en Belgique et aux Pays-Bas', *Belgisch Tijdschrift voor Oudheidkunde en Kunstgeschiedenis*, 70, 3–111.

Coomans, T (2004). 'The medieval architecture of Cistercian nunneries in the Low Countries', *Koninkiijke Nederlandse Oudheidkundige Bond Bulletin*, 3, 62–90.

Coomans, T (2005). 'From Romanticism to New Age: the evolving perception of a church ruin', *Téoros. Revue de recherche en tourism*, 24, 47–57.

Coomans, T (2012). 'Reuse of sacred places: perspectives for a long tradition', in T Coomans, H De Dijn, J De Maeyer, R Heynickx and B Verschaffel, eds, *Loci Sacri: Understanding Sacred Places*, Leuven University Press, pp. 221–41.

Coomans, T (2018). *Life Inside the Cloister: Understanding Monastic Architecture*, Leuven University Press.

Coomans, T, De Dijn, H, De Maeyer, J, Heynickx, R and Verschaffel, B eds (2012). *Loci Sacri: Understanding Sacred Places*, Leuven University Press.

Coomans, T and Grootswagers, L (2016). 'Developing a European network for the future of religious heritage', in K Van Balen and A Vandesande, eds, *Heritage Counts: Reflections on Cultural Heritage Theories and Practices 2*, Garant, pp. 221–8.

Cooney, G (1996). 'Building the future on the past: archaeology and the construction of national identity in Ireland', in M Díaz-Andreu and T Champion, eds, *Nationalism and Archaeology in Europe*, UCL Press, pp. 146–63.

Coppack, G (1990). *Abbeys and Priories*, Batsford/English Heritage.

Cormack, W F (1995). 'Barhobble, Mochrum: excavation of a forgotten church site in Galloway', *Transactions of the Dumfriesshire and Galloway Natural History and Antiquarian Society*, 70, third series, 5–106.

Courtney, P, Egan, G and Gilchrist, R (2015). 'Small finds', in R Gilchrist and C Green, *Glastonbury Abbey: Archaeological Investigations 1904–79*, Society of Antiquaries of London, pp. 293–311.

Cowan, E J and Henderson, L eds (2011). *A History of Everyday Life in Medieval Scotland, 1000–1600*, Edinburgh University Press.

Cowan, I B and Easson, D E (1976). *Medieval Religious Houses, Scotland*, Longman.

Cowell, M (1928). 'The French-Walloon church at Glastonbury, 1550–1553', *Proceedings of the Huguenot Society of London*, 13, 483–515.

Cramp, R J (2005). *Wearmouth and Jarrow Monastic Sites, Volume I*, English Heritage.
Cramp, R (2014). *The Hirsel Excavations*, The Society for Medieval Archaeology Monograph 36.
Crone, A and Hindmarch, E with Woolf, A (2016). *Living and Dying at Auldhame, East Lothian*, Society of Antiquaries of Scotland.
Cruden, S (1950–1). 'Glenluce Abbey: finds recovered during excavations. Part I', *Transactions of the Dumfriesshire and Galloway Natural History and Antiquarian Society*, 29, third series, 177–94.
Cruden, S (1952). 'Scottish medieval pottery: the Melrose Abbey collection', *Proceedings of the Society of Antiquaries of Scotland*, 87, 161–74.
Cruden, S (1955–6). 'Scottish medieval pottery', *Proceedings of the Society of Antiquaries of Scotland*, 89, 67–82.
Cunningham, J (2009). 'A young man's brow and an old man's beard: the rise and fall of Joseph of Arimathea in English Reformation thought', *Theology*, 112, 251–9.
Curle, A O (1924). 'A note on four silver spoons and a fillet of gold found in the nunnery at Iona', *Proceedings of the Society of Antiquaries of Scotland*, 58, 102–11.
Curran, K (2005). 'Religious women and their communities in late medieval Scotland', PhD thesis, University of Glasgow.
Curran, K (2015). '"Through the keyhole of the monastic library door": learning and education in Scottish medieval monasteries', in R Anderson, M Freeman and L Paterson, eds, *The Edinburgh History of Education in Scotland*, Edinburgh University Press, pp. 25–38.
Dalglish, C (2012). 'Scotland's medieval countryside: evidence, interpretation, perception', in N Christie, and P Stamper, eds, *Medieval Rural Settlement: Britain and Ireland, AD 800–1600*, Windgather Press, pp. 270–86.
Dalglish, C and Driscoll, S (2010). 'An international Scottish Historical Archaeology?', *International Journal of Historical Archaeology*, 14, 309–15.
Dallen, J T and Olsen, D H eds (2006). *Tourism, Religion and Spiritual Journeys*, Routledge.
Darvill, T (2002). 'White on blonde: quartz pebbles and the use of quartz at Neolithic monuments in the Isle of Man and beyond', in A Jones and G MacGregor, eds, *Colouring the Past: The Significance of Colour in Archaeological Research*, Bloomsbury, pp. 73–91.
Davies, O (2015). 'The material culture of post-medieval domestic magic in Europe: evidence, comparisons and interpretations', in C Houlbrook and N Armitage, eds, *The Materiality of Magic: An Artefactual Investigation into Ritual Practices and Popular Beliefs*, Oxbow Books, pp. 379–417.
Davis, A (2019). 'Plant remains', in C Harward, N Holder and C Thomas with D Bowlsher, M McKenzie and K Pitt, *The Medieval Priory and Hospital of St Mary Spital and Bishopsgate Suburb: Excavations at Spitalfields Market, London E1, 1991–2007*, Museum of London Archaeology.
De Dijn, H (2012). 'The scandal of particularity: meaning, incarnation and sacred places', in T Coomans, H De Dijn, J De Maeyer, R Heynickx and B Verschaffel, eds, *Loci Sacri: Understanding Sacred Places*, Leuven University Press, pp. 39–48.
De Rubeis, F and Marazzi, F eds (2008). *Monasteri in Europa occidentale (secoli VIII–XI): topografia e strutture*, Viella.
Dellheim, C (1982). *The Face of the Past*, Cambridge University Press.
Destefanis, E (2011). 'Archeologia dei monasteri altomedievali tra acquisizioni raggiunte e nuove prospettive di ricerca: strutture materiali, organizzazione, gestione territorial', *Post Classical Archaeologies*, 1, 349–82.
Díaz-Andreu, M and Champion, T (1996), 'Nationalism and archaeology in Europe: an introduction', in M Díaz-Andreu and T Champion, eds, *Nationalism and Archaeology in Europe*, UCL Press, pp. 1–23.
Dickson, C (1996). 'Food, medicinal and other plants from the fifteenth-century drains of Paisley Abbey, Scotland', *Vegetation History and Archaeobotany*, 5(1–2), 25–31.
Dickson, C and Dickson, J (2000). *Plants and People in Ancient Scotland*, Tempus.
Dictionary of Scottish Architects, Ian Gordon Lindsay [www.scottisharchitects.org.uk/architect_full.php?id=202407].

Dilworth, M (1995). *Scottish Monasteries in the Later Middle Ages*, Edinburgh University Press.

Dingwall, H M (2002). *A History of Scottish Medicine: Themes and Influences*, Edinburgh University Press.

Ditchburn, D (2010). 'The "McRoberts Thesis" and patterns of sanctity in late medieval Scotland', in S Boardman and E Williamson, eds, *The Cult of Saints and the Virgin Mary in Medieval Scotland*, Boydell Press, pp. 177–94.

Donoho, E (2014). 'The madman amongst the ruins: the oral history and folklore of traditional insanity cures in the Scottish Highlands', *Folklore*, 125(1), 22–39.

Driscoll, K (2015). 'The role of quartz in Neolithic lithic traditions: a case study from the Thornhill early Neolithic palisaded enclosure, Co Londonderry, Northern Ireland', *Proceedings of the Royal Irish Academy. Section C: Archaeology, Celtic Studies, History, Linguistics, Literature*, 115C, 1–27.

Driscoll, S T (2002). *Excavations at Glasgow Cathedral 1988–1997*, Society for Medieval Archaeology Monograph 18, Maney.

Driscoll, S T (2010). 'Scottish Historical Archaeology: international agendas and local politics', *International Journal of Historical Archaeology*, 14, 442–62.

Dubisch, J (1995). *In a Different Place: Pilgrimage, Gender and Politics of a Greek Island Shrine*, Princeton University Press.

Duffy, E (1992). *The Stripping of the Altars: Traditional Religion in England 1400–1580*, Yale University Press.

Dugdale, W (1817–30). *Monasticon Anglicanum*, Volume VI, London.

Dunbar, J G and Fisher, I (1974). 'Sgor nam Ban-Naomha ("Cliff of the Holy Women"), Island of Canna', *Scottish Archaeological Forum*, 5, 71–5.

Dyas, D (2004). 'Medieval patterns of pilgrimage: a mirror for today?', in C Bartholomew and F Hughes, eds, *Explorations in Christian Pilgrimage*, Ashgate, pp. 92–109.

Dyas, D (2017). 'Place, spirituality and mission', unpublished paper presented at *Cathedrals, Mission, and the Power of Place, Past, Present and Future*, Lambeth Palace.

Egan, G (1997). 'Non-ceramic finds', in C Thomas, B Sloane and C Phillpotts, eds, *Excavations at the Priory and Hospital of St Mary Spital, London*, Museum of London Archaeological Service Monograph, pp. 201–10.

Emerick, K (2014). *Conserving and Managing Ancient Monuments: Heritage, Democracy, and Inclusion*, Boydell & Brewer.

Ervynck, A (1997). 'Following the rule? Fish and meat consumption in monastic communities in Flanders (Belgium)', in G De Boew and F Verhaeghe, eds, *Environment and Subsistence in Medieval Europe. Papers of the 'Medieval Europe Brugge 1997' Conference*. Volume 9, Instituut voor het Archeologisch Patrimonium, pp. 67–81.

Evans, C (1998). 'Historicism, chronology and straw men: situating Hawkes' "Ladder of inference"', *Antiquity*, 72(276), 398–404.

Evans, J (1922). *Magical Jewels of the Middle Ages and Renaissance*, Constable.

Everson, P and Stocker, D (2011). *Custodians of Continuity? The Premonstratensian Abbey at Barlings and the Landscape of Ritual*, Lincolnshire Archaeology and Heritage Reports Series 11, Heritage Trust of Lincolnshire.

Ewart, G (1996). 'Inchaffray Abbey, Perth and Kinross: excavation and research, 1987', *Proceedings of the Society of Antiquaries of Scotland*, 126, 469–516.

Ewart, G (2001). *Dundrennan Abbey: Archaeological Investigation within the South Range of a Cistercian House in Kirkcudbrightshire (Dumfries and Galloway), Scotland*, Scottish Archaeological Internet Report 1, Society of Antiquaries of Scotland with Historic Scotland and the Council for British Archaeology.

Ewart, G and Gallagher, D B (2013). *Monastery and Palace: Archaeological Investigations at Holyroodhouse 1996–2009*, Archaeology Report 6, Historic Scotland.

Ewart, G, Gallagher, D and Sherman, P (2009). 'Graveheart: cult and burial in a Cistercian chapter house – excavations at Melrose, 1921 and 1996', *Proceedings of the Society of Antiquaries of Scotland*, 139, 257–304.

Falk, A-B (2008). *En Grundläggande Handling. Byggnadsoffer Och Dagligt Liv i Medeltid*, Nordic Academic Press.

Fawcett, R. (1994a). *Scottish Abbeys and Priories*, Historic Scotland.

Fawcett, R (1994b). *Scottish Architecture: From the Accession of the Stewarts to the Reformation, 1371–1560*, Edinburgh University Press.

Fawcett, R (2002). *Scottish Medieval Churches: Architecture and Furnishings*, Tempus and Historic Scotland.

Fawcett, R (2011). *The Architecture of the Scottish Medieval Church 1100–1560*, Yale University Press.

Fawcett, R and Oram, R (2004). *Melrose Abbey*, Tempus.

Feld, S and Basso, K H eds (1996). *Senses of Place*, School of American Research Press.

Ferguson, R (2001). *George MacLeod: Founder of the Iona Community*, Wild Goose Publications.

Fergusson, P, Coppack, G, Harrison, S and Carter, M (2016). *Rievaulx Abbey*. English Heritage Guidebooks, English Heritage.

Fernie, E (1980). 'The spiral piers of Durham Cathedral', in N Coldstream and P Draper, eds, *Medieval Art and Architecture at Durham Cathedral*, British Archaeological Association Conference Transactions 3, British Archaeological Association, pp. 49–58.

Fernie, E (1983). *The Architecture of the Anglo-Saxons*, Holmes & Meier.

Fernie, E (1986). 'Early Church Architecture in Scotland', *Proceedings of the Society of Antiquaries of Scotland*, 116, 393–411.

Finnernan, N (2012). 'Hermits, saints and snakes: the archaeology of the early Ethiopian monastery in wider context', *International Journal of African Historical Studies*, 45(2), 247–71.

Finucane, R C (1977). *Miracles and Pilgrims: Popular Beliefs in Medieval England*, Dent.

Fiorin, E, Sáez, L and Malgosa, A (2018). 'Ferns as healing plants in medieval Mallorca, Spain? Evidence from human dental calculus', *International Journal of Osteoarchaeology*, preprint doi: 10.1002/oa.2718

Flakney, K (2015). 'Detecting past medieval medical practices through trace element analysis of dental calculus', unpublished undergraduate dissertation, University of Reading.

Fogelin, L (2003). 'Ritual and presentation in early Buddhist religious architecture', *Asian Perspectives*, 42, 129–54.

Fogelin, L (2007). 'The archaeology of religious ritual', *Annual Review of Anthropology*, 36, 55–71.

Foley, R (2011). 'Performing health in place: the holy well as a therapeutic assemblage', *Health & Place*, 17(2), 470–79.

Fontein, J (2006). *The Silence of Great Zimbabwe: Contested Landscapes and the Power of Heritage*, University of Edinburgh.

Foot, S (1991). 'Glastonbury's early abbots', in L Abrams and J P Carley, eds, *The Archaeology and History of Glastonbury Abbey: Essays in Honour of the Ninetieth Birthday of C. A. Ralegh Radford*, Boydell & Brewer, pp. 163–89.

Forsyth, K and Maldonado, A (2013) 'The early sculpture of Kirkmadrine', unpublished report commissioned by Historic Scotland.

Foster, S M (1998). 'Discovery, recovery, context and display', in S M Foster, ed, *The St Andrews Sarcophagus: A Pictish Masterpiece and its International Connections*, Four Courts Press, pp. 36–62.

Foster, S M and Cross, M eds (2005). *Able Minds and Practised Hands: Scotland's Early Medieval Sculpture in the 21st Century*, Society for Medieval Archaeology Monograph 23, Maney.

Foucault, M (1986). 'Of other spaces', *Diacritics*, 16(1), 22–7.

Fowler, C (2004). *The Archaeology of Personhood: An Anthropological Approach*, Routledge.

Fowler, C and Harris, O (2015). 'Enduring relations: exploring a paradox of new materialism', *Journal of Material Culture*, 20(2), 127–48.

Fowles, S M (2013). *An Archaeology of Doings: Secularism and the Study of Pueblo Religion*, School for Advanced Research Press.

Fredengren, C (2016). 'Unexpected encounters with deep time enchantment. Bog bodies, crannogs and "otherworldly" sites: the materializing powers of disjunctures in time', *World Archaeology*, 48(4), 482–99.

Frey, N (1998). *Pilgrim Stories: On and Off the Road to Santiago*, University of California Press.

Gaimster, D (2014). 'The Hanseatic cultural signature: exploring globalization on the micro-scale in late medieval northern Europe', *European Journal of Archaeology*, 17(1), 60–81.

Gaimster, D and Gilchrist, R eds (2003). *The Archaeology of Reformation, 1480–1580*, The Society for Post-Medieval Archaeology Monograph 1, Maney.

Galliot, S (2015). 'Ritual efficacy in the making', *Journal of Material Culture*, 20(2), 101–25.

Gardiner, M (2012). 'Oral tradition, landscape and the social life of place-names', in R Jones and S Semple, eds, *Sense of Place in Anglo-Saxon England*, Shaun Tyas, pp. 16–30.

Garrow, D (2012). 'Odd deposits and average practice: a critical history of the concept of structured deposition', *Archaeological Dialogues*, 19(2), 85–115.

Gavin-Schwartz, A (2001). 'Archaeology and folklore of material culture, ritual and every-day life', *International Journal of Historical Archaeology*, 5(4), 263–80.

Geary, P J (1986). 'Sacred commodities: the circulation of medieval relics', in A Appadurai, ed, *The Social Life of Things: Commodities in Cultural Perspective*, Cambridge University Press, pp. 169–91.

Gerrard, C (2003). *Medieval Archaeology: Understanding Traditions and Contemporary Approaches*, Routledge.

Gesler, W M (2003). *Healing Places*, Rowman & Littlefield.

Gilchrist, R (1989). 'Community and self: perceptions and use of space in medieval monasteries', *Scottish Archaeological Review*, 6, 55–64.

Gilchrist, R (1994). *Gender and Material Culture: The Archaeology of Religious Women*, Routledge.

Gilchrist, R (1995). *Contemplation and Action: The Other Monasticism*, Leicester University Press.

Gilchrist, R (2005). *Norwich Cathedral Close: The Evolution of the English Cathedral Landscape*, Boydell Press.

Gilchrist, R (2008). 'Magic for the dead? The archaeology of magic in later medieval burials', *Medieval Archaeology*, 52, 119–59.

Gilchrist, R (2012). *Medieval Life: Archaeology and the Life Course*, Boydell Press.

Gilchrist, R (2013). 'Courtenay Arthur Ralegh Radford', *Biographical Memoirs of Fellows XII, Proceedings of the British Academy*, 341–58.

Gilchrist, R (2014). 'Monastic and church archaeology', *Annual Review of Anthropology*, 43, 235–50.

Gilchrist, R (2015). 'Transforming medieval beliefs: the significance of bodily resurrection to medieval burial rituals', in M Prusac and R Brandt, eds, *Ritual Changes and Changing Rituals: Function and Meaning in Ancient Funerary Practices*, Oxbow Books, pp. 379–96.

Gilchrist, R (2019). 'Magic and archaeology: ritual residues and "odd" deposits', in S Page and C Rider, eds, *Routledge History Handbook of Medieval Magic, ca 1000–1500*, Routledge, pp. 383–401.

Gilchrist, R, Allan, J and Bell, J (2017). *Glastonbury Abbey Guidebook*, Trustees of Glastonbury Abbey.

Gilchrist, R and Green, C (2015). *Glastonbury Abbey: Archaeological Investigations 1904–79*, Society of Antiquaries of London.

Gilchrist, R and Mytum, H eds (1993). *Advances in Monastic Archaeology*, British Archaeological Report 227, Tempus Reparatum.

Gilchrist, R and Sloane, B (2005). *Requiem: The Medieval Monastic Cemetery in Britain*, Museum of London Archaeology Service.

Giles, K (2000). *An Archaeology of Social Identity: Guildhalls in York, c.1350–1630*, British Archaeological Report British Series 315, Oxford.

Glastonbury Abbey Conservation Plan 2018, unpublished, Keystone Historic Buildings Consultants for Glastonbury Abbey Trustees.

Glenn, V (2003). *Romanesque and Gothic Decorative Metalwork and Ivory Carvings in the Museum of Scotland*, National Museum of Scotland.

Gofton, R and McVerry, J (2014). 'Glastonbury Abbey visitor results 2014', unpublished report for the Glastonbury Abbey Trustees by Heritage and Community.

Goodall, J A (1986). 'The Glastonbury Abbey Memorial Plate reconsidered', *The Antiquaries Journal*, 66, 364–7.

Gooder, J, Bush, H, Crowley, N and Heald, A (2004). 'Excavations at Newbattle Abbey College Annexe, Dalkleith, Midlothian', *Proceedings of the Society of Antiquaries of Scotland*, 134, 371–401.

Götlind, A (1993). *Technology and Religion in Medieval Sweden*, Falun.

Gough, P (2007). '"Contested memories: contested site": Newfoundland and its unique heritage on the Western Front', *The Round Table*, 96(393), 693–705.

Gowlland, G (2011). 'The "matière à penser" approach to material culture: objects, subjects and the materiality of the self', *Journal of Material Culture*, 16(3), 337–43.

Grabar, O and Kedar, B Z eds (2010). *Where Heaven and Earth Meet: Jerusalem's Sacred Esplanade*, Jamal and Rania Daniel Series in Contemporary History, University of Texas Press.

Graham, E, Simmons, S E and White, C D (2013). 'The Spanish conquest and the Maya collapse: how "religious" is change?', *World Archaeology*, 45(1), 161–85.

Gransden, A (2001). 'The growth of the Glastonbury traditions and legends in the twelfth century', in J P Carley, ed, *Glastonbury Abbey and the Arthurian Tradition*, Arthurian Studies 44, D. S. Brewer, pp. 29–54.

Grau-Sologestoa, I (2018). 'Pots, chicken and building deposits: the archaeology of folk and official religion during the High Middle Ages in the Basque Country', *Journal of Anthroplogical Archaeology*, 49, 8–18.

Graves, C P (2000). *The Form and Fabric of Belief: The Archaeology of Lay Experience in Medieval Norfolk and Devon*, British Archaeological Report British Series 311, British Archaeological Reports.

Graves, C P (2008). 'From an archaeology of iconoclasm to an anthropology of the body: images, punishment and personhood in England, 1500–1660', *Current Anthropology*, 49(1), 35–57.

Graves, C P (2015). 'Stained and painted window glass', in R Gilchrist and C Green, *Glastonbury Abbey: Archaeological Investigations 1904–79*, Society of Antiquaries of London, pp. 320–37.

Green, M (2009). 'Salerno on the Thames: the genesis of Anglo-Norman medical literature', in J Wogan-Browne, ed, *Language and Culture in Medieval Britain: The French of England, c.1100–c.1500*, York Medieval Press, pp. 220–231.

Greene, J P (1992). *Medieval Monasteries*, Leicester University Press.

Greenfeld, L and Eastwood, J (2009). 'National identity', in C Boix and S C Stokes, eds, *The Oxford Handbook of Comparative Politics*, Oxford University Press [www.oxfordhandbooks.com/view/10.1093/oxfordhb/9780199566020.001.0001/oxfordhb-9780199566020-e-11, accessed 17 December 2018].

Greilsammer, M (1991). 'The midwife, the priest, and the physician: the subjugation of midwives in the Low Countries at the end of the Middle Ages', *The Journal of Medieval and Renaissance Studies*, 21, 285–329.

Groves, S, Roberts, C, Johnstone, C, Hall, R and Dobney, K (2003). 'A high status burial from Ripon Cathedral, North Yorkshire, England: differential diagnosis of a chest deformity', *International Journal of Osteoarchaeology*, 13(6), 358–68.

Gruber, C (2012). 'The Martyr's Museum in Tehran: visualizing memory in post-revolutionary Iran', *Visual Anthropology*, 25 (1–2), 68–97.

Gruber, S (2002). 'Archaeological remains of Ashkenazic Jewry in Europe: a new source of pride and history', in V Leonard and V Rutgers, eds, *What Athens has to do with Jerusalem: Essays on Classical, Jewish and Early Christian Art and Archaeology in Honour of Gideon Foerster*, Peeters, pp. 267–301.

Gullbekk, S H (2018). 'Scandinavian women in search for salvation: women's use of money in religion and devotional practices', in N Myrberg Burström and G Tarnow Ingvardson, eds, *Divina Moneta: Coins in Religion and Ritual*, Routledge, pp. 209–27.

Gullbekk, S H, Kilger, C and Myrberg Burstrom, N (2016). 'Religion and money', unpublished Conference session: *Medieval Religion and Archaeology*, Gotland [www.khm.uio.no/english/research/projects/religion-and-money/church-and-money/].

Habu, J, Fawcett, C and Matsunaga, J M eds (2008). *Evaluating Multiple Narratives: Beyond Nationalist, Colonialist, Imperialist Archaeologies*, Springer.

Hall, D W (1995). 'Archaeological excavations at St Nichols Farm, St Andrews, 1986–87', *Tayside and Fife Archaeological Journal*, 1, 48–75.

Hall, D W (2006). *Scottish Monastic Landscapes*, Tempus.

Hall, D W and Bowler, D (1997). 'North Berwick, East Lothian: its archaeology revisited', *Proceedings of the Society of Antiquaries of Scotland*, 127, 659–75.

Hall, D W, Haggarty, G and Hughes, M (in prep). 'The ceramics', in A Cameron, *Excavations at Marischal College, Aberdeen.*

Hall, M A (2007). 'Crossing the pilgrimage landscape: some thoughts on a Holy Rood reliquary from the river Tay at Carpow, Perth and Kinross, Scotland', in S Blick, ed, *Beyond Pilgrim Souvenirs and Secular Badges: Essays in Honour of Brian Spencer*, Oxbow Books, pp. 75–91.

Hall, M A (2011). 'The cult of saints in medieval Perth: everyday ritual and the materiality of belief', *Journal of Material Culture*, 16(1), 80–104.

Hall, M A (2012). 'Money isn't everything: the cultural life of coins in the medieval burgh of Perth, Scotland', *Journal of Social Archaeology*, 12(1), 72–91.

Hall, M A (2016a). '"Pennies from Heaven": money in ritual in medieval Europe', in C Haselgrove and S Krmnicek, eds, *The Archaeology of Money. Proceedings of the Workshop 'Archaeology of Money', University of Tübingen, October 2013*, Leicester Archaeology Monograph 24, School of Archaeology and Ancient History, pp. 137–59.

Hall, M A (2016b). 'Playing the dark side: a look at some chess and other playing pieces of jet and jet-like materials from Britain', in F Hunter and A Sheridan, eds, *Ancient Lives: Object, People and Place in Early Scotland. Essays for David V Clarke on his 70th Birthday*, Sidestone Press, pp. 359–81.

Hallbäck, D-A (1976–7). 'A medieval(?) bone with a copper plate support, indicating an open surgical treatment', *Ossa*, 3(4), 63–82.

Hamerow, H (2006). '"Special deposits" in Anglo-Saxon settlements', *Medieval Archaeology*, 50, 1–30.

Hamerow, H (2012). *Rural Settlements and Society in Anglo-Saxon England*, Oxford University Press.

Hamilakis, Y and Yalouri, E (1999). 'Sacralising the past', *Archaeological Dialogues*, 6(2), 115–35.

Hamilton, D (1981). *The Healers: A History of Medicine in Scotland*, Canongate.

Hamlin, A and Brannon, N (2003). 'Northern Ireland: the afterlife of monastic buildings', in D Gaimster and R Gilchrist, eds, *The Archaeology of Reformation, 1480–1580*, The Society for Post-Medieval Archaeology Monograph 1, Maney, pp. 252–66.

Hammond, M (2006). 'Ethnicity and the writing of medieval Scottish history', *Scottish Historical Review*, 85(1), 1–29.

Hammond, M (2010). 'Royal and aristocratic attitudes to saints and the Virgin Mary in twelfth- and thirteenth-century Scotland', in S Boardman and E Williamson, eds, *The Cult of Saints and the Virgin Mary in Medieval Scotland*, Boydell & Brewer, pp. 61–86.

Hammond, M (2013). 'Introduction: the paradox of medieval Scotland, 1093–1286', in M Hammond, ed, *New Perspectives on Medieval Scotland 1093–1286*, Boydell Press, pp. 1–52.

Harbison, R (1991). *Pilgrimage in Ireland*, Barrie and Jenkins.

Hardy, K, Buckley, S, Collins, M J, Estalrrich, A, Brothwell, D, Copeland, L, García-Tabernero, A, García-Vargas, S, de la Rasilla, M, Lalueza-Fox, C and Huguet, R (2012). 'Neanderthal medics? Evidence for food, cooking, and medicinal plants entrapped in dental calculus', *Naturwissenschaften*, 99(8), 617–26.

Hare, J N (1985). *Battle Abbey: The Eastern Range and the Excavations of 1978–80*, Historic Buildings & Monuments Commission for England, Archaeological Report 2.

Harris, N E (2016). 'Loadstones are a girl's best friend: lapidary cures, midwives and manuals of popular healing in medieval and early modern England', in B Bowers and L M Keyser, eds, *The Sacred and the Secular in Medieval Healing: Sites, Objects, and Texts*, Routledge, pp. 182–218.

Harrison, R (2012). *Heritage: Critical Approaches*, Routledge.

Harvey, B (1993). *Living and Dying in England 1100–1540: The Monastic Experience*, Clarendon Press.

Harvey, D C (2002). 'Constructed landscapes and social memory: tales of St Samson in early medieval Cornwall', *Environment and Planning D: Society and Space*, 20(2), 231–48.

Harvey, D C (2008). 'The history of heritage', in B Graham and P Howard, eds, *The Ashgate Research Companion to Heritage and Identity*, Ashgate, pp. 19–36.

Harward, C, Holder N and Thomas, C with Bowlsher, D, McKenzie, M and Pitt, K (2019). *The Medieval Priory and Hospital of St Mary Spital and Bishopsgate Suburb: Excavations at Spitalfields Market, London E1, 1991–2007*, Museum of London Archaeology.

Hawkes, C (1954). 'Archaeological theory and method: some suggestions from the Old World', *American Anthropologist*, 56(2), 155–68.

Haycock, D B (2002). *William Stukeley: Science, Religion, and Archaeology in Eighteenth-Century England*, Boydell & Brewer.

Hedeager, L (2011). *Iron Age Myth and Materiality: An Archaeology of Scandinavia AD 400–1000*, Routledge.

Heelas, P, Woodhead, L, Seel, B, Tusting, K and Szerszynski, B (2005). *The Spiritual Revolution: Why Religion is Giving Way to Spirituality*, Blackwell.

Heighway, C and Bryant, R (1999). *The Golden Minster: The Anglo-Saxon Minster and Later Medieval Priory of St Oswald at Gloucester*, Council for British Archaeology Research Report 117.

Higham, N (2002). *King Arthur: Myth-Making and History*, Routledge.

Hildburgh, W L (1908). 'Notes on some amulets of the Three Magi Kings', *Folklore*, 19, 83–7.

Hill, P (1997). *Whithorn and St Ninian: The Excavation of a Monastic Town, 1984–91*, The Whithorn Trust/Sutton Publishing.

Hindman, S with Fatone, I and Laurent-di Mantova, A (2007). *Toward an Art History of Medieval Rings: A Private Collection*, Paul Holberton.

Hinton, D (2005). *Gold, Gilt, Pots and Pins: Possessions and People in Medieval Britain*, Oxford University Press.

Historic England (2016). *Research Strategy* [https://content.historicengland.org.uk/images-books/publications/research-strategy/research-strategy.pdf/].

Historic Environment Scotland (2016). *Scotland's Archaeology Strategy* [http://archaeologystrategy.scot/files/2016/08/Scotlands_Archaeology_Strategy_Aug2016.pdf].

Hobsbawm, E J (1983). 'Introduction: inventing tradition', in E J Hobsbawm and T O Ranger, eds, *The Invention of Tradition*, Cambridge University Press, pp. 1–14.

Hodder, I (1998). 'The past as passion and play: Çatalhöyük as a site of conflict in the construction of multiple pasts', in L Meskell, ed, *Archaeology under Fire: Nationalism, Politics and Heritage in the Eastern Mediterranean and Middle East*, Routledge, pp. 124–39.

Hodder, I (2008). 'Multivocality and social archaeology', in J Habu, C Fawcett and J M Matsunaga, eds, *Evaluating Multiple Narratives: Beyond Nationalist, Colonialist, Imperialist Archaeologies*, Springer, pp. 196–200.

Hodges, R (1997). *Light in the Dark Ages: The Rise and Fall of San Vincenzo al Volturno*, Duckworth/Cornell University Press.

Holbrook, N and Thomas, A (2005). 'An early-medieval monastic cemetery at Llandough, Glamorgan: excavations in 1994', *Medieval Archaeology*, 49, 1–92.

Hollinrake, C and Hollinrake, N (2003). 'An archaeological watching brief at Glastonbury Tor during the entrances and pathways enhancement', unpublished report No 312, copy in Somerset Heritage Environment Record file.

Holtorf, C (2013a). 'On pastness: a reconsideration of materiality in archaeological object authenticity', *Anthropological Quarterly*, 86(2), 427–43.

Holtorf, C (2013b). 'The need and potential for an archaeology orientated towards the present', *Archaeological Dialogues*, 20(1), 12–18.

Holtorf, C and Fairclough, G (2013). 'The new heritage and re-shapings of the past', in A

González-Ruibal, ed, *Reclaiming Archaeology: Beyond the Tropes of Modernity*, Routledge, pp. 197–210.

Holtorf, C and Williams, M R (2006). 'Landscapes and memories', in D Hicks and M Beaudry, eds, *Cambridge Companion to Historical Archaeology*, Cambridge University Press, pp. 235–54.

Hopkinson-Ball, T (2007). *The Rediscovery of Glastonbury Abbey: Frederick Bligh Bond, Architect of the New Age*, Sutton.

Hopkinson-Ball, T (2008). 'Trouble at the abbey', *British Archaeology*, Jan.–Feb., 33–7.

Hopkinson-Ball, T (2012). 'The cultus of Our Lady at Glastonbury Abbey: 1184–1539', *The Downside Review*, 130, 3–52.

Horden, P (2007). 'A non-natural environment: medicine without doctors and the medieval European hospital', in S B Bowers, ed, *The Medieval Hospital and Medical Practice*, Ashgate, pp. 133–45.

Horning, A, Breen, C and Brannon, N (2015). 'From the past to the future: integrating archaeology and conflict resolution in Northern Ireland', *Conservation and Management of Archaeological Sites*, 17(1), 5–21.

Houlbrook, C (2015). 'The wishing-tree of Isle Maree: the evolution of a Scottish folkloric practice', in C Houlbrook and N Armitage, eds, *The Materiality of Magic: An Artefactual Investigation into Ritual Practices and Popular Beliefs*, Oxbow Books, pp. 124–42.

Houlbrook, C and Armitage, N eds (2015). *The Materiality of Magic: An Artefactual Investigation into Ritual Practices and Popular Beliefs*, Oxbow Books.

Howard, M (2003). 'Recycling the monastic fabric: beyond the act of dissolution', in D Gaimster and R Gilchrist, eds, *The Archaeology of Reformation, 1480–1580*, The Society for Post-Medieval Archaeology Monograph 1, Maney, pp. 221–34.

Huggon, M (2018). 'Medieval medicine, public health and the medieval hospital', in C M Gerrard and A Gutiérrez, eds, *The Oxford Handbook of Later Medieval Archaeology in Britain*, Oxford University Press, pp. 836–55.

Hukantaival, S (2013). 'Finding folk religion: an archaeology of "strange" behaviour', *Folklore: Electronic Journal of Folklore*, 55, 99–124.

Hutchinson, F (2001). 'Archaeology and the Irish rediscovery of the Celtic past', *Nations and Nationalism*, 7(4), 505–19.

Hutton, R (2003). *Witches, Druids and King Arthur*, Hambledon Continuum.

Hutton, R (2014). *Pagan Britain*, Yale University Press.

Hutton, R (2015). 'Contemporary religion in historical perspective: the case of modern paganism', *Alternative Spirituality and Religion Review*, 6, 101–13.

Hutton, R (2016). 'Introduction', in R Hutton, ed, *Physical Evidence for Ritual Acts, Sorcery and Witchcraft in Christian Britain: A Feeling for Magic*, Palgrave Macmillan, pp. 1–14.

ICOMOS (1994). *The Nara Document on Authenticity*, ICOMOS.

Immonen, V and Taavitsainen, J-P (2014). 'Finger of a saint, thumb of a priest: medieval relics in the Diocese of Turku, and the archaeology of lived bodies', *Scripta Instituti Donneriani Aboensis*, 23, 141–73 [https://ojs.abo.fi/ojs/index.php/scripta/article/view/311].

Insoll, T (2004). *Archaeology, Ritual, Religion*, Routledge.

Jackson, R (2006). *Excavations at St James Priory, Bristol*, Oxbow Books.

James, H F, Henderson, I, Foster, S M and Jones, S (2008). *A Fragmented Masterpiece: Recovering the Biography of the Hilton of Cadboll Pictish Cross-Slab*, Society of Antiquaries of Scotland.

James, H F and Yeoman, P (2008). *Excavations at St Ethernan's Monastery, Isle of May, Fife, 1992–7*, Tayside and Fife Archaeological Committee Monograph 6.

James, T (1997). 'Excavations at Carmarthen Greyfriars, 1983–1990', *Medieval Archaeology*, 41, 100–94.

Jamroziak, E (2008). 'Cistercians and border conflicts: some comparisons between the experiences of Scotland and Pomerania', in J Burton and K Stöber, eds, *Monasteries and Society in the British Isles in the Later Middle Ages*, Studies in the History of Medieval Religion Volume 35, Boydell Press, pp. 40–50.

Jamroziak, E (2011). *Survival and Success on Medieval Borders: Cistercian Houses in Medieval Scotland and Pomerania from the Twelfth to the Late Fourteenth Century*, Brepols.

Jamroziak, E (2013). 'Cistercian identities in twelfth- and thirteenth-century Scotland: the case of Melrose Abbey', in M Hammond, ed, *New Perspectives on Medieval Scotland 1093–1286*, Boydell Press, pp. 175–82.

Janes, D and Waller, G F eds (2010). *Walsingham in Literature and Culture from the Middle Ages to Modernity*, Ashgate.

Janssens, P A (1987). 'A copper plate on the upper arm in a burial at the church in Vrasene, Belgium', *Journal of Paleopathology*, 1, 15–18.

Jeffrey, S (2015). 'Challenging heritage visualization: beauty, aura and democratisation', *Open Archaeology*, 1(1) [https://doi.org/10.1515/opar-2015-0008].

Johanson, K and Jonuks, T (2015). 'Superstition in the house of God? Some Estonian case studies of vernacular practices', *Mirator*, 16(1), 118–40.

Jolly, K (2002). 'Medieval magic: definitions, beliefs, practices', in K Jolly, C Raudvere and E Peters, eds, *Witchcraft and Magic in Europe: The Middle Ages*, Athlone, pp. 1–71.

Jones, S (2010). 'Negotiating authentic objects and authentic selves: beyond the deconstruction of authenticity', *Journal of Material Culture*, 15(2), 181–203.

Jones, S (2012). '"Thrown like chaff in the wind": excavation, memory and the negotiation of loss in the Scottish Highlands', *International Journal of Historical Archaeology*, 16(2), 346–66.

Jones, S (2017). 'Wrestling with the social value of heritage: problems, dilemmas and opportunities', *Journal of Community Archaeology & Heritage*, 4(1), 1–17.

Jones, S and Leech, S (2015). *Valuing the Historic Environment: A Critical Review of Existing Approaches to Social Value*. AHRC: Cultural Value Project Report, University of Manchester [www.escholar.manchester.ac.uk/uk-ac-man-scw:281849].

Jonsson, K (2009). *Practices for the Living and the Dead: Medieval and Post-Reformation Burials in Scandinavia*. Stockholm Studies in Archaeology 50, Stockholm University.

Kapaló, J A (2013). 'Folk religion in discourse and practice', *Journal of Ethnology and Folkloristics*, 7(1), 3–18.

Karlström, A (2005). 'Spiritual materiality: heritage preservation in a Buddhist world?', *Journal of Social Archaeology*, 5(3), 338–55.

Kedar, B Z (2014). *Rival Conceptualizations of a Single Space: Jerusalem's Sacred Esplanade*, Nehru Memorial Museum and Library.

Keevil, G, Aston, M and Hall, T eds (2001). *Monastic Archaeology*, Oxbow Books.

Kelleher, R (2012). 'The re-use of coins in medieval England and Wales c.1050–1550: an introductory survey', *Yorkshire Numismatist*, 4, 183–200.

Kelleher, R (2018). 'Pilgrims, pennies and the ploughzone: folded coins in medieval Britain', in N Myrberg Burström and G Tarnow Ingvardson, eds, *Divina Moneta: Coins in Religion and Ritual*, Routledge, pp. 68–86.

Kelly, S E (2012). *Charters of Glastonbury Abbey*, Anglo-Saxon Charters 15, Oxford University Press.

Kennedy, M (2015). 'Glastonbury's myths made up by twelfth-century monks', *The Guardian*, 23 November [www.theguardian.com/science/2015/nov/23/glastonbury-myths-made-up-by-12th-century-monks].

Kent, O (2015). 'Wares associated with specialist scientific and technical activities', in R Gilchrist and C Green, *Glastonbury Abbey: Archaeological Investigations 1904–79*, Society of Antiquaries of London, pp. 276–8.

Kieckhefer, R (1994). 'The specific rationality of medieval magic', *American Historical Review*, 99, 813–36.

Kieckhefer, R (2000). *Magic in the Middle Ages*, Cambridge University Press.

Kinder, T N (2012). 'What makes a site sacred? Transforming "place" to "sacred space"', in T Coomans, H De Dijn, J De Maeyer, R Heynickx and B Verschaffel, eds, *Loci Sacri: Understanding Sacred Places*, Leuven University Press, pp. 195–208.

Kindon, S, Pain, R and Kesby, M eds (2007). *Participatory Action Research Approaches and Methods: Connecting People, Participation and Place*, Routledge.

Kingdom, M (forthcoming). 'The past people of Exeter: health, social standing and well-being in the Middle Ages and early modern period', PhD thesis, University of Exeter.

Klamer, A (2014). 'The values of archaeological and heritage sites', *Public Archaeology*, 13, 59–70.

Klemperer, W D and Boothroyd, N (2004). *Excavations at Hulton Abbey, Staffordshire 1987–1994*, Society for Medieval Archaeology Monograph 21, Maney.

Knott, K, Krech, V and Meyer, B (2016). 'Iconic religion in urban space', *Material Religion*, 12 (2), 123–36.

Knowles, D and Hadcock, R N (1971). *Medieval Religious Houses: England and Wales*, Longman.

Knüsel, C J, Kemp, R L and Budd, P (1995). 'Evidence for remedial treatment of a severe knee injury from the Fishergate Gilbertine monastery in the city of York', *Journal of Archaeological Science*, 22, 369–84.

Koopmans, R (2016). '"Water mixed with the blood of Thomas": contact relic manufacture pictured in Canterbury Cathedral's stained glass', *Journal of Medieval History*, 42, 535–58.

Kornbluth, G (2016). 'Early medieval crystal amulets: secular instruments of protection and healing', in B Bowers and L M Keyser, eds, *The Sacred and the Secular in Medieval Healing: Sites, Objects, and Texts*, Routledge, pp. 143–81.

Krasnodebska-D'Aughton, M and Lafaye, A (2018). 'Material culture of mendicant orders in medieval Ireland', in M M de Cevins, ed, *Marginalité, économie et christianisme. Les frères mendiants dans l'économie du sacré en Europe centrale*. Rennes University Press, pp. 119–44.

Kristjánsdóttir, S (2010). 'The tip of the iceberg: the material of Skriðuklaustur monastery and hospital', *Norwegian Archaeological Review*, 43 (1), 44–62.

Kristjánsdóttir, S (2015a). 'Becoming Christian: a matter of everyday resistance and negotiation', *Norwegian Archaeological Review*, 48(1), 27–45.

Kristjánsdóttir, S (2015b). 'No society is an island: Skriðuklaustur Monastery and the fringes of monasticism', *The Journal of Medieval Monastic Studies*, 2015(4), 153–72.

Kristjánsdóttir, S (2017). *Leitin Ad Klaustrunum. Klausturhald Á Íslandi Í Fimm Aldir*, Midstöd Íslenskra Bókmennta.

Kristjánsdóttir, S, Larsson, I and Åsen, P A (2014). 'The Icelandic medieval monastic garden: did it exist?', *Scandinavian Journal of History*, 39, 560–79.

Krochalis, J (1997). 'Magna Tabula: the Glastonbury tablets (part 1): preface', in J P Carley and F Riddy, eds, *Arthurian Literature 16*, Boydell & Brewer, pp. 93–183.

Lafaye, A (2018). 'Spiritual renewal and changing landscapes: the mendicant orders in Ireland, 13th–16th century', in J Lyttleton and M Stout, eds, *Church and Settlement in Ireland*, Four Courts Press.

Lagorio, V (2001). 'The evolving legend of St Joseph of Glastonbury', in J P Carley, ed, *Glastonbury Abbey and the Arthurian Tradition*, D. S. Brewer, pp. 55–81.

Laing, L R (1971–2). 'Medieval pottery from Coldingham Priory, Berwickshire', *Proceedings of the Society of Antiquarians of Scotland*, 104, 242–7.

Landy, J and Saler, M eds (2009). *The Re-Enchantment of the World: Secular Magic in a Rational Age*, Stanford University Press.

Lash, R (2018). 'Pebbles and peregrinatio: the taskscape of medieval devotion on Inishark Island, Ireland', *Medieval Archaeology*, 62(1), 83–104.

Lev, E (2002). 'Medicinal exploitation of inorganic substances in the Levant in the medieval and early Ottoman periods', *Adler Museum Bulletin*, 28(2–3), 11–16.

Lewis, J H and Ewart, G J (1995). *Jedburgh Abbey: The Archaeology and Architecture of a Border Abbey*, Society of Antiquaries of Scotland Monograph 10.

Lewis, M (2016). 'Life (and after-life) insurance in the medieval period: insights offered by the distribution of pilgrim badges recorded by the Portable Antiquities Scheme in England', in B S Bowers and L M Keyser, eds, *The Sacred and the Secular in Medieval Healing: Sites, Objects, and Texts*, Routledge, pp. 266–304.

Lewis, M E (2007). *The Bioarchaeology of Children: Perspectives from Biological and Forensic Anthropology*, Cambridge University Press.

Lindley, P (2007). *Tomb Destruction and Scholarship: Medieval Monasteries in Early Modern England*, Shaun Tyas.

Ljungkvist, J and Frölund, P (2015). 'Gamla Uppsala: the emergence of a centre and a magnate complex', *Journal of Archaeology and Ancient History*, 16, 1–29.

Lloyd, R L (1971–2). 'Medieval pottery from Coldingham Priory, Berwickshire', *Proceedings of the Society of Antiquaries of Scotland*, 104, 242–7.

Locker, M and Lewis, M (2015). 'Landscapes of devotion: pilgrim signs in their wider context', *Church Archaeology*, 17, 49–61.

Lowe, C (2005). 'New light on Kelso Abbey: archaeological interventions on the Bridge Street Garage site, 1996–8', *Proceedings of the Society of Antiquaries of Scotland*, 135, 319–42.

Lowe, C (2006). *Excavations at Hoddom, Dumfriesshire*, Society of Antiquaries of Scotland.

Lowe, C ed (2008). *Inchmarnock: An Early Historic Island Monastery and its Archaeological Landscape*, Society of Antiquaries of Scotland.

Lowe, C (2009). *'Clothing for the Soul Divine': Burials at the Tomb of St Ninian. Excavations at Whithorn Priory, 1957–67*, Historic Scotland.

Luxford, J M (2005). *The Art and Architecture of English Benedictine Monasteries, 1300–1540*, Boydell Press.

Luxford, J M (2012). 'King Arthur's tomb at Glastonbury: the relocation of 1368 in context', in E Archibald and D F Johnson, eds, *Arthurian Literature 29*, Boydell & Brewer, pp. 41–51.

Lyons, W J (2014). *Joseph of Arimathea: A Study in Reception History*, Oxford University Press.

MacDonald, I G (2014). 'The church in Gaelic Scotland before the Reformation', in T O O'Hannrachain and R Amrstrong, eds, *Christianities in the Early Modern Celtic World*, Palgrave Macmillan, pp. 17–28.

MacGregor, N (2018). *Living with the Gods: On Beliefs and Peoples*, Allen Lane.

MacKinlay, J (1893). *Folklore of Scottish Lochs and Springs*, William Hodge.

MacLennan, W J (2001). 'Fractures in medieval Scotland', *Scottish Medical Journal*, 46, 58–60.

Macquarrie, A (1992). 'Early Christian religious houses in Scotland: foundation and function', in J Blair and R Sharpe, eds, *Pastoral Care before the Parish*, Leicester University Press, pp. 110–33.

Maddrell, A (2009). 'A place for grief and belief: the Witness Cairn, Isle of Whithorn, Galloway, Scotland', *Social & Cultural Geography*, 10 (6), 675–93.

Maddrell, A (2015). 'Renewing pilgrimage practices in the Celtic West: the Isle of Man', in A Maddrell, V della Dora, A Scafi and H Walton, eds, *Christian Pilgrimage, Landscape and Heritage: Journeying to the Sacred*, Routledge, pp. 131–79.

Maddrell, A, della Dora, V, Scafi, A and Walton, H (2015). 'Introduction: pilgrimage, landscape, heritage', in A Maddrell, V della Dora, A Scafi and H Walton, eds, *Christian Pilgrimage, Landscape and Heritage: Journeying to the Sacred*, Routledge, pp. 1–21.

Magilton, J, Frances L and Boylston, A eds (2008). *Lepers Outside the Gate: Excavations at the Cemetery of the Hospital of St James and St Mary Magdalene, Chichester, 1986–1987 and 1993*, Council for British Archaeology Report 158.

Malden, R J ed (2000). *The Monastery and Abbey of Paisley*, Renfrewshire Local History Forum.

Malik, K (2015). 'The struggle for cultural heritage' [https://kenanmalik.wordpress.com/2015/11/11/the-struggle-for-cultural-heritage/].

Mallory, J P (2016). *In Search of the Irish Dreamtime: Archaeology and Early Irish Literature*, Thames and Hudson.

Malone, C, Barrowclough, D and Stoddart, S (2007). 'Introduction', in D Barrowclough and C Malone, eds, *Cult in Context: Reconsidering Ritual in Archaeology*, Oxbow Books, pp. 1–7.

Maltwood, K E (1964). *A Guide to Glastonbury's Temple of the Stars: Their Giant Effigies Described from Air Views, Maps, and from 'The High History of the Holy Grail'*, James Clarke & Co.

Manning, M C (2014). 'Magic, religion, and ritual in historical archaeology', *Historical Archaeology*, 48(3), 1–9.

Marks, R (2004). *Image and Devotion in Late Medieval England*, Sutton.

Márkus, G (2016). 'Faith in Cowal: a pilgrimage project and an early medieval cross', in S Foster, K Forsyth, S Buckham and S Jeffrey, eds, *Future Thinking on Carved Stones in Scotland*, Scottish Archaeological Research Framework [www.scottishheritagehub.com/content/case-study-faith-cowal-pilgrimage-project-and-early-medieval-cross].

Martinón-Torres, M and Rehren, T (2005). 'Alchemy, chemistry and metallurgy in Renaissance Europe: a wider context for fire-assay remains', *Historical Metallurgy*, 39(1), 14–28.

Mather, J D (2009). '"Wonder-working water": the history and hydrogeology of the Chalice Well and other Glastonbury springs', *Geoscience in South-West England*, 12(2), 115–24.

Mauss, M (2006 [1936]). 'Techniques of the body', in N Schlanger, ed, *Techniques, Technology and Civilisation*, Berghahn Books, pp. 77–95.

Mawrey, R (2012). 'The mystery of the Glastonbury cross', *History Today*, 6(4) [www.historytoday.com/richard-mawrey/mystery-glastonbury-cross].

Maxwell-Stuart, P G (2001). *Satan's Conspiracy: Magic and Witchcraft in Sixteenth-Century Scotland*, Tuckwell Press.

McCann, J M (1952). *The Rule of St Benedict*, Burns & Oates.

McClain, A N (2010). 'Cross slab monuments in the late Middle Ages: patronage, production and locality in northern England', in S Badham and S Oosterwijk, eds, *Monumental Industry: The Production of Tomb Monuments in England and Wales in the Long Fourteenth Century*, Shaun Tyas, pp. 37–65.

McGuire, B (1982). *The Cistercians in Denmark*, Cistercian Publications.

McNeill, P G B and MacQueen, H L eds (1996). *Atlas of Scottish History to 1707*, The Scottish Medievalists and Department of Geography, University of Edinburgh.

McRoberts, M D (1968). 'The Scottish church and nationalism in the fifteenth century', *Innes Review*, 19(1), 3–14.

Meaney, A L (1981). *Anglo-Saxon Amulets and Curing Stones*, British Archaeology Report 96.

Meier, T and Tillessen, P (2014). 'Archaeological imaginations of religion: an introduction from an Anglo-German perspective', in T Meier and P Tillessen, eds, *Archaeological Imaginations of Religion*, Archaeolingua Series Minor 31, Archaeolingua Alapítvány, pp. 11–248.

Melville, G, Schneidmüller, B and Weinfurter, S eds (2014). *Innovationen durch Deuten und Gestalten. Klöster im Mittelalter zwischen Jenseits und Welt*, Klöster als Innovationslabore: Studien und Texte 1, Schnell & Steiner.

Melville, G, Silberer, L and Schmies, B eds (2015). *Die Klöster der Franziskaner im Mittelalter. Räume, Nutzungen, Symbolik*, Vita regularis, Abhandlungen 63.

Merrifield, R (1987). *The Archaeology of Ritual and Magic*, Batsford.

Meskell, L ed (2009). *Cosmopolitan Archaeologies*, Duke University Press.

Meskell, L (2012). *The Nature of Heritage: The New South Africa*, Wiley-Blackwell.

Meskell, L (2016). 'World heritage and WikiLeaks', *Current Anthropology*, 57(1), 72–95.

Meyer, B and de Witte, M (2013). 'Heritage and the sacred: introduction', *Material Religion*, 9 (3), 274–81.

Meyer, B, Morgan, D, Paine, C and Plate, S B (2010). 'The origin and mission of material religion', *Religion*, 40(3), 207–11.

Miller, J (2004). *Magic and Witchcraft in Scotland*, Goblinshead.

Miller, P and Saxby, D (2007). *The Augustinian Priory of St Mary Merton, Surrey: Excavations 1976–90*, Museum of London Archaeology Service.

Moffat, B (1988–98). *SHARP Practice 2, 3, 4, 5, 6: Second, Third, Fourth, Fifth, Sixth Reports on Researches into the Medieval Hospital at Soutra, Lothian Region, Scotland*, SHARP.

Moffat, B (2014). 'Archaeological sources for the history of herbal medicine practice: the case study of St John's Wort with Valerian at

Soutra medieval hospital', in S Francia and A Stobart, eds, *Critical Approaches to the History of Western Herbal Medicine: From Classical Antiquity to the Early Modern Period*, Bloomsbury, pp. 253–70.

Mohan, U and Warnier, J-P (2017). 'Marching the devotional subject: the bodily-and-material cultures of religion', *Journal of Material Culture*, 22(4), 369–84.

Møller-Christensen, V (1969). 'A rosary bead used as tooth filling material in a human mandibular canine tooth: a unique case from the Danish Middle Ages', in *21st International Congress of the History of Medicine, Siena. Atti del Congress Internazionale di Storia Dela Medicina, Siena*, pp. 800–11.

Monastic Iceland [https://notendur.hi.is/~sjk/AR.htm].

Monastic Ireland [www.monastic.ie/].

Monastic Wales [www.monasticwales.org/].

Monteiro, L D (2011). 'The Mezquita of Córdoba is made of more than bricks: towards a broader definition of the "Heritage" protected at UNESCO world heritage sites', *Archaeologies*, 7(2), 312–28.

Moorhouse, S (1972). 'Medieval distilling-apparatus of glass and pottery', *Medieval Archaeology*, 16, 79–121.

Moorhouse, S (1977). 'The glass', in K J Barton and E W Holden, 'Excavations at Bramber Castle, Sussex, 1966–7', *The Archaeological Journal*, 134, 70–2.

Moorhouse, S (1983). 'Vessel glass', in P Mayes and L A S Butler, *Sandal Castle Excavations 1964–73*, Wakefield Historical Publications, pp. 225–30.

Moorhouse, S (1993). 'Pottery and glass in the late medieval monastery', in R Gilchrist and H C Mytum, eds, *Advances in Monastic Archaeology*, British Archaeological Reports 227, Tempus Reparatum, pp. 127–48.

Moorhouse, S and Wrathmell, S (1987). *Kirkstall Abbey Volume 1. The 1960–64 Excavations: A Reassessment*, West Yorkshire Archaeology Service.

Moran, B T (2006). *Distilling Knowledge: Alchemy, Chemistry, and the Scientific Revolution*, Harvard University Press.

Morgan, D (2010). 'Introduction', in D Morgan, ed, *Religion and Material Culture: The Matter of Belief*, Routledge, pp. 1–18.

Morris, R (1989). *Churches in the Landscape*, Dent.

Morris, R K (2003). 'Recycling the monastic fabric: beyond the act of dissolution', in D Gaimster and R Gilchrist, eds, *The Archaeology of Reformation, 1480–1580*, The Society for Post-Medieval Archaeology Monograph 1, Maney, pp. 235–51.

Moss, R (2008). 'Appropriating the past: Romanesque spolia in seventeenth-century Ireland', *Architectural History*, 51, 63–86.

Muir, A (2011). *Outside the Safe Place: An Oral History of the Early Years of the Iona Community*, Wild Goose Publications.

Müldner, G, Montgomery, J, Cook, G, Ellam, R, Gledhill, A and Lowe, C (2009). 'Isotopes and individuals: diet and mobility among the medieval bishops of Whithorn', *Antiquity*, 83 (322), 1119–33.

Müldner, G and Richards, M P (2005). 'Fast or feast: reconstructing diet in later medieval England by stable isotope analysis', *Journal of Archaeological Science*, 32(1), 39–48.

Müldner, G and Richards, M P (2007). 'Diet and diversity at later medieval Fishergate: the isotopic evidence', *American Journal of Physical Anthropology*, 134(2), 162–74.

Murray, E, McCormick, F and Plunkett, G (2004). 'The food economies of Atlantic island monasteries: the documentary and archaeo-environmental evidence', *Environmental Archaeology*, 9(2), 179–88.

Murray, M (1934). 'Female fertility figures', *Journal of the Royal Anthropological Institute*, 64, 45–57.

Myrberg, N (2004). 'False monuments? On antiquity and authenticity', *Public Archaeology*, 3(3), 151–61.

Myrberg Burström, N (2018). 'Introduction. Faith and ritual materialised: coin finds in religious contexts', in N Myrberg Burström and G Tarnow Ingvardson, eds, *Divina Moneta: Coins in Religion and Ritual*, Routledge, pp. 1–10.

Myrberg Burström, N and Tarnow Ingvardson, G eds (2018). *Divina Moneta: Coins in Religion and Ritual*, Routledge.

Naum, M (2015). 'Material culture and diasporic experiences: a case of medieval Hanse merchants in the Baltic', *Archaeological Papers of the American Anthropological Association*, 26(1), 72–86.

Niklasson, E and Hølleland, H (2018). 'The Scandinavian far-right and the new politicisation of heritage', *Social Archaeology*, 18(2), 121–48.

Nilsson Stutz, L (2016). 'Building bridges between burial archaeology and the archaeology of death: where is the archaeological study of the dead going?', *Current Swedish Archaeology*, 24, 13–70.

Noppen, L, Coomans, T and Drouin, M (2015). *Des couvents en héritage/Religious Houses: A Legacy*, Presses de l'Université du Québec.

Norton, C (1994). 'The buildings of St Mary's Abbey, York and their destruction', *Antiquaries Journal*, 74, 256–88.

Nyberg, T (2000). *Monasticism in North-Western Europe: 800–1200*, Ashgate.

Oakley, G E (1978). 'The vessel glass', in J H Williams, 'Excavations at Greyfriars, Northampton 1972', *Northamptonshire Archaeology*, 13, 153.

Ó Carragáin, T (2010). *Churches in Early Medieval Ireland: Architecture, Ritual and Memory*, Paul Mellon Centre for Studies in British Art, Yale University Press.

O'Connor, T (2007). 'Thinking about beastly bodies', in A Pluskowski, ed, *Breaking and Shaping Beastly Bodies: Animals as Material Culture in the Middle Ages*, Oxbow Books, pp. 1–10.

O'Keeffe, T (2003). *Romanesque Ireland: Architecture and Ideology in the Twelfth Century*, Four Courts Press.

Olsan, L T (2003). 'Charms and prayers in medieval medical theory and practice', *Social History of Medicine*, 16, 343–66.

Opie, I and Opie, I (1997). *The Oxford Dictionary of Nursery Rhymes*, 2nd edn, Oxford University Press.

Oram, R (2009). 'A note on the dating of Barhobble Chapel bones and the historical context of their deposition', *Transactions of the Dumfriesshire and Galloway Natural History and Antiquarian Society*, 83, Third Series, 51–4.

Oram, R D (2011). 'Disease, death and the hereafter in medieval Scotland', in E J Cowan and L Henderson, eds, *A History of Everyday Life in Medieval Scotland, 1000–1600*, Edinburgh University Press, pp. 196–225.

Orser Jr, C E (2010). 'Twenty-first-century historical archaeology', *Journal of Archaeological Research*, 18(2), 111–50.

O'Sullivan, J (1994). 'Excavations of an early church and a women's cemetery at St Ronan's medieval parish church, Iona', *Proceedings of the Society of Antiquaries of Scotland*, 124, 327–65.

O'Sullivan, J (1998). 'Nationalists, archaeologists and the myth of the golden age', in M A Monk and J Sheehan, eds, *Early Medieval Munster: Archaeology, History and Society*, Cork University Press, pp. 178–89.

O'Sullivan, J (1999). 'Iona: archaeological investigations 1875–1996', in D Broun and T O Clancy, eds, *Spes Scotorum, Hope of Scots: Saint Columba, Iona and Scotland*, T & T Clark, pp. 215–43.

O'Sullivan, A, McCormick, F, Kerr, T R and Harney, L (2014). *Early Medieval Ireland AD 400–1100: The Evidence from Archaeological Excavations*, Royal Irish Academy.

Page, S (2013). *Magic in the Cloister: Pious Motives, Illicit Interests and Occult Approaches to the Medieval Universe*, University of Pennsylvania Press.

Paphitis, T (2013). '"Have you come to take the king away?" A survey of archaeology and folklore in context', *Papers from the Institute of Archaeology*, 23(1), Art. 16 [http://doi.org/10.5334/pia.434].

Parker Pearson, M and Ramilisonina (1998). 'Stonehenge for the ancestors: the stones pass on the message', *Antiquity*, 72(276), 308–26.

Pérez-Arantegui, J, Ribechini, E, Colombini, M P and Escudero, F (2011). 'Characterization of an ancient "chemical" preparation: pigments and drugs in medieval Islamic Spain', *Journal of Archaeological Science*, 38(12), 3350–7.

Pestell, T (2004). *Landscapes of Monastic Foundation: The Establishment of Religious Houses in East Anglia, c.650–1200*, Boydell Press.

Pestell, T (2005). 'Using material culture to define holy space: the Bromholm Project', in A Spicer and S Hamilton, eds, *Defining the Holy: Sacred Space in Medieval and Early Modern Europe*, Ashgate, pp. 161–86.

Peterson, J B (1999). *Maps of Meaning: The Architecture of Belief*, Psychology Press.

Petts, D (2011). *Pagan and Christian: Religious Change in Early Medieval Europe*, Bristol Classical Press/Bloomsbury Academic.

Phillpots, C (2003). 'The houses of Henry VIII's courtiers in London', in D Gaimster and R Gilchrist, eds, *The Archaeology of Reformation, 1480–1580*, The Society for Post-Medieval Archaeology Monograph 1, Maney, pp. 299–309.

Pierce, E (2013). 'Jet cross pendants from the British Isles and beyond: forms, distribution and use,' *Medieval Archaeology*, 57, 198–211.

Pluskowski, A ed (2017). *The Ecology of Crusading, Colonisation and Religious Conversion in the Medieval Eastern Baltic: Terra Sacra II*, Brepols.

Pluskowski, A, Boas, A J and Gerrard, C (2011). 'The ecology of crusading: investigating the environmental impact of Holy War and colonisation at the frontiers of medieval Europe', *Medieval Archaeology*, 55(1), 192–225.

Porter, J (1998). 'The folklore of northern Scotland: five discourses on cultural representation', *Folklore*, 109, 1–14.

Potts, C (1997). *Monastic Revival and Regional Identity in Early Normandy*, Boydell Press.

Poulios, I (2014). *The Past in the Present: A Living Heritage Approach – Meteora, Greece*, Ubiquity Press.

Power, R (2006). 'A place of community: "Celtic" Iona and institutional religion', *Folklore*, 117(1), 33–53.

Price, R with Ponsford, M (1998). *St Bartholomew's Hospital, Bristol: The Excavation of a Medieval Hospital, 1976–8*, Council for British Archaeology Research Report 110.

Principe, L M (2013). *The Secrets of Alchemy*, University of Chicago Press.

Puhvel, J (1987). *Comparative Mythology*, Barnes and Noble.

Radford, C A R (1951). 'The excavations at Chapel Finian, Mochrum', *Transactions of the Dumfriesshire and Galloway Natural History and Antiquarian Society*, 28, Third Series, 28–40.

Radford, C A R (1957). 'Excavations at Whithorn: Final Report', *Transactions of the Dumfriesshire and Galloway Natural History and Antiquarian Society*, 34, Third Series, 131–96.

Radford, C A R (1967). 'The early church in Strathclyde and Galloway', *Medieval Archaeology*, 11, 115–16.

Radford, C A R (1968). 'Glastonbury Abbey', in G Ashe, ed, *The Quest for Arthur's Britain*, Praeger, pp. 119–38.

Radford, C A R (1981). 'Glastonbury Abbey before 1184: interim report on the excavations, 1908–64', in N Coldstream and P Draper, eds, *Medieval Art and Architecture at Wells and Glastonbury*, British Archaeological Association Conference Transactions IV, pp. 110–34.

Radford, C A R and Swanton, M J (1975). *Arthurian Sites in the West*, University of Exeter.

Radini, A, Nikita, E and Shillito, L M (2016). 'Human dental calculus and a medieval urban environment', in B Jervis, L G Broderick and I G Sologestoa, eds, *Objects, Environment and Everyday Life in Medieval Europe*, Brepols, pp. 297–313.

Raglan, J (1939). 'The Green Man in church architecture', *Folklore*, 50(1), 45–57.

Rahtz, P and Watts, L (2003). *Glastonbury: Myth and Archaeology*, Tempus.

Randla, A (1999). 'The mendicant orders and their architecture in Scotland', in J Sarnowsky, ed, *Mendicants, Military Orders, and Regionalism in Medieval Europe*, Ashgate, pp. 243–81.

Rankin, A (2013). *Panaceia's Daughters: Noblewomen as Healers in Early Modern Germany*, University of Chicago Press.

Rasmussen, K, Skytte, L, Jensen, A and Boldsen, J (2015). 'Comparison of mercury and lead levels in the bones of rural and urban populations in Southern Denmark and Northern Germany during the Middle Ages', *Journal of Archaeological Science: Reports*, 3, 358–70.

Rasmussen, K, Skytte, L, Ramseyer, N and Boldsen, J L (2013). 'Mercury in soil surrounding medieval human skeletons', *Heritage Science*, 1(16) [www.heritagesciencejournal .com/content/1/1/16].

Rawcliffe, C (1995). *Medicine and Society in Later Medieval England*, Sutton.

Rawcliffe, C (1998). 'Hospital nurses and their work', in R Britnell, ed, *Daily Life in the Late Middle Ages*, Sutton, pp. 43–64.

Rawcliffe, C (1999). *Medicine for the Soul: The Life, Death and Resurrection of an English Medieval Hospital*, Boydell Press.

Rawcliffe, C (2002). 'On the threshold of eternity: care of the sick in East Anglian monasteries', in C Harper-Bill, C Rawcliffe and R G Wilson, eds, *East Anglia's History: Studies in Honour of Norman Scarfe*, Boydell Press, pp. 41–72.

Rawcliffe, C (2005). 'The earthly and spiritual topography of suburban hospitals', in K Giles and C Dyer, eds, *Town and Country in the Middle Ages: Contrasts, Contacts and Interconnections, 1100–1500*, Society for Medieval Archaeology Monograph 22, Maney, pp. 251–74.

Rawcliffe, C (2006). *Leprosy in Medieval England*, Boydell Press.

Rawcliffe, C (2008). '"Delectable sightes and fragrant smelles": gardens and health in late medieval and early modern England', *Garden History*, 36, 3–21.

Rawcliffe, C (2011). 'Health and disease' and 'Medical practice and theory', in J Crick and E van Houts, eds, *A Social History of England, 900–1200*, Cambridge University Press, pp. 66–75 and 391–401.

Rawcliffe, C (2013). *Urban Bodies: Communal Health in Late Medieval English Towns and Cities*, Boydell Press.

Rawcliffe, C (2017). 'Christ the physician walks the wards: celestial therapies in the medieval hospital', in M P Davies and A Prescott, eds, *London and the Kingdom: Essays in Honour of Caroline M Barron. Proceedings of the 2004 Harlaxton Symposium*, Shaun Tyas, pp. 78–97.

Ray, H P (2014a). 'Introduction', in H P Ray, ed, *Negotiating Cultural Identity: Landscapes in Early Medieval South Asian History*, Routledge, pp. xi–xix.

Ray, H P (2014b). *The Return of the Buddha: Ancient Symbols for a New Nation*, Routledge.

RCAHMS (1982). *Argyll: An Inventory of the Ancient Monuments, Volume 4: Iona*, Royal Commission on the Ancient Historical Monuments of Scotland (RCAHMS).

Redknap, M (2005). 'An early medieval girdle from burial 631', in N Holbrook and A Thomas, 'An early medieval monastic cemetery at Llandough, Glamorgan: excavations in 1994', *Medieval Archaeology*, 49, 53–64.

Reece, R (1981). *Excavations in Iona 1964–1974*, UCL Institute of Archaeology.

Reid, A G and Lye, D M (1988). *Pitmiddle Village and Elcho Nunnery*, Perthshire Society of Natural History.

Richardson, J S (2006). *Sweetheart Abbey*, Historic Scotland.

Riddle, J (1992). *Contraception and Abortion from the Ancient World to the Renaissance*, Harvard University Press.

Rider, C (2012). *Magic and Religion in Medieval England*, Reaktion Books.

Riegl, A (1982 [1903]). 'The modern cult of monuments: its character and its origin', *Oppositions*, 25(Fall), 21–51.

Rippon, S (2013). 'Historic landscape character and sense of place', *Landscape Research*, 38(2), 179–202.

Ritchie, A (1997). *Iona*, Batsford/Historic Scotland.

Roberts, C (2004). *Heavy Words Lightly Thrown: The Reason Behind the Rhyme*, Granta Books.

Roberts, C A (2017). 'Applying the "index of care" to a person who experienced leprosy in late medieval Chichester, England', in L Tilley and A Schrenk, eds, *New Developments in the Bioarchaeology of Care*, Springer, pp. 101–24.

Roberts, C A and Cox, M (2003). *Health and Disease in Britain: From Prehistory to the Present Day*, Sutton.

Robertson, I ed (2012). *Heritage from Below*, Ashgate.

Rodwell, W (2001). *Wells Cathedral: Excavations and Structural Studies, 1978–93*, 2 vols, English Heritage.

Rodwell, W J (2005). *The Archaeology of Churches*, Tempus.

Rodwell, W, Hawkes, J, Howe, E and Cramp, R (2008). 'The Lichfield Angel: a spectacular

Anglo-Saxon painted sculpture', *The Antiquaries Journal*, 88, 48–108.

Roffey, S (2006). 'Constructing a vision of salvation: chantries and the social dimension of religious experience in the medieval parish church', *The Archaeological Journal*, 163(1), 122–46.

Roffey, S (2012). 'Medieval leper hospitals in England: an archaeological perspective from St Mary Magdalen, Winchester', *Medieval Archaeology*, 56, 203–34.

Roffey, S and Tucker, K (2012). 'A contextual study of the medieval hospital and cemetery of St Mary Magdalen, Winchester', *International Journal of Paleopathology*, 2, 170–80.

Rosenwein, B H (1999). *Negotiating Space: Power, Restraint and Privileges of Immunity in Early Medieval Europe*, Manchester University Press.

Rountree, K (2006). 'Performing the divine: neo-pagan pilgrimages and embodiment at sacred sites', *Body & Society*, 12(4), 95–115.

Ruggles, D F (2010). 'The stratigraphy of forgetting: the Great Mosque of Cordoba and its contested legacy', in H Silverman, ed, *Contested Cultural Heritage: Religion, Nationalism, Erasure and Exclusion in a Global World*, Springer, pp. 51–67.

Sampson J (1995). *Glastonbury Abbey: The Painted Decoration of the Lady Chapel, Glastonbury* [http://archaeologydataservice.ac.uk/archives/view/glastonbury_abbey_2007/lady_chapel/index.cfm].

Sampson, J (2015). 'Gothic sculpture and worked stone', in R Gilchrist and C Green, *Glastonbury Abbey: Archaeological Investigations 1904–79*, Society of Antiquaries of London, pp. 358–82.

ScARF (2012). *Medieval Scotland: A Future for its Past*, Summary Medieval Panel Document, Scottish Archaeological Research Framework [www.scottishheritagehub.com/sites/default/files/u12/ScARF%20Medieval%20September%202012.pdf].

Scarre, G (2003). 'Archaeology and respect for the dead', *Journal of Applied Philosophy*, 20(3), 237–49.

Scholkmann, B (2000). 'Die Zisterzienser und ihre Wassernutzung: die Mühlen des Klosters Bebenhausen', in B Scholkmann and S Lorenze, eds, *Von Cîteaux nach Bebenhausen: Welt und Wirken der Zisterzienser*, Attempto, pp. 153–73.

Scott, J ed (1981). *The Early History of Glastonbury. An Edition, Translation and Study of William of Malmesbury's De Antiquitate Glastonie Ecclesie*, Boydell Press.

Semple, M C (2009). 'An archaeology of Scotland's early Romanesque churches: the Towers of Alba', PhD thesis, University of Glasgow.

Semple, S (2013). *Perceptions of the Prehistoric in Anglo-Saxon England: Religion, Ritual and Rulership in the Landscape*, Oxford University Press.

Shackley, M (2001). 'Sacred world heritage sites: balancing meaning with management', *Tourism Recreation Research*, 26(1), 5–10.

Shackley, M (2002). 'Space, sanctity and service: the English cathedral as heterotopia', *International Journal of Tourism Research*, 4(5), 345–52.

Sharpe, R (1995). *Life of St Columba by Adomnán of Iona*, Penguin.

Shaw, J (2013a). 'Archaeologies of Buddhist propagation in ancient India: "ritual" and "practical" models of religious change', *World Archaeology*, 45(1), 83–108.

Shaw, J (2013b). 'Archaeology of religious change: introduction', *World Archaeology*, 45(1), 1–11.

Sheehy, J (1980). *The Rediscovery of Ireland's Past: The Celtic Revival 1830–1930*, Thames and Hudson.

Shiels, J and Campbell, S (2011). 'Sacred and banal: the discovery of everyday medieval material culture', in E J Cowan and L Henderson, eds, *A History of Everyday Life in Medieval Scotland, 1000–1600*, Edinburgh University Press, pp. 67–88.

Silberman, N A (2001). 'If I forget thee, O Jerusalem: archaeology, religious commemoration and nationalism in a disputed city, 1801–2001', *Nations and Nationalism* 7(4), 487–504.

Singh, R P (2016). 'The contestation of heritage: the enduring importance of religion' in B Graham and P Howard, eds, *Ashgate Research Companion to Heritage & Identity*, Ashgate, pp. 125–42.

Sims-Williams, P (1986). 'The visionary Celts: the construction of an "ethnic preconception"', *Cambridge Medieval Celtic Studies*, 11, 71–96.

Skemer, D C (2006). *Binding Words: Textual Amulets in the Middle Ages*, University of Pennsylvania Press.

Skinner, T and Tyers, T (2018). 'Introduction: the garden at the intersection of pleasure, contemplation and cure', in T Skinner and T Tyers, eds, *The Medieval and Early Modern Garden in Britain: Enclosure and Transformation, c.1200–1750*, Routledge, pp. 3–14.

Sloane, B (2012). *The Augustinian Nunnery of St Mary Clerkenwell, London: Excavations 1974–96*, Museum of London Archaeology.

Smith, A D (2001). 'Authenticity, antiquity and archaeology', *Nations and Nationalism*, 7(4), 441–9.

Smith, A W (1989). '"And did those feet . . .?": the legend of Christ's visit to Britain', *Folklore*, 100, 63–83.

Smith, C, Burke, H, de Leiuen, C and Jackson, G (2016). 'The Islamic State's symbolic war: Da'esh's socially mediated terrorism as a threat to cultural heritage', *Journal of Social Archaeology*, 16(2), 164–88.

Smith, G H (1979). 'The excavation of the hospital of St Mary of Ospringe, commonly called Maison Dieu', *Archaeologica Cantiana*, 95, 81–184.

Smith, L (2006). *The Uses of Heritage*, Routledge.

Smith, R (2013). 'Monks, myths and multivocality: presenting the ruins of Glastonbury Abbey', PhD thesis, University of Reading.

Sotres, P G (1998). 'The regimens of health', in M D Grmek, ed, *Western Medical Thought from Antiquity to the Middle Ages*, Harvard University Press, pp. 291–318.

Southwest Heritage Trust (2017). 'Earliest monastery in the British Isles discovered in Somerset'. Supporting Information [www.swheritage.org.uk/earliest-monastery-discovered].

Spelman, S H (1639). *Concilia, Decreta, Leges, Constitvtiones, Re Ecclesiarum Orbis Britan.*

Spencer, B (1998). *Pilgrim Souvenirs and Secular Badges: Medieval Finds from Excavations in London*, HMSO.

Spicer, A (2000). '"Defyle not Christ's kirk with your carrion": burial and the development of burial aisles in post-Reformation Scotland', in B Gordon and P Marshall, eds, *The Place of the Dead: Death and Remembrance in Late Medieval and Early Modern Europe*, Cambridge University Press, pp. 149–69.

Spicer, A (2005). '"What kinde of house a kirk is": conventicles, consecrations and the concept of sacred space in post-Reformation Scotland', in W Coster and A Spicer, eds, *Sacred Space in Early Modern Europe*, Cambridge University Press, pp. 81–103.

Spiritual Capital (2012). *Spiritual Capital: The Present and Future of English Cathedrals. Findings of a Research Project carried out by Theos and the Grubb Institute* [www.theosthinktank.co.uk/cmsfiles/archive/files/Reports/Spiritual%20Capital%2064pp%20-%20FINAL.pdf].

Stalley, R (1987). *The Cistercian Monasteries of Ireland*, Yale University Press.

Stallibrass, S (2007). 'Taphonomy or transfiguration: do we need to change the subject?', in A Pluskowski, ed, *Breaking and Shaping Beastly Bodies: Animals as Material Culture in the Middle Ages*, Oxbow Books, pp. 52–65.

Standley, E R (2013). *Trinkets and Charms: The Use, Meaning and Significance of Dress Accessories 1300–1700*, Oxford University School of Archaeology Monograph 78, Institute of Archaeology, University of Oxford.

Standley, E R (2016). 'Spinning yarns: the archaeological evidence for hand spinning and its social implications c. AD 1200–1500', *Medieval Archaeology*, 60(2), 266–99.

Stausberg, M (2011). *Religion and Tourism*, Routledge.

Stöber, K and Austin, D (2013). 'Culdees to canons: the Augustinians of North Wales', in J Burton and K Stöber, eds, *Monasteries and Society in the British Isles in the Later Middle Ages*, Studies in the History of Medieval Religion Volume 35, Boydell Press, pp. 39–54.

Stocker, D (1997). 'Fons et origo: the symbolic death, burial and resurrection of English font stones', *Church Archaeology*, 1, 17–25.

Stocker, D and Everson, P (2003). 'The straight and narrow way: fenland causeways and the conversion of the landscape in the Witham Valley, Lincolnshire', in M Carver, ed, *The Cross Goes North: Processes of Conversion in Northern Europe, AD 300–1300*, Boydell & Brewer/York Medieval Press, pp. 271–88.

Stones, J A (1989). *Three Scottish Carmelite Friaries: Excavations at Aberdeen, Linlithgow and*

Perth, 1980–1986, Society of Antiquaries of Scotland Monograph 6.
Stopford, J (1994). 'Some approaches to the archaeology of Christian pilgrimage', *World Archaeology*, 26(1), 57–72.
Stout, A (2008). *The Thorn and the Waters: Miraculous Glastonbury in the Eighteenth Century*, Green and Pleasant Publishing.
Stout, A (2012). 'Grounding faith at Glastonbury: episodes in the early history of alternative archaeology', *Numen*, 59, 249–69.
Stout, A (2014). 'After the end: Glastonbury Abbey, 1539–1825', *Somerset Archaeology and Natural History*, 157, 72–93.
Stringer, K J (2000). 'Reform monasticism and Celtic Scotland: Galloway, c.1140–1240', in E J Cowan and A McDonald, eds, *Alba: Celtic Scotland in the Medieval Era*, Tuckwell Press, pp. 127–65.
Stronach, S (2005). 'The Anglian Monastery and Medieval Priory of Coldingham: *Urbs Coludi* revisited', *Proceedings of the Society of Antiquaries of Scotland*, 135, 395–422.
Swedish National Heritage Board (2016a). *Kulturarvsarbetet i samhällsutvecklingen*. Report from the Swedish National Heritage Board.
Swedish National Heritage Board (2016b). *Vision för kulturmiljöarbetet 2030*. Report from the Swedish National Heritage Board.
Swenson, E (2015). 'The archaeology of ritual', *Annual Review of Anthropology*, 44, 329–45.
Sykes, N (2005). 'Hunting for the Anglo-Normans: zooarchaeological evidence for medieval identity', in A Pluskowski, ed, *Just Skin and Bone? New Perspectives on Human–Animal Relations in the Historical Past*, BAR International Series 1410, Archeopress, pp. 73–80.
Tabraham, C J (1984). 'Excavations at Kelso Abbey', *Proceedings of the Society of Antiquaries of Scotland*, 114, 365–404.
Tarlow, S (2006). 'Archaeological ethics and the people of the past', in C Scarre and G Scarre, eds, *The Ethics of Archaeology: Philosophical Perspectives on Archaeological Practice*, Cambridge University Press, pp. 199–216.
Thomas, C (1971). *The Early Christian Archaeology of North Britain*, Oxford University Press.
Thomas, C, Sloane, B and Phillpotts, C eds (1997). *Excavations at the Priory and Hospital of St Mary Spital, London*, Museum of London Archaeology Service Monograph 1.
Thomas, G (2013). 'Life before the minster: the social dynamics of monastic foundation at Anglo-Saxon Lyminge, Kent', *The Antiquaries Journal*, 93, 109–45.
Thomas, G, Pluskowski, A, Gilchrist, R, Andrén, A, Augenti, A, García-Contreras Ruiz, G, Valk, H, Stäcker, J and Astill, G (2017). 'Religious transformations in medieval Europe: towards a new archaeological agenda', *Medieval Archaeology*, 16(2), 300–29.
Thompson, J D A (1956). *Inventory of British Coin Hoards, AD 600–1500*, Royal Numismatic Society Special Publication No. 1.
Thorn, J (1980). 'Small finds report', in S Johnson, 'Excavations at Conisborough Castle 1973–1977', *Yorkshire Archaeological Journal*, 52, 82–3.
Thorpe, D E (2017). 'Lighting the way. Lithuanian Vėlinės: visuality as participation, resistance, rupture, and repair', *Journal of Material Culture*, 22(4), 419–36.
Thurlby, M (1995). 'The Lady Chapel of Glastonbury Abbey', *The Antiquaries Journal*, 75, 107–70.
Tilley, L (2107). 'Showing that they cared: an introduction to thinking, theory and practice in the bioarchaeology of care', in L Tilley and A Schrenk, eds, *New Developments in the Bioarchaeology of Care*, Springer, pp. 11–43.
Todd, M (2000). 'Profane pastimes and the reformed community: the persistence of popular festivities in early modern Scotland', *Journal of British Studies*, 39, 123–56.
Tranvouez, Y (2015). 'Friches monastiques en longue durée: les ruines de l'ancienne abbaye de Landévennec, entre réinvestissement religieux et remploi culturel', in L Noppen, T Coomans and M Drouin, eds, *Des couvents en héritage/Religious Houses: A Legacy*, Presses de l'Université du Québec.
Travaini, L (2015). 'Saints, sinners and . . . a cow: offerings, alms and tokens of memory', in E M Giles, M Gaspar and S H Gullbekk, eds, *Money and the Church in Medieval Europe*,

1000–1200: Practice, Morality and Thought, Ashgate, pp. 209–21.

Treasure Trove in Scotland: Report by Queen's and Lord Treasurer's Remembrancer 2008/2009 [https://treasuretrovescotlandorg.files.wordpress.com/2017/01/ttu_annual_report_08_09.pdf].

Treasure Trove in Scotland: Report by Queen's and Lord Treasurer's Remembrancer 2012/2013 [https://treasuretrovescotlandorg.files.wordpress.com/2017/01/ttu_annual_report_12_13.pdf].

Treasure Trove in Scotland: Report by Queen's and Lord Treasurer's Remembrancer 2013/2014 [https://treasuretrovescotlandorg.files.wordpress.com/2017/01/ttu_annual_report_13_14.pdf].

Treasure Trove in Scotland: Report by Queen's and Lord Treasurer's Remembrancer 2015/2016 [https://treasuretrovescotlandorg.files.wordpress.com/2017/01/ttu_annual_report_15_16.pdf].

Trigg, S (2005). 'Walking through cathedrals: scholars, pilgrims, and medieval tourists', *New Medieval Literatures*, 7, 9–33.

Trigger, B G (1984). 'Alternative archaeologies: nationalist, colonialist, imperialist', *Man*, 19 (13), 355–70.

Tsivolas, T (2014). *Law and Religious Cultural Heritage in Europe*, Springer.

Tuan, Y (1990). *Topophila: A Study of Environmental Perceptions, Attitudes and Values*, Columbia University Press.

Tuan, Y (2005). *Space and Place: The Perspective of Experience*, University of Minnesota Press.

Turner, S, Semple, S and Turner, A (2013). *Wearmouth and Jarrow: Northumbrian Monasteries in an Historic Landscape*, University of Hertfordshire Press.

Tyson, R (2000). *Medieval Glass Vessels found in England, c. AD 1200–1500*, Council for British Archaeology.

UNESCO (2003). *Convention for the Safeguarding of the Intangible Cultural Heritage*.

Untermann, M (2001). *Forma ordinis: die mittelalterliche Baukunst der Zisterzienser*, Volume 89, Deutscher Kunstverlag.

Van Arsdall, A (2014). E'valuating the content of medieval herbals', in S Fancia and A Stobart, eds, *Critical Approaches to the History of Western Herbal Medicine: From Classical Antiquity to the Early Modern Period*, Bloomsbury, pp. 47–66.

Van Dyke, R M and Alcock, S E eds (2008). *Archaeologies of Memory*, John Wiley & Sons.

van Gennep, A (1960 [1909]). *The Rites of Passage* (trans. M B Vizedom and G B Caffee), University of Chicago Press.

Veitch, K (1999). 'The conversion of native religious communities to the Augustinian rule in twelfth- and thirteenth-century Alba', *Records of the Scottish Church History Society*, 29, 1–22.

Verschuuren, R, Wild, R, McNeely, J and Oviedo, G eds (2010). *Sacred Natural Sites: Conserving Nature and Culture*, Earthscan.

Voigts, L E and Payne, P (2016). 'Medicine for a Great Household (c.1500): Berkeley Castle Muniments Select Book', *Studies in Medieval and Renaissance History: Third Series*, AMS Press, 99–264.

Voyé, L (2012). 'The need and the search for sacred places', in T Coomans, H De Dijn, J De Maeyer, R Heynickx, and B Verschaffel, eds, *Loci Sacri: Understanding Sacred Places*, Leuven University Press, pp. 73–91.

Waddell, J (2014). *Archaeology and Celtic Myth*, Four Courts Press.

Walker, D (2012). *Disease in London, 1st – 19th Centuries*, Museum of London Archaeology Monograph 56.

Wallis, R J and Blain, J (2003). 'Sites, sacredness and stories: interactions of archaeology and contemporary paganism, *Folklore*, 114(3), 307–21.

Walser, J D, Kristjánsdóttir, S, Gowland, R and Desnica, N (2018). 'Volcanoes, medicine, and monasticism: investigating mercury exposure in medieval Iceland', *International Journal of Osteoarchaeology* 2018, 1–14 [https://doi.org/10.1002/oa.2712].

Walsham, A (2004). 'The Holy Thorn of Glastonbury: the evolution of a legend in post-Reformation England', *Parergon*, 21(2), 1–25.

Walsham, A (2011). *The Reformation of the Landscape: Religion, Identity, and Memory in Early Modern Britain and Ireland*, Oxford University Press.

Walsham, A (2012). 'Sacred topography and social memory: religious change and the landscape in early modern Britain and Ireland', *Journal of Religious History*, 36(1), 31–51.

Walton, H (2015). 'Theological perspectives on Christian pilgrimage', in A Maddrell, V della Dora, A Scafi and H Walton, *Christian Pilgrimage, Landscape and Heritage: Journeying to the Sacred*, Routledge, pp. 22–42.

Warinner, C, Speller, C and Collins, M J (2015). 'A new era in palaeomicrobiology: prospects for ancient dental calculus as a long-term record of the human oral microbiome', *Philosophical Transactions of the Royal Society B*, 370 (1660), 20130376. doi: 10.1098/rstb.2013.037.

Warnier, J P (2013). 'The sacred king, royal containers, alienable material contents, and value in contemporary Cameroon', in H P Hahn and H Weiss, eds, *Mobility, Meaning and Transformations of Things*, Oxbow Books, pp. 50–62.

Waterton, E and Watson, S (2013). 'Framing theory: towards a critical imagination in heritage studies', *International Journal of Heritage Studies*, 19(6), 546–61.

Watson, G (2018). *Monastic Magic and Healing*. University of Reading, Dataset [http://dx.doi.org/10.17864/1947.152].

Weiner, A B (1992). *Inalienable Possessions: The Paradox of Keeping-While-Giving*, University of California Press.

White, E D (2016). 'Old stones, new rites: contemporary pagan interactions with the Medway Megaliths', *Material Religion*, 12(3), 346–72.

White Marshall, J and Walsh, C (2005). *Illaunloughan Island: An Early Medieval Monastery in County Kerry*, Wordwell.

Wijesuriya, G (2000). 'Conserving the temple of the tooth relic, Sri Lanka', *Public Archaeology*, 2, 99–108.

Williams, D (2013). 'Musical space and quiet space in medieval monastic Canterbury', in J Day, ed, *Making Senses of the Past: Toward a Sensory Archaeology*, Southern Illinois University Press, pp. 196–220.

Williams, H (2006). *Death and Memory in Early Medieval Britain*, Cambridge University Press.

Willmott, H and Bryson, A (2013). 'Changing to suit the times: a post-Dissolution history of Monk Bretton Priory, South Yorkshire', *Post-Medieval Archaeology*, 47(1), 136–63.

Willows, M (2015). 'Palaeopathology of the Isle of May', in K Gerdau-Radonić and K McSweeney, eds, *Trends in Biological Anthropology 1*, Oxbow Books, pp. 42–53.

Winterbottom, M and Lapidge, M eds (2012). *The Early Lives of St Dunstan*, Clarendon Press.

Woodland, R R (1981). 'The pottery', in J E Mellor and T Pearce, *The Austin Friars, Leicester*, Council for British Archaeology Report 35, pp. 81–129.

Wyckoff, D (1967). *Albertus Magnus Book of Minerals*, Clarendon Press.

Yelton, M (2006). *Alfred Hope Patten and the Shrine of Our Lady of Walsingham*, Canterbury Press.

Yeoman, P (1995). *Medieval Scotland: An Archaeological Perspective*, Batsford/Historic Scotland.

Yeoman, P (1999). *Pilgrimage in Medieval Scotland*, Batsford.

Yeoman, P (2009). 'Investigations on the May Island, and other early medieval churches and monasteries in Scotland', in N Edwards, ed, *The Archaeology of the Early Medieval Celtic Churches*, Society for Medieval Archaeology, pp. 227–44.

Zarnecki, G ed (1984). *English Romanesque Art 1066–1200*, Weidenfeld & Nicolson.

INDEX

Lightning Source UK Ltd.
Milton Keynes UK
UKHW050814181219
355581UK00007B/56/P